PETHYBRIDGE, Roger. The social prelude to Stalinism. St. Martin's, 1974. 343p tab bibl 74-75011. 18.95

Pethybridge is the director of the Centre of Russian Studies at the University College of Swansea, Wales, and the author of three previous studies on Soviet history. This volume treats social conditions existing in Russia during the New Economic Policy of the 1920s. Pethybridge demonstrates that the Bolshevik leaders failed to perceive social reality in Russia and that forces such as the small-scale organization of Russian society and illiteracy adversely affected Soviet plans to construct a new society. The study is based upon primary sources as well as the latest research in sociology and political science and is a valuable contribution to the ongoing debate on the origin of Stalinism. It should be read in conjunction with such works as Stephen F. Cohen's *Bukharin and the Bolshevik Revolution* (CHOICE, May 1974), Roy Medvedev's *Let history judge* (CHOICE, Apr. 1972), and Robert Tucker's *Stalin as revolutionary, 1879-1929* (CHOICE, Jan. 1974). Highly recommended for all upper-division undergraduates and graduate students in political theory and history.

The Social Prelude
to Stalinism

The Social Prelude to Stalinism

ROGER PETHYBRIDGE

1015509

ST. MARTIN'S PRESS   NEW YORK

AFFILIATED PUBLISHERS : Macmillan Limited, London –
also at Bombay, Calcutta, Madras and Melbourne

For my father

Contents

1 Bolshevik Ideas and Social Realities

The Bolshevik party was the prime political motivating force in the Soviet state and society in the 1920s. Since it was authoritarian, partly by choice, partly as the result of external pressures, both before and after it came into power in October 1917, it is natural that historians should have concentrated their attention above all on the party's development, functions and power over a backward nation. They have tended to study Soviet history *de haut en bas*, politically speaking. Other factors have served to reinforce this approach. Increasing specialisation amongst historians in this century has led to what J. H. Hexter calls the 'tunnel' method. Historians 'split the past into a series of tunnels, each continuous from the remote past to the present, but practically self-contained at every point and sealed off from contact with or contamination by anything that was going on in any of the other tunnels. At their entrances these tunnels bore signs saying diplomatic history, political history ... and so on.' [1] From the early days of foreign interest in Soviet affairs, the political tunnel has been dug the deepest, though it is rapidly being superseded by the economic tunnel, which is being increasingly and effectively exploited.

Another reason for concentrating on high politics has been the comparative accessibility of source materials. This is particularly the case up to the late 1920s, when Bolsheviks and political exiles alike produced a wealth of evidence of considerable value, a flood which was to dry up in the 1930s. Finding sources on local and social history has proved to be far more difficult. Given a multinational, disparate society, spread out over the largest inhabited land mass in the world, a society that was fifty per cent illiterate as late as 1926, the hazards of interpretation are clear. Historians also tend to dwell in time sections within their subject tunnels, and

1917 has often loomed as an almost insuperable barrier. The effort and knowledge required to bridge the gap between Tsarist and Soviet history, especially social history, has intimidated many scholars. The general result has been, as Walter Laqueur puts it in an interesting work on interpretations of Soviet history, that 'Most Western studies have been preoccupied with the "commanding heights" and the institutions'.[2] A similar preoccupation was apparent in the earlier stages of the historiography of the French Revolution. Professor A. Cobban thought that the last great primitive was Taine, who wrote nearly ninety years after the Revolution. It was not until well into this century that historians like Lefebvre, Mornet, Soboul and Rudé firmly placed the earlier political approach in the wider historical matrix.

It would be succumbing to the narrowness of the tunnel makers to insist that, since Russian social history in the twentieth century has been relatively neglected, it should be pursued in a vacuum. There is also the danger of ascribing a paramount role to the social interpretation of history. If 'social' is defined in the way that Durkheim defined it, one may be tempted to wield this approach so as to encompass all the social sciences and to let it become the main agent of their unity and synthesis. This leads to methodological imperialism, or what Raymond Aron has called 'sociologism'[3] – the effort to explain all phenomena as arising from society. Such an exercise is self-defeating. It is pointless to use a theory as the criterion for the selection of the relevant facts, and then on the basis of those facts to illustrate and confirm the theory by which they have been chosen.

Moreover any attempt in writing on social history to formalise causal description is worthless. This is because it is impossible to emulate the precision of formulae in science like, for example, a formula in chemistry by which a compound requires several elements in stated proportions. Whereas the natural sciences can abstract and isolate their data from the total world of experience, social history more than all other approaches to history must apply to society as a whole, from which nothing can be excluded.

In their flight from the rigid Marxist (and Soviet) socio-economic interpretation of Russian history, many foreign scholars have to some extent overemphasised the belief that the organisation of men in a community is primarily political. They have rightly laid stress on Lenin's political voluntarism[4] in 1917 but have also tended to play down the subtle interaction of subsequent Bolshevik political and social ideas with the various features of Soviet society. In order to understand the early Soviet period in the round, the political ideas of the central policy makers about the special problems of Soviet society should be studied more closely. The coexistence in NEP of a revolutionary party in the process of working out the future of Russia and a society which was not merely recuperating from the exhaustion of a world war, revolution and a civil war, but was actually moving retrogressively in several ways, created great tensions. This Janus-headed situation was aggravated because the Bolshevik party was to some extent out of touch with Russian society. For centuries every government of Russia had held itself aloof from the society under its control, but particular influences were at work in the early years of the Soviet regime which tended to reinforce this effect.

Inside the party the apparatus was the real driving force in the 1920s. Lenin's concept of a highly centralised, élitist group acting within the general party body led to its partial estrangement from the lower ranks of the party and a fortiori from the mass of the population. The links between the *apparat* and the proletarian ranks of the party were far weaker in NEP than they had been in the winter of 1917–18, when one can with some justice speak of an *apparat* which tried to reflect the characteristics of the leading workers of Petrograd, Moscow and the big industrial towns. By the end of the Civil War working-class support for the Bolsheviks had disintegrated. Military recruitment, disease, and lack of employment and food in the cities caused urban depopulation on a vast scale. Most of the 400,000 men lost by the Red Army were workers. At the start of NEP Russia no longer possessed a working class, conscious of its own identity, assuming that such a class had ever existed. Between 1921 and 1924 a new type of young worker evolved, interested in material questions rather than in any political ideal. This malleable generation was drawn into the lower ranks of the party through a series of campaigns until a record figure of 459,067 worker communists was reached in 1928. After 1925 the party *apparat* did not always hide its opinion of worker members as backward and lacking in initiative.[5]

Within the *apparat* itself, as Professor W. E. Mosse has noted, 'one can speak – with due caution – of separate revolutionary generations'.[6] From information given in the encyclopedic dic-

tionary *Granat*, it appears that leading Bolsheviks born between
1860 and 1874 were more likely to be of non-Russian extraction,
to come from an upper-middle- or middle-class background, and
to have received a higher education. A second age group born between 1883 and 1891 had a higher proportion of persons of
Russian extraction from a lower-class background equipped with
an elementary education. The point that concerns us here is that
the small central leadership core in the Central Committee, which
really controlled the policies and basic outlook of the party from
1917 into the mid-1920s, retained the characteristics of the first
rather than the second generation. These characteristics were unusual in the wider party membership of the 1920s and were rarely
found combined in a single member. It is significant that Stalin
stood virtually alone among the central leaders in the period
1917–21 with regard to his lower social background and education. As Professor Mosse says, he was 'the prototype and, at the
same time, the forerunner of the "new men"'.[7] He was also more
pragmatic and less inclined to remain withdrawn in the isolated
position of the central leadership during the later NEP period.

The attitudes of the Old Bolshevik leadership were substantially
different from those of the newer *apparatchiki* who came into
power after October 1917. Most of these differences tended to
isolate the first generation of leaders from the realities of the postrevolutionary situation. Repression, imprisonment and exile had
induced them to formulate abstract, preconceived ideas about the
nature of Russian society, since it could not be studied at close
hand nor at the grass roots level for much of the time. During the
periods when they managed to be politically active in Russia, they
were forced to adopt secretive underground methods which they
found hard or impossible to discard once they achieved power in
1917.

Many of the leading Old Bolsheviks were intellectuals. Some of
them had a keen interest in political theory and the study of history, and almost none of them had been engaged in the day-to-day
running of any medium-sized administrative organisation prior
to 1917, much less the giant Russian state machine.[8] In the years
before the Revolution, and particularly before the escapist movements in literature and art had gained impetus, there had been
lively political contact between the revolutionary and the cultural
sectors of the intelligentsia : indeed the two sectors overlapped in

their social background, education and interests, as indicated above. Before the events following on the February Revolution showed up irreconcilable political divisions of opinion on the left, this link permitted some of the Old Bolsheviks, despite Lenin's personal love-hate relationship with the intelligentsia, to exert indirect pressure against the Tsarist regime through the cultural channel. After October the intelligentsia was deprived of many of its more brilliant representatives, who now found themselves too far to the right to stay in the country. The middle and the left in the guise of the fellow-travellers and *Proletkult* both caused embarrassment to the Bolshevik leaders subsequently. Thus by the 1920s the Old Bolshevik intellectuals were in some ways more rather than less culturally isolated than they had been prior to the Revolution.

So often in NEP the arguments of the Old Bolshevik *apparatchiki* appear highly academic, unrelated to the details of the actual social situation in Russia. This is scarcely surprising. Due to the chaotic condition of the country after 1917, statistical evidence on any matter was either fragmentary or unobtainable.[9] The majority of the Bolshevik leaders had not lived in the midst of Russian society through the war period 1914–17 which witnessed many fundamental changes in the social and economic structure of the country. The lack of information and experience reinforced each other, and may have appeared as a positive release to the leaders who became involved in violent polemical discussion in the 1920s. They could and did distort their scanty evidence on the nature of Soviet society in order to suit their scholastic arguments and improve their personal status vis-à-vis their rivals. The changing definition of a *kulak* or a *seredniak* (middle peasant) was geared closely to the state of affairs in the Stalin-Trotsky debate and had rather less to do with the actual condition of the peasantry, in so far as this was known in all its complexity.[10]

Even if in some ways the actual state of affairs could be properly examined in NEP, it was often neglected in favour of the future or the foreign situation. The existing state of society seemed such a rebuttal of Bolshevik aspirations that it was more comforting to neglect it by looking beyond. Abortive, short-term practical experiments like workers' control in the years prior to NEP had taught the Bolshevik policy makers to divorce their theoretical ideals from the recalcitrant nature of society and to plan optimistically for the future on more abstract lines. To do this was to revert to what they had been used to doing during the long years out of power before 1917. It came easily to the Old Bolsheviks, and they re-entered this realm with enthusiasm after the years of War Communism. The twin ingredients of continuing fanaticism and a backward nation kept alive and refreshed that brand of maximalism which had infused Bolshevik thought prior to the Revolution. Throughout NEP one wing of the ruling élite escaped not merely into the future, but into the future of other countries too, which were expected to link up with Russia politically after undergoing violent revolution.

During the whole of the Great Debate in the party leadership over the development of Russia, the high-level claustrophobia was rarely pierced by opinion intruding from the Bolshevik rank and file. In 1925 the Leningrad party organisation, although it had ceased to be representative of the city's workers, nevertheless spoke out against Bukharin's neo-Populism in its defence of the proletariat of the old capital, which more than any other section of the working class had suffered from the slowing down in industrial activity. For once, broadly based resentment led to real pressure being exerted on the formulation of future national policy. Otherwise the arguments within the party élite left both the lower party cells and the working class in a state of perplexity and boredom. The Trotsky Opposition spent much of its energy arguing about Permanent Revolution, Thermidor, the Kuomintang, Clemenceau, etc. Occasionally the sparring contestants made artificially contrived appeals to the rank and file, as did the Opposition in the summer of 1926, but for the most part they were met with uncomprehending apathy.

Thus there were several walls within walls which guarded the ivory tower of the party leadership. The Old Bolsheviks were set apart in many ways from the newer members of the Central Committee : in their turn the latter rarely heeded the opinions of the lower party membership.

The organisational and intellectual isolation of the Bolsheviks, who were a small body of townsmen in a huge peasant population, led them into many practical difficulties concerning the government of the country. It is not the aim of this book to investigate these administrative problems in their own right. Many competent and systematic analyses of the impact of the governmental machine during the years 1917–29 on various sections of the populace – workers, peasants, intellectuals, managers [11] and so on, have already been carried out, together with studies of early Soviet legislation on social problems and of such matters as education, family law, and religion. A general survey of the same areas would amount to little more than a synthesis of scholarly monographs already written and to this degree would be superfluous. Furthermore, the emphasis in this study is somewhat different. Whereas a scholar like Olga Narkiewicz in her book, *The Making of the Soviet State Apparatus* sees specific forms of Bolshevik social administration in NEP creating problems which eventually led to pressure from precise organizational changes, the present author is looking less at institutional questions and more at the reverberation of certain Bolshevik political and social ideas against the sounding board of Soviet social realities. In adopting this emphasis there is no wish to minimise the significance of the institutional and administrative approach. Elsewhere the author also has laid stress on technical and administrative problems as they affected the political course of events during the Russian Revolution of 1917.[12]

A strictly institutional approach, or one based on distinctions of class and social occupation, would tend to cloak the naked confrontation between Bolshevik aspirations and social backwardness, partly because the study would have to be arranged according to organisations or social groups rather than on the basis of idea-fact collisions and solutions : partly for the reason that the considerable discrepancies between Bolshevik theories and social realities would be less clear if the main accent were put on administration in action, with all that this implies in terms of political expediency and dilution of original ideals.

Most accounts of the Russian Revolution tend to shy away from the problem of reconciling the elegantly and rationally conceived humanitarian ideals of the Bolshevik party with the ugly details of actual Soviet history as it developed into what has come to be known, for better or for worse, as Stalinism. Historians have concentrated on one facet or the other, for various reasons. It is frequently hard to find in one and the same observer a sympathetic and sensitive reaction to two themes which, though definitely related, require a very different kind of understanding. Considerable intellectual and emotional strain becomes apparent in the effort to link up the two approaches. This is particularly strong in the case of Soviet Russia : the gap between Bolshevik hopes and the social heritage from the prerevolutionary era was enormous. Polemical inclinations with regard to the Russian Revolution have tugged writers either to the left, which over-indulges in fantasy and hides from harsh realities, or to the right, where too much emphasis is put on sordid episodes and not enough on the nobility or influence of ideology. One of the great virtues of de Tocqueville consisted in his sincere admiration of the force of values behind the French Revolution, although he felt he had to condemn the facts of the Revolution.

The Bolsheviks immediately after 1917 wished to transform long-rooted social institutions, like the family in a patriarchal peasant society. They wanted to dismantle Russia's enormous standing army, to inculcate deep culture through education rather than by means of quick propaganda in an illiterate nation, to impose large-scale social and economic forms of life on a small-scale system, and to abolish bureaucracy at one stroke in a country whose cumbersome state administration was as notorious as that of Austro-Hungary. Here in a nutshell are some of the conflicts that are examined in later chapters. The aim of the book is not merely to examine these confrontations *per se*, but to see how the tensions between theory and reality in the social sphere eventually contributed to the political climate that led to Stalinism.

Some of the reasons for Bolshevik isolation from society in the years after 1917 were ascribed above to party organisation and composition. One should not assume that there is an automatic link between the outlook of a party and its composition : a party run by white-collar intellectuals by no means always acts solely in harmony with the wishes of those social groups from which it stems. But in the case of the leading Bolsheviks the political theory to which they clung tended to reinforce their estrangement from society during NEP. The picture seen through Marxist eyes was often badly out of focus. The difficulties experienced by the Bolsheviks in adapting Marxist theory to Russian conditions are notorious and too well rehearsed to need much comment here. The peculiarities of Russia's history in European terms – her lack of long-established industry, her small proletariat, and her unique class structure – caused enough doctrinal worries before 1917. After the Revolution the problems of applying hitherto abstract theories to a real and chaotic social structure became overwhelming.

Rather less attention has been paid to the impact of Marxist-Leninist social theories on early Soviet social life, and less still to their political repercussions. Besides being of interest in its own right, the study of social origins may help to lend historical perspective to the many recent sociological studies of contemporary Soviet Russia.[13] History is sociology in movement, 'the empirical evidence of societies in action', as Professor Trevor-Roper has put it.[14] A defect of much social theory, Russian studies included, is that it often neglects historical evidence and depends too heavily on a small range of contemporary material. Thus the language of social theory is sometimes inappropriate to past conditions, though it has no qualms about trying to describe them.

One area of Marxist-Leninist social thought that has already been compared with actual conditions in NEP is the Bolshevik theory of class structure, particularly as it related to the various categories of the peasantry.[15] The social theories of Marx and Engels were crude and vague where peasants were concerned. The peasantry, even less than the proletariat and bourgeoisie of Western Europe, could not be dealt with in broad categories. Professor S. Ossowski has pointed out how Marx, when in a relaxed, philosophical frame of mind, refined his notions of class structure, allowing for subtleties that on other occasions were swept aside by Marx the revolutionary, who blunted his tools in his passion to convince and activate his audience.[16] It was the second strain in Marxist thought which the Bolsheviks naturally took over. The Tsarist legal approach to class status had been even more *simpliste* than the Marxist-Leninist point of view. Until 1917 every Russian was born into an ascribed legal position as a member of a social estate or *soslovie*.

Until recently students of NEP tended either to adopt Bolshevik class terminology which embodied a specific theory of the Russian Revolution, or, even if they were not hypnotised by this terminology, remained content with broad generalisations possessing only a very rough relation to realities, which meant merely repeating the defects of the Bolshevik approach in another guise.[17] Apart from a brief excursus into the slippery question of class definition,[18] there is no intention to go further into this field here. Like the major problem of trying to fit Marxist theory on to a recalcitrant substructure, the subject of class has already received close scrutiny.

In the chapters which follow, less carefully examined areas of social life, and the theoretical debates and political influences they generated, are considered. Chapter 2 deals with the sharpest contrast of all between Bolshevik ideals and the underdeveloped features of postrevolutionary society. Maximalist theories were applied almost without compromise to many forms of social life in the period of euphoria immediately following the revolution. In all sectors a similar pattern of bold experimentation led to early disillusionment and the postponement of projects. Chapter 3 is set in contrast to Chapter 2. The powerful influence of military conditions on social and political affairs before and during the Civil War is treated here. Not only were social conditions far too backward for them to be leavened at once by the Bolsheviks' plans; they were in a regressive state in some ways due to the physical impact of war and the gradual permeation of quasi-military thought. An attempt is made to show why this occurred despite the party's aversion to the notion of a standing army in a socialist system. Chapters 4 and 5 take a closer look at two features of Soviet society which acted as severe brakes on the implementation of social, economic and political progress over the whole period 1917–29. The contrast between the avowed aim of the dictatorship of the proletariat and the prevailing fifty per cent adult illiteracy rate of the Soviet peoples as late as 1926 is studied in Chapter 4. Lenin's long-term educational ideals are compared with the ways in which the literacy campaign was used in fact as an opportunity to imprint on ignorant minds monolithic political preconceptions. Chapter 5 deals with the persisting small-scale structure and relationships of Soviet society up to the period of collectivisation and the Five-Year Plans. The economic consequences of the Bolsheviks' efforts during NEP and after to apply large-scale theories inherited from Marx and Engels have been researched in great detail, but the ways in which small-scale social structure remained impervious to Marxist-Leninist political designs has received far less attention. The chief reason was the overwhelming peasant basis of society. Three interlocking centralised organisations – the party, the army (especially in the Civil War period) and the new state administration – became increasingly authoritarian in their struggle to coordinate and push fragmented Soviet society in the direction of communism. The network of local Soviets, the co-operative movement and the handicraft (*kustarnyi*) system in the period 1921–8 are studied in their roles as potential links between the political centre and the small-scale grass roots of society.

The party bureaucracy grew rapidly in size and importance through the period 1921–9. It is well known that both Marx and Lenin took an adverse view of bureaucracy and expected it to decline and eventually disappear in a proletarian society. The Bolsheviks, internal heretics like Trotsky, and foreign observers have all given reasons for the perpetuation of a massive bureaucracy in the Soviet period. All three groups have concentrated on political and economic factors. The aim of Chapter 6 is to show how the social influences reviewed in Chapters 1 to 5 acted as strong consolidators and, at the same time, helped to shore up increasing political authoritarianism, which with the passage of the years came to be clearly embodied in institutional terms by the party bureaucracy.

The final chapter assesses the ways in which the influences described in the rest of the book coalesced by the end of NEP and helped to swing the balance in favour of Stalin's political methods. In the course of the first six chapters mutually reinforcing bonds between the various developments are examined in so far as they contributed to greater political authoritarianism. Although it is impossible in the final analysis to accord exact weight to the various factors involved, an attempt is made to juxtapose social problems with high-level political and economic decisions, and also the personality of Stalin, as ingredients of 'Stalinism'. In conclusion one must speculate why similar social backwardness in other contemporaneous regimes did not produce similar political results, and also why an apparently high level of social development in a country like Germany nevertheless led to a totalitarian system.

The main purpose in selecting the subject matter for the first six chapters is to highlight those points of irritation between social ideals and practice in the postrevolutionary period which contributed to the subsequent political climate. Raymond Aron in discussing types of industrialising societies has noted that one cannot say that in principle all economic planning of the kind Stalin resorted to necessarily excludes the competition of political parties for the exercise of power; the essential point is probably the division between the desires of the governed and the will of the rulers.[19] In the case of Soviet Russia's early social history one could rephrase 'the desires of the governed' in a more passive way as the lethargies or backwardness of the governed. The Bolsheviks' arguments for being the living embodiment of the aspirations of the working masses and so unable to act against their interest are well known. A second argument was that the party aimed at the creation of a society having nothing in common with existing society, and not only in Russia. On the basis of these vast ambitions the Bolsheviks claimed a monopoly of political activity and social coercion. F. Dzerzhinsky, the fanatical head of the *Cheka*, stated the view in this way : 'The hunger and sufferings of the masses of the people, the weeping of children and the despair of their mothers are the sacrifices which the people must make in order to overcome the enemy and to triumph.' [20] Ivan in Dostoevsky's *Brothers Karamazov* had upheld a different opinion : 'If the sufferings of children go to make up the sum of sufferings which is necessary for the purchase of truth, then I say beforehand that the entire truth is not worth such a price.'

There are two other important motives for choosing the topics examined in the book. Areas neglected by other writers on early Soviet Russia have been singled out, partly just because they have been largely overlooked, but also because it is thought that further study of these particular aspects may throw light on the main political problem of the Soviet era – the phenomenon of Stalinism. Secondly, some common themes run through the topics and link them together. If all social facts were incoherent, as Max Weber believed, then every interpretation would be little more than a highly personal juggling act regulated by individual social historians. The author feels that Soviet social and political life in the years of 1917–29 was not completely incoherent. Like Soviet society itself, it contained many semi-organised parts with interconnecting influences. But no clear total order is evident, so that ties between separate topics and chapters cannot be rigidly defined nor rendered all-embracing. Any attempt to do this would be to fall into the trap of imagining, together with Soviet Marxist historians, that social reality can be completely structured, or that a part of it can regulate all the rest. This would imply that there can be only one correct sociological theory.

Any discussion of social influences on political thought and action must for similar reasons be relatively loosely structured in terms of time periods covered. The subject matter is evolutionary by nature and demands historical perspective. It is essential to show the cumulative pressure of social forces within a flexible chronological framework : this method may also help to accentuate their significance vis-à-vis more dramatic and short-lived political outbursts. The repercussions of events strictly limited in time, like the Bolshevik *coup d'état* of October 1917, the Kronstadt revolt, the Tambov uprising, or Stalin's decision to collectivise agriculture, are more obvious and have been more closely studied, but it is not, for the present author at least, a foregone conclusion that they are therefore necessarily more important milestones on the road to Stalinism. In any case they cannot be arbitrarily separated from ongoing social developments and considered in a vacuum. The political events listed above were all stamped with the seal of Bolshevik achievement over recalcitrant forces. Although they were in themselves signs of a high-handed manner, they represented less of an explanation for the eventual drift to the totalitarian system of the 1930s than did the creeping and unconquered effects of social backwardness. With regard to the prelude to Nazism, R. Dahrendorf makes a similar point : 'Adducing specific events as causes is only seemingly precise and concrete; upon closer reflection it turns out to evade the issue by leaving its solution implicit and in terms of little plausibility at that. However one wants to assess the weight of specific events in the prehistory of National Socialism, there is no getting away from the social basis on which they occurred and from which the political reactions of people become understandable.' [21]

Although the motor is always hard to locate in social change, we are also concerned with political dynamics which can easily be pinned down in time, and so the chapters in this book are arranged in some sort of chronological order. Chapters 2 and 3 deal for the most part with the years 1917–21, whereas Chapters 4 and 5 span the whole period 1917–29 and overflow it at both ends. The growth of bureaucracy, analysed in Chapter 6, occurred mainly in the latter portion of these years. Stalin, whose influence was closely associated with the rise of the party bureaucracy, came to sole power in 1929.

As has been said, the year 1917 serves as a kind of unfortunate mental barrier to research. Because of the evolutionary nature of our interests, it will be necessary to delve back before 1917 on many issues. We have already looked at some of the differences in outlook between the Old Bolsheviks and those who joined the party after 1917. The leading Bolsheviks' ideas on the family, traditional military organisation, education and the need for large-scale socio-economic units, all of which are treated in this book, were inherited from their prerevolutionary body of thought, gestated in a long political wilderness. Likewise it would be impossible to examine the problems of illiteracy, small-scale social groupings or even the question of why bureaucracy reappeared, unless their roots in the pre-1917 period are at least recognised, if not discussed at length.

The need to adopt an evolutionary stance has nothing to do with any political prejudices in the author's mind, and everything to do with the special nature of the subject involved. There is no doubt, however, that the evolutionary method has often been used by conservative interpreters of Russia for all kinds of topics. This is only natural, since they see themselves as corrective agents of the revolutionary disposition to clear away the past and begin all over again. The Bolsheviks and their historians, like all revolutionaries, have asserted activity as against passive continuity. They hate the past, just because in the light of history the pressures and conditions of human affairs often seem to be ineluctable.

Many instances of exaggerated stress on continuity even within the sphere of social history, do seem to occur in the Soviet field. The events of 1917 are reduced to little more than a passing mirage or sleight of hand. On the other hand scholars who lean much more to the left have perhaps taken too strong a whiff of the antidote to this affliction. E. H. Carr states that the institutional and social framework was smashed to a greater extent by the Russian Revolution than its equivalent in the English and French Revolutions. He ascribes this greater thoroughness partly to the ruthlessness of the Bolsheviks, partly to the call of Marx and Lenin to smash the pre-existing state machinery.[22] He also adds that it was due 'most of all to the weakness of the old Russian social and political order, which showed none of the tenacity and power for survival of its western counterparts'.[23] Isaac Deutscher agrees about the lack of social continuity but gives a slightly different reason. He sees all social classes, with what he calls 'the partial exception of the peasantry', as either exhausted and prostrate or pulverised under the impact of the Civil War.[24] The Bolsheviks found themselves surrounded by a social vacuum. Their earlier habit of regarding themselves as the sole interpreters of the class interest was now cultivated further by the actual state of society.[25]

The attitudes of these two scholars seem to be slightly too negative. If they mean only that as a class neither the proletariat nor the peasantry played an active role in Bolshevik high politics after 1917, then one must agree. But they appear to go further than that. E. H. Carr concludes that 'in Russia, after the Civil War, only individuals survived',[26] not classes. One of the aims of this book is to try to show that although pre-existing social forces may not have played an active, dynamic role in politics after 1917, they did have a deep and lasting negative influence on the attainment of Bolshevik social, economic and political goals. Deutscher makes a partial exception with regard to the peasantry, and he is surely right. This heavy millstone, eighty per cent of the national population, hung round the necks of the Bolsheviks, and made them adjust their policies on every issue studied in subsequent chapters of this book.

Before we enter into a more detailed survey, a word on sources may be appropriate here. Throughout this section reference has frequently been made to social realities. How close to those realities can we actually get? It has been asserted elsewhere that with regard to economic and social development 'by the mid twenties the Bolsheviks must have been amongst the best informed of all national leaders'.[27] We beg to differ, unless Soviet information is compared only with sources available in countries then at a similar or lower stage of development. The vagaries of the Central Statistical Board have been pointed out above.[28] It is true that many social surveys were carried out during NEP, but they were mainly indiscriminate samples according to no regular chronological or geographical pattern. Some of the most useful information came from ex-Mensheviks,[29] but this rendered it suspicious in the eyes of the Bolsheviks. Again one only has to compare Russia's almost complete lack of a backlog of social statistics with that of Britain, say, to realise how flimsy a base the party had to build upon. Russia's first national census was held in 1897. It had many defects. By the second half of the nineteenth century, every British town of any size possessed small-scale survey maps, on which one can still discern such inconsequential items as individual shrub-beries in private suburban gardens.

Lenin himself realised that in the years immediately following the Revolution the amount of sources which could be collated and published was severely limited by lack of paper, printing presses and human skills.[30] Soviet historians of the present day concur with Lenin's rather pessimistic view, despite the fact that since 1956 more sources have been published on Soviet history than in all the previous years of the Soviet period. They acknowledge that countless primary and secondary sources were destroyed or lost in the Revolution and Civil War. In the effort to preserve vital docu-ments on high political issues, seemingly less important materials of social interest were neglected or even torn up methodically, without any particular motive for obliterating them.[31] Original sources were also often lost when documents wrongly supposed to be duplicates were thrown away.[32]

Large lacunae appear in the sources for these reasons, so that it is often difficult to find single pieces of evidence let alone to cor-roborate sources so as to allow cross-checking. These difficulties are compounded by the bureaucratic hiatus that occurred over the revolutionary years, so that details of social administration are lost for ever. In a vast, centralised, largely illiterate country, where the bureaucracy was essential as a recorder and scribe, this was even more serious. The small portion of the nation which was literate was so engrossed by the accelerated tempo of the epoch that, unless it could emulate Lenin's energy, it found little time to write down accounts of contemporary events. This is visible to anyone who studies the microfilms of the Smolensk archives in the first years after 1917, where pressure of other business has left its trace in scant, untidy notes, quite unlike the fuller and more orderly ar-chives of later years.[33]

Observing early Soviet Russia at a distance of fifty years or so, we have a clear advantage over Soviet commentators in the chaotic years 1917–29, when it was hard to acquire a rounded view of any subject. It may also be an advantage to stand outside historio-graphical controversies which still rage in the USSR. An authorita-tive article of 1961 declared that it was no longer *de rigeur* to judge every source by its class origin and political inclination : a knowledge of the psychological attitude of the author of the source was sufficient.[34] This approach was criticised as unwise in a counter-attack of 1965. Vigilance over class bias was still necessary, since bias nullified any value that a source might appear to have.[35]

Soviet and foreign scholars suffer equally from the fact that throughout the period under review they are investigating a largely oral tradition. This is particularly crippling where sources for social history are concerned. Oral information was rarely trapped and set down in writing. The author of a recent detailed and interesting study of the peasant commune and gathering (*skhod*) over the years 1925–30 has to admit that he found 'virtually no direct evidence on the internal social dynamics of the commune'.[36] When we come to look at the problem of illiteracy in Chapter 4, we shall discover how difficult it is to know how far Bolshevik indoctrination struck a responsive chord among the recently literate masses and how far it conflicted with their inherited beliefs. The response, even if it ever came in articulate form from such apolitical areas of society, was evanescent because it was mostly oral. It is therefore hard to distinguish how far the political malleability of the masses in the 1930s was due to deliberate manipulation or instinctive prejudice. Yet all these drawbacks give one no reason for throwing in the sponge. After all, many scholars continue to spend a lot of time investigating other 'traditional societies'. The quality of Soviet political life in the 1930s was undoubtedly affected by mass illiteracy and deserves to be assessed qualitatively, even if one cannot reduce the answer to pseudo-scientific quantitative proportions.

The comparative rarity of sources is also affected by something else. Soviet historians have noted that collections of published documents, such as the ones in celebration of the fortieth anniversary of 1917, use Petrograd- or Moscow-based materials as prototypes for the whole of Russia, the largest country in the world.[37] This is often the case for the whole period 1917–29. It is usually due to sheer lack of local archives but is sometimes caused by overreliance on easily accessible central sources. For example, Soviet and foreign scholars often refer to statistics on cooperation collected expressly for the Fifteenth Party Congress.[38] Yet if one can compare them with primary local archives on the same topic (and only Soviet scholars can do this, for reasons of security), it evidently becomes clear that they are not comprehensive and are somewhat distorted for central purposes.[39]

In 1921 an obscure but literate peasant from the Vladimir *guberniia* wrote his memoirs of the Russian Revolution. He warns the reader that the names of Kerensky, Miliukov or Trotsky will only appear fleetingly in his book. 'My chief hero is the Russian people, which in the last resort decides the fate of the Revolution.' [40] The present author is by no means confident that such a generalisation could be upheld in the light of the successful political authoritarianism which the Bolsheviks wielded from the start. However, he is well aware of the dangers expressed in the advice given to this same peasant by Leo Tolstoy at the time of the 1905 revolution : 'Write down, write down, write down everything that you see and hear ! Because afterwards they will make of all this what they did with the French Revolution, some sort of learned sausage, and they will poison millions of people with it. Certainly you should write and as truthfully and precisely as possible . . .' [41]

1 J. H. Hexter, *Reappraisals in History* (London, 1967) p. 194.

2 W. Z. Laqueur, *The Fate of the Revolution: Interpretations of Soviet History* (London, 1967).

3 See his *Eighteen Lectures on Industrial Society* (London, 1967) p. 23.

4 Since Lenin's voluntarism is often referred to subsequently, it should be explained at this point. Lenin's decision to take political power in October 1917 appears as an act of voluntarism for two main reasons, though many other subtleties are also involved. First, Russia's socio-economic stage of development was not ripe for a Marxist-type revolution. Second, Lenin's personal intervention in 1917 seemed to stretch Marx's allowance for the role of the individual in history beyond plausible bounds.

5 As might be expected, Trotsky was one of the first to comment on this when he told the Central Committee on 8 October 1923, 'There has been created a very broad stratum of Party workers, entering into the apparatus of the government of the Party, who completely renounce their own Party opinion, at least the open expression of it, as though assuming that the secretarial apparatus is the apparatus which creates Party opinion and Party decisions. Beneath this stratum, there lies the broad mass of the Party, before whom every decision stands in the form of a summons or a command.' Quoted in L. Trotsky, *New Course* (New York, 1943) p. 154.

6 W. E. Mosse, 'Makers of the Soviet Union', in *The Slavonic and*

East European Review (1968), pp. 141–54. Another useful article on a related theme is R. V. Daniels, 'Intellectuals and the Russian Revolution', in the *American Slavic and East-European Review* (April 1961) pp. 270–8.

7 Op. cit., p. 152.

8 A study of writings by members of the Politburo shows a definite dividing line with the ascendancy of Stalin and his supporters. There is a clear trend away from theoreticians, who wrote a great deal, towards organisers who wrote little or nothing. See G. K. Schueller, in H. D. Lasswell and D. Lerner (editors), *World Revolutionary Elites: Studies in Coercive Ideological Movements* (Cambridge, Mass., 1965) pp. 135–8.

9 Although prolific, the output of the *Tsentral'noe Statisticheskoe Upravlenie* (1918–29) had many faults. It did not cover the nationalised sector, nor economic planning. This agency competed with other bodies also collecting data, and its evidence often clashed with theirs. It was too academic for the needs of *Gosplan* and the political leaders. Reformed in 1926–7, it was too late to have much impact on party opinion.

10 E. H. Carr gives an acute description of political juggling of this type in his *A History of Soviet Russia: Socialism in One Country, 1924–1926*, vol. 1 (London, 1958) pp. 95–9.

11 Studies on Soviet workers include P. H. Avrich, 'The Russian Revolution and the Factory Committee', unpublished thesis (Ann Arbor, 1961); A. Broderson, *The Soviet Workers: Labour and Government in Soviet Society* (New York, 1966); M. Dewar, *Labour Policy in the USSR, 1917–1928* (London, 1956); I. Deutscher, *Soviet Trade Unions: Their Place in Soviet Labour Policy* (R.I.I.A., London, 1950); F. I. Kaplan, *Bolshevik Ideology and the Ethics of Soviet Labour* (London, 1969); J. B. Sorenson, *The Life and Death of Soviet Trade Unionism, 1917–1928* (New York, 1969). For the peasantry see M. Lewin, *Russian Peasants and Soviet Power* (London, 1968); D. J. Male, *Russian Peasant Organisation Before Collectivisation* (Cambridge, 1971); T. Shanin, *The Awkward Class: Political Sociology of Peasantry in a Developing Society: Russia 1910–1925* Oxford, 1972). On the intelligentsia see Daniels, op. cit.; S. Fitzpatrick, *The Commissariat of Enlightenment: Soviet Organisation of Education and the Arts under Lunacharsky* (Cambridge, 1970); V. S. Frank, 'Lenin and the Russian Intelligentsia', in L. Schapiro (editor), *Lenin, the Man, the Theorist, the Leader: A Reappraisal* (London, 1967); M. Hayward and L. Labedz (editors), *Literature and Revolution in Soviet Russia* (London, 1963); R. A. Maguire, *Red Virgin Soil: Soviet Literature in the 1920s* (Princeton, N.J., 1968).

On the managers, see J. R. Azrael, *Managerial Power and Soviet Politics* (Cambridge, Mass., 1966); J. Berliner, *Factory and Manager in the USSR* (Cambridge, Mass., 1957); D. Granick, *The Red Executive* (London, 1960). General works covering these fields include the monumental series on the period by E. H. Carr, aided in later volumes by R. W. Davies; and O. Narkiewicz, *The Making of the Soviet State Apparatus* (Manchester, 1970).

12 See R. W. Pethybridge, *The Spread of the Russian Revolution: Essays on 1917* (London, 1972).

13 These include D. Lane, *Politics and Society in the USSR* (London, 1970) and M. Matthews, *Class and Society in Soviet Russia* (London, 1972). The latter records in his preface the need for what he calls 'temporal profundity'.

14. H. Trevor-Roper, 'What is Historical Knowledge for us Today?' in *Survey*, No. 3 (1971) p. 10.

15 See Lewin, op. cit., and Shanin, op. cit. A brilliant discussion of the relationship between Bolshevik notions of class and early Soviet social structure as a whole is to be found in Carr, op. cit., pp. 89–136.

16 S. Ossowski, *Class Structure in the Social Consciousness* (London, 1963) pp. 76–88.

17 It is interesting to note that the same historiographical process has gone on with regard to class studies of the French Revolution. See A. Cobban, *The Social Interpretation of the French Revolution* (Cambridge, 1965) pp. 21–2.

18 See Chapter 5, pp. 197–9.

19 Aron, op. cit., p. 96.

20 Quoted in *Dzerzhinsky* (Moscow, 1947), p. 13.

21 R. Dahrendorf, *Society and Democracy in Germany* (London, 1968).

22 Carr, op. cit., pp. 125–6.

23 Ibid., p. 126.

24 I. Deutscher, *The Prophet Unarmed: Trotsky 1921–1929* (London, 1960) p. 5.

25 Ibid., pp. 11, 13.

26 Carr, op. cit., p. 126.

27 Matthews, op. cit., p. 38.

28 See note 9 on p. 19.

29 See N. Jasny, *Soviet Economists of the Twenties: Names to be Remembered* (Cambridge, 1972) for remarks on non-Bolshevik interpreters of NEP.

30 See V. I. Lenin, 'Statistika i sotsiologiia', in *Proletarskaia revoliutsiia*, no. 1 (1921) p. 4.

31 For example, see G. F. Kozlova, 'Ekspertiza tsennosti dokumentov narodnykh sudov', in *Voprosy arkhivovedeniia*, no. 4 (1962) pp. 91–3. 32,861 law-suits on peasant affairs were destroyed from 1924 in a single *oblast'*, that of Gomel'sk.

32 M. P. Gubenko, in *Istoriia SSSR*, no. 1 (1962), pp. 114–21.

33 On this subject see also Chapter 4, p. 158, note 73.

34 V. P. Danilov and S. I. Yakuboskaia, 'Istochnikovedenie i izuchenie istorii sovetskogo obshchestva', in *Voprosy Istorii*, no. 5 (1961) pp. 3–24.

35 M. P. Gubenko and B. G. Litvak, 'Konkretnoe istochnikovedenie istorii sovetskogo obshchestva', in *Voprosy Istorii*, no. 1 (1965) pp. 5–6.

36 Male, op. cit., p. 210.

37 Gubenko *et. al.*, op. cit., pp. 12–13.

38 *Kooperatsiia k XV s"ezdu VKP (b)* (Moscow, 1927).

39 Gubenko, *et. al.*, op. cit., p. 14.

40 I. Navizhin, *Zapiski o revoliutsii* (Vienna, 1921) p. 5.

41 Ibid.

2 Social Visions 1917–21

Those social and intellectual characteristics which tended to set most of the leading Old Bolsheviks apart from the masses were mentioned in the preceding chapter. More important within the context of this chapter, it has been hinted that the vulgarised Marxist theories the Bolsheviks inherited were ill-suited to Russia's specific social conditions. Yet during the first years of Soviet rule certain aspects of these scarcely adumbrated ideas of Marx and especially of Engels were seized, enlarged upon and immediately applied in an extreme form to Russian society. Had Marx survived to witness these short-lived experiments, it is more than likely that he would have branded them as 'utopian' and therefore quite alien to his own social aims as they were expressed in his maturity. In order to understand the problem, Marx's attitude to utopia must be summarised, then set beside the more usual non-Marxist view. In the light of these two disparate approaches the impulses of the Bolsheviks can be diagnosed and the social experimentation in the period 1917–21 examined in a few selected case studies.

The bold projects of War Communism [1] were doomed to failure almost before they got off the ground : but the very fact that they were ever undertaken at all shows how some, if not all, the Bolshevik leaders were as sanguine about the outcome of a lightning social revolution as they had been (with some justification in retrospect) about the possibility of a quick and successful political *coup d'état* in October 1917. They did not realise in the period immediately after 1917, and only dimly during NEP, to what extent Russia's prolonged social backwardness would tend to shore up the more authoritarian elements in the Leninist political model.

When the word 'socialism' first came into currency in France and England in the 1830s, it was at first used to describe imaginary systems which were completely antithetical to real ones. Marx and

Engels subsequently attacked the early socialists like Saint-Simon, Fourier and Owen for their chimeric idealism which in their view lacked any grounding in the scientific analysis of society. As Engels put it in *Socialism: Utopian and Scientific,*

> The solution of the social problems, which as yet lay hidden in undeveloped economic conditions, the Utopians attempted to evolve out of the human brain. Society presented nothing but wrongs; to remove them was the task of reason. It was necessary, then, to discover a new and more perfect system of social order and to impose this society from without by propaganda, and, wherever it was possible, by the example of the model experiments. These new social systems were foredoomed as Utopian; the more completely they were worked out in detail, the more they could not avoid drifting off into pure fantasies.

For Marx and Engels, as Georges Sorel explained,[2] to give a theoretical analysis of the future socio-economic order would be to try to erect an ideological superstructure in advance of the conditions of production on which it had to be built.

Despite Marx's categorical condemnation of what he called 'utopian' thinkers, his own ideas at some points verge on the utopian in the sense ascribed to this term by non-Marxist political theorists. This is important, since it will help us to understand why utopian traits in the more usual sense of the term reappear in Lenin's social policies in War Communism, and *a fortiori* in the visions of other Bolsheviks who adopted Marx in an even more vulgarised form.

Traditionally, the definition of an utopian cast of mind has not been determined according to whether it is founded on moral or economic postulates, as Marx claimed, but is generally characterised by an orientation towards ends which do not exist in the actual world. It is impossible to give a descriptive definition of utopias, since if one had ever existed it would presumably no longer have been an utopia. One must therefore rely on an exemplary definition culled from specimens of utopian thought through the ages. Two main streams are apparent. One looks for the perfect society through material abundance, the merging of man's selfish individuality into the collective, and the greatness of the State. The other concentrates more on happiness through the freedom to express human personality without sacrificing anything to a given moral code or to the interests of the State. The second stream is by far the smaller, and includes a minority of writers, among whom one may count William Morris, M. Bakunin and P. Kropotkin.

The young Marx's first attempt to reveal Hegel's errors and to search for new directions was made entirely on the political plane, with no reference to economic dogma. His introduction to *Zur Kritik der Heqelschen Rechtsphilosophie* contains a vision of revolution which is based above all on messianic impulse. The description is unlike other utopian structures of the nineteenth century, however, in that it is not encumbered by detailed explanations. It remains vague and magnificent. Yet it is not possible to agree with Marx's rigid division of his own social philosophy from that of the earlier socialists. Both fitted into the wider movement of visionary schemes fired by moral postulates which spanned the nineteenth century as a whole.

It can also be argued, and with justice, that the mature Marx fastened upon 'scientific' proof for his theories in order to give greater conviction to his youthful impulses, which never failed to suffuse his later thought. Some critics have gone further and have tried to show that Marx expected an automatic release from the social ills of capitalism through the scientific working of iron economic laws, and that this was in fact more utopian than the hopes of Saint-Simon or Fourier. The latter were at least well aware that an ideally constituted division of labour on the basis of social ownership was in itself no harbinger of complete accord between the individual and society. One of Marx's harshest critics, Ludwig von Mises, claims that Marx believed that no one could advance 'any definite proposals for the construction of the Socialist Promised Land. Since the coming of Socialism was inevitable, science would best renounce all attempts to determine its nature'.[3]

This view exaggerates what is mistakenly called 'Marxist materialism', and is an interpretation of Engels' writings after Marx's death rather than of Marx's own thought. Reality for Marx is not mere objective data, external to human influence, but is moulded by men through consciousness. Marx takes up a central stance between classical materialism and traditional idealism, bridging the dichotomy between subject and object. 'Productive forces' may include human activity and thought, although this is a controversial point. Because of this, it is possible for men to lessen the birth-pangs of the historical process rather than be mere spectators of a scientific process.

The notion that Marx believed in the automatic birth of a communist utopia may thus be discarded, but there is another aspect of his thought which tends to set him in the utopian camp. Karl Popper has made a famous distinction between what he calls utopian and piecemeal engineers. The former search and fight for the greatest ultimate good of society as a whole, whereas the latter deal with specific, urgent evils of society as it is. Marx adopted a characteristic of the utopian approach to society in his sweeping effort to get to the root of the total system. He too envisaged an apocalyptic revolution which would change the social world out of recognition.[4]

Although, for reasons already mentioned, Marx himself refused to spell out in detail how society would be reconstructed, the practical consequences of planning rationally for the whole of society could not be ignored by the Bolsheviks after 1917. Even in the 1970s our factual knowledge of the intermeshed forces at work in society is inadequate. In the preceding chapter it has been pointed out why much less was known, particularly by the Bolsheviks, of the actual state of Russia just after the Revolution. Our present-day expertise in the formulation of general sociological theories is still insufficient for large-scale 'engineering'. In their time the early Bolsheviks possessed a single theory which, for all its brilliance, contained the inevitable crudities of pioneer theories, and it fitted Russian social conditions like a saddle on a cow's back. With limited practical experience and an ill-adapted theory which had already suffered at the hands of vulgarisers and revisionists, the Bolsheviks introduced radical changes whose consequences were of necessity very hard to calculate.

In the *Communist Manifesto* Marx and Engels again showed how much they owed to the Utopian Socialists, although the latter were bitterly attacked in this work. One significant exception who was treated much more favourably was F. Babeuf. It is difficult to see why he should have escaped severe criticism since he clearly comes within Marx's special definition of an Utopian Socialist, unless one realises that Babeuf's followers were Marx's most useful allies at the time of writing the *Communist Manifesto*.[5] Furthermore the 'positive precepts' of the early socialists for a better society, such as the transformation of the State into a mere managing authority for production and the elimination of the family, are not considered to be erroneous. They are nevertheless dubbed utopian for the reason that class contradictions were not fully developed at the time they were conceived. Thus it is not the contents of the Marxist blueprint for a new social structure which are original, but the broader philosophical foundation on which the blueprint is built.

It is no coincidence that Lenin, like Marx before him, took particular care to indicate the differences that separated his thought from that of the Utopians, including both Marx's Utopian Socialists and other writers more generally considered to be utopian. Lenin was peculiarly sensitive on this point, knowing that many political opponents and neutral observers could not see the differences clearly. In fact there were a number of pressures on the Bolsheviks besides the utopian aspects of the Marxist heritage which sometimes led them to adopt what others were to call utopian attitudes. These are discussed below, but first Lenin's debt to Marx can be isolated. It was psychologically natural that the young messianic Marx had a great attraction for Lenin in the period of War Communism. Lenin himself was still a comparatively young man. He had taken Marxist voluntarism to extremes in the political sphere by prematurely staging a *coup d'état* in the name of a proletariat which hardly existed in the Russia of 1917 in Marx's sense of the term. Lenin took the bit between his teeth with regard to both the time and place of the Marxist political revolution. Almost by force of circumstance and under the impetus of this political success, some Bolsheviks went on in War Communism to implement a highly voluntarist application of Marx's more utopian social theories. Lenin initially agreed to this sequence, since he had been the strongest advocate of political voluntarism, but soon withdrew in the face of the experimental excesses which flourished briefly under War Communism. Thereafter, as we shall see, he reverted to a more orthodox position, professing that the time was not ripe according to Marxist laws for such advanced social changes, which could only be realistically effected after the establishment of the requisite economic substructure and after international revolution.

It was difficult for Lenin in other ways to resist the temptation to agree to social experiments which he later branded as utopian.

Unlike Marx, he was confronted with an actual society of some 145 millions of which he was the nominal leader. He was surrounded by supporters who had helped him to power and who were now eager to introduce immediate social changes. Marx had been so deliberately vague as to the details of the future society that it was not possible for Lenin to refer back explicitly to his writings in order to condemn the improvisations which sprang up in War Communism : but at least Lenin shared Marx's view that the details of the future order could not be known in the era of transition. This was all the more the case in a society which in some particulars was making a direct transition from a pre-capitalist system to socialism. 'It is a very difficult thing,' wrote Lenin, 'to find transitional measures. We have not succeeded in doing this by a quick and straight road, but we shall not lose heart, we shall come into our own.'[6] Lenin thus avoided falling into the trap which has snared so many utopian thinkers. Their suggestions for the idyllic regulation of the minutiae of everyday social life have often turned out to be highly authoritarian. On the other hand Lenin's rejection of piecemeal engineering in specific social institutions entailed advocating sweeping changes for the future which were continually postponed until a later date, and were subsequently never realised in his, or in Stalin's, lifetime.

Many non-Marxist influences were at work on the Bolsheviks which pushed them into undertaking utopian experiments during War Communism. It has often been the case in history that brilliant intellectual élites in backward states have inclined towards utopian theories in the face of the discrepancies between their progressive ideas and the actual situation. As we have noted in Chapter 1, the Old Bolsheviks were the direct intellectual and even social heirs of a prominent section of Russia's prerevolutionary intelligentsia, which found itself in just such a position in the second half of the nineteenth century.

Russia's decisive entry into the mainstream of European culture after the Napoleonic wars coincided in time with the Romantic movement, which helped to foster utopian visions of man's emancipation from a repressive environment. The heyday of literary utopias occurred in the 1830s and 1840s before being cut short in Western Europe by the failures of the revolutions of 1848. The different course of events in Russia and the continuing rift between the intelligentsia and the regime were conducive to the survival of utopian thought there. As E. H. Carr has observed, two generations of Russian radicals used Chernyshevsky's utopian work, *What is to be Done?*, as their bible.[7] They also adopted and perpetuated some of the most outré and utopian strands of thought from the Romantic movement, particularly from the German Romantics. This was no mere accident. Before the age of Bismarck and the unification of the German states, pockets of isolated intellectuals survived under similar political conditions to those which prevailed in Russia until a later date. The German tradition survived amongst the Old Bolsheviks : there are many instances besides that of Marx and Engels of the continued borrowing of extremist social ideas from Germany in the period of War Communism.

For reasons that were peculiar to Russia, her intellectuals were apt to seize upon the more extreme forms of West European thought. Isaiah Berlin has expressed some of these motives so succinctly that it is worth quoting him here.

> In a country like Russia, cut off from the West in the first place by the great medieval religious schism, into which few ideas from outside were allowed to penetrate, in which literacy was very low, almost any idea which came in from the West – provided that it possessed any degree of initial attractiveness – fell upon marvellously rich and virgin soil, and was taken up with a passion hardly imaginable in the West. If there is a large vacuum, and a very fresh and untutored people, many of them eager for light, then almost any idea – no matter how fanciful or obsolete – is likely to find some ready response somewhere. This was the position in Russia in the second quarter of the last century. Hence the immense addiction to theories and doctrines – not merely as something of intellectual interest, not merely as something to while away an idle hour, but to some a source of salvation, something which, if believed in and acted upon, might lead people to a better life, like that which some of them fondly imagined was being led in the West.[8]

The Bolsheviks patronised the authoritarian wing of the utopian tradition. They were dealing with a rigid opposition in the shape of the Tsarist autocracy, so they naturally clung to rigid theories with which to counter it. This is also one reason why the Russian Social Democrats did not abandon the European fashion in the 1860s for scientific materialism once it had swept by in other countries. The dogmatic nature of Marxism had definite long-term attractions for them in a tactical sense. Intellectually they stayed fixed in the generation of Turgenev's Sons, and never became reconciled to the regime as some of the intellectuals of the following generation did, by entering state service in an effort to reform it from within, or by refusing to face political realities and withdrawing into a *fin de siècle* pose, as did many representatives of the literary intelligentsia.

Towards the close of the nineteenth century increasing signs of industrial progress and a series of booms followed by recessions brought the problem of Russia's economic modernisation to the fore. The discrepancy between her apparently inexhaustible supply of raw materials and labour and her backwardness compared with Western Europe and North America led both Sergei Witte and Lenin in turn to the same conclusion, namely that their task was to introduce modern technology as fast as possible. Both men also realised that for lack of time and given the untutored character of the Russian masses, they would have to provide the total framework of socio-political organisation as well.[9] The means which the two men used to this end were of course very different from each other. So too was the source of their inspiration. In Lenin's case the sense of urgency appealed to his chiliastic conception of time in the light of his hopes for the future. The utopian streak in his makeup, which became so prominent for a brief moment in his *State and Revolution*, led him to place the industrial future of Russia at an almost specific and prematurely determined point of time.

Lenin was also specific with regard to some economic projects conceived in the Civil War period. His personal interest in Taylorism and schemes for the electrification of the country contained frequent utopian implications that remind one directly of Saint-Simon's technological daydreams. These two interests of Lenin are discussed below. Russia had to wait until the end of NEP for the large-scale imposition from above of thoroughgoing industrialisation. It was left to Stalin to carry out Witte's and Lenin's vision in a way which might well have shocked both his predecessors. There were also some utopian features (in the authoritarian tradition) amongst the details of Stalin's First Five-Year Plan. Simone Weil's rejection of technological utopias with their insistence on man's subservience to machines is pertinent to the Soviet situation in the 1930s.[10]

At the turn of the nineteenth century the Russian Social Democrats and the Socialist Revolutionaries were affected in part by another aspect of the *Zeitgeist* which tended to enhance the visionary influences at work on the Bolsheviks. Some of the greatest contemporary figures in Russian literature, from Chekhov to Blok, were drawn into apocalyptic descriptions of Russian society. Many intellectuals were attracted by mysticism, which found expression in a wide variety of media, including philosophy and the visual arts. Whereas the majority used the fashion as a means of escaping from the unpleasant realities of late Tsarist Russia, the Bolsheviks added its eschatological overtones to their practical schemes for the staging of a successful revolution. Virtually all intellectuals of whatever political persuasion were aware that political revolution was an imminent possibility, although few were prepared to prophesy exactly when it might occur, and all of them were surprised at the moment when it finally took place. The general sense of foreboding helped to account for the apocalyptic influences at work. These in turn were kept alive by that messianic consciousness which, according to N. Berdiaev, is more characteristic of the Russians than of any other people except the Jews.[11] Literary influences from Western Europe during the same period also had their effect on Russian thought, imbuing it with Symbolist and mystical ideas. These influences are examined in more detail below, particularly with regard to Maiakovsky.

The utopian ideal was at first promoted rather than retarded by the success of the February Revolution in 1917. Widespread euphoria and over-optimistic hopes for the immediate future prevailed in the initial stages of both the French and the Russian Revolutions. It was not only the revolutionary leaders who held out plans for the future. A scholar who has investigated the aspirations of Russian society as expressed in over 4,000 letters, telegrams and motions sent to the Moscow Soviet in March 1917, puts it thus: 'The dream of Russian liberty had come true, and the people saw themselves as . . . professional statesmen, each having in his pocket a proposal for changing and modernizing the country.'[12] The human individuals in the society on which the Bolshevik leaders imposed their temporary social utopia during War Communism were thus quite different in their expectations as a result of the

Revolution. The peasants seized the land, the workers tried to take over the running of the factories, and libertarians defied the laws of 'bourgeois' morality. Bolshevik notions at the political centre, coupled with social aspirations from below, culminated in the peculiar amalgam of War Communism which, 'although to some it seemed the embryo of the future communist millennium, was neither a coherent whole nor a logically necessary projection of Marxist theory'.[13]

After the success of the Bolshevik *coup d'état* in October 1917 a new stimulus served to uphold the utopian tradition. As was mentioned in the preceding chapter, the existing state of society in the Civil War seemed to be such a rebuttal of Bolshevik prognostications that it became more comforting to neglect it by looking beyond to the domestic future or to the prospects for international revolution. Promises of improvement are implicit to some extent in most social movements, but there is great variation in the realism with which intervening problems are assessed. The Bolsheviks, and especially the Left Bolsheviks after 1917, resorted to offering blind hopes and easy escape through their utopian panaceas. They sometimes used illusions as solutions. The Bolsheviks as a whole tended to believe in the short term that revolution in itself led to the abolition of problems.[14] The Leftists found a receptive audience. The formal expression of their views at their utopian climax, in Bukharin's *Programme of the Communists (Bolsheviks)*, sold a million copies in Russia within three months of its publication in May 1918.

Such illusions were also kept alive by the awakened interests and grievances of social groups and intellectual movements which the Bolsheviks had tried their best to arouse before and during 1917. Probably the most articulate social group of this kind were the leading factory workers who tried to perpetuate workers' control after the Revolution. Their demise is reviewed below. Amongst the intellectuals Lenin had to confront the libertarians in the immediate postrevolutionary period, including those within his own party. On the extreme left there were those who looked to a Third Revolution beyond February and October 1917 for the achievement of their maximalist aims.

When one surveys the accumulated motives for utopian speculation in Bolshevik thought as it was eventually expressed concretely in the social experiments of War Communism, it is possible to see that some Bolshevik leaders, at least in this short period of their intellectual history, did not lie outside the mainstream utopian tradition dating back to the 1830s and earlier in Western Europe. They were particularly close to that group of early socialists whom Marx classified as 'Utopian'. Four parallels between the social ideas of the two groups may be listed in order to show this. Robert Owen combined industry and agriculture in his optimistic blue-print for villages of cooperation, a scheme which was in accord with Marx's later ideas and was taken over by the Bolsheviks. Owen, Fourier and Weitling wanted to abolish criminal law, as did the more impatient Bolshevik legal theorists during the Civil War. Fourier and Owen made education the responsibility of the com-munity as a whole. This was the aim of the Bolsheviks, whose early highly experimental schemes for education also resembled in fact the paper projects of the early socialists. Free love was widely favoured by the early socialists, and although some Bolshevik legis-lation on marriage immediately after 1917 was partly influenced by Engels and early twentieth century German writers, it also bears a close resemblance to the views of the early socialists.

The foreign inspiration behind the social experiments during the period of War Communism can now be seen to be the cul-minating point of a long tradition rather than the start of a new movement. By the time it was being implemented the intellectual tide outside Russia was turning against that tradition. The most prolific period in Western Europe for the output of utopian theories had occurred prior to the 1850s. The decline of interest in the second half of the century was followed in the twentieth century by an actual revulsion against the authoritarian dangers inherent in utopian systems. H. G. Wells' *A Modern Utopia*, pub-lished in 1905, agrees with Marx's reticence with regard to the ideal society. Both men refuse to describe the utopia in any detail. But Wells goes beyond this and breaks with the utopian tradition (and with Marx) by refusing to give an exclusive and final social solution, however vague it might be. His utopia is not static, but admits of other utopias. 'There will be many Utopias. Each generation will have its new version of Utopia, a little more certain and complete and real . . .' [15]

Wells offered a very qualified and cautious version of the nine-teenth century utopian model. After him other thinkers directly attacked the tradition and constructed nightmare utopias intended to reveal the authoritarian excesses to which they were prone. It is significant that one of the earliest and greatest of these was E. Zamiatin, a Russian who had firsthand knowledge of War Communism and who wrote his satire, *My*, in 1920–21. From him Orwell took some of his ideas for *1984*.[16]

The mixed sources of utopian social thought in the ideas of the Old Bolsheviks had a strong influence on the views which Lenin and his colleagues evolved in the critical years immediately before and after 1917. The equivocal attitude to utopian views that Lenin inherited from Marx developed into an increasingly violent oscillation between sympathy and antipathy as the Revolution approached and was won. This was because the problems of the actual situation in Russia, which were far greater than any Marx had to face personally, changed swiftly from month to month, affecting both Lenin's psychological motivation and his general political tactics. Lenin's mind in the years 1914–17 was racked by two polar views, the one coldly materialist, the other utopian in its exaggerated application of the Hegelian dialectic. In solitary exile during the First World War, Lenin yielded to the solace of voluntarist phantasy at a moment when a successful revolution in Russia seemed as remote as ever. He then wrote in his notebook :

> The approach of the mind to a particular thing . . . is complex, split into two, zig-zag like, which *includes it in* the possibility of the flight of phantasy from life; more than that : the possibility of the transformation (moreover, an unnoticeable transformation, of which man is unaware) of the abstract concept, idea into a *phantasy* . . . For even the simplest generalization, in the most elementary general idea . . . *there is* a certain bit of phantasy. (Vice versa : it would be stupid to deny the role of phantasy, even in the strictest science : cf. Pisarev on useful dreaming, as an impulse *to* work, and on empty day-dreaming.)[7]

In just such a way as this Lenin transformed the abstract concept of the dialectic, which he studied in depth during the war years and applied in a phantastic form to his two most famous works of social interpretation : *Imperialism: The Highest Stage of Capitalism* and *State and Revolution*. In order to give continued assurance to his will to revolution, Lenin turned the dialectic into a tool for personal wish fulfilment. The dialectical logic of

Hegel as interpreted by Marx provided Lenin with a formal means of allowing humanity to make totally unrealistic leaps into a new social world, to smash imperialism, the state and bureaucracy and, as he wrote in *State and Revolution*, to substitute the 'whole people in arms' for the capitalists and bureaucrats in the control of production within twenty-four hours of the fall of the latter.[18] Neither before nor after the writing of *State and Revolution* in the summer of 1917, at the climax of his utopian trend, did Lenin ever yield to such phantasy, especially such detailed phantasy. It contradicted his adherence to the doctrine of scientific materialism and his training as a statistical sociologist. He was spurred on at this particular moment in time, exiled in Finland after the abortive Bolshevik coup of July, by the need to inspire both himself and his followers with a vision of the future which had to be bright enough and near enough to give them the vital sense of urgency required to put through the boldest political coup in all history.

Lenin's views were to swing drastically away from the apocalyptic mood of *State and Revolution* with the onset of the Civil War in 1918, but during the first months of Bolshevik rule a modified type of utopianism still affected Lenin's approach to most socio-economic and administrative problems. In his article *Will the Bolsheviks Retain State Power?* Lenin expanded his plans for instant management by workers and peasants. Harsh military realities eventually compelled those who led the fight for the survival of the Soviet state to jettison their utopian projects. Lenin's severe treatment of workers' control is considered below as an important example of this in civilian life. In the military sphere it was remarkable how that arch romantic, Trotsky, bowing at once to the need to defend Petrograd from the Germans and to organise the eastern front, rejected earlier utopian projects for a socialist militia and relied on a regular army of the traditional type.[19]

Lenin's political tactics as well as his psychological reactions altered radically with the changed position after October 1917. Between the February Revolution and October he deliberately played down his earlier insistence ever since *What is to be Done?* on a centrally controlled political organisation. His views in 1917 were a peculiar mixture of utopian beliefs, a desire to use anarchist movements in order to smash the Provisional Government, and the determination ultimately to 'organise everything, take everything into our hands', in the words he used later to rephrase the centralist outlook in 1918. But the utopian and anarchic streaks appeared to prevail momentarily in 1917, so much so that Lenin's soft handling of the factory committees seemed to place him for once squarely on the libertarian wing of the utopian tradition. Previously and subsequently he always adhered to the authoritarian wing.

The October coup in Petrograd was in itself less of a major turning point in Russian history than Lenin's dramatic switch in political tactics on taking over the power of the state. A Petrograd-centred *coup d'état* with a minimal exchange of physical force took place rather than an All-Russian Revolution. Only a prolonged Civil War could alter this balance : yet the success of the War depended on the ruthless centralisation of all forms of power in Lenin's hands. The new leader allowed his utopian views to linger on in the social sphere until the actual outbreak of the Civil War, but clamped down immediately after October in all areas where his political authority was at stake. With fierce realism he at once imposed a strict censor on the press, though he had clamoured for it to be lifted from February to October. Similar *voltes-face* were imposed on all central institutions which might influence the political process.

Thus in the course of a few months in the winter of 1917–18 Lenin successively abandoned his previously held utopian ideas, at first in the political sphere and then on social matters. After the start of the Civil War only two utopian social interests of apparently minor importance were allowed to survive in Lenin's mind. They are worth examining here, since they represent the idiosyncratic swan song of this side of his thought. Lenin became deeply intrigued by the possibility of providing electrification for the entire country, and by the relevance of Taylorism to Soviet labour conditions. Both interests lay directly in the Russian tradition of fascination with technological progress.

A long-term plan of electrification (GOELRO) was first outlined to the Party Congress in 1920 by an engineer, G. M. Krzhizhanovsky, with Lenin's personal backing. After discussing these ideas with Lenin, H. G. Wells characterised them as 'senseless dreams amid universal ruin'.[20] The fact that most of Moscow's electricity had to be cut off so as not to overstrain the city power station when a large map lit up to show Russia's future hydroelectric plants to the Congress, seemed to be a pathetic illustration of Wells' point. The famous slogan coined by Lenin, 'Communism is Soviet power plus the electrification of the whole country',[21] was not a naive momentary aberration, nor even a careful vulgarisation of his own more sophisticated view, but a firmly held belief. Lenin called electrification the 'second programme of our party'[22] and devoted much of his speeches and writing to this theme.[23] At one point in his reflections on electrification he considers technological utopias in general. If a Bolshevik dreamt of altering the economic basis of Russia in three years, 'he would of course be a dreamer of phantasies. And – there's no need to hide the fact – there have been quite a few dreamers of this kind in our country. There's nothing particularly bad about this. In what way could a socialist revolution be begun in such a country without dreamers of phantasies?'[24] Lenin went on to point out that widespread electrification would provide the requisite base for a rationalised economy, but he realised that it would take decades to achieve.

Thus as far as timing was concerned he was not utopian, and his economic opinions on this subject have been dubbed 'interesting pioneering efforts at thinking out means of developing Russia's natural resources on a large scale'.[25] It is when one looks at the *social* results which Lenin predicted would follow immediately on electrification that we are back in the realm of utopias. He saw electrification as a magic catalyst which would automatically sweep away centuries of social backwardness. Patriarchal Russian society could be obliterated, 'thanks to one huge, crowning scientific enterprise'.[26] 'Without electrification, a return to capitalism is inevitable.'[27] Lenin had some strange bedfellows who agreed with him. On the extreme left the maximalists held very similar views, except that they were also totally unrealistic as to the timing of the project, which Lenin was not. Writing on the tasks of maximalism in May 1917, an obscure author built his whole programme on the foundation of common labour in the fight against nature. Primitive man had wielded the club, then the axe, but now electricity was the only tool for transforming society.[28] Lenin's views were also taken up by the poet Maiakovsky, whose vulgarised and unorthodox social ideas on many other subjects incurred Lenin's criticism, but escaped as far as electrification was concerned. In one of his poster-poems, Maiakovsky chides the bourgeois for his sceptical approach to the social results of electricity.

'At electrification his eyes bulged a bit.
"Utopia", he said, "nothing
   Will come of it".
Just you wait, bourgeoisie.
There'll be New York in Tetushakh,
   There'll be paradise in Shuee.' [29]

The notion of waving a scientific or pseudo-scientific wand in order to produce fast social changes is a perennial favourite in utopian thought, as a perceptive Russian author noted in a survey of the history of utopias written in 1910.[30] He put the Russian Social Democrats' fascination with technology in a direct line of tradition dating back not only to Saint-Simon, but beyond to the alchemists and the astrologists. It was easy for the Russian Marxists to fit into this particular tradition. Like the Japanese in another country with vast industrial potential, they were inclined to exaggerate the immediate benefits of applying West European technology to their society. As good Marxists, they stressed the connection between economic changes and social and psychological advancement. When Lenin deals with electrification in this way, however, he finds another odd bedfellow. A. A. Bogdanov, whose unorthodox Marxist views are also considered in Chapter 4, believed that the collective ideal arose in proletarian psychology purely on the basis of large-scale machine production.[31] Lenin thought that electrification would serve to break up Russia's small-scale peasant economy and narrow-minded peasant psychology at the same time.[32] He even implied that if the future national grid could be extended to cover a series of neighbouring countries, their national prejudices might be replaced by an international outlook.

Lenin's vague optimism was not unlike the poetic phantasies of the Futurists and Constructivists whose ideas were prevalent in artistic circles during the Civil War. Men like V. Tatlin saw technology as the major source of power in the modern world, releasing men from labour, which would be transformed into an art. The mechanical projects of these men were confined to the world of the theatre, since the real Soviet world outside was far too backward to make use of them.[33] Even by the partly disillusioned mid-1920s, after Lenin's death, writers inspired by his enthusiasm described the new hydroelectric schemes in terms which are reminiscent of the romantic approach to early industrialisation in Western Europe a hundred years before: 'Sixty thousand electric horses will stay in harness for whole decades.'[34] Lenin preferred to leave the details of GOELRO's plan in vague outline. He mentioned in a letter of 23 January 1920 to Krzhizh-anovsky that the non-technical members of his government and the public needed a popular project to arouse their interest.[35] Yet despite the vagueness and the utopian social predictions, the long-term economic results of Lenin's vision were impressive. In 1920–21 a mere extra 12,000 kilowatts were produced. By 1935 the figure was 6.9 millions and by 1940 11.2 millions.[36]

The social effects of electrification remained hypothetical in the Civil War period, but they were immediate with regard to Lenin's other surviving interest that had utopian implications. Lenin's dalliance with Taylorism, or scientific management, may appear to be of minor significance, but on closer scrutiny it fore-shadows Stalin's interpretation of the authoritarian utopia in general, and his interest in Stakhanovites in particular.[37] It is also directly concerned with the treatment of the central social class, the proletariat. The American F. W. Taylor set in motion a far reaching revolution in the industrial process. Working on the assumption that labour scarcity was permanent and that costs had to be minimised, Taylor tried through precise calculation to break down each working procedure into its components and then put together the combination of job aggregates and work motion that would bring about the most productive results. He was well aware that he was subordinating man to the machine, in the social and psychological sense as well as economically. Thus he recom-mended, 'One of the first requirements for a man who is fit to handle pig iron as a regular occupation is that he shall be so stupid and so phlegmatic that he more nearly resembles an ox than any other type.'[38]

Lenin's stress on obligatory labour and labour mobilisation in *State and Revolution* became a fundamental tenet of Soviet social policy. His interest in technocracy, inherited indirectly from Saint-Simon, also led him to adopt Taylor's theories. Lenin, like Marx, was caught between admiration and fear of the industrial process, which dehumanised man but which could also organise methods of production and distribution on scientific lines. Unlike Marx he could not maintain an equivocal position when faced with the collapse of Russian industry after the 1917 Revolution. Although he had reacted against over-rationalised labour methods in his youth,[39] he now advocated Taylorism. Neither did he relax his views after the end of the Civil War. During NEP wage and labour adjustments were made so that the party in the name of the Trade Unions aimed only at maximising output and minimising costs.

The application of Taylorism to factory workers did not go uncriticised during the Civil War and in NEP, when it was still possible to argue against the party line. In a bitter article published in the railwaymen's journal for 1920, the author complained that Taylorism allowed the Bolsheviks to 'exploit the worker to the maximum'. Wagon-loaders using Taylor's methods could handle 3,000 *puds*[40] instead of 750 within the same period of time, but surely it would benefit the workers more if they were given a mechanical loader? Foremen were even advised, following Taylor's practice, to designate the return walk from the wagon to the goods for loading as free time. The author concluded that the party looked as though it would end by exhausting its most precious material, the proletariat, and would repeat American mistakes which led to social tension and exploitation.[41]

The false premises on which Taylor's theories were built, the exaggerated claims for the method and the ruthless neglect of the human factor in the search for perfection, all smacked of the authoritarian utopian tradition. Taylorism came to be applied consciously or unconsciously to many other aspects of Soviet life besides factory labour organisation. Trotsky insisted that it be introduced into the army and even into the education of 10 to 15-year-olds in preparation for military service.[42] Lenin, and to a much greater extent Stalin, envisaged a whole society run like a workshop in the most efficient way for what they took to be the common good: but as N. Berdiaev observed, 'Lenin did not believe in man . . . he had a boundless faith in the social regimentation of man. He believed that a compulsory social organization could create any sort of new man.'[43] In his nightmare version of utopia, written at the height of the Soviet vogue for Taylorism, Zamiatin portrays the future social ideal as the perfection of the human machine. Taylorism is applied to each step, each movement that men make. They eat synthetic food, dress in synthetic uniforms, and are taught at school by time-saving robots.

The burden of responsibility that fell on Lenin's shoulders after the coup of October 1917 caused him to confine his interest in social experimentation to areas of life which had no deleterious effects on his political rule. Trotsky was to move in the same direction, at least as far as military affairs were concerned, when he had to answer for the efficiency of the Red Army. Other Bolsheviks in less vulnerable positions did not shed their utopian inheritance so quickly. Bukharin, Kollontai and Bogdanov, to name three of the leaders of the Left Communists, as they came to be called in 1918, pursued social chimeras throughout the Civil War and often came into sharp conflict with Lenin.

Lenin had already taken issue with many aspects of their thought prior to the Revolution. On tactical grounds he had disagreed with their hopes for a renewed armed uprising on the model of Moscow in 1905. In his *Materialism and Empirio-Criticism* he attacked the theoretical speculations of the Leftists as upheld by Bogdanov, and in 1909 he went so far as to summon a meeting of the Bolshevik leadership to exclude the group he called 'Left fools'. Bogdanov's role in prompting utopian views among the Leftists is important, since his sophisticated and unorthodox philosophy of knowledge was an early general foundation on which Bukharin, Kollontai, Lunacharsky and others elaborated their detailed structures for social revolution in the various aspects of life that interested them in particular. This is not the place to enter into an explanation of Bogdanov's theories [44] (his views on education and culture are treated in the chapter on illiteracy). Less well known are his two 'phantastic' novels, as he named them, which are descriptions of the future Soviet utopia.[45] One of them is set on Mars after the victorious revolution of the Martian working class which occurred in 1560 A.D. The engineers of the new regime work out the answers to social problems by scientific mathematical analysis instead of relying on biased individual human talent, so that 'when the epoch of radical transformation of all the social structure began, it was possible to overcome the very great difficulties of the new organisation relatively easily and completely systematically'.[46] Bogdanov's hopes expressed through fiction are reminiscent of Taylorism.

Between the outbreak of the First World War and January 1918 the issue of the war served to reconcile Lenin in some ways, though not in all, to the Leftists. Trotsky's theory of permanent revolution and Bukharin's writings on imperialism were taken up by Lenin in support of his views on internationalism and defeatism. The new relationship was cemented when Lenin returned to Russia in April 1917 and openly declared his aim as defeatism and the overthrow of the Provisional Government. He thus agreed with the Leftists that Western Europe was on the brink of proletarian revolution. Indeed, both he and they thought that without international uprisings backward Russia would be incapable on her own of effecting a social revolution.

Lenin temporarily abandoned the internationalism of the Left under the pressure of military necessity in the winter of 1917-18. His victory over the Leftists in signing the peace of Brest-Litovsk with the Central Powers was soon followed by the need to form a regular army for the defence of the eastern front rather than for revolutionary war in Western Europe. Despite this change of heart, Lenin allowed War Communism to be introduced, although he admitted later that it was a mistaken attempt to stage social and economic transformations without international support which might provide the correct economic basis for such changes.[47] January 1918 marked the final parting of the ways between Lenin and the Leftist utopians as far as social experiments were concerned. He subsequently quarrelled in turn with Bogdanov, Bukharin, Kollontai and others when they persisted in continuing with root-and-branch social reforms. In his *The Infantile Disorder of 'Leftism' in Communism* Lenin publicly condemned the faults of the romantics. The main targets of his attack were leaders of foreign communist parties, but he also by inference wished to discredit domestic utopians. It is of some interest to note that the precondition of an international structure for a social utopia was not confined to Marxist-Leninist theory. In *A Modern Utopia* Wells also claimed, though on different grounds, that only a world system could uphold an ideal social life.

The stress which Bukharin laid prior to 1918 on the need for Russia to join up with international revolutionary movements in order for her to survive and to develop into a mature communist society should have led him logically, with Lenin, to discard utopian social schemes with the onset of the Civil War, but the romantic in him produced a new gloss on the previous orthodoxy which enabled him to maintain his original position. In his *Historical Materialism: A System of Sociology*, first published in 1921, he defined society as 'the broadest system of mutually interacting persons, embracing all their permanent mutual interactions, and based on their labour relations'.[48] He went on to argue that since society is not merely an aggregate of persons, it cannot in any way be reduced to its parts and retain the same meaning. The component parts of a watch are its sum, but not the watch itself. Only a certain arrangement of people, 'connected by the labour bond between them', constitutes a real society.[49] In periods of temporary retrogression and revolutionary transition, such as the one through which Russia was passing in the Civil War, the growth of production forces was thwarted and therefore the social bonds of labour were severed. At this point Bukharin showed his trump card (it was not new since he followed Bogdanov's ideas closely here) : during these periods of history productive forces were in retreat and under the greater influence of superstructures. Thus there was no especial need to have the right kind of economic base in order to carry out advanced social experiments, which for a time could develop a life of their own, although even this life was circumscribed by the prerevolutionary state of productive forces.[50]

In the political sphere the utopians never succeeded in organising mass support. They were broken by Lenin's coercive pressure from the very start of the Bolshevik regime. Moreover some of them were placated by the introduction of War Communism, which seemed to suit their leanings. As so often in the early history of the party, Lenin also stood to gain politically when schisms began to appear among the Leftists. Those who adhered rigidly to their prerevolutionary libertarian notions now organised themselves into two separate groups – the Democratic Centralists and the Workers' Opposition. Both were increasingly opposed by the authoritarian utopians, Trotsky and others; most of whom were former Left Mensheviks. The Democratic Centralists in particular attacked Trotsky's changed views on the role and organisation of the Red Army, to which reference has already been made. Trotsky was the most imaginative of all the leading Communists in his vision of man's future, but at the same time he was a rational pragmatist. Faced with the practical problems of the Civil War, he acted as a true dialectician. He did not envisage an early finality in the political nor in the social spheres, but only an adaptable process. For this reason military realities made him less rather than more utopian. They could have had a very different effect, as indeed they did on less flexible visionaries who argued that wars 'easiest of all and most often of all in history bring about the realisation of utopias'.[51] A protagonist of this view in the Civil War quoted with approval the slogan of that wild romantic Georges Sand : 'Struggle or death : bloody war or nothing – thus the question is posed without end !'[52]

This strange marriage of ideas was typical of the muddled views of the lesser known figures who formed the rank and file of the Democratic Centralists and the Workers' Opposition, or were even too libertarian to fit into either of these groups. They had fewer political responsibilities than Kollontai or Bukharin, let alone Lenin or Trotsky, and were correspondingly detached from the pressure of events. Their eclectic views on social problems were culled from such a wide variety of theoretical sources that their debt to Marxism was often quite obfuscated. This was unconsciously reflected in a history of ideas published in 1922 entitled *From Thomas More to Lenin, 1516–1917*.[53] The author included under what he called a history of Marxist socialism all types of utopians, anarchists and other strange bedfellows.

The most important unorthodox influences on the lesser Bolsheviks and fellow-travellers were, as might be expected, imported from Germany. It was in line with a tradition which dated back at least as far as the early German Romantics.[54] Translations of all kinds of German works on utopian themes, from A. Voigt's *Social Utopias* to A. Bebel's *Future Society*[55] were eagerly read. Their ideas reappeared in ill-digested form in the writings of minor Russian theorists. Rosa Luxemburg's views were anathema after 1917 for Lenin and other orthodox leaders, but at these lower levels her opinions on social policy were repeated and welcomed.[56] Any foreign grist to the utopian mill that could be found was incorporated. The progressive optimism of Darwin was put to use in many works.[57] In one short book alone the ideas of such heterogeneous thinkers as Heine, Schiller, Shelley and that 'well-known Englishman [sic] William James'[58] were regurgitated. Small wonder that Lenin grew impatient with the superficial nature of this advocacy of instant millennium.

Maiakovsky is an interesting example of the unorthodox maximalist tendency that so irritated Lenin. Maiakovsky was not a threat at the highest political level, but he was a great writer and propagandist, and Lenin feared that his extravagant ideas would therefore reach a wide audience. Maiakovsky's views on revolution in early Soviet society were an amalgam of nearly all the utopian strands which have been discussed in this chapter. His ideas are also fascinating because their evolution through his personal career reflected in microcosm the progressive disillusionment of the ultra-Leftists. Maiakovsky's interest in utopian themes long preceded the Revolution. As a leader of the Russian Futurist movement before 1917, he already looked to technological progress as the panacea for his country's social backwardness. He was also chiliastic in the broader utopian tradition. His constant impatience with menial, customary daily life (*byt*) and his need to realise future benefits in an accelerated process of time was at first satisfied by the speed of the 1917 Revolution. He celebrated the Bolshevik victory with his drama *Mystery–Bouffe*, of which the first version was completed in September 1918. This play combined a brief account of the Revolution with a vision of a future utopia on earth. His optimism in *Mystery–Bouffe* and in many of his poems in the Civil War period was focused on social affairs, but an ever increasing tide of personal pessimism crept into his work. The optimistic element was based on his earlier Futurist and chiliastic views, but also on Marxism, which coloured the philosophy of history expressed in *Mystery–Bouffe*. Maiakovsky's early membership in the Social Democratic Party was more than a formal gesture, and he probably read widely in Marxist thought.[59]

The second version of *Mystery–Bouffe*, dating from 1920, revealed a decline of Maiakovsky's hopes for the social revolution. He became more troubled by *byt*, which for him summed up the reactionary weight of slow tradition in both social and personal life. It was this stubborn adherence to prerevolutionary customs in most social classes that was the main stumbling block of the Leftists, and we shall see in successive chapters of this book how its heavy influence continued to have an adverse effect on political theories and on political organisation through the 1920s.

Marx had not specified the amount of time that would elapse between the Revolution and the advent of the classless society. The Bolshevik party slowly adapted itself to the slowness and imperfection of this world, but the poet's solution was uncompromising in the case of Maiakovsky and Esenin, who both committed suicide. Maiakovsky eventually retreated into a private world, waiting with eschatological hope for what he called the 'third revolution of the spirit' : it had its political equivalent in the Anarchists' belief in their 'Third Revolution', which would achieve what the February and October Revolutions had failed to do. From social revolution in historical time, Maiakovsky finally turned to individual rebellion against time by putting an end to his own life. In his career he almost turned full circle. At the end he returned to the escapism which had characterised his earliest prerevolutionary outlook, and also, as we have seen, the outlook of so many other Russian intellectuals in the first seventeen years of the twentieth century. One can but guess how many other romantic enthusiasts for the Revolution, whose lives are less well documented, followed a similar trajectory of illusion and disillusionment.

In the realm of actual social planning and achievement, rather than in poetic descriptions of their eventuality, an analogous pattern can be observed. The highly placed Leftists in the Civil War tried to realise the social utopia of free and equal individuals in all spheres simultaneously. In politics they usually tended to be anarchistic : in economics they were anti-centralist and democratic. On social matters they thought that Bogdanov's doctrine of revolutionary culture necessitated the immediate abandonment of 'bourgeois' social constraints over the individual. Through a wide range of social institutions various experiments motivated by similar ideals flourished briefly until they were cut short by the final defeat of the Left at the Tenth Party Congress in March 1921. Split between the Trotskyist authoritarians and the libertarian wing, and embarrassed by the Kronstadt rebellion, the utopians were defeated by Lenin's attack on factionalism within the party. Experimentation in the role of the family (Kollontai's special interest), in the Trade Unions (Trotsky and Bukharin), in the law (P. I. Stuchka and B. Pashukanis), in education (V. N. Shulgin) and a whole series of other social fields petered out, leaving only literature and one or two other lesser areas where innovations still continued into NEP.

On every front except electrification and Taylorism, Lenin now opposed social utopianism. A mere six months after writing *State and Revolution* he virtually contradicted his earlier opinions by telling Bukharin that he was violating historical perspective by talking of the state withering away.[60] Turning quickly from political to social questions, he attacked over-fast changes in labour management, family structure, education and *belles-lettres* (these attacks are discussed later), as well as in many other fields. In this he was often supported by Stalin. Of all the major Bolshevik leaders, Stalin was by far the most taciturn on the subject of the ideal society. He just repeated the orthodox and vague Marxist teaching about the future,[61] whilst acting pragmatically as he always did. The only exception to this rule in the period 1917–21 resulted from his flattery of Lenin combined with his envy of Trotsky. In a letter he sent to Lenin in March 1921 he compared Lenin's magnificent projects for electrification with Trotsky's scheme for the militarisation of labour : 'What poverty of thought, what backwardness compared with the GOELRO plan !' He went so far as to suggest that the party devote a third of all its working time to electrification.[62]

The remainder of this chapter is devoted to a closer examination of two areas of social life that were the subject of controversy between Lenin and the Leftists in the Civil War. The family and the role of workers in the management of the economy have been chosen as case studies. More than any other area, experiments in the family and theoretical disputes over its function reveal the immense gap that lay between revolutionary aspirations and the backward reality. Whereas the peasantry dominates any discussion of family life, workers' control concentrates on the proletariat and has a higher level of political significance, since it was intended at different times by different Bolshevik leaders to progress from an instrument of socio-economic control to a substitute for the political bureaucracy of the past. Both subjects are studied here less from above than from below. This means that it is not a sufficient explanation for the failure of these early social experiments to point to the unrealistic nature of the theories that were applied from the centre. It is also just as important, if not more so, to look at the effect of social recalcitrance on the part of the masses.

Nevertheless one cannot approach the problem of the family in the early Soviet period with no knowledge of the ideological motives of the Bolsheviks. The Social Democrats cannot be given all the credit for trying to reform family life in Russia. From the turn of the century until 1917 liberals of all hues had more practical influence than the Marxists in this sphere. Serious nationwide discussion of the family structure began at meetings like the first All-Russian Women's Congress of 1908, which mustered over 900 delegates.[63] Liberal writers who managed to avoid the censor began to support social and even political rights for women, claiming vaguely that whereas men ruled Russia by force, women would do it through Christian love.[64] The emphasis remained on the rights of women up to 1917. This was a fashionable cause in Germany and Britain at the time, whilst nearer to home the Grand Duchy of Finland granted the vote to women in 1906. At the first Congress for the Education of Women, held in 1915, a speaker reminded the audience that in one part of the Empire (Finland) no less than twenty-six bills on the family had been presented to the government.[65] Alexandra Kollontai's name does not figure in the list of delegates to either of the Congresses.

When the Provisional Government lifted the censorship after February 1917 the literature on the social and political rights of women and the family proliferated. The political emancipation of women in Britain in the summer of 1917 led to more vociferous Russian claims. One woman author noted that although there had been much theorising during the French Revolution on sexual equality and freer family ties, little had actually been achieved. She praised G. E. Lvov, the first leader of the Provisional Government, for granting political rights to women : 'Only a free mother can bring up free citizens.' [66] Another woman writer recalled the role played in the Russian revolutionary movement by women like Vera Figner, Vera Zasulich and Sofia Perovskaia.[67] Industrial development and the need to find women to replace men called up for the war were seen as ways in which women were being freed from the bonds of the patriarchal family. It was also noted in 1917 that women's battalions were formed in many other Russian cities besides Petrograd.[68]

The liberals wanted to reform the legal status of the family under the Provisional Government. An eminent jurist, G. Grigorovsky, described the plight of families in Tsarist Russia as 'separate pairs of swallows which made their nests at the window of a huge state building'. In 1902 Russia refused to join the Hague international convention on family law. She continued to depend on Meyer's book on civil law, which had been a student text for sixty years, and which considered family affairs as moral matters to be dealt with mainly by the obscurantist ecclesiastical courts. Divorce, for example, was entirely within their powers. Grigorovsky ridiculed the Holy Synod, which in 1917 tried to think in terms of reform by amending the rigid divorce laws but still intended to confine them to church courts. He was adamant that the government through the civil code should be responsible for the family, which was the backbone of Russia's population and her whole social future.[69]

The Bolsheviks inherited many of the reformist ideas current in Russia before 1917. They agreed with Grigorovsky that so long as the family remained a key area in the socialisation of children it must be protected and reformed by the state. They also agreed that the Tsarist regime relied on the conservative structure of the family as a bastion of reaction. But they added new ideological arguments taken from Marx and especially from Engels. These arguments can be read in the original texts or in summaries of them,[70] and are merely adumbrated here. In the capitalist system, according to Engels, marriage has an economic basis. It is used for the transmission of property and is tainted by private wealth. Genuine human love in such a society only exists in working class families. A socialist system would free all families from economic and legal barriers by abolishing private wealth and basing them on free choice. Women would become the equals of men : housekeeping and child care would become the common concern of society as a whole.

In the Civil War, A. Balabanova, a famous Bolshevik, waxed lyrical on the immediate effects the October Revolution would have on the nature of the family and the role of women : 'And now in our society, hallowed by unheard-of sufferings and the workers' struggles, the female toiler throws away her crown of thorns, that centuries old crown woven through and knit together with so much degradation, suffering, tears, sweat and blood.'[71] Balabanova, like Kollontai, wrote under the influence of many previous thinkers, both Marxist and non-Marxist. This accounts in part for the considerable element of unorthodoxy in the two women's ideas, particularly Kollontai's. The enormous volume of foreign literature and the discussions of the liberals have already been noted. Kollontai made her own translation from the German of A. Bebel's utopian work.[72] The utopian streak was also to be found in indigenous Russian authors prior to 1917. Some of Kollontai's more fanciful ideas were rehearsed ten years before she publicised them in books like M. Eletsky's *Free Love*. Strongly influenced by foreign romantics like Rousseau and Shelley, Eletsky evaluated free love in an almost mystical way, giving it creative and noble attributes.[73]

All the Bolsheviks, from Lenin to Kollontai, seemed at first sight to be adopting a libertarian attitude to the family. Without a doubt the Russian family system before 1917 helped to preserve many conservative features of the old regime, although some of Engels' economic strictures were exaggerated and partly irrelevant to the Russian case. Peasant social mores were all-important for the family structure in Tsarist Russia since the peasants comprised the vast majority of the population. The peasant family was strongly patriarchal. Male dominance was based on economic and religious grounds as well as on long social tradition. The head of each extended family controlled the management and repartition of the whole family plot in the agricultural system of the *mir*, or commune. His economic rights were bolstered by the analogy drawn by the church between the natural authority of God the Father and the head of each human family. The mutual support of the Orthodox Church and the peasant family meant that to attack one was to attack the other, which the Bolsheviks set out to do. The extended family system and cramped living conditions helped to ensure that the superstitions, illiteracy and backwardness of the grandparents were handed on by them to the second and even to the third generation.

The Tsarist government and its propagandists made full use of the family, which acted as a discreet fourth pillar to the official creed of Autocracy, Nationality and Orthodoxy. On the eve of the First World War apologists for the regime were still recommending that parents should see to it that their children be educated exactly as they themselves had been, in the interest of morality and stability.[74] The place of women was by the fireside. As guardians of the future generation, their aim was to use their natural gentleness to stress the avoidance of force, and to fight against atheism and anarchy in their children.[75] A magnificently naive theory on the political role of the family was produced for the regime by 'the peasant N. Bogachev', as the author was styled on the title page. The first power in the world had been the ownership and education of children by Adam and Eve. The first family grew into a tribe, and tribes grew into kingdoms (*tsarstva*). Since the Tsar was sent by heaven to be the protector of all parents, he was called the Father of the people and was the second power in the world. It would be working against nature to preserve the second power without the first. They had to support each other. If marriage contracts were broken, life became 'cattle-like' (*skots-*

kaia). If the Tsar did not uphold the old family laws, human society would descend to the order of sheep, asses and pigs : 'Life flourishes when members of the family are in their place, that is, when the father rules and the children obey.'[76]

Bogdanov thought that in many spheres of social life the authoritarian yoke typical of feudal systems would be thrown off under the dominance of the bourgeoisie. Capitalist pressures would create specialisation in the economic and social systems, leading to some measure of individual choice. One sphere he excluded was the family, where he believed the bourgeoisie had kept up an authoritarian approach in spite of economic pressures.[77] The social progress that had to be made from Russia's quasi-feudal system to a socialist one, bypassing capitalism, was enormous in Lenin's opinion as well.

Lenin and Kollontai differed in their motives for smashing the traditional family nexus. Lenin viewed the social influence of the family as a rival to the political centre. Its reactionary hold on individuals had to be loosened. Kollontai agreed that there should be a new 'family of the collective of workers, in which people will be bound together not by blood relationships, but by their common interests, aspirations and aims and which will make them brothers in spirit'. Lenin went beyond this stage. For him detachment from the family did not lead to rootless freedom, but to reliance on the party. After Lenin's death this attitude was reinforced. The Komsomol Pavlik Morozov, who was killed by his uncle after denouncing his father to the Soviet authorities for harbouring kulaks, was raised to the status of a martyr by the regime for putting the party before the family. Lenin's constant insistence on the replacement of small-scale structures, whether political, social or economic, which might set themselves up as semi-autonomous units apart from the one party system, is the subject of a later chapter. The role of the family as a small-scale social unit is discussed there, but at this point it should be noted that Bukharin agreed with Lenin on the *economic* need to smash the peasant family, although his libertarian views during the Civil War would not permit him to draw Lenin's political conclusions. In *Historical Materialism* Bukharin wrote that the Russian peasant family was a small-scale economic unit, based directly on production : 'The economic significance of the family is so great that marriages are dictated by specific economic calculation : "there is no woman in the house".' The proletarian family was more progressive. It had no private economy, but merely consumed its wages paid out by large-scale industry which split up the peasant family geographically by drawing it into factories and replacing the public social attractions of the city for the now superfluous household.[78]

Lenin's politicised view of the family had forebears in the utopian tradition. Many social engineers wished to subordinate the role of the family to the state. They condemned the family as they did property, since both encouraged selfish instincts and had a disintegrating effect on the community. Kollontai might have been shocked if she had realised the affinity of her 'liberal' views with Plato's. Her dictum on the family quoted above virtually repeats Plato's advice to his guardians: 'in everyone he meets he will think he has a brother or sister, or father or mother, or son or daughter, or grandchild or grandparent'.[79] After Kollontai Aldous Huxley realised the dangers in his satire on utopia, *Brave New World*, where sexual passion is regarded as a danger to the stability of the State and is replaced by promiscuous sexual intercourse as a purely therapeutic measure. As is so often the case in utopian thought, what appears to be liberal becomes harshly authoritarian when the details are spelt out. The gap between Lenin and Kollontai was not so wide as it appeared to be. One of the German left-wing writers on the family, approved by Kollontai, recommended that the government should investigate and punish all young people under the age of eighteen who indulged in sexual relationships. It should also carry out compulsory checks on all citizens for sexual diseases.[80] One is reminded of that seventeenth century fanatical friar, Tommaso Campanella. In his utopia the rules decreed that men and women wrestle together in public like the Greeks, so that the rulers could see who was impotent and which organs were suited to each other.[81]

Although Lenin and Kollontai had common predecessors, they disagreed in several ways. Lenin was a much more cautious exponent of social revolution than Kollontai, who said that making love was of no more consequence than taking a sip of water. Even Friedländer, the German Marxist quoted above, agreed with Lenin that in the Civil War the time was not ripe to implement the reforms Kollontai desired immediately. Material conditions had to change before they could support new family relationships.[82] Lenin did agree to radical legislation on the family soon after 1917, but he and others became critical of the irresponsible way in which the new laws were applied.[83] Lenin also took good care to distinguish between the various types of family structure in the country, and dealt differently with the Moslem polygamy of Central Asia than with the Christian peasant monogamy of European Russia. Kollontai was more sweeping, less interested in careful detail : for all 'worker-mothers', whether Russian, Turkic or Jewish, children would become universally owned, not 'yours and mine'. There would only be two restrictions on the sexual union, that neither the race nor economic progress be adversely affected.[84]

Kollontai's unorthodox views are well known. She was supported by lesser campaigners whose ideas on the family were, if anything, still more extravagant. One propagandist began his book on women's rights with a depiction of Russia, so soon after the Revolution, as a shining example of 'the justification of Fourier's thoughts'.[85] He had forgotten, or had never read, Marx's criticism of the Utopian Socialists. The dependent position of women in the family unit was seen as a class inequality in the Marxist sense, thus splitting each family into two socio-economic classes and making nonsense of Marx's actual ideas.[86] If the theories of Moscow and Petrograd intellectuals were so wildly constructed, it was hardly surprising that the party rank-and-file in the provinces interpreted the new ideas in garbled ways. In Vladimir a decree was passed in the Civil War which made every virgin over eighteen years state property. Kollontai appeared to be positively cautious compared with this. Although she usually ignored the materialist argument for regulating social advance on the basis of economic progress, she agreed with Bogdanov that it would take a radical transformation of the average Russian's psychological makeup to achieve quick results.[87] Lenin was too preoccupied with matters of high policy to devote much time to criticising the views of Kollontai and others.[88] He approved of any changes which would bring the family closer to communal life, but the ascetic in him disapproved of 'free love', which he attacked for reflecting the decadence of 'lower middle-class radicalism'.

The gulf between Bolshevik theories on the family and the reality prior to 1917 was enormous. Neither did the actual course of events after the Revolution fit into the pattern hoped for by either Lenin or Kollontai. They put too much faith in legislation and political intervention from above, and did not reckon sufficiently with social pressures from below.

To begin with, the old family structure they assailed in their writings no longer existed in Russia by the time of the Civil War, except for the deep countryside and some non-European parts of the country. It was disintegrating under the impact of the World War, the Revolution and internal strife. Families were decimated, scattered, deprived of housing and affected more fundamentally than they ever would be by a whole decade of subsequent Bolshevik social legislation on the family. More often than not, as an investigation pointed out in 1920, the break-up of the family and loose morals were caused by the chaotic situation in Russia rather than by political enforcement from the centre. Marriage registration books were only retrieved from the local clergy and checked by the civil authorities at the end of 1918 or even late in 1919 for some areas.[89] The increased number of divorces in the Civil War resulted more from general disruption than from any reaction to new Bolshevik legislation. The number was artificially swollen, since many divorce cases were waiting to be heard which had accumulated during the Revolution.[90]

The Soviet government passed a considerable body of laws on the family in 1917 and 1918,[91] but through Lenin's influence the legislation did not go so far in abolishing the family as a social institution as Kollontai demanded. Its main effect was to transfer family affairs from the religious to the civil authorities. By 1921 Lenin could declare that *according to the law* not a trace of sexual inequality remained, but the law did not penetrate into real life for many years after that date. The economic independence of the family seemed to be shattered by the abolition of inheritance in 1918, but by 1922 anyone could inherit 10,000 roubles, and after 1926 this limit was rescinded. Many similar developments in family life were mere genuflections to the ideological theories but were little affected by them. The ideas which flourished in the Civil War were often counteracted subsequently.

Sexual inequality was a case in point. Kollontai did her best to prove that women were taking on increasingly important roles in the Civil War as military nurses, factory workers, teachers, telephonists, etc., but the peace and the transition to NEP brought with them the dismissal of women in such numbers that by February 1922 a decree had to be issued to the effect that in the case of dismissal from jobs women and men had to be treated on an equal basis.[92] Even this did not stop discrimination, as later Soviet authors observed.[93] In political matters also, women did not live up to the expectation of the law. In 1928, 19 million were free to vote, but only 6 million took the trouble to do so.[94]

Even if Soviet women had made full use of their opportunities, there was not enough money to fulfil plans thought out on paper in the period 1917–21. Funds did not exist for the thousands of crèches and public dining rooms that were supposed to replace family rearing.[95] Until 1921 the few nurseries established were all confined to towns in the Russian republic (RSFSR).[96] Statistics on social affairs, and especially on the family, are hard to come by and difficult to assess for the Civil War years, but one thing is clear : none of the social experiments in all spheres, including the family, had any effective practical impact beyond the towns of European Russia, and even in the towns they were mainly confined to small numbers of the younger section of the population. It was not simply that ideas were unrelated to the facts. Russia was too large, her communications were in disorder, and much of the country was under White control. The Bolsheviks were a tiny minority intent above all on political survival. It is a cause for wonder and admiration that some of them could find the time to write on and indulge in social experimentation of this kind.

Lenin's aversion to the harmful moral features of Leftist thought on the family became more widespread in party and non-party circles as time went by. Ironically, the real damage to the social structure was caused less by the irresponsible theories of Kollontai and others which came under fire, than by the cumulative after-effects of prolonged war and famine. Intellectuals who were city dwellers and most closely influenced by 'free love' ideas were apt to exaggerate the theories' impact, ignoring the mass of the population which was illiterate and rural. A representative of this élite, P. Romanov, wrote a series of novels and short stories in NEP depicting the moral breakdown of Russia. He contrasted the clean, new life created by Bolshevik power with the rotten inner life of women who had forgotten the deeper meaning of love and had abandoned themselves to sex. Sometimes the city heroines of his stories reacted against the fashionable ideas of the Civil War.[97] In a more light-hearted vein, M. Zoshchenko wrote of a dandy from Saratov who induced a girl friend to sign a receipt denying all claims on him if a child resulted from their love affair. The unmarried mother later took him to court, where the judge pronounced Soviet law to be on the side of the child and denounced the father's immorality.[98]

Serious sexual scandals in the ranks of the party were sometimes due to garbled interpretations of the utopian theories. The resulting moral debauchery caused considerable concern at high political levels in the 1920s.[99] Far more often adverse social conditions were the reason. Romanov normally confined his interests to city life but could not totally ignore the wider Soviet scene. He described the disruptive effect of the population drift from the country to the towns. Married males in search of work contracted extramarital ties in the city and lost touch with their families.[100] Prostitution probably became more rather than less widespread for some years after the Revolution, in spite of Bolshevik efforts and prophecies. This was due to social disorder rather than to the doctrine of 'free love'. Statistics are of negligible value here, but some broad evidence is available. Women were much in excess of the male population after the war years. 1,300,000 domestic servants, most of them women, were counted in the 1897 census. Nearly all lost their jobs in the Revolution and female unemployment remained at a far higher level than male until the close of NEP.[101]

Separation of man from wife in Russia's chaotic years broke up thousands of families. In the same way hundreds of thousands of children were cut adrift from their married or unmarried parents. The plight of Russia's orphans in the period 1917–28 is relatively well documented, because the shocking situation led to many official surveys. Probably more than any other social pressure, these children were the cause of a general reversion to a more traditional view of the family. They roamed the towns and the countryside in packs, robbing and killing in the brutal need to survive.

The peasantry never ceased to be the main source of opposition to the destruction of the family nexus. As late as 1925 over 75 per cent of peasant weddings were performed in church, contrary to the Bolsheviks' secularisation of marriage. The peasant divorce rate remained much lower on average than in the towns. The economic structure of NEP encouraged the peasants to cling to family life and male heirs as preservers of their small-scale farms. By 1928 the social, religious and economic motives for the protection of the family persisted as strongly as ever. The peasants began to be joined in their views by literate townspeople by the end of NEP. At a youth conference held in February 1929 the tide was clearly turning. Romanov's stories on sexual life were criticised as an evil influence (though they were models of propriety compared with *Lady Chatterley's Lover*, published in 1928). The conference argued that 'Every young worker must remember that he is a deputy of society in the family', and should uphold morality and the family.[102]

Thucydides, in a passage analysing the general trend of morality immediately after a revolution, writes of the family, 'the tie of blood was weaker than the tie of party, because the partisan was more ready to dare without demur'.[103] This was not unlike Kollontai's point of view. After the mid-1930s Stalin took a different line. Like the youth conference of 1929, he did not wish to create a conflict between the individual's loyalty to the social and to the political institution, but preferred to subsume the family under the aegis of the party. Political advocates of the family in history have seen in it the basis for a stable State, the indispensable social cell, the training ground for the virtues of obedience and loyalty required by the State, especially the authoritarian State. As Stalin became increasingly conservative, he realised that the family, far from presenting a danger by inducing individualist tendencies in the young, accustomed them, on the contrary, to respect the authority of the father : they would later obey the orders of the Party-State just as unquestioningly. From the 1940s until 1953 the Soviet family proved to be a useful tool for attuning children to a rapidly changing society which, paradoxically, became more and more conservative politically.

Stalin's manipulation of the family as an adjunct of political control lies beyond the scope of this study. What is important to stress here is that the path to his eventual negation of Engels' theories on the family was cleared for him by the reaction which Kollontai's interpretations provoked and, more significantly, by the devastating effects of war and revolution on family life. These effects were feared and countered by the peasantry, which made up the great majority of the population, and on their natural conservatism Stalin later came to rely. The peasant-turned-worker in the industrial revolution from the 1930s onwards did not shed his social prejudices with his rural background.

Workers' control and its decline shortly after the Revolution has been treated in several recent secondary studies.[104] It is only discussed briefly here as a utopian project. Lenin eventually willed it to fail, but it also faded out as a utopian dream because of social inadequacy on the part of the working class. In this respect the reasons for the demise of workers' control have close connections with the low standards of literacy and education amongst the masses, which are treated at much greater length in a subsequent chapter. The void left by the incapacity of the proletariat to help in the management of the economy, let alone of society and the political structure, also led to the reintroduction of bureaucracy, which is treated in Chapter 6.

Considered as a socio-political experiment, workers' control differed in several respects from the attempts to dissolve the family. The proletariat was a progressive minority, whereas the family nexus formed the backward majority. Marx's intended role for the proletariat placed this class squarely at the political helm of the socialist state system from the outset. It would have been ludicrous to conceive of a Family Opposition party, but the workers gave their name, if little else, to a splinter group which obstructed Lenin's majority faction. Workers' control was also more influential because as an experiment it was promoted by Lenin before the October coup, at a time when no central authority could control its progress. By the winter of 1917–18 it had become an important, if confused, movement, under the personal sponsorship of the leader of the Bolshevik party. Experiments with the family had not yet got off the ground and were only of secondary interest to Lenin in any case.

The main political question to be posed with regard to workers' control is at what point in time did Lenin relegate the idea of the dictatorship of the proletariat as a whole to second place after the dominance of the party. Lenin embarked in active politics firmly convinced of the truth of Marx's doctrine concerning the political leadership of the proletariat during and after a socialist revolution. In the course of his practical revolutionary activities he suffered two disillusionments; or perhaps it was only one, for the second one may have been feigned. Lenin was never closer to the proletariat than in 1895, at the time of the factory strikes in St. Petersburg. After 1897 the emergence of Economism and Bolshevism both resulted from the irreconcilable aims of labour and the Social Democrats over an extended period dating from 1885. The coolness of the factory proletariat towards political aims led directly to Lenin's formulation in *What is To Be Done?* of an élitist party acting independently, but in the name of the working class. This was Lenin's major, and perhaps final, disillusionment over the capacity of the Russian proletariat to stage a revolution and straight away run a backward country.

Lenin's genius, however, lay in his flexibility, and during the 1905 Revolution he temporarily advocated broader party membership and spontaneous political movement from below. This created a precedent for 1917, when he again invoked spontaneity in any quarter that might aid the Bolsheviks to wreck the Provisional Government. Lenin relied on the factory committees and workers' control in 1917 and for a very brief period afterwards for two practical reasons. The Bolsheviks' popularity among the factory committees and their only coercive tool, the Red Guard, depended on Lenin's approval of workers' control. His small party relied on the committees too as a means of capturing the national economy. Workers' control helped to keep unruly factory owners in check until industry could be nationalised.

Both of these aims were clearly temporary. Moreover, the meaning the leading Bolsheviks attached to the Russian word *kontrol'* was different from the one given to it by proletarian activists. As early as August 1917 a party spokesman warned that the workers 'did not distinguish between the concept of control and the concept of taking possession (*zakhvat*)'.[105] A year later a Bolshevik apologist stressed the well known usual meaning in Russian of *kontrol'* as checking rather than controlling : 'Control is not concerned with administration. Control is the examination of how the fulfilment corresponds to the task.'[106] In his concrete dealings with the factory workers in 1917 and during the Civil War, Lenin never appeared to view workers' control as the first stage of the early and therefore utopian introduction of the political dictatorship of the proletariat. It was only when he was momentarily detached from the reality of Russia's backward working class, writing *State and Revolution* in Finnish exile, that he dreamt not only of workers running the state, but even of peasants managing the bureaucracy. Workers' control in practice was little more than a makeshift tool for the achievement of immediate aims, comparable to the committees of poor peasants in the countryside. Lenin's ambivalence on this question, as on so many others in the period 1917–21, can never be clarified completely, since it boils down in the final analysis to a knowledge of the workings of his private conscience.[107] Whether Lenin suffered a second disillusionment in 1917–18 over the economic and political capabilities of the proletariat, or whether he was a cynical tactician, rests on this.

The reason why workers' control became far more important as a social and political idea than the committees of poor peasants was that some high ranking Bolshevik Leftists in the Workers' Opposition tried to turn Lenin's temporary advocacy of workers' control into permanent economic and political management by the proletariat. This utopian wing was naturally supported by a section of the workers themselves who had misinterpreted Lenin. The familiar pattern of utopian thought in the years 1917–21 is again revealed. When Lenin stopped short after October, others continued. Lenin's motives for abandoning the notion of workers' control by January 1918 were the same as in other spheres. The factory committees had helped the Bolsheviks to power in October, but now the conservation of that power, Lenin's main obsession, seemed to be threatened. The factory committees were rife with anarchists, and at the lower levels they refused to obey the orders of the Bolshevik dominated Central Soviet of Factory Committees. The ways in which Lenin eliminated workers' control have been examined elsewhere. The fiction used to support the move was that the party, Soviets and trade unions were all similar organs through which the proletariat could express its wishes. This rendered heretical any claim to independence on the part of the unions, let alone the factory committees or individual workers; so that if Lenin inclined to Taylorism in industry, it meant that the workers had to agree, even though they were bound to suffer from its harsh methods.

Lenin could also have reiterated his orthodox Marxist argument after 1917 that the socio-economic basis did not yet exist for allowing the proletariat to run the political life of the country. He used this weapon against the utopians in nearly every other sphere, but not here, since he did not dare to do so. Having just acted in a highly voluntarist manner by pushing through the October coup in the name of the proletariat, Lenin had to cover up his utopian traces in more discreet ways. Hence the fiction of the dictatorship of the proletariat through the party. The Workers' Opposition attacked this myth until their final defeat at the Tenth Party Congress in 1921. Lenin was menaced from the right as well as from the left, because it was only after October that he made a dramatic switch to the right, when it was too late to reverse the effect of his previous policy. In an open letter to the Petrograd workers, written on 28 October 1917, G. V. Plekhanov replied to attacks they had made on him, accusing him of going over to the 'bourgeois' cause because he was opposed to the October coup. He reminded them that Engels had stated that a great historical error would be made if the proletariat were encouraged to take the power before the substructure was ripe for it. Plekhanov was saddened by the Petrograd coup, 'not because I do not want to see the working class triumph; on the contrary I sought its triumph with all the strength of my spirit and at the same time I see how far off these events postpone it.' [108]

Plekhanov's prophetic judgment, just before his death in 1918, was ignored by the optimistic Left, and by an articulate minority of the new Soviet proletariat which still took what they thought to be Lenin's 1917 view of the factory committees seriously after October. It is very difficult to ascertain how the workers themselves actually envisaged workers' control, since their spokesmen were so often not factory proletarians, and Bolshevik historiography has contrived to obscure those of their aims which did not coincide with the party line. Since the Mensheviks after 1917 had to depend for their fast declining influence on the workers' support, their expression at home and abroad of workers' views might be taken to be more authentic : but we know from surviving Menshevik archives that their spokesmen amongst foreign trades unions were threatened and blackened by Bolshevik agents.[109] Contemporary Soviet journals do, however, include a few articles and speeches by genuine rank-and-file workers. From these skeletal sources it appears that they were poorly acquainted with either Bolshevik or Anarchist objectives. The workers above all were concerned with their rights to the property they had seized and sometimes shared out between themselves. They interpreted control as ownership and made unrealistic claims for their ability to run large industrial plants.[110]

The ways in which the Bolsheviks divided and ruled the various organisational channels originally open to the proletariat have often been described. The factory committees were set against the trade unions, and the bourgeois 'specialists' against both. Rather less emphasis has been put on partly self-induced reasons for the lack of influence of the articulates from the factory floor. At the higher levels, personal political ambition rather than altruistic support for fellow workers may well have caused trade union leaders like A. Lozovsky to oppose Bolshevik domination over the proletariat in 1918. Having failed to make a successful bid for personal power through the trade unions, he reverted in 1919 to an adherence to Bolshevik policies. At the lower levels, genuine proletarians were often attracted by promises of better social and economic status to accept white-collar jobs in the new bureaucracy, which meant that they became alienated from the class they claimed to serve, and as Bolshevik officials they often found themselves subsequently opposing workers' demands in the name of the party.

So far we have been talking of the cream of the proletariat. If several historical stages of the working classes of Western Europe prior to 1917 could have been telescoped and combined, they would have corresponded very roughly to the mixed nature of the Russian proletariat. The low educational standards and initiative of the average Soviet worker-peasant created a vicious circle, since the proletariat for ideological reasons did not have the right not to work, and there was scant leisure for acquiring literacy or new skills. During the Civil War Petrograd labour organisations were reputed to have stated at a secret meeting, 'Never before has overtime work been practised so widely as now : the worst of it is that more than ninety per cent of the overtime is compulsory and any refusal on the part of the workers is severely punished.' [111] In their depressed state even the leading workers engaged in workers' control at the start of 1818 did not elaborate an independent role for the proletariat. At conferences they tended to ask the political centre for instructions and expected orders to be handed down to them.[112]

The idea that workers could control their own destiny within their factory walls, let alone on a larger scale, became more rather than less remote as time went on. This was by no means merely the result of deliberate Bolshevik attempts to suppress them. As of

1917 Trotsky could declare with pride that the proletariat of Petrograd, Moscow and the big European cities of Russia formed the concentrated geographical as well as the political spearhead of the Revolution. By the end of the Civil War this working class support had virtually disintegrated, due to those social and military reasons already mentioned in the previous chapter.[113] In NEP the Bolsheviks had little fear that their dependence upon a weakened labour force would become a bargaining point for economic and political concessions to the working class. The last squib of genuine proletarian opposition came from the Workers' Group headed by A. F. Miasnikov at the Twelfth Party Congress in 1923. Lack of morale, cohesion, political interest and above all the desire to avoid the threat of the widespread unemployment of NEP, ensured a quietist attitude thereafter.

The last cry of the proletariat as expressed by Miasnikov was directed mainly against the exploitation of the workers by the privileged party bureaucrats. In *State and Revolution* Lenin had claimed, or pretended, that workers' control would rapidly become a substitute for bureaucracy. This soon proved to be utopian, and also ran counter to Lenin's post-1917 strategy. The easy demise of the dictatorship of the proletariat was a leading cause of the resurrection of bureaucracy to fill the gap. The process is described in Chapter 6. This bureaucracy in Stalin's hand was to become the chief instrument of the political system of the 1930s. The close tie between social backwardness and political authoritarianism is readily apparent.

In conclusion it should be clear that social experimentation during the Civil War hardly amounted to an effective movement among the general population. The Bolsheviks were divided over it : few Russians actually participated, except in the towns. None of the experiments survived long after the Civil War, and several of them perished at its very outset. Lenin's political act of voluntarism in October 1917 could not be reversed without a counter-revolution, but voluntarism in the social sphere could be stemmed with small cost to the regime. Marx's vagueness on the social future after a revolution allowed the Party to hurry up or slow down the implementation of social change as it thought fit without losing credibility. A few high ranking enemies were made, like Bogdanov and Bukharin, but the latter was subsequently converted to the Leninist line, whilst the former was discredited.

The political future of the Soviet Union was foreshadowed by the Tenth Party Congress in 1921, when the dying embers of all forms of organised opposition to the Bolshevik party were quenched for at least half a century, although this could not be clear at the time. The fate of the social dreams of the Left opposition was not sealed in the same way. The orthodox Leninist stance assumed that the social utopias would be merely delayed for a brief period. Social time was now determined, as Karl Mannheim has put it, as a series of strategical points based on the development of the Marxist *Unterbau*. The unorganised, oscillating experience of the ecstatic utopia seemed to be largely abandoned, although various minority groups like survivors of the Workers' Opposition and the Democratic Centralists, and occasionally the trade unions and the Communist League of Youth, still chased social visions throughout NEP. For the most part lethargy and caution, born of the exhaustion of earlier years and efforts, induced leading social thinkers to become orthodox gradualists. Of these Bukharin was the outstanding example of utopian-turned-realist.

Nevertheless, the utopian tradition left indelible marks on Soviet social progress. The enormous discrepancies that lay between Russia's actual condition in 1917 and the communists' dreams tended to act as brakes on social change. The maximalist experiments of the Civil War backfired because they were so unrealistic. They had a minimal effect on social life, and led to disillusionment and criticism. Less optimistic schemes on a smaller scale might have produced modest successes and fewer disappointments. In NEP the same mistake was made, though it was now largely confined to the realm of ideas. The great debate on future plans for Soviet society and the economy that raged in the Bolshevik hierarchy through the 1920s was almost unconcerned with bridging the gap between the ideal and the reality. Other reasons, besides the utopian background, why many Party leaders ignored the petty realities of NEP in their yearning for the future have been explored in the previous chapter.[114] Some less influential social engineers were more practical, but their careful statistical researches and pioneer sociological work on Soviet problems carried little weight. This was because they were *spetsy* (bourgeois specialists) and ex-Mensheviks, whose views were sometimes indistinguishable from those of the Right Opposition within the party. General economic and social strategy was therefore determined at a higher, purer party level, above the heads of these astute but politically unreliable advisors.

After the death of Lenin and the rise of Stalin, it might be thought that the utopian elements would have perished with the disappearance of their original architect and the assumption of power by a more pragmatic leader, who brought with him in the 1930s a new generation of like-minded technical intelligentsia. This was not the case, although the utopian ideal suffered a further sea change with the start of the Five-Year Plans. Lenin presented Stalin with the same irreversible problem he had created. The political voluntarism of 1917 still led ineluctably to the need for social voluntarism, since economic activity on the part of the masses had not created the right base for gradual social reforms even by the close of NEP. The future of Soviet Russia after 1928 still depended on the wishes of a single individual which could not be sociologically determined with any measure of exactness. It is true that in time the charismatic achievements of Stalin were translated (by force) into the collective life of the people, but as of 1928–9 Marx's attack on the Utopian Socialists in *The Communist Manifesto* could apply equally to Stalin :

'In their case, individual inventiveness had to take the place of social activity, imagined conditions of liberation must serve their turn instead of historically extant ones, a social organisation evolved out of the thinker's inner consciousness was the only available substitute for the gradually developing organization of the proletariat to form a class. To them, the history of days to come presented itself as nothing more than propaganda and the practical realization of their social phantasies.'

The economic and social stagnation which lasted through most of NEP made it scarcely easier for Stalin than for the Civil War utopians to effect a smooth transition from a small-scale to a large-scale economy. The bridge had not been built. Stalin's postponement of international revolution and his belief in the Soviet Union's ability to provide socialism in one country swept away the main orthodox argument against the viability of radical social change. It made no difference that the original diagnosis was probably a false one in any case, and remains to this day untested in international political experience. The new accent on nationalism after 1928 also gave freer rein to that brand of traditional Russian messianism which had had close connections with utopian thought in the past. In a sense, maximalism appears to be a permanent feature of the Russian mind, although it crops up in differing guises at different times. Exaggerated social hopes born of Russia's increasing self-confidence in the technological field reappeared in 1961 with the promulgation of the Third Party Programme. Many of the detailed visions outlined on that occasion had much in common with the early Soviet technological utopias.

There was one important shift of emphasis in Stalin's imposition of the second utopia in 1929. All the libertarian strands in the Civil War experiments were eliminated, whilst the authoritarian features remained. Stalin's character and political manner ensured this, and widespread Bolshevik impatience over the delays and set-backs of NEP reinforced the trend. The need for urgency revived the chiliastic sense. In 1931 Stalin told a conference of industrial managers : 'We are fifty or a hundred years behind the advanced countries. We must make good this lag in ten years. Either we do it, or they crush us.' [115] The stress on a centralised economy and the reduction of private fields of economic and social activity was enhanced. The notion of law as a means of healing rather than as an act of retribution was rejected. The Marxist interpretation of the relationship between the sexes was transmuted almost beyond recognition in the Stalinist era. The emphasis placed on education by the Utopian Socialists as a liberating influence on the masses has never been abandoned in theory by the Bolsheviks, and the Soviet practical record is impressive in many ways. In some vital respects, however, the abolition of mass illiteracy and the advent of universal education were used as political instruments by Stalin to promote an oppressive political system.

It is strange that the Bolsheviks, trained in a determinist school of thought, could not or would not see how their early social ideals were destined to undergo drastic changes. As Karl Mannheim has said, Bolshevism 'which hitherto has unmasked all its adversaries' utopias as ideologies, never raised the problem of determinateness about its own position. It never applied this method to itself and never checked its own desire to be absolute.' [116] Changes seemed inevitable in the process of adapting social theories taken from a West European matrix and applied to a very different society. Russian society had deep roots dating from its own unique past that could not be wholly eradicated in the fleeting years of the Civil

War, nor even a decade later. Maiakovsky's *byt* acted as a heavy drag on both the social and political ambitions of the party. Two important aspects of this social backwardness are studied in Chapters 4 and 5.

Another determining factor which the Bolsheviks largely ignored was the result of the violence which they employed in order to come to power and stay there, supported only by a minority of popular opinion. Subsequently they used this power for preconceived ends not sanctioned in the social experience of the masses. The strain thus imposed on the party led it to be motivated primarily by the cruel necessities of the power it had taken over. The prerevolutionary social ideals became a consideration of secondary importance, and were hammered by Stalin into a convenient authoritarian mould to suit his political aims. The second Bolshevik social utopia of the 1930s was of far more consequence than the first, since it was not confined to the cities of European Russia, but engulfed the whole Soviet population. It also came to stay.

One determining consideration that Lenin at least did acknowledge was the failure for the time being of international revolution after 1917 and the domestic social consequences of this for the Soviet Union. There is every reason to believe that the Left Communists would have lost hope eventually on this count too if they had survived beyond the Tenth Party Congress. The authoritarian branch of the left, including Trotsky, had already modified the position of the left as a whole by making common cause with Lenin during War Communism. By the 1930s the only libertarian ideal left standing in the Bolshevik armoury was one that could not be put to the test – the concept of the withering away of the State. This is the most conspicuous utopian feature in Marxist-Leninist doctrine, derived in part from the widespread nineteenth-century tendency to idealise society and to regard the State as evil. It is also the most abstract and vague feature, yet remains a central tenet of Bolshevik theory. It was the subject of prolonged discussion in the Soviet Union during War Communism, and again in 1936, 1949, 1952 and more recently in 1961. The vision still remains for future realisation.

One sequence of events which closely determined the failure of the first utopia was the course of the Civil War and the brutal influence on many facets of social life precisely at the time when the latter were the subject of experimentation. The contrast between the optimistic projects described in this chapter and the military realities depicted in the next is a tragic one. When they are considered together, it will be seen that, in the light of the years 1917-21 in Russia, to posit violent revolution and war as a rational way of bringing about social change was like imagining that an earthquake is a good way of producing a lake.

1 For the meaning of the term 'War Communism' see Chapter 3, pp. 96-9.

2 *Décomposition du Marxisme*, 3rd ed. (Paris, 1925) p. 37.

3 Ludwig von Mises, *Socialism* (New Haven, 1950) p. 16.

4 K. R. Popper, *The Open Society and Its Enemies*, vol. 1. *The Spell of Plato* (London, 1957) pp. 158-64.

5 Babeuf also pleased Marx by recognising the irreconcilable nature of class antagonisms and therefore the need for violence to produce a new order.

6 V. I. Lenin, *Selected Works*, vol. 9, p. 121.

7 Carr, 'The Bolshevik Utopia', in *1917: Before and After* (London, 1969) pp. 60-1.

8 Isaiah Berlin, 'The Role of the Intelligentsia', in *The Listener*, (2 May 1968) p. 563.

9 This is the nub of T. H. von Laue's argument in *Why Lenin? Why Stalin? A Reappraisal of the Russian Revolution 1900-1930* (London, 1966).

10 See Simone Weil, *La condition ouvrière* (Paris, 1951) amongst her other writings on this theme.

11 N. Berdiaev, *The Russian Idea* (London, 1947).

12 M. Ferro, 'The Aspirations of Russian Society', in R. Pipes (editor), *Revolutionary Russia* (Cambridge, Mass., 1968) p. 143.

13 T. H. Rigby, *Communist Party Membership in the USSR 1917-1967* (Princeton, 1968) p. 89.

14 For more detailed treatments of these tendencies, see Hans Toch, *The Social Psychology of Social Movements* (London, 1966) Chapter 2, and Isaiah Berlin, 'Political Ideas in the Twentieth Century', in *Foreign Affairs* (April, 1950) pp. 365-6.

15 *A Modern Utopia* (London, 1905) p. 354.

16 Huxley's *Brave New World* also has an affinity with *My*.

17 Lenin, *Philosophical Notebooks*, in *Collected Works*, vol. 38 (Moscow, 1961) pp. 372-3.

18 On the psychological motivation of the utopian side of Lenin's thought, see Lewis S. Feuer, 'Lenin's Phantasy – The Interpretation of a Russian Revolutionary Dream', in *Encounter* (December 1970) pp. 23–35. The Freudian speculation in this article lacks any scholarly foundation, but the discussion of Lenin's changing approach to materialism is acute.

19 For a more detailed treatment of the sudden decline of utopian plans for the new Red Army, see J. Erickson, 'The Origins of the Red Army', in R. Pipes (editor), *Revolutionary Russia* (London, 1968) pp. 224–58.

20 H. G. Wells, *Russia in The Shadows* (London, 1921) p. 135.

21 It was first used as the title of a speech Lenin made at the Moscow *guberniia* party conference on 20 November 1920.

22 In a speech to the Eighth All-Russian Congress of Soviets, 22 December 1920.

23 See the impressive amount of assembled materials in Lenin, *Ob elektrifikatsii* (Moscow, 1934).

24 Ibid., p. 11.

25 A. Nove, *An Economic History of the USSR* (London, 1969) p. 70.

26 *Ob elektrifikatsii*, pp. 14–15.

27 Ibid., p. 13.

28 D. Cheremin, *Zadachi maksimalizma*, no. 2 (Moscow, 1918).

29 These are two remote villages in the depth of the Russian countryside. The quotation comes from the poem-poster 'Then and Now' (1921).

30 A. Sventokhovsky, *Istoriia utopii* (Moscow, 1910).

31 For an elaboration of this view, see A. A. Bogdanov, 'Voprosy sotsializma', in *Novy Mir* (Moscow, 1919).

32 Lenin, *Ob elektrifikatsii*, pp. 11–12. M. Zoshchenko wrote a satirical gloss on this theme in his short story, *Bednost'* (*Poverty*), in which a householder was so horrified by the way the new electricity revealed her sordid surroundings that she cut the wires. 'I don't want to live in the light. I don't want my modest circumstances to be lit up for the bedbugs to laugh at.'

33 See C. Gray, *The Great Experiment: Russian Art 1863–1922* (London, 1962) pp. 244–52, for a description of these schemes.

34 V. Anan'in (editor), *Po fabrikam i zavodam, ocherki proizvodstva i byta* (Moscow, 1926) p. 31.

35 Lenin, *Ob elektrifikatsii*, p. 24.

36 *Metody i praktika opredeleniia effektivnosti kapital'nykh vlozhenii i novoi tekhniki* (Moscow, 1967) pp. 95–6.

37 A system named after the worker concerned whereby certain workers were helped to set high records of productivity, and the work norms for other workers correspondingly increased.

38 Quoted in Daniel Bell, *Work and Its Discontents* (Boston, 1956) p. 7.

39 See Lenin, *Collected Works*, vol. 2 (London, 1932) p. 89, for his distaste in 1895–6 for man's subservience to machines.

40 One *pud* equals 36 lbs.

41 From an article by Galaktinov in *Zheleznodorozhnik* (25 February 1920).

42 L. Trotsky, *Kak vooruzhalas' revoliutsiia*, vol. 2 (Moscow, 1923) p. 127 ff.

43 N. Berdiaev, *The Origin of Russian Communism* (Ann Arbor, 1960) p. 127.

44 Bogdanov's ideas may be studied in his *Filosofiia zhivogo opyta* (St. Petersburg, 1912); *Vseobshchaia organizatsionnaia nauka* (St. Petersburg, 1913); *Nauka ob obshchestvennom soznanii* (Moscow, 1914); *Sotsializm nauki* (Moscow, 1918); *Iskusstvo i rabochii klass* (Moscow, 1918).

45 These rare books are entitled *Krasnaia zvezda* and *Inzhener Menni*, and can be found in the Helsinki University Library.

46 *Inzhener Menni* (Petrograd, 1919) p. 149.

47 Lenin, *Collected Works*, 3rd edn., vol. 28, p. 29.

48 Authorised translation from the Third Russian edition (London, 1926) p. 90.

49 Ibid., p. 93.

50 Ibid., p. 264.

51 G. Borisov, *Diktatura proletariata* (Petrograd, 1919) p. 42.

52 Ibid.

53 B. I. Gorev, *Ot Tomasa Mora do Lenina, 1516–1917* (Moscow, 1922).

54 See p. 28 supra.

55 St. Petersburg, 1906, and Moscow, 1918, respectively.

56 See for example Bystransky, *Proletariat i nauka* (Petrograd, 1920) pp. 5–6, *et al.*

57 As in Borisov, op. cit., p. 41, etc.

58 Bystransky, op. cit.

59 We know from Maiakovsky's *Ia sam* that he had read, amongst other works, Engels's *Anti-Dühring*, the foreword to Marx's *Das Kapital* and some of Hegel's writings (probably including *The Philosophy of History*).

60 See L. B. Schapiro, *The Communist Party of the Soviet Union* (London, 1960) p. 206 and note 3.

61 Stalin's ideas are succinctly expressed in his *Sochineniia*, vol. 10 (Moscow, 1954) pp. 139–40.

62 Quoted in Stepanov, op. cit., p. 78. Corroborated, without a date in Stalin, *Sochineniia*, vol. 5, p. 50.

63 *Biulleteni pervogo vserossiisskogo zhenskogo s"ezda*, no. 1 (St. Petersburg, 1908) p. 78.

64 O. K. Grave, *Zhenskii vopros* (St. Petersburg, 1907) pp. 139–43.

65 *Trudy pervogo s"ezda po obrazovaniiu zhenshchin*, vol. 2 (Petrograd, 1915) p. 628.

66 A. Tyrkova, *Osvobozhdenie zhenshchin* (Petrograd, 1917) pp. 4–15.

67 T. Aleksinskaia, *Zhenshchina v voine i revoliutsii* (Petrograd, 1917).

68 Tyrkova and Aleksinskaia, op. cit.

69 G. Grigorovsky, *Grazhdanskii brak: ocherki politiki semeinogo prava* (Petrograd, 1917) pp. 7–14, 24, 136 ff.

70 See F. Engels, *The Origin of the Family, Private Property and the State*, in K. Marx and F. Engels, *Selected Works* (Moscow, 1951). For secondary accounts, see K. Geiger, *The Family in Soviet Russia* (Cambridge, Mass., 1968) and D. Lane, *Politics and Society in the USSR*, Chapter 1 (London, 1970).

71 A. Balabanova, *Ot rabstva k svobode* (Moscow, 1920) p. 16.

72 See p. 43, supra.

73 *Svobodnaia liubov'* (St. Petersburg, 1908), especially Chapter 6 and p. 169 ff.

74 V. A. Posse, *Brak, sem'ia i shkola* (St. Petersburg, 1913) p. 34.

75 A. I. Muranevich, *Sem'ia i zhenshchina* (Moscow, 1909) pp. 60–1.

76 N. Bogachev, *Sem'ia i gosudarstvo* (Moscow, 1903) pp. 5–7.

77 *Voprosy sotsializma*, pp. 113–16.

78 op. cit., p. 156.

79 Plato confined his advice to an élite, whereas Kollantai was prescribing for the masses.

80 P. Friedländer, *Polovoi vopros – gosudarstvo i kul'tura* (Petrograd, 1920) pp. 65–7.

81 T. Campanella, *Civitas Solis Poetica: Idea Reipublicae Philosophiae* (Frankfurt, 1623).

82 Friedländer, op. cit., p. 63.

83 See for instance P. V. Verkhovsky, *Novye formy braka i sem'i po sovetskomy zakonodatel'stvu* (Leningrad, 1925) p. 28 ff. The laws were so unclearly drafted and interpreted that marriage was possible before or even without registration, so that it was often difficult to distinguish marriage from prostitution and bigamy.

84 A. Kollontai, *Novaia moral' i rabochii klass* (Moscow, 1918), p. 46.

85 O. Bystransky, *Revoliutsiia i zhenshchina* (Petrograd, 1920) p. 1.

86 Ibid., p. 5.

87 Kollontai, op. cit., p. 57.

88 Trotsky wrote later : 'The party did not and could not accord specific attention to questions of the everyday life of the working masses. We have never thrashed out these questions concretely . . . We have as yet done nothing in regard to the family . . .' From *Voprosy byta* (Moscow, 1923) p. 83.

89 A. G. Goichbarg, *Brachnoe, semeinoe i opekunskoe pravo sovetskoi respubliki* (Moscow, 1920) p. 22.

90 Ibid., pp. 80–1.

91 For a detailed survey see G. Sverdlov, *Brak i sem'ia v SSSR* (Moscow, 1956).

92 *Sobranie uzakonenii i rasporiazhenii rabochego i krest'ianskogo pravitel'stva, 1917–1924* (1922) pp. 18–203.

93 See G. N. Serebrennikov, *Zhenskii trud v SSSR* (Moscow, 1934) p. 226.

94 E. J. Dillon, *Russia Today and Yesterday* (London, 1929).

95 See V. K. Nikol'sky, *Sem'ia i brak v proshlom i nastoiashchem* (Moscow, 1936) p. 68 ff.

96 N. T. Dodge, *Women in the Soviet Economy* (Baltimore, 1966) p. 76.

97 P. Romanov, 'Bez cheremukhi', in *Sbornik rasskazov* (Moscow, 1927).

98 M. Zoshchenko, *Raspiska (The Receipt)*.

99 For examples of this, see M. Fainsod, *Smolensk Under Soviet Rule* (Cambridge, Mass., 1958) pp. 48–9.

100 P. Romanov, *Chernye lepeshki* (Moscow, 1927).

101 A survey of unemployed women in 1923 revealed that 43 per cent had not worked for over a year. 13 per cent of all those questioned said that they might take up prostitution. See V. Bonner, *Bor'ba protiv prostitutsii v SSSR* (Moscow, 1936).

102 V. Ketlinskaia and V. Slepkov, *Zhizn' bez kontrolia* (Moscow, 1929) pp. 22, 86.

103 Thucydides, *History of the Peleponnesian War*, book 3, LXXXII, pp. 3–7.

104 See Deutscher, *Soviet Trade Unions, Their Place in Soviet Labour Policy*; M. Dewar, *Labour Policy in the USSR 1917–1928*; T. Hammond, *Lenin on Trade Unions and Revolution 1893–1917*; F. Kaplan, *Bolshevik Ideology and the Ethics of Soviet Labour 1917–*

1920: The Formative Years; J. Sorenson, *The Life and Death of Soviet Trade Unionism, 1917–1928.*

105 *Oktiabr'skaia revoliutsiia i fabzavkomy*, vol. 1 (Moscow, 1927) p. 171. This is from a statement by V. M. Levin at the Second Conference of Petrograd Factory Committees.

106 N. Osinsky, 'Stroitel'stvo sotsializma, obshchie zadachi organizatsii proizvodstva', in *Kommunist* (Moscow, 1918).

107 On this problem see an interesting essay by J. Rees, 'Lenin and Marxism', in L. Schapiro and P. Reddaway (editors), *Lenin, The Man, The Theorist, The Leader* (London, 1967) pp. 87–106 and especially pp. 103–4.

108 G. V. Plekhanov, *God na rodine. Polnoe sobranie statei i rechei 1917–1918 gg.*, vol. 2 (Paris, 1921) pp. 246–8.

109 See the Portugeis Archives in the International Institute of Social History, Amsterdam, where correspondence between W. A. Appleton and Samuel Gompers shows how Menshevik visitors were hounded by Bolshevik agents.

110 A. Smirnov, 'Rabochii kontrol'', in *Vestnik metallista* (June–August 1918). The opponents of workers' control and later accounts of it also include some direct evidence of this nature. See R. Rosenfeld, *Promyshlennaia politika SSSR* (Moscow, 1926). For an influential Leftist's advocacy of workers' control in an extreme form, see Iu. Larin, *Trudovaia povinnost' i rabochii kontrol'* (Petrograd, 1918).

111 Portugeis Archive.

112 See for instance *Pervyi vserossiskii s"ezd professional'nykh soiuzov 7–14 ianvaria 1918* (Moscow, 1918) pp. 221–2.

113 See p. 3 supra.

114 See p. 5 supra.

115 The chiliastic sense was also conspicuous in the experimental art forms of the postrevolutionary period. As V. Meyerhold translated it succinctly into his own idiom : 'We are too busy to spend one or two years on a single play; on our clock the second hand is all important.'

116 Karl Mannheim held a special view of the meaning of utopia, but it does not affect this criticism of the Bolsheviks.

3 The Impact of War

The regimentation of social and political life in Russia is often said to have come about in the Stalinist period, but in fact Russian society has been militarised to a greater or lesser extent since the sixteenth century. Tsarist Russia has been called a 'barracks state', with a rigid hierarchy of social and political command culminating in the person of the autocrat. Perhaps just because Russian society has been subject to military influences for so long, it is difficult to distinguish a specifically military role in the councils of the government, whether Tsarist or Soviet.[1] This leads to the central paradox of the present chapter, that although the Civil War had enormous influence on the character and organisation of early Soviet socio-political life, it did not mean that the military ceased to play its traditional Russian role of obedience to the ruler. Nevertheless the resuscitation in new guise of the militarised aspects of Russian society had a crushing effect on utopian experiments during the Civil War and continued to infiltrate Soviet life in the peace which followed.

Lenin adopted from Babeuf, via Marx, the optimistic conviction that regular armies should be abolished. Marx's view that the bureaucratic-military machine should be smashed and replaced by the armed people was stated forcefully in the Communist Manifesto. Regular army units were the tools used by nineteenth-century governments to squash left-wing movements, so that it is hardly surprising that most socialist intellectuals regarded them with such mistrust. After the February Revolution Lenin put renewed stress on the need to liquidate the Tsarist army and to rely on volunteer militiamen raised from the poorest classes.[2] The Red Guards were in practice only a dim reflection of Lenin's vision. They served their limited purpose in 1917 but were totally inadequate for ensuring the survival of the new Bolshevik regime.

The Red Guards sent out to deal with Krasnov's poorly mounted counter-offensive against Petrograd on 10 November 1917 only just won the day. The prospect of using them to face German troops was frightening, but it was a real one, as the Tsarist army was melting away through desertion and demobilisation. Against the White armies in December 1917 the Rostov Red Guards fought through the day, then returned to their families at night as if quitting a shift. The diminished, isolated troops still at the front were left to the mercy of the White Volunteer Army.[3]

Lenin was persuaded by the force of circumstances after October to allow a large-scale regular army to be built up once again, although this implied a reversal of the socialist view. However, Marx's opinion that the Paris Communards had acted correctly in forming an *ad hoc* military group rather than working on previously laid down principles made it easier for Lenin to change his mind with a clear conscience.[4] Both Trotsky and Lenin modified their ideas under the pressure of the German approach to Petrograd and the crisis on the eastern front.[5] Lenin expressed his shock on recognising the true state of the army in February 1918, when the capital had to be defended : 'We have no troops. None at all. The workers of Petrograd must take the place of the armed forces.'[6] A Soviet scholar calculated that as of April 1918 the core of the new Red Army centred on Petrograd consisted of a mere 25,000 men, of whom 10,000 were ex-Red Guards.[7] As his experience grew, Trotsky insisted on a disciplined, regular army in order to win the Civil War. Lenin concurred. In the autumn of 1918 the anticipated collapse of the Central Powers gave Lenin an additional reason : 'Let us increase our efforts to organize the Red Army ... It was our intention to have an army of a million men by spring, but now we need an army of three million.'[8] At first Lenin envisaged that the Soviet military might be able to give aid to the German people in revolution. In the event the Red Army was unable to keep its foothold in the Baltic states, but the Soviet-Polish War of 1920 gave Moscow a new chance of breaking through into Central Europe.

In view of Lenin's lack of interest before October 1917 in taking over or transforming the Tsarist army (as well as his incapacity to do so), it is surprising that there was no 18th Brumaire, no military coup to fill the power vacuum. Even if one can call the Kornilov affair an attempted coup of this kind, it turned out to be an im-

mediate failure, resulting only in the destruction of Kornilov and
the military and civilian conservatives who backed him. The great
majority of the Russian generals were not interested in politics,
either during or after 1917.[9] The White Army leaders left political
problems to the incompetent advice of the liberals who followed
in their camp, whilst a considerable number of high-ranking military figures agreed to fight as military *spetsy* in the Red Army.
Their energies before and after 1917 were directed primarily
against the German foe, not against any particular regime inside
Russia. Since the Germans in the first part of 1918 were the only
force capable of removing the Bolsheviks, the Russian officer class
was indirectly performing a great service to the infant regime.
Lenin encountered little serious political opposition from the
officers remaining in Bolshevik-controlled territory after October.
In any case it was useless to try to move troops against the Bolsheviks. By the end of November General Posokhov, the Chief of Staff
of the Twelfth Army, affirmed that '. . . the army just doesn't
exist'.[10]

One and a half years after its foundation, the Red Army had
surpassed the figure of three million proposed by Lenin. As in so
many other spheres, Lenin had retreated rapidly from his earlier
position. His dominating motive, as always, was the retention of
political power. The party could only be defended by a centralised,
regular army, not by a proletarian militia. Local initiative, as with
workers' control, was sacrificed to dictatorship over the proletariat.
Thus from the start the character of the Red Army had social and
political implications for the relationship between the party and
the workers. In 1919 and again in 1922 there were protracted
debates over the respective merits of a militia versus a regular
army, but to some extent they were conducted in a theoretical
and artificial vacuum against the *Realpolitik* background of a
large regular army. Bukharin and the Left Communists were to
some extent pacified by Lenin's declaration at the Seventh Party
Congress in March 1918 that the regular military system was only
a short-term measure to deal with the emergency situation.
Trotsky, cut off from the utopians by his military experience,
admitted later that the Red Army was similar to the Tsarist army
in many ways, but he claimed that it was quite different in its
political aims. This was undoubtedly the case, but one tradition
that was carried over was the existence of the close ideological and

organisational ties between the government and the military which in Tsarist Russia at least had tended to shore up social and political authoritarianism. The quarrels of 1919 and 1922 were partly artificial in that they were used as screens for the personal ambitions of those involved in them. The Military Opposition shifted its attack on Trotsky from one topic to another, and was joined by Stalin, an odd companion for a group of military thinkers who were largely anti-centralist, anti-bureaucratic and bordering on the utopian. But as was noted earlier with regard to Lenin's electrification projects, Stalin was willing to go against what fixed political ideals he had in order to inflict a tactical wound on Trotsky.

By December 1919 it was clear that the Bolsheviks would eventually win the Civil War, although this might not happen for some time. With the prospect of victory in sight, the idea of a militia system no longer seemed too remote, and Lenin's promise at the outset of the war was recalled. More important still, Trotsky reverted to his anti-centralist leanings in this respect and advocated the formation of a socialist militia, which would also allow for the establishment of localised labour and defence units. Those who came forward to oppose the idea of a national militia based their arguments less on the need for a large-scale, efficient coercive organ to defend the party (as Lenin had done in time of peril) than on the impossibility of establishing a socialist military structure in a backward economy and society. Once again, as in the case of the social experiments of War Communism, a progressive and libertarian project foundered on the rocks of Russia's slow socio-economic development.

The arguments outlined by I. Smilga and M. Tukhachevsky against the introduction of a militia system were as follows. Until the Soviet economy could be organised on a large-scale basis, the proletariat would remain in a small minority, and if it were scattered thinly over a large number of militia units, its social influence would be weakened.[11] Smilga pointed out also that, given the poor communications network and the size of the country, it would be difficult to mobilise and deploy militia troops.[12] Tukhachevsky's interest in a revolutionary offensive against other countries led him to agree to this argument. He added that a militia system would be encumbered by a large peasant majority which would lack political consciousness (he cited the example of Makhno's heretical local peasant army). How could a peasant rising like the Tambov rebellion be brought under control by a peasant militia?[13] Finally, Tukhachevsky argued that the notion of an 'armed people' had been imported from Germany (like so many other utopian ideas), where modern technology, heavy industry and good communications formed a more realistic basis for its implementation.[14]

M. Frunze's solution to the problem was a mixed army, part regular, part militia. By the winter of 1924 the territorial militia forces accounted for 52.4 per cent of the Red infantry. However, the new territorial groups did not correspond closely to the vision of the militia which had occupied the minds of the Left Communists; and as time went on, the territorial element weakened. By the mid-1930s 70 per cent of the Red Army consisted of cadre as opposed to militia troops.[15]

Thus a regular standing army persisted, despite the reservations of Lenin before 1917 and of the utopians after the Revolution. It is strange that the determinist Bolsheviks did not foresee that such an army would be needed to defend the socialist state. Lenin in particular was well aware of the close interrelationship between war and revolution. In his Theses of October, written in 1915, and again in the autumn of 1916, he pointed out how war begat revolution, and, in turn, revolution produced war. Lenin asked, 'Was there ever in history an example of a great revolution occurring by itself, not tied to war? Of course not.'[16] Bukharin on the other hand evolved an original and typically optimistic argument which forecast the opposite. Since the dictatorship of the proletariat was the pinnacle of the class struggle, he saw military coercion becoming historically valueless. Force passed into the hands of the majority, and the majority could put it aside for ever.[17]

Historians and political theorists since Lenin have tended to agree with his opinion rather than with Bukharin. A spate of studies on the role of the military in politics followed on the pioneer work of Katherine Chorley, who concluded that revolutionary situations were to be expected in the closing stages of an unsuccessful war.[18] In the nineteenth and early twentieth centuries, the Russian government survived military defeat in the Crimean War and the war with Japan, though these wars led directly to the Emancipation of the Serfs and the Revolution of 1905 respectively. Even the successful campaign against Napoleon was followed by the Decembrist revolt and the subsequent militarisation of society and politics under Nicholas I. The French invasion of Russia had more effect than the other two wars on the domestic life of the civilian population. This last point provides the clue to the devastating socio-political influence of World War I, which was the first major cataclysm in which the violence of modern warfare was unleashed upon the whole population of Russia and of other countries. Furthermore, Russia was well on the road to defeat in 1917 when revolution approached and the Tsarist government fell. The force of the war toppled not one, but two regimes, as the Provisional Government crashed under the impact of the same continuing onslaught. The Russian army abandoned its basic function of shielding domestic civilian life against the horrors of war. The historical distinction between civilian and military zones melted even further under the pressure of the Civil War which followed external war and internal revolution.

Indeed, international war was merely the prelude to the Revolution in terms of the spread of violence. Until 1917 the militarisation of daily life was more confined to the fighting fronts, although the army tussled increasingly with the government over the control of civilian areas behind the fronts. During 1917 violence spread to the interior of the country, although it was amazing how little blood was actually shed in February and October. But the infection was spreading from the military zones. It is significant that in the course of the thrusts to the left during the year, whereas only threats and insults were hurled at the heads of the more conservative figures in Petrograd and Moscow, their counterparts at the fronts and in the naval ports were murdered by soldiers and sailors. After their almost uncanny capture of the strategic hubs of political power with a minimal use of force in October, the Bolsheviks and the whole population found retribution in the all-enveloping violence of a prolonged Civil War.

It appears to be a common assumption among contemporary writers on the role of the military in politics that the 'military' can be categorised as something distinct from, and perhaps opposed to, the 'political'. In any analysis of the social or political role of the military it is perhaps convenient to identify two spheres – civil and military – and to proceed from there. But it leads to the danger of treating the 'military' as a completely independent variable and to assume its isolation from other variables. In the specific instance of Russia, throughout her modern history, and especially in her period of total internal war 1918–20, it is not possible to think in terms of the autonomy of the military from the social and political worlds : they are interfused. Hannah Arendt agrees to this as a general principle when considering revolutionary situations in this century, but believes that since violence is speechless, 'political theory has little to say about the phenomenon ... and must leave its discussion to the technicians'.[19] Whilst it may be true that man, to the extent that he is a political being, is endowed with speech, as Aristotle noted, speechless violence of the type that occurred in the Russian Civil War was surely the direct result of previous political action – Lenin's decision to assume the helm of the state without a general mandate. This same violence and general brutalisation during the Civil War was also to have widespread social and political after-effects.

Increasing military impingement on many aspects of Russian affairs was already apparent from 1914 onwards. The French Revolution, like the Russian Revolution of 1905 but unlike that of 1917, took place in time of peace. The energies of the French revolutionary armies were expended abroad, not at home in a defensive or a civil war. The general effect of war, whether international as for France, or mainly domestic as for Russia after 1917, led to political centralisation and military-type discipline in government. The crucial difference was that whereas the vigorous predominance of the army in France ended in Bonapartism, in Russia the Bolsheviks never lost their firm control over the combined political-military machine.

The Russian experience certainly confirmed the generalisation that total war and defeat are conducive to revolution. The World War was a merciless exponent of Russia's evils. In the economic sphere, S. Witte had realised very clearly as the government emerged from the Revolution of 1905 that the one thing it could not afford was to engage in another major military conflict. When the war against the Central Powers came, nearly all Russia's external trade was cut off. In time she lost her vital Polish and Baltic industrial areas. Most of the plant that remained had to be put to military use, since the Russian economy was not so diversified nor so developed as that of Germany. Even when war materials could be produced in sufficient quantity, the creaking communications network, as in the Crimean War, was unable to convey them fast enough to the widely spread fronts. When the inefficient manage-

ment of the war became increasingly apparent, political repercussions began to well up from the lower administrative levels. The
civilian Voluntary Organisations, which took on ever greater
duties connected with supplying the armed forces, were based on
Moscow and thus were well placed to oppose the Petrograd
bureaucrats and indirectly the Court. The Duma could not appeal
to the army for political support, since this was contrary to the
tradition that the military should remain subservient to the poli-
ticians, but the Voluntary Organisations, with the connivance of
the Progressive Bloc in the Duma, began to enlist the support of
leading military figures for constitutional reforms in order to win
the war : General M. Alekseev's connections with the Voluntary
Organisations in this way served to alienate him from the Tsar.

Political unrest due to the badly managed war effort spread to
the highest levels of government. The main reason behind the
changes in the Cabinet of August 1915 was the need to ensure
better military supplies. Subsequently the rumour spread that
Nicholas II was attempting to conclude a bilateral peace agreement with Germany. The German background of the Empress
tended to lend credence to this belief and involved her personally
in the political crisis. It was she who persuaded Nicholas to take a
firm stand on the cardinal point at issue – the timing of concessions
to the liberals in the Duma. The monarchy was determined to put
off until after the war those political and administrative reforms
which the Voluntary Organisations demanded immediately.

The failure of the Tsar and his government to channel and inspire the organised soicial energies at work in World War I led
directly to a revolutionary situation. Even in the total war situation so common in the twentieth century, it is not inevitable that
an inefficiently run war means the collapse of the government that
is to blame, but the Russian regime alienated precisely those social
forces which might have saved it. Not unnaturally, Nicholas II
and his advisors could neither understand nor adapt themselves to
the new type of war that overtook their country. The Voluntary
Organisations were more flexible from the start, and adapted
themselves progressively to the gradual involvement of society as
a whole in the fight. For instance, the Union of the Zemstvos
started out with few powers and an unclear programme, but soon
spread its work into the theatre of war and organised the care of
the wounded, the evacuation of refugees, etc.[20] The ties between

social work in the depths of the rear and the servicing of the fronts became much closer.[21] The military headquarters also came to the conclusion that the only way to make the military machine more efficient was to assert control over more and more of the civilian hinterland. This led to bitter confrontations between the military headquarters and the Ministry of War.

The composition of the army itself reflected this fusion of military and civil affairs. Before the outbreak of the war, the ranks of the military were more cut off from civilian influence than afterwards. The huge 1914 intake of new conscripts and reservists into the largest army in history meant that millions of older peasants had reluctantly to leave their domestic interests to serve at the front. By 1916, 36 per cent of the male population of working age was under arms. Since Russia suffered more casualties than any nation in the war, the ranks had to be continually replenished with hurriedly trained civilians. The composition of the officer corps also underwent great changes as a result of the war-time emergency officer-training courses. The young officers produced in this way were not interested in the army as a career. Their social background was more varied than that of the peacetime officer corps. Many of them had been involved in the Municipalities and Zemstvos, the basis of the Voluntary Organisations.

By February 1917 the army 'was no longer a select body largely secluded from the prevailing political climate, but had become merely part of the populace clothed in soldiers' greatcoats', in the words of a scholar who has studied military-civil relations during this period.[22] After February various new tensions were exerted on the armed civilians to go so far as to desert from their military obligations in favour of their private domestic interests. Rumours of famine in the cities, of the seizure of land in the countryside, gave proletarians and peasants alike reason to worry about the well-being of their families. Defeatist propaganda fell upon open ears.[23] During the same period the number of civilian factory workers, left-wing agitators and others who penetrated in the opposite direction to the fronts increased rapidly. Desertion from the ranks accelerated between February and October. According to a rough survey carried out on 25 October, there were then over 6,300,000 men left serving at the front : another 3,000,000 were stationed in the rear.[24] By the following spring most of them had literally melted away into civilian life.[25]

The high turnover due to casualties of civilians who acquired fighting experience became even faster with the onset of the Civil War. This was because one massive army disintegrated but was soon replaced by another, somewhat different in composition. The detailed ways in which the personnel of the new Red Army corresponded to or varied from the ranks of the Tsarist army will never be known. What is known is that by 1 July 1918 perhaps about 360,000 men had been enlisted, not including Red Guards and partisans.[26] The figure later rose to over 3,000,000. The borderline between military service and civilian life continued to be broken down by the huge number of deserters: in the course of about eighteen months nearly a million of them were arrested or else returned to their units; at one stage in 1919 they nearly equalled the combat strength of the whole of the Red Army.[27]

The new army still reflected broad strata of society, since it was by no means confined to the proletariat. On the contrary, by the end of the Civil War only 15–18 per cent of the total military strength were workers.[28] Most of the soldiers were peasants, as had been the case in the Tsarist army. Even the 'bourgeoisie' was not excluded, since its members were liable for mobilisation for labour service. Many command positions in the Red Army were also manned by ex-Imperial officers and NCOs. During the course of the Civil War, from 12 June 1918 to 15 August 1920, 48,409 ex-officers, 10,339 Tsarist administrative staff and 214,717 ex-NCOs were taken back into the Red Army as 'military specialists'.[29]

An anonymous author came to the conclusion in an article written for a military journal in 1919 that 'The large-scale structure of the Red Army as it is at present means that the interests of ever wider groups of the population are automatically bound up with military interests. The affairs of the Red Army are the business of all the toiling masses.'[30] The distinction between military and civil affairs also tended to be obliterated by the geographical and strategic aspects of the Civil War. The formalised military fronts of the World War vanished, and were replaced by a series of localised internal campaigns on Russian soil which swept backwards and forwards from month to month, reducing Bolshevik-controlled territory to roughly the size of Muscovy at one stage. Naval and air arms contributed little to the operations. The war was dominated by land engagements, in which, by their very nature, the civilian population was more embroiled. Instead of defending the abstract concept of the fatherland from a trench hundreds of miles away from home, peasants and workers in or out of uniform were fighting on their own doorsteps to preserve what was left of their personal estate. In the summer of 1919 the whole of Soviet territory was divided into regimental districts, and these areas were sub-divided into battalion, company and section areas. Local military organisations based on this military geography provided the army with reinforcements and also served as the basis for the later creation of the militia.[31]

The brutalisation of all aspects of life was overwhelming. Apart from the millions who died in uniform at the fronts in the World War or later in the Civil War, it has been estimated that 7,000,000 so-called civilians died from hunger and disease between January 1918 and July 1920, whilst the death rate doubled.[32] The horrors of war penetrated to the very heart of civilian culture and administration. Even before the outbreak of the Civil War in 1917, the capital city was declared to be part of the military zone. On 24 February 1918 the Germans captured Pskov. Two days later the Council of People's Commissars drew up a plan for the evacuation of Petrograd, and in March the government moved to the future capital of Moscow. In the interval civilian volunteers formed the hard core of the nascent Red Army. The hooters of Petrograd factories summoned volunteers to go out to fight. Workers remained civilians to the extent that their factory jobs were retained for them, and they were supposed to receive financial compensation if the plants were forced to close down through their absence. Student bodies established *ad hoc* sapper units, journalists were mobilised, and A. Lunacharsky geared all cultural institutions to the defence of the city.[33]

When Petrograd was threatened once more by General N. Yudenich in October 1919, Trotsky went so far as to suggest that the White forces should be let into the city and then attacked by street guerillas, who would trap them in the capital's labyrinth.[34] In *Peshchera* (The Cavern) a tale set in the beleaguered Petrograd of 1919, E. Zamiatin depicts the reduction of Russia to a state of primitive barbarity by using the image of the city as a prehistoric settlement, peopled by cavemen ruled by the basic needs for survival. His fears for the effect of internal war on society were reiterated in another article written in 1919: 'The proud *homo erectus* is getting down on all fours, is sprouting tusks and fur; the beast in man is triumphant.' [35]

In his role of Commissar for War, Trotsky underestimated the long-term dangers of total war for the future of social and political life. 'What does it mean to militarise?' he asked himself. 'It means to be prepared to take on responsibility and thus to create a better type of cultured person.' [36] The rigours of the Civil War conditioned him to expect and demand cruelty. The first known mention of concentration camps, and their usefulness, in any document from a Bolshevik leader, came from Trotsky's pen in a report to the Central Committee in May 1919. [37] Of course ruthless fanaticism was essential if Trotsky was to keep under control an ill-assorted peasant army afflicted by desertion and low morale. But the real threat to peacetime society came towards the end of the Civil War, when Trotsky, still immersed in his military experience, proceeded to apply the harshest disciplinary principles to his quasi-military visions of civilian institutions. During the transitional period at the close of the Civil War, Trotsky issued draconic instructions to the Third Army even when it was converted into the First Labour Army in preparation for a peacetime economy. Deserters from work, including malingerers and those who did not fulfil their work norm, were to be treated like deserters from battle, and shot. [38]

In different ways all the Bolshevik leaders were touched by the brutal character of the times. A vicious circle developed, since they used their authority to lash out ruthlessly in order to preserve themselves and the party, thus disseminating and perpetuating brutality from above. The harsh conditions of the Civil War taught Lenin to 'hit without mercy, even though in our ideal we are against using violence against people'. [39] Progress had to be delayed yet again, this time in the sphere of what Lenin called communist morality. It took the sensitivity of a literary genius like Gorky to stand firm against the encroachment of violence. During the Civil War, 'It often happened that I spoke with Lenin of the cruelty of revolutionary tactics and ways of life. "What do you expect?" – he asked in wonder and anger. "Is humanism possible in such an unheard of ferocious struggle? ..."' [40] Gorky was particularly concerned about the internal class war that Lenin waged against the civilian population behind the screen of the Civil War military operations. Only Gorky could have protested personally to Lenin about the fate of the Romanovs and actually saved the life of one of the Grand Dukes. The harsh fate of the intelligentsia, most of whom had been born into the wrong social classes, preoccupied Gorky in the war. As Curator of Culture he tried to protect artists of all kinds against class hatred and the abysmal living conditions in the towns. Gorky's conscience finally drove him to break with Lenin and leave the country in 1921. The cumulative impact of the treatment of the Kronstadt revolt, the arrest of the public members of the Famine Relief Commission and the deaths of A. Blok and N. Gumilev was too much for him. From his exile in Western Europe, he continued to do all he could to moderate Bolshevik terror, but in later years he had far less influence over Stalin than he had exerted over Lenin.

Among the Bolshevik leaders even Bukharin, the libertarian and persistent opponent of a standing army during the Civil War, succumbed unwittingly to the regimentation of social and political affairs. In his theoretical works of the period, *Historical Materialism* and *ABC of Communism*, he constantly used analogies taken from military life to illustrate his general points of analysis.[41] Perhaps the influence of Lenin and Trotsky was contagious: their writings were peppered with both pertinent and inept allusions to military models.[42] In the *ABC of Communism*, Bukharin stressed the need to destroy the old regime, and particularly the Tsarist army. He went on to admit that the new army would therefore be the first institution together with the party in the revolutionary regime.[43] He discounted the possibility that this priority of order for social reconstruction might give an overriding role to the military or to a combined political-military organ. After his conversion to the Right Opposition in NEP, however, Bukharin openly condoned the fusion of civil and military government in the Civil War: 'It was self-explanatory that the dictatorship of the proletariat took on the form of a proletarian military dictatorship.'[44] Zamiatin maintained in *Tserkov' boz'ia* (The Church of God), a story published during NEP, that the slaughter involved in the overthrow of the old order had undermined the moral authority of the new regime. The Bolsheviks claimed that they were acting in self-defence, but they had tolerated systematic lawlessness and violence from the first in the pursuit of their own particular aims. There is cumulative evidence for this, from Stalin's association with bloody ventures in Georgia long before 1917, to the armed dispersal of the Constituent Assembly in 1918. The arbitrary suppression of all critics by the Tsarist government had in time induced most left-wing parties to adopt similar methods. The political changes they sought by extra-legal means naturally led them on to violence.[45] Lenin seriously underestimated the long shadow that was to be cast over the future conduct of Soviet government by the Bolsheviks' long involvement in violence. On this cardinal point, as on several others, Rosa Luxemburg saw more clearly than Lenin did. Lenin welcomed the World War as a means of mobilising the hatred of the warring masses but she was so depressed by the inhuman effects of the fighting that for a period she seriously contempted suicide.

Against the background of the Civil War, involving the combined mobilisation of a revived standing army and the civilian population, let us now examine the specific ways in which first the party and then society were influenced by the war although never being subjected to naked military rule.

In very general terms it has already been noted by several scholars that as political forces the Bolshevik party and the Red Army had certain similarities. During the Civil War the party like an army tried to mobilise the whole population to engage in planned and coordinated activities leading towards a definite goal.[46] These activities were primarily of a military nature, though social, economic and even supranational aims were included. During NEP the similarity was no longer so apparent, but with collectivisation and the First Five-Year Plan it became more striking than ever, despite the fact that strictly military activities were no longer involved. Other similarities which also lingered on in peacetime were the quasi-military organisation and functions of the party based on the original need of an insurrectional political group to model itself on the military. Finally, both party and army were purposive instruments with similar characteristics: centralised command, hierarchy, discipline and self-sufficiency.

The ways in which the Bolsheviks organised themselves both before and during October 1917 seem to bear these points out. The theoretical basis for the party as laid down in *What is to be Done?* relies on military illustrations: '... It is necessary to have a strong organization of tried revolutionaries ... As we know, in time of war, it is not only of the utmost importance to imbue one's own army with confidence in its strength, but it is important also to convince the enemy and all *neutral* elements of this strength; friendly neutrality may sometimes decide the issue.'[47] In 1917 itself, Lenin eventually decided to apply a minimal amount of quasi-military force at the nodal point of Russian life in order to topple the weak Provisional Government: Bolshevik persuasion through propaganda had been powerful but incapable of ending the Kerensky regime by its own momentum alone. Lenin's decision entailed reliance on the Military Revolutionary Committee for two months after the October coup. It has been argued that during this short period the MRC held the balance of power between the Petrograd Soviet on the one hand and the Bolshevik Central Committee on the other.[48] If the October coup is viewed in terms of the abandonment of supreme state authority by the Provisional Government to a new organ of power, then one can point unswervingly to the break between the MRC and the Staff of the Petrograd Military District on the night of October 21–22 as the start of the coup.

In terms of technical control too, the MRC at first occupied a leading position. Its commissars were sent out to supervise the Petrograd garrison. No organ could supervise the whole of Russia between February 1917 and the close of the Civil War, but in October the MRC prevented the despatch of any military units to the front and broadcast revolutionary appeals in its own name to the fronts and the civilian areas. Given the apolitical attitude of most military officers, the demoralised state of the army, and the geographical impossibility that any foreign army could swiftly take over the power vacuum inside Russia, the MRC achieved considerable authority. Even before the foundation of the *Cheka* on 20 December 1917, the MRC contained a section for dealing with counter-revolution, headed by F. Dzerzhinsky. In embryo four constituents of political power already existed which jostled for position in the following period – the Soviet structure, the military, the police and the Bolshevik party. With the benefit of hindsight Soviet scholars have naturally wished to stress the prime legitimacy of the Bolsheviks at this early stage: for their part non-communist historians have tended to pre-date slightly the clear emergence of party dominance over the other organisations. It is true that the MRC soon after its creation by the Petrograd Soviet became a Bolshevik vehicle, but it was not inconceivable that Trotsky might have refused to allow the MRC to be dissolved on

5 December 1917, when Bolshevik influence was transferred to the Council of People's Commissars. Luckily for the party, neither Trotsky nor any other leader ever evinced the slightest trace of Bonapartism, either then or at the close of the Civil War. Yu. Martov was aiming wide of the mark when in 1921 he claimed from the safe haven of Berlin that NEP was 'the programme of a Bonapartist military-bureaucratic dictatorship'.[49]

The advent of the Civil War in a sense dealt another blow at the feasibility of Bonapartist rule. The limited quasi-military coup of October broadened into a nationwide political revolution involving the entire civilian population. The localised MRC was superseded by the all-Russian Soviet, and above all by the party, networks. If one looks at the wording of the 1918 Constitution and makes assumptions of the kind that a constitutional historian of another country would draw, then the party, which is nowhere mentioned in that document, can be considered as just one rival structure set against others that are named in the Constitution. But in the emergency of the Civil War, the centralised party soon drained power from all other less compact organs, at the same time continuing to work through the medium of those bodies it managed to control.

The new Red Army was one of these bodies. The political element was firmly predominant in the Revolutionary Military Council of the Republic, as it came to be called by the autumn of 1918. Civilians were also placed in similar organs at the fronts. At all levels the political commissars, assisted by the special sections of the *Cheka*, watched over military personnel. Trotsky stressed that it was impossible for the army to remain politically neutral, as some military specialists hoped, although they agreed to fight for the new regime. A firmly cemented political-military administration had to conduct the struggle.[50] This system throughout the Civil War avoided those clashes between the civil and military authorities that had in turn weakened the Tsarist and Provisional Governments. The linchpin of the combined operation was Lenin. He was a 'one-man political-military staff' as Louis Fischer aptly described him.[51] Learning as much from his reading of Clausewitz as from Marx, Lenin oversaw the military struggle, while never for one moment forgetting the social and political objectives of the war. For the first time in history, he claimed, war was based 'on the proximity, the insoluble proximity, or it might be said on the insoluble fusion of the Soviets and the army'.[52] Note the lack of reference to the party, the *éminence grise* which manipulated both organs. Lenin's theoretical knowledge, derived from his reading before the Revolution, happened to coincide nicely with the total character of the Civil War as it was actually revealed. It gave him superior insight into many problems. Whereas purely military minds continued to view the war in traditional, formal terms, Lenin at once grasped the need to link up activity between the civil and military zones in the struggle without set fronts.

Modern writers on the military often tend to suggest that in general a politician and a soldier are of different species,[53] but both Lenin and Trotsky seem to defy this proposition, as do the thirteen other Politburo members between 1917 and 1951 who likewise played joint political and military roles in the Civil War.[54] Both Lenin and Trotsky, the two leading party figures, avoided the Scylla of Bonapartism. When Trotsky wrote that the main guarantee against Bonapartism was that the Red Army was merely the tool of a specific political regime,[55] his was no idle boast. Some of the historical and organisational reasons for this have already been mentioned. Bukharin added another in 1919: 'Bonapartism is characterised by individual persons taking on a significance which has no correspondence at all to their real role. They have no self-sufficient social base under them, despite the fact that the power of the state belongs to them.'[56] Compared with the social support given to the Whites, the foundations on which Lenin relied grew stronger through persuasion and coercion as the war progressed. Kolchak in contrast asserted that the first essential in Siberia was an armed force. He neglected the need in time of civil war for carefully fostered mutual interests between the army, the civil authorities and the population at large. Kolchak, like Trotsky, earned the hatred of the peasants by taking their food and men, and both were feared by townsmen for unleashing peasant armies against the towns. The Bolsheviks survived the civilian hatred they stirred up because of their more tightly knit military-civil organisation and their better understanding of total warfare. Kolchak could have learnt many lessons from Makhno, whose peasant units lacked any formal cohesion but were closely integrated for a time with the surrounding population in the Ukraine.

In the English Puritan Revolution and the French Revolution the army emerged as the only group with sufficient unity to domi-

nate the situation. The Russian Revolution was unique in producing a disciplined party which became more than a substitute
for the traditional role played by the military in political up-
heavals. Whereas the Jacobins organised themselves for the duration of the revolutionary period only, and were doomed to
dispersal soon afterwards, it has been seen that the Bolsheviks
consciously modelled their party on quasi-military lines long before 1917. 'Take the army of today', wrote Lenin in exile : 'It is a
good example of organization. This organization is good only because it is flexible and is able at the same time to give millions of
people a single will.' [57]

The Bolshevik Revolution sailed safely past the Scylla of Bonapartism, but during the Civil War it started to veer towards the
Charybdis of what was later to be known as Stalinism. The final
contours of Stalinism are reviewed in the last chapter of this book :
at this stage attention is focussed entirely on the social origins of
that phenomenon. N. Podvoisky unconsciously adumbrated one
aspect of the future contours when he wrote in a military journal
in 1918 that the Red Army was not just a technical organ; it was
also a social body which therefore required a collective spirit. The
civilian leader of such an army, with strong roots in civilian life,
was a 'personal incarnation of this psychological unity'.[58] These
were strange words from the pen of a Marxist, but Stalin was later
to graft the idea of the supreme authority of the leader on to an
ideology that clearly minimised the role of the individual in
society. Podvoisky's comment is arresting, because it shows how
easily the notion of the all-important Leader could be transferred
from the military-political plane to the civil sphere. After 1928
Stalin *in peacetime* once more mobilised a population that had
been partially conditioned to regimentation in the Civil War. By
that time the armed forces had been ousted as an instrument of
domestic coercion by the secret police.

The dangers of Whig history must be carefully avoided, however. The political regimentation of society was only at a nascent
stage in the Civil War, compared with the 1930s. Anti-monolithic
pressures at the higher and lower levels of the political-military
organisation remained numerous. Just as the social experiments
of this early period scarcely extended beyond the urban centres, so
the militarised model of society was restricted in the main to the
army itself, though all men were touched by the prevailing chaos

and brutality, and military influences were increasingly felt in social and economic affairs. In the military organs themselves centrifugal trends were at work. The Red Army itself maintained independent control over its political and security organs. Although Bolshevik party members were the shock-troops of the armed forces, the central party authorities waged a continual battle against the tradition of independence in military communist cells which the Bolsheviks themselves had instilled between February and October 1917. Not until 1919 was any kind of central control asserted, and until 1924 the Central Political Administration (PUR) managed to operate separately from the Bolshevik Central Committee.

Close ties between the lower echelons of the party and the army were forged because enlistment into the military ranks became a passport to party membership, but entry was enlarged indiscriminately at the height of the Civil War, so that widespread purges had to be carried out later. During the war itself desertion took place on a gigantic scale. Of those Red troops taken prisoner by force rather than by desertion in the Polish Campaign, it was estimated that only 8 to 10 per cent were genuine party supporters.[59] The Red Army as a whole was never a homogeneous nor a safely pro-Bolshevik social unit during the Civil War. Armies in unevenly developed economies are often composed of highly stratified class groupings, and the Red Army was no exception, despite Bolshevik efforts to level its social composition. Too many aristocratic and middle-class officers survived from the Tsarist army, and there were not enough proletarians to put to rest the fear of a peasant-led independent military movement. Certainly it was risky to use peasant units to suppress peasant uprisings amongst the civilian population

Not until the late 1920s was the Red Army moulded into monolithic unity firmly under central Bolshevik political supervision. The same cannot be said of the secret police, which from its establishment in December 1917 was carefully subordinated in all ways to the party, although undesirable elements managed to enter its ranks during the Civil War. The rise of the *Cheka*, its relationship to the army and the party, and its use as a weapon of social control were crucial factors in the avoidance of Bonapartism and the drift towards permanent authoritarianism. Although the demarcation line between internal and external violence was hard to distinguish in an internal war, the *Cheka* gradually took over responsibility for domestic acts of coercion aimed primarily at the civilian population in the political and class struggle. Naked military force was directed more against external enemies and recalcitrant non-combatants in league with them. After the close of the Civil War the division of power became more obvious, when the Red Army was deprived of its coercive rationale in time of peace, whereas the secret police gained new powers over the civilian population.

Before the Revolution Lenin had prophesied that the struggle which would follow it would generate internal class war as well as international strife.[60] Yet when Bolshevik-inspired sailors in January 1918 killed two obvious class enemies of the Revolution, the Kadets A. Shingarev and F. Kokoshkin, the editors of *Izvestiia*, now a Bolshevik organ, commented : 'this murder . . . helps only the enemies of the Revolution, the Black Hundred . . . The murderers must be found and brought before the revolutionary court. There must be no stain on the Revolution.'[61] With the outbreak of the Civil War and the attempt on Lenin's life in August 1918, Lenin's prophesy came true on both fronts. In order to deal with sudden threats on every side, the Bolsheviks leant heavily on three institutional controls inherited from the period before October : namely a standing army, a secret police and a system of political commissars in the army. Just as Trotsky felt it necessary to convince critics that the new army was only like the old one in form, but not in content,[62] so M. Latsis, an apologist for the *Cheka*, in which he came to occupy an eminent position, declared : 'Those who see no difference between the Tsarist police and our Extraordinary Commissions are unable to see or understand anything, they have slept through the February and October Revolutions and now expect others to do all the dirty work in creating the new communist society . . .'[63] Certainly the *Cheka* was at this early period intended to serve as a sharp-edged instrument of social progress rather than as the preserver of the *status quo*, which had been the role assigned to the Tsarist *Okhrana*. In time this distinction was to become far more blurred. Even in the initial stages of the new regime, the changes in the organisational arrangements of the coercive tools, if not in their ideological motivation, resembled much more a process of *Gleichschaltung* than a thoroughgoing revolution.

The situation was almost ideal for the resurrection of the secret police. The catastrophic speed of events was conducive to mental inertia as a kind of reaction, even in the most progressive sectors, so that just as all the parties of the Left fell back on the 1905 Soviet system in February, so the Bolsheviks looked to the secret police after October. In the chaotic constitutional situation it was possible for the *Cheka* to arise and extend its powers without the publication of any formal legislation on it whatsoever. It was only in 1924 that a statement was issued which may be taken as the official establishment of the secret police system.[64] The climate of total war and universal violence also made it easier for the *Cheka* to emerge under the cover of the military and to assert gradual control over internal social affairs.

The details of this unobtrusive peeling-off from the military are of some interest. Feliks Dzerzhinsky, in August 1917, was placed together with Ya. Sverdlov in joint control of the All-Russian Central Bureau of Military Organisations. For a short period he also supervised the editing of the newspaper *Soldat*, which appeared between July and October 1917. After the October coup it was natural that persons arrested on charges of counter-revolution were brought to the offices of the Petrograd Military Revolutionary Committee. A special section under Dzerzhinsky was set up to deal with them,[65] and it survived the curtailment of the powers of the MRC which took place only fifteen days after the October coup. Until its final dissolution in mid-December 1917, the MRC, and its special section in particular, acted as the Bolsheviks' temporary apparatus for repression.[66] This role was superseded immediately with the formation of the *Cheka* as a separate body on 20 December 1917. Its first recruits were 50 volunteers and 60 soldiers who had helped to storm the Winter Palace in October.[67] By the end of July 1918 the *Cheka* wielded 35 battalions.[68] On 1 July 1919 the *Cheka* Staff was given much wider powers. It was reconstituted as the Staff for Troops of Internal Security (*VOKhR*), gathering under its command all the Units of Special Purpose (*ChON*) which had previously been subject to various military and civil authorities. Dzerzhinsky later succeeded in weaning these units further away from military influences by freeing them from guard duties and garrison chores.[69]

Behind the organisational screen of the military, the *Cheka* took on more and more powers for dealing with political foes and the civilian population. These powers have often been described and are therefore not treated in any detail here.[70] In addition to his post as head of the *Cheka*, Dzerzhinsky was appointed Commissar of Internal Affairs in March 1919.[71] Thus the Tsarist connection between the two bodies was reconstituted. It was yet another example of organisational inertia. When the *Cheka* was abolished in February 1922 it was replaced by the State Political Administration (*GPU*) which was now formally attached to the Commissariat of Internal Affairs. The fact that the Civil War was total in nature, lacked defined fronts and involved civil and military lives indiscriminately, provided wide scope for the *Cheka* to manoeuvre without incurring so much hostile publicity as it would have done in time of peace, or in a war of a more traditional type. Even before 1917 the weapons of coercion were viewed by the Tsarist regime as being of service in domestic affairs in a situation of increasingly total warfare. On enlisting in the World War, Russian soldiers had to swear to defend the throne and the fatherland against both external and internal foes.[72]

The *Cheka*'s area of activity had no set limits. In the territorial sense Latsis proclaimed that the secret police was acting on the internal front of the Civil War . . . It is a fighting organ of Soviet power, ensuring the possibility of peaceful reconstruction by the massed millions of workers and peasants who hold the power.'[73] But a little further on in the same book he also ascribed considerable importance to the special *Cheka* units at the shifting military fronts, though he thought that they would be abolished at the end of the Civil War.[74] When peace came, the secret police actually gained extra control over the peacetime frontiers of the country, in February 1921.[75] In the legal sense too, the *Cheka* had a completely free hand. It claimed absolute autonomy for its searches, arrests, trials and judgements. Dzerzhinsky drew a telling analogy between the police and military in a press interview given in June 1918 : 'The *Cheka* is not a court. The *Cheka* is the defence of the Revolution as the Red Army is. And just as in the Civil War the Red Army cannot stop to ask whether or not it may harm individuals but is obliged to act with the one thought of securing the victory of the Revolution over the bourgeoisie, the *Cheka* is obliged to defend the Revolution and conquer the enemy even if its sword does by chance sometimes fall upon the heads of the innocent.'[76] The Commissar of Justice, I. Steinberg, who happened to be a

Left SR, protested against such arbitrary behaviour, as did his successors, but Lenin gave his support to the *Cheka*.[77] Latsis considered that many of the 'crimes' committed in the Civil War were not counter-revolutionary, but merely a reflection of the transitional phase from a bourgeois to a socialist society. Both types of crime, however, 'are usually so closely interwoven that it is hard in the first instance to differentiate between them'. He concluded from this that the *Cheka* must first survey crimes, classify them, and then pass on crimes incurred against the existing laws to the ordinary courts.[78] The fact that the secret police was permitted to be the prime arbiter had implications that were to cast a long authoritarian shadow over the workings of the civil and criminal law. In the 1930s the earlier blurring of categories provided a precedent for the Great Purge.

The institutionalisation of social terror in the shape of the Soviet secret police was a gradual process which was directly engendered by the atmosphere of mass violence promoted by the World War, the Revolution and Civil War. Arising in the first place from largely spontaneous causes, it developed fast when the process of normal legal enforcement broke down. After October the Tsarist and Republican legal system collapsed, to be replaced for a prolonged period by reliance on 'revolutionary conscience'. Mass terror took over from sporadic acts of violence in the summer of 1918, with the assassinations of the Bolshevik leader, V. Volodarsky, the chief of the Petrograd *Cheka*, M. Uritsky, and the attempt on Lenin's life. The deliberate and formal organisation of violence through the *GPU* only took place after the end of military violence. The secret police benefited from its para-military origin and guise, but avoided the decline which the military suffered as a force in peacetime politics. With party backing the police could also circumvent the entire legal system, the only other institution of formalised coercion.

The new *GPU* was more centralised than the military. A strict hierarchy of lower agencies was set up under the overriding control of the Moscow *GPU*. Unlike the army, which in spite of the experience of the Civil War still retained some measure of traditional institutional independence, the *GPU* was intimately connected with the party, so that in time it became difficult to distinguish which was in command of the other. The informal development of the police helped in this respect. For these reasons the secret police came to occupy a leading position in the administration of coercive measures against Soviet society. During the 1920s most of its earlier wartime powers for dealing with the population remained submerged, but when Stalin again mobilised the entire country in agricultural collectivisation and the Five-Year Plans, its latent uses came to the surface. Once the external military enemy and then internal high-level political foes had been defeated, the party finally turned its sword against the broad masses in a renewed situation of total violence. Those civil powers which the secret police assumed in the course of the Civil War were wielded once more, this time against literally millions of civilians rather than against thousands. The *ad hoc* revolutionary tribunals of the Civil War were blown up into the nationwide legalised police system of N. Ezhov. The original limited target of the *Cheka* in the winter of 1917–18 had been the 'bagmen', the speculators who followed in the wake of economic and social chaos. At the end of the 1920s the Nepmen were pursued on a far vaster scale, but for similar reasons. The *Cheka* hunted the upper and middle classes as the main class foes in the Civil War. The *OGPU* later transferred this strategy to the kulaks and a section of the intelligentsia. The control which the police had come to assert over labour camps, the communications network, warehouses and granaries, together with its particular interest in sabotage, was given enormously wider scope in the industrialisation process of the 1930s.

The various developments that took place as a result of the military situation in the political structure and the secret police were accompanied during the Civil War by direct military pressures on other aspects of social life and political institutions. Before examining these pressures, however, it may be useful to enter into a short digression concerning the conflicting interpretations that have been made of War Communism. This will serve to emphasise the sincere ideological motives of the Bolsheviks for introducing certain influences into social and economic life which were not entirely due to the military situation. It will also bring into play once more the theoretical beliefs behind the social experiments of the Civil War period that were discussed in the previous chapter.

Whereas Soviet and non-communist scholars have devoted scant attention to the social utopias of these early years, the economic characteristics of War Communism have been studied in detail. Broadly speaking, there have been two schools of thought among Western observers. The more recent group, including M. Dobb and E. H. Carr, has tended to view the short-lived economic phenomenon known as War Communism as an empirical creation, unconnected with Marxist economic theory. They tend to think that scarcity of essential goods and military necessities drove the Bolsheviks to act as they did, rather than any tenacious reliance on the ideology they inherited. Carr does in fact give an account of the Bolsheviks' prerevolutionary economic programme, but he views it as secondary to military expediency after 1917.[79] During the 1920s and 1930s Western students of War Communism made a more convincing effort to interpret its economic measures as an outcome of Marxist-Leninist reasoning. Writers like B. Brutzkus and L. Lawton agreed that the Civil War had an enormous impact on the manner in which ideological precepts were applied, but the two writers did not obfuscate the rigorous and deep sources of those precepts.[80] Brutzkus observed that at the time the Bolsheviks did not view their economic projects as temporary stop-gaps caused by the harsh requirements of the Civil War : War Communism still flourished in the winter of 1920 during a relatively tranquil interlude in the war.[81] As an economic system it suffered from some organisational defects which had little or nothing to do with the running of military operations. Finally, it survived for four months after the end of the Civil War.[82]

Although the present writer does not pretend to be an expert on economic affairs, the view held by Brutzkus and others seems to bear a closer relationship to the real balance of motives for introducing War Communism, not only on the basis of the internal arguments given by them, but also when comparison is made with the reasoning behind the social experiments analysed in the foregoing chapter. A similar brand of deep-seated Marxist inspiration played an equally important part in the social and economic projects of the Civil War. Both were derived from the more utopian trends in Marxist thought, though both suffered considerable distortion due to the military realities of the period. A reading of Lenin's *The Immediate Tasks of the Soviet Government*, published in April 1918,[83] leads to the conclusion that he genuinely believed in the instant need for socialist economic organisation. Even Lenin at this stage was imbued by that eager chiliasm which kept other Bolsheviks involved in utopian social experiments well into the Civil War. Lenin imagined that the principle of surplus appropriation, eliminating purchase and sale on the market and substituting socialist distribution of products in kind for the private exchange of goods between agriculture and industry, could be introduced immediately, as the title of his article implied.

One of the differences between the social and economic spheres was the greater Marxist orthodoxy of the economic theories. We have seen that the social projects were infused by a curious amalgam of fashionable ideas, many of which were prevalent in Germany at the time. Another difference was that whereas Lenin turned his face against social experimentation in 1918, he remained more sanguine on the economic front until the final collapse of War Communism. Social progress was much less vital to the successful outcome of the Civil War than the requisitioning of food supplies from the peasantry, which was a central feature of War Communism. It is significant that Taylorism and electrification, the two utopian schemes with social implications that lingered on as interests in Lenin's mind, were closely connected with the economic features of War Communism. The main reason why Lenin eventually abandoned War Communism was the same one that had led him at an earlier stage to curb workers' control and the radical reform of the family structure. The socialist plan to cut out commodity production was shelved because it led to economic chaos and social unrest of such dimensions that the political power of the Bolsheviks was threatened. The economic threat was far more serious than the menace of anarchic, anti-central social experiments. 'War Communism', as it misleadingly came to be called *after* it was over, was not stopped because it was a measure intended for wartime purposes only, but because Bolshevik sovereignty was at stake.

One further parallel became evident in the subsequent revival of ambitious social and economic planning at the end of NEP. Just as the more authoritarian elements in the social theories current during the Civil War were taken up and adapted to the situation in the 1930s, so the accent changed in economic planning. Historians of the Soviet period seem to have almost forgotten that brutally rapid and highly centralised industrialisation was not the Bolsheviks' primary aim from the very first. The elimination of commodity production and the direct exchange of products in a socialist community freed from the dichotomy between town and country, between proletarian and peasant, were their chief objectives in War Communism. The question of tight political and therefore of economic centralisation only arose as a permanent peacetime objective under Stalin. The fact that through military necessity the initial scheme was centralised from the start must not obscure the general principles involved, which by no means automatically required an authoritarian political framework.

At this point we may return to the main theme of this chapter and examine direct military influences on social organisation in the Civil War. In retrospect it will be seen that disciplined regimentation of this kind was revived in the 1930s, although no longer administered by the military authorities.

The way in which the supply problem in time of war affected socio-economic life adversely is of interest, since the question of supplies was regulated in War Communism by *a priori* Marxist theory as well as by the practical need to furnish the Red Army with all its requirements. Any proper analysis of the social effects of the supply problem entails an examination of the crescive influences which built up during the war prior to October 1917, since they laid the foundations for what was to follow. The cumulative supply crisis and its social and political repercussions by 1917 have been studied in another place by the present author.[84] A few major points may suffice here. The condition of a nation's stomach seems to be a vital factor in political revolutions. The French Revolution was finally touched off by the acute rise in the price of bread in Paris, and the February Revolution of 1917 by unruly queues outside the Petrograd bakeries which were short of supplies. It would also not be an exaggeration to say that the state of social unrest provoked by the supply problem was one of the main impulses behind the eventual collapse of the Provisional Government. The role of the army in this crisis was crucial. It had a gargantuan appetite for supplies of all kinds, and this appetite increased. Prior to September 1915 the ranks comprised between three and four millions. By January 1916 this figure rose to over six millions, and on the eve of the February Revolution stood at approximately seven millions.[85] Strategic military advances, retreats and concentrations repeatedly altered the supply problem on the long fronts from the Baltic to the Black Sea, and in the Caucasus. Lack of co-operation between the civil and military authorities exacerbated the situation. The chaotic state of military supplies was chiefly responsible for the decline of morale in the army. Lack of rifles, boots, greatcoats and food provided more telling arguments in favour of Lenin's defeatist platform than reams of propaganda. As disorder multiplied throughout 1917, scapegoats were looked for and found. Among the civilian population the townsmen came to believe that the peasants were grain profiteers, whereas the peasants blamed the cities for the lack of basic commodities. On the whole the peasants were less reluctant to give up their crops to the army than to the urban centres. They had been compelled to send their sons to the front, so they reckoned that their grain should follow them.

The political coup of October did nothing to stem the supply crisis. In a letter from the Secretariat of the Bolshevik Central Committee sent out to local cells shortly after Lenin's victory, the problem was categorised as 'the burning question of the moment, which could bring all the gains of the Revolution to naught'.[86] With the onset of the Civil War the situation took a new turn for the worse, since the important grain-producing regions of the Ukraine, the Don, the northern Caucasus and Siberia were cut off from Central Russia. In general, apart from grain, the Civil War had peculiarly severe dislocating effects on all supplies. Military operations damage an economy more on account of their dislocating influence than because of direct destruction; in an internal war military action may run through heavily populated civilian areas, cutting one part of the country off from the other. This was certainly the often repeated case in the Russian Civil War.

As early as January 1918 the alarming character of the supply problem was evident in Lenin's advice that all food speculators should be 'shot on the spot' by mixed detachments sent out by regiments and factories.[87] Once more the military-civil borderline was ignored. On February 15 an Extraordinary Commission on Food and Transport was established under the joint supervision of the Chairman of the Central Committee on Army Supplies, the Commissar of Railways, and the Vice-Chairman of the Council of Supply.[88] In May 1918 Ya. Sverdlov, the Chairman of the Bolshevik Central Executive Committee, declared that the class struggle had to be carried into the villages. Armed detachments of city workers were sent to the countryside to requisition surplus grain. The importance attached by Lenin to the supply crisis in the army and the towns may be judged from his *Theses on the Current Situation*, issued on May 26, which suggested that 'the Commissariat for War be converted into a Commissariat for War and Food – i.e., nine-tenths of the work of the Commissariat for War to be concentrated on reorganizing the army for the war for grain . . .'[89] Thus the effect of the military situation on the supply crisis led to the violent confiscation of grain. But that was not the whole story. Although the methods used were brutal, they had a real connection with the Marxist principle of surplus appropriation with the aim of ending purchase and sale on the market. It was not merely the cruel necessities of the Civil War which inspired the requisitions. The idea of consciously destroying capitalist commercial principles was also inherent in the Bolsheviks' action. Already in May 1917 Lenin had realised that the chaotic state of Russia's supplies could be used as a political lever for the future nationalised control of the country's resources. He then foresaw that 'the aim of a state organization should be to organize on a broad regional and subsequently country-wide scale the exchange of agricultural for manufactured goods'.[90]

The consumer needs of the military and the cities rapidly became an instrument of social warfare in the Bolsheviks' hands. Lenin knew that close party control over food supplies would enable him to use the food scarcity as a means of compelling the 'bourgeois' to work for the new regime or else starve. He also used the upper classes as scapegoats for the difficulties. In a letter to the workers of Petrograd he wrote : 'The famine is not due to the fact that there is no grain in Russia, but to the fact that the bourgeoisie and the rich generally are putting up a last decisive fight against the rule of the toilers, against the state of the workers, against Soviet power, on this most important and acute of issues, the issue of bread.'[91] The *Cheka* was instructed to deal with this menace, thus for the first time channelling armed coercion against the internal class enemy for socio-economic reasons. The system was to be applied on a far grander scale in later years. Lenin also whipped up hatred of the rich peasants amongst the poor with the formation of the Committees of the Poor, which were incited to requisition grain by force. Maxim Gorky viewed this aspect of social war and its implications for the future with particular anguish.

By the winter of 1918 the organisation of supplies was completely fused with the military-political decision-making process. On 30 November 1918 the Soviet of Workers' and Peasants' Defence was created under the presidency of Lenin. It acted as a sort of war cabinet and ministry of supply and labour rolled into one. In July 1919 A. Rykov was appointed as Extraordinary Plenipotentiary of the Red Army Supply Council, with the powers to carry out requisitions of all kinds of supplies : the entire country's available resources were open to violent extraction.[92] These were the almost inevitable results of earlier trends. When it had appeared that supply trains between Orel and Kursk would be held up in 1918, Lenin had ordered the army as well as local Soviet organs to move in.[93] He suggested that nineteen-year-olds should be called up, given military training, and then sent out as a *Prodarmiia* (Supply Army) to find grain and fuel.[94] By 1920 roughly half Russia's total output of sugar, fish, fat, tobacco, soap, textiles and footwear was being consumed by the Red Army.[95]

The Soviet transport system was the most severely affected by military supply demands. The policy of labour militarisation, which was another important aspect of the encroachment on civil affairs, was ruthlessly applied on the railways under Trotsky's control. He reorganised the Central Political Administration of the Railways (*Glavpolitput'*) on lines similar to the Red Army organ with the same title. The need for efficient supplies came before political or social justice. Trotsky agreed that his methods were violent, but he thought that they were in inverse proportion to the powers of the administrative machinery : 'The stronger we are,' he stressed, 'the less frequent are the instances of hostility to our orders.'[96] If one reads through Trotsky's account of the Civil War, however, it is clear that he often advocated and used draconic methods to satisfy his personal frustration. When his private train was blocked, or the snow was not cleared from the line he was travelling along at the time, he was apt to work up his anger into a scheme for the militarisation of all forms of transport in the entire country.[97]

Trotsky's treatment of the supply crisis had repercussions that influenced long-term trends beyond the technical problem of how to feed the army and the cities. His high-handed treatment of labour and his manipulation of *Tsektran*, the body which combined the two main transport Trade Unions, was vigorously opposed by the All-Russian Central Council of Trade Unions, led by M. Tomsky. The internal revolt which took place within *Tsektran* was the beginning of the end of the policy of labour militarisation, at least at this stage of Soviet history. It also led, together with other causes, to a fundamental weakening of Trotsky's political position and the ascendancy of Stalin, who managed to take Trotsky's control over transport away from him. As in so many other areas, the secret police eventually took over supervision of the means of communication from the military-civil authorities.

In the light of Russian history the treatment of the supply problem during the Civil War may be seen as a temporary eruption in a much longer continuum. Before the October coup, the peasants had viewed Kerensky's grain monopoly as nothing better than legalised robbery. The Provisional Government might well have acted as the Bolsheviks did subsequently, by using military detachments on a large scale to get the grain to the towns and fronts, but it was incapable of controlling them. Again in the 1930s, as a result of the economic policy formulated by E. Preobrazhensky, the peasantry was forced to supply the food for the army and the rapidly increasing urban population without obtaining the sort of equivalent in industrial goods which it would have received in the conditions of a capitalist market. Preobrazhensky's premises for the reimposition of socio-economic conditions, which in their actual operation were somewhat reminiscent of War Communism, differed in theoretical terms from the hypotheses formulated by the Bolsheviks in the earlier period. Taking a leaf out of the Marxist theory of capitalist development, Preobrazhensky assumed that socialist development likewise had to rely on primitive accumulation in order to build up a superior mode of production organization. Capitalism had achieved its purpose in this way by the social and economic plunder of colonial areas and their inhabitants. In Preobrazhensky's view, primitive Socialist accumulation could be achieved in Soviet Russia if the millions of small-scale peasant farms took the place of external colonies as a source of accumulation.

Although the shift of emphasis between War Communism and the period of collectivisation from one facet of Marxist theory to another was considerable, the practical social effects, and to some extent the economic effects, were not so dissimilar. A precedent on a limited basis and under peculiar military conditions was established in the Civil War. In the 1930s a peacetime system was established. Once the peasants had been forced into the collective farms, they were submitted to pressures which subsequently involved less naked military violence and much more sophisticated manipulation than under War Communism, but they were nevertheless once more condemned to be social and economic subordinates in a network of compulsory supply. Even on the theoretical level, the fundamental aim of Marxist planning to cut out commodity production and introduce direct products-exchange within a totally socialised economy, which orginally lay at the root of the supply methods of War Communism, was not entirely lost sight of in the period of rapid industrialisation under Stalin. In his *Economic Problems of Socialism in the USSR* Stalin reasserted this principle once again.[98]

The close connection between the militarisation of the supply system and of labour, particularly in the communications sector, has already been noted. Forced labour on military lines, like forced supply, was already part of Russia's historical experience long before the Soviet period. A method of militarised labour employment had been established during the reign of Alexander I by A. Arakcheev, the Minister of War. Army units in the provinces were linked up to agricultural production in addition to their normal military duties. When Trotsky prepared to introduce the militarisation of labour towards the close of the Civil War, Trade Union and Menshevik opponents declared that he was harking back to the Arakcheev regime. Trotsky countered them by wielding the same argument that was used to defend the resuscitation of a standing army and a secret police. The outward form might appear to be similar, but the inward inspiration was quite new :

An ideological struggle must be carried out against the prejudices of the petty intelligentsia and Trade Unionists who regard the militarisation of labour and the employment of military units in the production process as a return to the Arakcheev regime. It is necessary to explain the inevitability and the progressive character of military compulsion aimed at economic improvement on the basis of universal compulsory labour . . .[99]

As for the old-fashioned mould which contained the novel policy, Trotsky cleared himself of conservatism by stating that the war authorities were the best equipped to control civilian labour, since the economic administration was brand new and as yet incapable of dealing with labour questions on a national scale.[100] The drift towards militarised forms of civilian labour before Trotsky introduced a definite plan of action for it in December 1919 was indicative of the way in which the course of the internal war quickly poisoned the conduct of social affairs. In November 1917 Lenin wrote that universal compulsory labour was no better than 'military penal servitude', but he went on to suggest that the ex-capitalists at least be subjected to compulsory work by the new government.[101] Trotsky suggested that the 'bourgeoisie' be employed for menial work in battalions at the rear. By 1919 the state of the economy was such that military-type discipline came to be asserted over the proletariat as well. The elimination of any distinction between military fronts and the civilian rear went on apace. A significant article in *Izvestiia* put it thus :

On every front a struggle which calls for sacrifice for the sake of an ideal is now being waged. Some fighters understand this ideal and sacrifice everything for it. Others, however, required the application of severe disciplinary measures. This has been the situation at the front. But what about the people behind the front line? The rear is undermining the front because it disorganises the national economy.[102]

One month later, in April 1919, *Izvestiia* published a decree setting up forced labour camps for workers found guilty of transgressing the harsh provision for labour discipline.

Trotsky's fully fledged idea of turning the Soviet population into a vast army of labour was embodied in twenty-four propositions submitted to the Bolshevik Central Committee in December 1919. He claimed that the concept of militarisation was 'only an analogy', though he went on, 'but an analogy which is very rich in content. No social organisation, except the army, has ever considered itself justified in subordinating citizens to itself in such a measure and in subjecting them to its will to such an extent as the state of the proletarian dictatorship considers itself justified in doing.' [103] The analogy was indeed a close one in Trotsky's mind. He wanted all women and male age groups not included in the

ranks to be called up for the new labour armies.[104] In his opinion
the best generals in the civilian armies would be those workers 'who
have gone through the school of war and are accustomed to handling masses and leading them under the most difficult conditions'.[105]

Trotsky's proposals met with sharp criticism from the Mensheviks and from within the Bolshevik party. V. Osinsky struck at
the root of Trotsky's position and the atmosphere created by the
Civil War. He fought against 'the blind imitation of military
models'. 'Comrade Trotsky has posed the question from the point
of view of a man who came from the sphere of military culture;
we are approaching it from the point of view of the civilian sphere.'
But Osinsky grasped the fact that in many Bolsheviks' minds the
distinction between broad military influences on social life and 'the
complete and formal militarisation' of labour had been drowned.[106]
Despite these warnings, the Ninth Party Congress in March 1920,
fully approved the call for the general mobilisation of labour for
compulsory work, the organisation of production on military lines,
and the employment of army groups for civilian labour. The Third
Fighting Army was directly converted into the First Labour Army
as a pilot scheme.

Lenin's attitude towards Trotsky's plans was in some ways
equivocal, although he certainly supported compulsory labour at
the Ninth Party Congress and did not oppose the final resolution
in favour of labour armies. Lenin did not believe that the system
had been forced on the Bolshevik party by the Civil War, nor did
he think that it would be a temporary method only. Disillusioned
by the experience of workers' control, he saw the militarisation of
labour as the solution to the problem of securing greater participation by the masses in building socialism. The enthusiastic
discipline of the Red Army would provide a fillip to the apathy of
the civilian proletariat. Lenin's decision marked another step on
the road to future designs for an authoritarian social structure. Not
only was the loosely organised system of workers' control rejected,
but also the much better ordered Trade Union movement, for as
Trotsky said at the time, 'Since we find it necessary to make the
transition to compulsory labour on a large scale, we shall not be
able to utilise the Trade Unions in drafting hundreds of thousands
and millions of peasants for production. They can be mobilised
only by the use of military methods.' [107] Lenin's earlier interest in
Taylorism, with its harsh disciplinary implications, led him on to

support Trotsky's grandiose military schemes. Trotsky also took a keen interest in Taylorism, and hoped that it would be applied in civilian and military life alike.[108]

Trotsky's plans for the militarisation of labour were by no means inspired solely by the expediencies of the Civil War. They were also squarely based on long-term considerations of a more theoretical nature. Since the socialist society of the future was to be developed according to an all-Russian economic plan, the interests of the nation as a whole could not be catered for with a fluid, unpredictable labour force. The only way to restore the ruined economy was to make manpower available in the same way as soldiers were. This motive was neatly linked up to another theoretical design that Trotsky revived at the close of the Civil War — the conversion of the standing army into a militia system. In a speech given on 25 January 1920, he proposed that 'A military region is to be established wherever there is an industrial region. With the contraction of the military fronts, we shall gradually make the transition to a militia system.' He advocated extremely close organisational ties between economic and militia organs. 'The agricultural periphery should come under the undivided leadership of the industrial centres. In this way a given region, with the industrial plants at the centre, will become at one and the same time an industrial region, a militia region, and a militia division.' [109]

Trotsky argued that a method by which proletarians and peasants could go on working in the factories and villages while spending part of their time in military training would approximate more closely to the model of the socialist system. 'In the factory a citizen would feel himself to be a part of his regiment.'[110] Trotsky's theoretical propositions found support in strange quarters. In the *ABC of Communism* we find Bukharin and Preobrazhensky also arguing the need to coordinate the military as just another unit of economic production.[111] Tukhachevsky firmly opposed Trotsky's militia scheme, but he agreed that the militarisation of labour was advisable to mop up the reserve labour force that could not be used by the permanent peacetime army which he advocated.[112]

The desperate state of the economy drove odd bedfellows to the same conclusion, but nevertheless militarised labour did not survive for long. The peasant rebellion in Tambov, the Kronstadt uprising, fears at high party levels of Trotsky's military power, and the eventual proclamation of NEP with all that this entailed for the relaxation of the hold over the labour force, combined to put an end to the militarisation of the economic apparatus. Yet is it true to say that 1921 witnessed the final eclipse of the militarisation of labour as a recurring phenomenon in Russian history? Trotsky envisaged it as a long-term venture in 1920, and he believed that it would only die out 'in proportion as the socialist economic system becomes more developed, as the conditions of work become more favourable, and as the educational level of the growing generation improves'.[113] None of these three prerequisites existed in sufficient strength by the end of NEP (the next chapter lays particular stress on the third aspect).

In 1927–8, as in 1920, quasi-military methods were advocated so as to avoid complete economic ruin. The threat of external intervention was also resurrected as a reason for dragooning the civil population in the First Five-Year Plan. The juridical compulsion to work under Stalin's government was not new in itself either. In their objections to Trotsky's 1920 plans, the Mensheviks had already tried to oppose the introduction of legal obligation, although they conceded the ethical and economic pressures to make men work. Even in some of its details, the actual working of the labour system in the 1930s was similar to the one which prevailed in the Civil War : a parallel similarity has already been noted in connection with the supply problem.

The similarities that exist between the two periods with regard to the manipulation of labour should not be overdrawn. Some definite changes of emphasis took place in the latter period. The full-blown system of forced labour which developed after 1928 was supervised by the security police and the party bureaucracy. The *NKVD* became a great industrial concern in its own right, based on slave labour. During the Civil War it was the army, together with the political hierarchy, which wielded that portion of the working population which fell under its somewhat limited control. Yet this organisational difference does not represent an unbridgeable gap, because, as we have seen, the police came to substitute the military as the party's main instrument of social coercion. The *NKVD* merely added a new dimension of terror to the domestic scene.

Another difference lies in the ideological sphere. Genuine attention was paid to theoretical Marxist problems in the first postrevolutionary years, and a certain logic knits together even the most authoritarian strands in Trotsky's views on labour. These sensibilities were to disappear completely in the 1930s. Moreover, if Trotsky's theoretical plans had become an actuality, they would probably have taken on increasing syndicalist features. Trotsky tried to conceal this possibility, probably because he knew that Lenin would object to a trend of this kind. Certainly the militia-based economy was a far cry from the totally centralised system of the First Five-Year Plan. The fact that the Civil War schemes were never tried out beyond a few model prototypes like the First Labour Army, also separates them from the large-scale implementation of forced labour under Stalin. Yet, when all the evidence is assessed for and against a useful comparison between Trotsky's vision and Stalin's realisation, some measure of continuity and garnered experience is apparent. The seeds were sown and the Soviet population was conditioned in the harshness of the Civil War for the fate that lay a mere eight years ahead after the interlude of NEP.

It cannot be maintained that all the military pressures on social life during the Civil War and thereafter were conducive to authoritarian methods. Certain influences had positive long-term effects. The Red Army and the Bolshevik party were the only mass organisations acting effectively over widespread areas during the Civil War. The ranks of the military inevitably became a social melting pot for peasants, proletarians and fugitives from the higher classes of the pre-Soviet era. The latter were able to escape into the political haven of the army, since the twenty-three sections of the conscript's *lichnaia kartochka*, or personal paper, omitted any reference to class origins or political affiliations. The records of mobilisations during the Civil War and afterwards would be invaluable primary sources of social information, but unfortunately only a fraction of them are obtainable. At the fronts different classes were momentarily bound together in the common fight: the landlord was the enemy of worker and countryman alike. An unconscious process of *smychka* began as class horizons slowly broadened, some time before *smychka* (the forging of ties between town and country) became a deliberate central policy. The lasting effect of this process is hard to assess, but it can easily be exaggerated. Allegiances rarely spread outside individual military units: in some cases separate socio-economic groups joined up as a united cadre, like the famous weavers of Ivanovo-Voznesensk. Peasant risings directed against the towns as much as against the Bolsheviks at the end of the Civil War gave definite proof that the traditional rift between city and peasant in Russia would take a long time to be eliminated.

Perhaps the most important method of breaking down class barriers was to educate the Russian peasant in uniform so that he could appreciate the political significance of what he and the military-political complex were fighting for. At the first All-Russian Congress of Internationalist Teachers in June 1918, Lenin likened the civilian educational cadres to an army of socialist enlightenment: for him knowledge was a weapon in the fight for national freedom.[114] The Red Army during the Civil War was probably a more efficient eradicator of illiteracy than any other agent, including the dislocated educational system. By a Decree of April 1918 compulsory teaching was introduced for all ranks. The role of the military as an indispensable large-scale educational machine is examined further in the chapter on illiteracy.[115]

The beneficial unifying role of the army was restricted, both in time and in scope. After the end of the Civil War it reverted to a narrower professional programme, and the peace tended to loosen bonds forged in the heat of battle. Even during the military operations the scope of the Red Army was limited. Its primary aim was to beat off the Whites, and social schemes naturally took second place. At the outset of the War the military was hardly influential in terms of the proportion of the population it contained – about 50–60,000 men at the end of January 1918.[116] Later it grew in size too fast to allow of properly organised social activities, although by avoiding a militia basis it gained in efficiency as a more centrally run structure.

After 1920 the intrusion of the military in fact receded in all spheres, so that the Red Army soon lost its supreme position as twin coordinator of the regime with the party. At this point a careful distinction should be made between the postwar decline of direct military control in political and social affairs and continuing and pervasive indirect wartime influences in civilian institutions. The Red Army was cut down in size, reduced to dealing mainly with its own internal problems, but other sectors remained permanently coloured by the experience of total war during the formative stages of the Soviet system. At the close of NEP an acute observer of social and political trends in the USSR was still very much aware of 'all this brutalization of life, which is the outcome of unbelievably cruel wars, Imperialist and Civil. Fighting went on for all of six years – from 1914 to 1920. We're getting away from it slowly.' [117] He was mistaken on this last point. The cruel necessities of collectivisation and the First Five-Year Plan led to the resurgence of harsh social conditions not altogether unlike those which prevailed in the years 1917–20.

The break-up of the joint political-military government of the Civil War period and the replacement of the army by the growing bureaucracy and secret police as superior instruments of party administration and coercion in time of peace form a suitable postscript to this chapter. Within the course of a few years Trotsky's all-powerful machine sank from its position as the near equal of the party to fourth place in the hierarchy of ruling organs. The political decline of the military apparatus vis-à-vis the party and the concurrent eclipse of Trotsky by Stalin have been described in scholarly detail elsewhere. [118] They are merely given in adumbrated form here, with the emphasis laid on the continuing paramilitary influences at work in the party and on Stalin.

By the second half of 1920 the outcome of the Civil War was clear. After the final defeat of Wrangel it was no longer imperative to bolster the army in preference to all other competitors. The ruined economy now claimed the main attention of the party, since the privation which war and the severities of War Communism brought in their wake led to widespread social and political unrest. The army forsook its right to a virtual monopoly of supplies, released its grip over forced labour and severed many connections with factories which had been converted to wartime production. Lenin's decision to embark on NEP meant that heavy industrial development stagnated, and with it the influential economic ties that might have grown up between the Soviet High Command and the state planning agencies.

The subordination of the military to the party was not achieved quite as rapidly as the loss of economic power. The appointment of V. Antonov-Ovseenko as head of the Red Army Political Administration in 1922 warded off the efforts of his predecessor, S. Gusev, to impose stringent centralised party controls over all ranks. Under Antonov-Ovseenko, who was sympathetic to Trotsky's views, some measure of democratic decentralisation took place. But from

1923 onwards a long purge was initiated with the combined aim of bringing the Soviet armed forces firmly under the heel of the ruling group in the party, and of getting rid of the vestiges of Trotsky's previous powers by consolidating the position of the new Red command. Frunze was the main initiator of these moves, acting with the full approval of Stalin. The older military *spetsy* who had surrounded Trotsky in the Civil War were ousted in favour of younger men of lower-class origins, thus allowing an outlet for frustrated ambitions. Party members were brought into the military apparatus in greater numbers than previously: this was particularly noticeable in the central administration, where the percentage of Communists increased rapidly from 12 to 25 per cent.[119]

The struggle for political power in the Bolshevik Central Committee lay at the root of the changing relationship between the army and the party. The rivalry between Trotsky and Stalin over military affairs can be traced back long before the conclusion of the Civil War, but it came to a head at the same time as the economic crisis, in the second half of 1920. The complicated debate over the future structure and role of the Red Army that raged between Trotsky and Frunze in 1920–1 was to a great extent a smoke screen for wider political issues. Stalin supported the platform of the emerging Red command, and the elections to the Central Committee at the Tenth Party Congress in 1921 ushered in his military associates, including Frunze, Voroshilov and Gusev. The next major turning point in Trotsky's military decline came in January 1924 when the Central Committee set up a special commission to look into army affairs. With Frunze, Gusev and Voroshilov figuring in the commission, it was almost inevitable that Trotsky's handling of the Red Army should come in for criticism on many counts. On 11 March 1924 Frunze was named as the successor to E. Sklyansky, Trotsky's deputy. Voroshilov was appointed commander of the influential Moscow Military District. The Soviet military establishment passed once and for all out of Trotsky's hands and into the hands of the Red command in alliance with Stalin. Trotsky was removed from the Revolutionary Military Soviet in January 1925.

The staff of the Political Administration was cut by 40 per cent in 1924 and packed with reliable henchmen of Stalin and Frunze. By an instruction of 8 September 1925, supervision of the Political

Administration was detached from the Revolutionary Military Soviet and placed under the direct control of the Central Committee. At the end of October 1925 Frunze was obliged by a party edict instigated by Stalin to undergo a medical operation which killed him. Irrespective of whether Frunze was intentionally murdered or not, the removal of the leader of the Soviet army definitely set the seal on Stalin's triumph over the military. In his closing manoeuvres Frunze had given evidence of increasing reluctance to allow the party complete control over the war machine. Through Voroshilov Stalin now proceeded to tie the Red Army permanently to the party with a very different status to the one it had assumed during the Civil War.

The shift in the balance of power after 1920 did not mean that the Bolsheviks managed to shake off more intangible military influences at the same time. Lenin had modelled the party apparatus on quasi-military lines sixteen years before the outbreak of the Civil War. The test of revolution and internal struggle only served to enhance a well-rooted tradition that easily survived the termination of armed hostilities. Those party characteristics which bore most similarity to military organisation were reinforced rather than weakened after Lenin's death and the rise of Stalin. Centralised command, hierarchy, discipline and self-sufficiency were extended in the 1920s and 1930s. During NEP the Bolshevik party, like a besieged fortress, put its own quarters in fighting order although faced with increasing social and economic disarray in the country at large. The military model left its mark despite the splicing of the army-party political nexus. The survival of military traces was apparent in the personnel of the party at all levels. The Politburo cherished among its full members, until two years before Stalin's death, no less than thirteen leaders who had exercised joint military and political authority in the Civil War. An essential difference after 1924 was that those army figures who survived, like Voroshilov, became Stalin's pawns compared to the military giants of the Civil War period, but their background still lent a definite martial air to the conduct of civilian affairs. Immediately below the political summit a new type of political soldier emerged. Nearly always closely associated with Stalin, these men were often indifferent military experts of NCO stock who had a weak grasp of Marxist ideology but proved to be efficient administrators on army lines. At the lower levels, though still useful as human levers to Stalin and the Red command, nearly 4,000 officers were brought into the party by the special Leninist enrolment in 1924.[120]

Stalin's motives and character provided two other potent reasons for the survival of paramilitary ingredients in the political structure. Much of the jealousy which stirred up his hatred of Trotsky in the Civil War was derived from his envy of Trotsky's mastery over the bureaucratic military machine which at that time extended its powers over so many areas of Soviet life. Stalin's efforts to weaken this machine (it was he who saw to the introduction of political instructors (*politruks*) in the army) and his claim to be attacking party bureaucracy in his position as head of the Workers' and Peasants' Inspectorate (*Rabkrin*) must not be taken as signs of disapproval of hierarchical bureaucracy *per se*. Once Trotsky as the manipulator of the machine had been removed, Stalin had no objection to taking over the inheritance. Indeed, it appealed to his cast of mind. Some adjustments had to be made. With the arrival of peace and the weakening of Trotsky's position, the political decline of the army was inevitable. But in many ways powers that had belonged to the military in the Civil War were merely transferred under party supervision to other instruments of rule, whilst retaining a military aura. The secret police took over the responsibility for coercive measures, and the developing Stalinist bureaucracy subsumed the temporary *ad hoc* role of the Red Army between 1918 and 1920 as the large-scale overseer of many aspects of society and the economy.

The way in which the *Cheka* originated and grew under the cover of total war has been described above. In the confused state organisation of the Civil War period its coercive powers overlapped those of the military in many spheres, although even before 1920 Dzerzhinsky was trying to build up an autonomous position. During NEP the party, under Stalin's guidance, asserted complete control over the police. As a member of the Politburo, Stalin sat on the collegium of the *Cheka* before 1922.[121] He had close personal connections with Dzerzhinsky, and also with G. Yagoda, who was gradually given more power over the day-to-day administration of police affairs when Dzerzhinsky turned his attention to the organisation of Soviet transport and industry. Stalin acquired control over the secret police more quickly than he did over the military, since the *GPU* had always been more centralised than the Soviet army.

Another difference between the development of the police and the military in the 1920s was that whereas the army lost virtually all its coercive powers in time of peace, except those which it exercised as a matter of internal discipline, the police retained its wide authority derived from its origins, and even added to it with the indulgence of the party. The armed forces of the secret police actually grew in size during NEP. Other aspects of its power remained dormant, to be revived and extended in the 1930s. At the height of the first wave of compulsory Soviet labour, in 1920, the Commissariat of War together with the *Cheka* were the main agencies of control. The military lost these powers for good after 1920, but the police was to take over its former role again in the years of Stalin's industrialisation drive. It also never relinquished its extra-legal authority to deal with internal enemies of the regime through its own tribunals. Whereas the scope of the Red Army came to be strictly confined to the special military courts, the police gradually broadened its grasp over civilian affairs.

We know from the Smolensk Archives that many ex-military personnel joined the secret police after the Civil War. It is probable that this was an all-Russian phenomenon, since there appears to be no special reason why a sideways move of this nature should be concentrated in one particular region. In this way the military ethos would be preserved to some extent in the ranks of the police, which had been permeated from the start by army personnel and organisation. A watershed in the relationship between the police and the party was reached in 1923, when the former was used for the first time to crush opposition in the latter,[122] thus proving decisively its superior political status to the army and its broader powers. It is hardly surprising that men with careers to advance often preferred the *GPU* to the barracks.

The military machine became a stop-gap bureaucracy in the Civil War, handling aspects of socio-economic affairs such as civilian labour and supply which in stable peacetime conditions would normally be dealt with by the relevant ministries. In order to defend this policy, Trotsky pointed to the nature of the beleaguered Soviet camp, which required complete militarisation since the entire energies of the system were channelled into surviving the White onslaught. There was also no time to replace or reconstruct the shattered Tsarist ministries which had largely collapsed through the recalcitrance or flight of white-collar workers. Before the Revolution it is interesting to observe how the interlocking Voluntary Organisations had already thrown up a second unofficial bureaucracy with a much better grasp of special wartime problems than the hidebound imperial civil service, which failed to adapt itself quickly enough after 1914, just as it had been unable to do so in the Crimean War. These new bodies collaborated closely with the fronts, although they remained distinct civilian agencies.[123] Lenin and Trotsky moved one stage further by establishing an extempore joint system to run both the war and the Soviet state together.

Trotsky carried his ideas too far, partly in the effort to convince others. He declared that the army should take the lead in all administrative questions, since it decided 'matters concerning the life and death of nations, states and ruling classes'.[124] That acute critic of Trotsky's methods, V. Osinsky, predicted at the Ninth Party Congress in 1920 that the head of the Red Army was 'implanting bureaucracy under the flag of militarisation'. He also foresaw the way in which the peacetime administration of the future would evolve out of the Civil War embryo : 'We do not need militarisation, because within our civilian apparatus there is an organic gravitation towards military methods of operation.'[125] Trotsky upheld a philosophy of administration that held dangers for the peacetime management of the state and the economy. He maintained a view that reminds one strangely of the nineteenth-century British amateur tradition : 'In the area of administration a good administrator of a factory or plant will also be a good military administrator. The methods of administration in general and on the whole are identical. Human logic is applied in much the same way in the military field as in others.'[126]

Students of bureaucracies have noted how the new type of total war in the twentieth century brought in its train a vast extension in the scope of central state administration. In almost every case this growth, due mainly to the need to coordinate combined civil-military exercises on a huge scale, was not reversed after the return to peacetime conditions. Total war involves slow recovery. Russia is perhaps the example *par excellence* of this phenomenon. The protracted length of the war, the fury of the civil conflict, the enormous areas and numbers of people involved, required a gigantic administrative machine. As we have seen, only the Bolshevik party and the Red Army in partnership could attempt to cope with the problems. The strain of war and revolution was such that the end of the Civil War did not bring any immediate release of tension. The implementation of NEP was an emergency measure to avoid complete social, economic and ultimately political ruin. The elimination of rival left-wing factions *after* the end of the war shows how serious the situation was considered to be. In administrative and political terms, the cessation of hostilities presented no hiatus at all.

Slowly, however, a large-scale bureaucracy more oriented towards civilian problems, though frequently using wartime procedures, replaced the Civil War machinery. The stratification which Trotsky had found to be ineluctable in the organisation of the army crept into the peacetime administration. Indeed, the military model acted as a prototype. Reverting to a more idealist attitude in 1923, Trotsky attacked the older Soviet bureaucrats who, he claimed, had still not struggled free from the red-tape methods engendered by the complexity of the Civil War.[127] Not only the structure but also many of the staff of the infant bureaucracy derived from the armed forces. The original and most important *spetsy* were those military officers and administrators who agreed to work for the Bolsheviks. Their example influenced all later types of *spetsy* : their methods and ideas had an incalculable effect on the conversion of the military machine into a civil one.

Many army *spetsy* stayed on to work in the post-1920 administration. In various spheres they became the natural leaders, so long as they could be trusted politically, of the large numbers of demobilised men who sought and obtained jobs in the swelling bureaucracy. The exact extent of this influx, which had its counterpart in the secret police, can never be estimated with any precision, but Trotsky's opinion is on record that 'the demobilization of the Red Army of 5 million played no small role in the formation of the bureaucracy. The victorious commanders assumed leading posts in the local Soviets, in economy, in education, and they persistently introduced everywhere that regime which had ensured success in the Civil War.'[128] The flood did not dry up with the end of demobilisation. Frunze's reforms of both the central and regional military bureaucracy led to the reduction at the centre alone of 947 men out of a total of 3,732.[129] Many of them must have entered the civil administration subsequently.

Less tangible traces of the military ethos in the new bureau-cracy had a more lasting effect on the manners of Soviet official-dom than is generally believed. When the Commissariats in the 1930s once again goaded the entire population into fighting harder (this time on the industrial and agricultural fronts, in the words of the military phraseology so prevalent in that later period), linger-ing military influences revived. As I. Il'f and E. Petrov slyly observed in a short story of 1934 entitled *On the Grand Scale*, 'The Admin. Officer (*of a Rubber Combine*) was wearing riding-breeches with knee-patches of yellow leather. For some reason, Admin. Officers like to clothe their civilian bodies in para-military garments, as if their work consisted not in peacefully counting electric-light bulbs and hammering copper inventory tags on to cupboards and chairs, but in endless show-riding and violent cavalry manoeuvres.'

The social origins of the Stalinist bureaucracy were manifold, and the military background forms only one thread in the woof and warp of its complexity. The military experience will be re-called once again when Soviet bureaucracy is discussed in its own right in Chapter 6.

Methods and memories culled from the Civil War percolated far beyond governmental institutions. The whole population was saturated by them. When one reads the biographies and eye-witness accounts of the period, the impress of the national upheaval on the psychology of the people, or what one percipient memoirist has called the 'inner life of revolution',[130] is far more striking than all the statistics and official data. Civil War stories and myths, and above all its songs, still live on in the mind of the Russian people. When millions of soldiers either deserted or were demobilised towards the end of the war, they carried with them vivid experi-ences unlike any others to which their previous lives had accus-tomed them. Some of them followed the often repeated course of not returning to the remote countryside from which they origin-ated. They moved to the towns, more suited to their restless mood, and thus extended the process of *smychka* (the linking of town and country) which had begun in their army careers. Most of the peasantry went back to the villages, however, since the hungry, cold towns could not support them, and each plot of agricultural land had to be guarded and rehabilitated.

The rebellions which stirred up the countryside at the end of

1920 were often instigated or inflamed by deserters and ex-servicemen, who carried their violent methods to the villages far from the shifting fronts of the Civil War.[131] These peasant revolts, of which the Tambov uprising was the most dramatic, were directed mainly against the Bolsheviks in the cities. In an effort to ward off unspent wartime energies, Bolshevik manuals in 1921–2 encouraged ex-Red Army peasants to stir up class war against the kulaks in the villages. Under headings such as 'The conqueror of Kolchak and Wrangel is the light of the world in the darkness of the village', ex-soldiers were urged to link up with the authentic local Bolsheviks in one united 'shock regiment' to agitate against the rich peasants. They were reminded that it was due to the direction of the military commanders that the Red Army had triumphed, and that 'the same principle applies to working life in time of peace'.[132] By these means internal aggression, stopping just short of military action, was deliberately transferred to the countryside in peacetime.

Demobilised soldiers were also of great potential use to the central civil authorities as agents of bureaucracy at the grass-roots level. As the manual quoted above put it, the local Soviets were distant from the towns and frequently misunderstood the new regulations handed down to them. Red Army men should be responsible for carrying information about the course of the Revolution to the far corners of Russia.[133] In many areas local Bolshevik cells were very thin on the ground, and since many servicemen had recently joined the party, they were encouraged to lead campaigns like the eradication of illiteracy. As late as three years after the end of the Civil War, the political organs of the Red Army were still being advised to correspond with military veterans in order to get them to collaborate in party affairs.[134] Discharged soldiers were exhorted to help with the revival of the rural Soviets in a resolution of the Twelfth Party Congress in 1923 and in the election campaigns of 1924.[135] Despite party pressure from the centre, this policy met with little success according to M. Kalinin. He declared at a conference of secretaries of rural party cells held in October 1924 that it was much easier to defeat the Whites in the Civil War than to get rid of peasant inertia. Some Red Army men became submerged in their peasant background before they could transform it.[136] Nevertheless a strikingly large proportion of all the chairmen of rural Soviets and of the chairmen of the *volost*

Executive Committees were ex-Servicemen even by 1925–6 : the rates were 63 per cent and 70 per cent, respectively.[137]

Military contacts with the population as a whole were kept fresh from 1923 onwards by the establishment of territorial divisions, which were a much modified form of the militia system. This arrangement served the Soviet state for many years until it was overtaken by a mass army. Recruits entered a division for four years, spending not more than five months of service in mobilisation, and not over two months in any one year.[138] They were subjected to political indoctrination from party and trade union officials during their training, and the Political Administration of the Red Army issued special directives in 1923 for its political organs in the territorial divisions. By these means the military spirit was kept alive over a much wider range of the nation than it was possible to encompass by the regular army, which was now reduced in size. During the lean years in the first half of the 1920s, many over-worked and under-paid proletarians looked back with nostalgia on their military careers, and newly employed men as well as their elders often preferred camp life to factory conditions which were far from stable in this period.[139]

We have seen how wartime influences emanated from the political-military regime of the Civil War and infused leading political institutions and society as a whole. They were disembodied in the sense that they came to be manipulated, not by the army itself, but by other organs which had collaborated with it in the years 1917–20. Bonapartism and even militarism [140] as such were thus avoided, but the after-effects of war were all-pervasive. The Bolshevik Jacks-of-all-trades who had acted as soldiers in in the Civil War were apt to retain their habits in the peace which followed : and as Edward Gibbon has eloquently written, 'The temper of soldiers, habituated at once to violence and to slavery, renders them very unfit guardians of a legal or even a civil constitution. Justice, humanity, or political wisdom, are qualities they are too little acquainted with in themselves to appreciate them in others.' [141] Striking evidence of this temper was given just after the Civil War, when the basis of the Bolsheviks' rule was challenged, once any hope of restoring the previous order had faded. Widespread fear that the Whites might prevail had preserved unity until the close of 1920. The party leadership now wielded the combined political and military machine for the last time, before it was superseded by the party and the secret police, in order to smash the Kronstadt, Tambov and many smaller peasant rebellions by armed force. The violent methods Trotsky had applied to the external foe he now turned against internal enemies on the island fortress of Kronstadt with equal ruthlessness. Only the political factions which rose up in debate against the Bolsheviks were spared the sword, though many of their members were later persecuted by the secret police which took over so many of the violent methods of the revolutionary period.

In this century militarism has been at the root of many successful attempts to overthrow governments by force. Such changes have sometimes cleared the way for modernisation, but they have rarely prompted social egalitarianism. Often military coups were instigated precisely in order to prevent the latter. If revolution is viewed as social change, then the military is not frequently a revolutionary, but a counter-revolutionary force.[142] At this point we must re-examine another aspect of the central paradox of this chapter, that although wartime influences loomed large before and after 1920 in the Soviet Union, they did not prevent the supremacy of a political party which survived and went on to implement the most sweeping social revolution the world has ever seen.

Apart from the loose analogies drawn by Lenin between the structure of an army and his party in *What is To Be Done?*, no organisational connections whatsoever existed between the Bolsheviks and the military in any form until after October 1917. Indeed, as has been noted, ideological revulsion was expressed against the very notion of a standing army. The uprising of February 1917 was a mass revolution and therefore quite alien in nature to a military-inspired coup. Prior to October the Bolseviks were unable to wrest an overwhelming majority of the army ranks from a position of politial neutrality. The success of the October coup did rely on a minimum of armed force, but most of it was supplied by the Red Guard unaided by military units. Only after their precarious victory in the cities of European Russia did the Bolsheviks' intimate reliance on a large army begin to have great influence on the direction of government. It was precisely in these years (1918–20) that premature social change was discussed and implemented in the teeth of the Civil War. The priority given to social progress and the determination with which it was pursued clearly showed how the mainsprings of the Bolshevik Revolution flowed from theories of human betterment that could not be stopped up even by war in the most adverse conditions.

In Russia there was no Thermidor which could effect a decisive alteration in the leadership or the course of the Revolution. For this reason the events of the formative period 1917–21 cast Soviet institutions and practices in an inalienable mould. Most of the major and unique features of Soviet life were generated within a very short period of time. The system of Soviets, the secret police, the network of political commissars in the army and many other aspects of government were hurriedly established, but they came to stay. It was the same with the mentality which controlled these institutions. For instance, the conspiratorial attitudes inherited from their underground past survived in everything the Bolsheviks managed after 1917. Thus they came to prefer the secret police to the military and the open law courts as their chosen instrument of social coercion. Lenin's voluntarist decision in October 1917 to stage a coup without a mandate from the Russian nation as a whole led inevitably to military involvement with that section of the population which did not agree. The prolonged and bitter wartime experience had a telling effect on the impressionable minds of men for whom every day brought fresh insights into the problems of practical government. They had never ruled a village, let alone a continent, before coming to power.

Lenin's political voluntarism implied social voluntarism, and its fruits were the utopian experiments of the immediate post-revolutionary years. But of the two forces at work that have been described in this and the preceding chapter, the impact of war became the stronger. Radical departures in the social sphere were mainly confined to the towns and to intellectuals : the Civil War tended to prevent their extension through the country, and military needs sucked up all material and human resources that might have been used for social progress. Lenin had to pursue military victory to the exclusion of all else. Whereas few benefited from social reform in this period, all were scarred by the war. The introduction of NEP entailed the further delay of many aspects of the socio-economic revolution. The failure of social progress in the Civil War meant that during NEP there were few bridges on which to build up a gradual transition from a backward economy to one of the most advanced in the world. In fact several retrogressive social features developed in this period of relative stagnation. As a result the social revolution which occurred after NEP was cataclysmic in its violence, while Russia went through in the course of a few years what had taken many generations to accomplish in Western Europe. The years of NEP added few new ingredients to the social basis of Stalinism. Rather they showed up in ever clearer outline, through the process of passing time and growing Bolshevik impatience, the political implications of continuing social backwardness. The next two chapters are devoted to social aspects of this period which acted like millstones round the neck of political democracy. The Bolsheviks might be capable of staging a lightning *coup d'état* and improvising a huge army in a matter of months, but social forms could not be revised in the same way nor at the same rate.

Collectivisation and industrialisation on a huge scale at the end of the 1920s required the total mobilisation of the masses. Their violent side-effects were nearly as ruthless and even more widespread than the experience of Civil War, which in many ways had prepared men and institutions for this new crisis. Stalin, the engineer of the second revolution, had been personally inured to violence long before 1917 but had learnt new lessons through the Civil War and later marshalled the party apparatus as strictly as any army. Latent wartime influences in the bureaucracy and the secret police were brought to the surface after 1928 and exploited in the service of Stalin's aims. Even the psychological fears of the Civil War period were revived by Stalin's renewed emphasis on the threat of imminent external intervention. Under these compulsive stresses the Soviet population was coerced into making fundamental socio-economic changes. Of the national societies of Europe, it is perhaps significant that Germany and Russia, the two countries which had experienced the greatest degree of both civil and military involvement in the First World War, succumbed most easily in the 1930s to recurring pressures of a quasi-military kind. A major difference between Hitler's and Stalin's experience, however, was that whereas in the Soviet Union the direct intervention of the military in political life was most unlikely after 1920, Hitler never entirely separated his coercive powers from those of the German army. He always envied Stalin's control over the military.[143]

The adult Soviet population was conditioned by earlier memories of violent social disruption and foreign intervention.

Instead of being drafted into the Red Army to fight for their lives, or else suffering the privations of total war in their homes, they were cajoled or forced during the 1930s into draconic projects for economic construction. The analogy drawn in a resolution of the Third Trade Union Congress of 1920 still lived on in the period of the Five-Year Plans : 'Just as a conscientious Red Army soldier is ready to sacrifice his life at any moment for the workers' cause, so every honest worker, man and woman, must be ready to strain himself to the utmost in the cause of the economic salvation of the socialist republic.' [144] A second generation was paying a high price, often with its lives once again, in the hope of future gain. The social millennium envisaged in the Civil War had to be deferred a second time. Lenin once said to Gorky while stroking the heads of some children, 'Their life will be better than ours; much of what we have lived through they will be spared. Their life will be less cruel.' [145] Lenin did not survive to witness or comment on the hard road taken by Russia's masses after 1928.

1 See G. H. N. Seton-Watson, 'Russia. Army and Autocracy', in M. Howard (editor), *Soldiers and Governments* (London, 1957) p. 101 ff. Of course military influences in the Tsarist period fluctuated greatly according to the period concerned, and countervailing pressures were also at work. Peter the Great's state system was clearly monolithic and orientated towards military victory, but the nineteenth century poses more of a problem. The reign of Nicholas I was a period of militarisation in so far as the discipline and harshness associated with military life were applied to society as a whole, yet the professional soldier's life was quite divorced from civil affairs. Under Alexander III it is true that the civilian bureaucracy was subservient to governors-general who were also usually military district commanders; yet during the same period some sectors of civilian society and the bureaucracy managed to achieve a certain amount of pluralism. This is not the place to enter into the subtler details of the Tsarist period. Suffice it to note that during the Soviet Civil War and afterwards none of the countervailing effects listed here survived.

2 See his *Letters From Afar*. Lenin's idea was well within the mainstream revolutionary tradition of nineteenth century Europe. In 1789, 1848 and 1871 the formation of the National Guard in the revolutionary capital was common form.

3 See *Illustrierte Geschichte des Bürgerkrieges in Russland 1917–1921* (Berlin, 1929) p. 239.

4 See K. Marx and F. Engels, *Ausgewählte Schriften* (Berlin, 1959) pp. 453–4.

5 See Chapter 2, p. 34. Lenin and Trotsky are reputed to have had talks with the Chief of the Naval Staff on the reorganisation of the armed forces very soon after the October coup. See D. F. White, *The Growth of the Red Army* (Princeton, 1944) p. 28.

6 Quoted in M. D. Bonch-Bruevich, *Vsia vlast' sovetam* (Moscow, 1958) p. 129.

7 V. Startsev, *Ocherki po istorii petrogradskoi krasnoi gvardii i rabochei militsii* (Moscow–Leningrad, 1965) pp. 286–7.

8 Lenin, *Sochineniia*, 4th edn., vol. 23, pp. 216–17.

9 After the February Revolution, General M. Alekseev tried to call a meeting of the commanders-in-chief of the various fronts, which might have led to the formation of a military *junta*, but he was opposed by General N. Ruzsky. The General Staff at Mogilev represented the greatest focus of possible resistance to the Bolsheviks in October, but it crumbled fast. See J. Erickson, *The Soviet High Command: A Military-Political History 1918–1941* (London, 1962) pp. 14–15.

10 Kh. Muratov, *Revoliutsionnoe dvizhenie v russkoi armii v 1917 g.* (Moscow, 1958), p. 313.

11 I. Smilga, *Ocherednye voprosy stroitel'stva krasnoi armii* (Moscow, 1920) p. 16.

12 Ibid., p. 10.

13 M. Tukhachevsky, *Krasnaia armiia i militsiia* (Moscow, 1921) p. 13.

14 Ibid., p. 6. For a more theoretical analysis of the need for a suitable substructure as a precondition for abolishing standing armies, see N. Bukharin, *ABC of Communism* (Ann Arbor, 1966) pp. 205–9.

15 Erickson, op. cit., p. 405.

16 Lenin, 'Otchet Tsentral'nogo Komiteta', *Sochineniia*, vol. 24, p. 122.

17 N. Bukharin, *Okonomik der Transformationsperiode* (Hamburg, 1922) pp. 182–3.

18 K. Chorley, *Armies and the Art of Revolution* (London, 1943) p. 20.

19 H. Arendt, *On Revolution* (London, 1963) p. 9.

20 See *Vserossiiskii zemskii soiuz. Sobranie upolnomochennykh gubernskikh zemstv v Moskve 7–9 sentiabria 1915 goda; doklad glavnogo komiteta* (Moscow, 1916).

21 See *Obshchestvennaia rabota v glubokom tylu* (Moscow, 1915) for details of early collaboration between the front and the rear.

22 G. Katkov, *Russia 1917: The February Revolution* (London, 1967) p. 35.

23 For a discussion of political propaganda among the military in 1917, see Pethybridge, *The Spread of the Russian Revolution – Essays on 1917*, pp. 154–64.

24 L. Gavrilov and V. Kutuzov, 'Perepis' russkoi armii 25 oktiabria 1917 goda', in *Istoriia SSSR*, no. 2 (1964) pp. 87–91.

25 See E. Gorodetsky, *Rozhdenie sovetskogo gosudarstva 1917– 1918 gg.* (Moscow, 1965) p. 399, for figures.

26 This is an optimistic figure, based on Soviet scholarship. See N. Shatagin, *Organizatsiia i stroitel'stvo Sovetskoi Armii v period inostrannoi interventsii i grazhdanskoi voiny (1918–1920 gg.)* (Moscow, 1954) p. 63.

27 V. Klyatskin, in *Istoricheskie zapiski*, no. 8 (Moscow, 1956) p. 32.

28 Ibid., p. 36.

29 See N. Efimov in *Grazhdanskaia voina 1918–1921*, vol. 2 (Moscow, 1928) p. 95.

30 *Krasnyi komandir*, no. 3 (1919) p. 6.

31 See I. Berkhin, *Voennaia reforma v SSSR (1924–1925 gg.)* (Moscow, 1958) p. 83, for the origins of the militia.

32 L. Kritsman, *Geroicheskii period velikoi russkoi revoliutsii*, second edition (Moscow, 1926) p. 187. S. Strumilin worked out that the number of military personnel killed in the World War was two to three times higher than during the Civil War, but losses amongst the civilian population were two to three times lower in the first period when compared with the second. See S. Strumilin, 'Trudovye poteri Rossii v voine in *Narodnoe khoziaistvo* (December, 1920), p. 105.

33 See A. Fraiman, *Revoliutsionnaia zashchita Petrograda, fevral'– mart 1918* (Moscow, 1964) pp. 119–78.

34 Trotsky, *Kak vooruzhalas' revoliutsiia*, vol. 2 (Moscow, 1923) pp. 383–4.

35 E. Zamiatin, 'Zavtra', in *Sobranie sochinenii* (Moscow, 1929).

36 Trotsky, op. cit., vol. 2, p. 127.

37 See B. Wolfe, 'The Influence of Early Military Decisions Upon the National Structure of the Soviet Union', in the *American Slavic and East European Review* (1950) pp. 175–6.

38 Trotsky, op. cit., vol. 3, p. 41.

39 Quoted in M. Gorky, *Lenin* (Moscow, 1931).

40 Ibid.

41 See for instance Bukharin's analysis, in *Historical Materialism*

pp. 98–9, of the role of the individual in *civil* society, which draws on the part played by general staff members in the army for illustrative inspiration.

42 For an imprecise analogy given by Lenin in 1920, see his *Collected Works*, 4th edn., vol. 31, p. 96 : 'One will readily agree that any army which does not train to use all the weapons, all the means and methods of warfare that the enemy possesses, or may possess, is behaving in an unwise or even criminal manner. This applies to politics even more than it does to the art of war.' For a typical example of Trotsky's many analogies, see *The New Course* (New York, 1943) pp. 103–4.

43 *ABC of Communism*, p. 262.

44 *Weg zum Sozialismus* (Vienna, 1925) p. 92.

45 Terrorism on behalf of the *status quo* or of revolutionary groups has been divided into the two categories of 'enforcement terror' and 'agitational terror' respectively. See T. Thornton, 'Terror as a Weapon of Political Agitation', in H. Eckstein (editor), *Internal War* (New York, 1964) p. 73.

46 See for instance G. Ionescu, *The Politics of the European Communist States* (London, 1967) pp. 74–6, and L. Schapiro, 'Totalitarianism Reconsidered', in *Survey* (Autumn 1969) p. 101. Ample detailed corroboration of these two writers' views may be found if one studies the Smolensk party archives over the Civil War period. In particular, see the minutes of the Smolensk *oblast'* party committee for 1920, in file WKP 6.

47 Lenin, *What is to be Done?* 3rd edn. (Moscow, 1964) p. 121.

48 W. Pietsch, *Revolution und Staat: Institutionen als Träger der Macht in Sowjetrussland 1917–1922* (Cologne, 1969) p. 40 *et al.*

49 Quoted in R. C. Williams, *Culture in Exile. Russian Emigrés in Germany, 1881–1941* (London, 1972) p. 232.

50 Trotsky, *Organizatsiia krasnoi armii* (Moscow, 1918) pp. 3–4.

51 L. Fischer, *The Life of Lenin* (London, 1968) p. 330.

52 Quoted in Shatagin, op. cit., p. 148.

53 Finer and Janowitz, to be fair to them, deal with *coups d'état* rather than with mass revolutionary situations. They also ascribe a greater degree of exclusiveness to the military than to the political ethic.

54 See G. Schueller, 'The Politburo', in H. Lasswell and D. Lerner (editors), *World Revolutionary Elites: Studies in Coercive Ideological Movements* (Cambridge, Mass., 1965) pp. 123–4. Of the thirteen, only K. Voroshilov could possibly be described as a professional soldier.

55 Trotsky, *Kak vooruzhalas' revoliutsiia*, vol. 1, p. 193.

56 Bukharin, *Vom Sturze des Zarismus bis zum Sturze der Bourgeoisie* (Berlin, 1919) p. 61.

57 Lenin, 'The Collapse of the Second International', in his *Collected Works*, 4th edn., vol. XXI, p. 283.

58 N. Podvoisky, in *Krasnyi ofitser*, no. 2, 1 November 1918, p. 1.

59 M. Weygand, 'The Red Army in the Polish War, 1920', in B. Liddell Hart (editor), *The Soviet Army* (London, 1956) p. 48. This estimate is taken from Polish intelligence reports and statements by Russian prisoners-of-war : it may therefore give rather a low percentage.

60 Lenin based his view on the experience of the Paris Commune : see an article on this by Lenin in *Sotsial-Demokrat*, 1 November 1914.

61 *Izvestiia* (22 January 1918) p. 1.

62 Cf. supra, p. 75.

63 M. Latsis, *Chrezvychainye Kommissii po bor'be s kontrrevoliutsiei* (Moscow, 1921) p. 13.

64 See Ya. Peters, 'Vospominaniia o rabote v VChK v pervyi god revoliutsii', in *Proletarskaia revoliutsiia*, no. 10 (1924).

65 See A. Joffe, in *Kommunisticheskii internatsional*, no. 6 (Petrograd, October 1919).

66 This repressive function is documented in an article by R. Pipes in *Kritika*, vol. 4, no. 3 (Cambridge, Mass., 1968) p. 23.

67 A. Tishkov, *Pervyi Chekist* (Moscow, 1968) p. 26.

68 Ibid., p. 28.

69 Ibid., p. 32, 35.

70 See Fainsod, *How Russia is Ruled*, pp. 425–33, and E. J. Scott, 'The *Cheka*', in *St. Antony's Papers*, no. 1 (London, 1956).

71 *Izvestiia*, 28 March 1919, p. 4.

72 See *Chto takoe soldat krasnoi armii* (Moscow, 1918) p. 1.

73 Latsis, op. cit., p. 8.

74 Ibid., p. 30. Through its 'special departments' the *Cheka* came to exercise great authority over large areas, and operated independently of the political commissars by 1921. See the *Report of the Committee to Collect Information on Russia* (London, 1921) p. 41, for corroboration of Latsis.

75 See *Pravda*, 13 February 1956, p. 3, for an article on the history of the border troops. Tishkov, op. cit., pp. 41–2, mentions that they were actually established on an informal basis as early as 1918. This is corroborated by an unpublished decree of 1918 (see S. Wolin and R. Slusser (editors), *The Soviet Secret Police* (London, 1957) p. 35, note 20, for a reference to this).

76 *Svoboda Rossii*, 9 June 1918.
77 M. Latsis, 'Tov. Dzerzhinskii i VChK', in *Proletarskaia revoliutsiia*, no. 9 (1926) p. 85.
78 Latsis, op. cit., p. 24.
79 For a fuller analysis of Carr's and Dobb's interpretation of War Communism, see P. C. Roberts, ' "War Communism" : A Reexamination', in the *Slavic Review* (June 1970) pp. 238–61.
80 B. Brutzkus, *Economic Planning in Soviet Russia* (London, 1935); L. Lawton, *An Economic History of Soviet Russia*, 2 vols. (London, 1932).
81 Brutzkus, op. cit., p. 102.
82 Ibid., p. 108.
83 *Pravda*, 28 April 1918.
84 See Pethybridge, op. cit.
85 These figures, which cannot be estimated with greater precision, are taken from N. Golovine, *The Russian Army in the World War* (New Haven, 1931) ch. 9.
86 *Perepiska Sekretariata TsK RSDRP(b) s mestnymi organizatsiiami*, vol. 2 (Moscow, 1957) p. 52.
87 Lenin, *Sochineniia*, 4th edn., vol. 26, p. 458.
88 *Pravda*, 15 February 1918.
89 Lenin, *Collected Works*, vol. 27, p. 406.
90 Ibid., vol. 24, p. 514.
91 Ibid., vol. 27, p. 391.
92 See Erickson, op. cit., p. 38.
93 *Leninskii sbornik*, vol. 18, p. 75.
94 S. A. Sokolov, *Revoliutsiia i khleb* (Saratov, 1967) p. 29.
95 *Prodovol'stvennaia politika* (Moscow, 1920) p. 236.
96 See Trotsky, *Sochineniia*, vol. 15, pp. 412–14.
97 See his *Kak vooruzhalas' revoliutsiia*, vol. 3 (Moscow, 1923) p. 69 *et al.*
98 See J. Stalin, *Economic Problems of Socialism in the USSR* (London, 1952) p. 70.
99 Trotsky, *Sochineniia*, vol. 14, pp. 112–14.
100 Trotsky, *Kak vooruzhalas' revoliutsiia*, vol. 3, p. 73.
101 Lenin, *Sochineniia*, vol. 21, p. 262.
102 *Izvestiia*, 26 March 1919.
103 Trotsky, *Sochineniia*, vol. 12, p. 129.
104 Trotsky, *Kak vooruzhalas' revoliutsiia*, vol. 3, p. 45.
105 Trotsky, *Sochineniia*, vol. 15, p. 113.
106 *Deviatyi s"ezd' Rossiiskoi kommunisticheskoi partii, stenograficheskii otchet* (Moscow, 1920) p. 99–100.
107 Trotsky, *Sochineniia*, vol. 15, p. 76.

108 Trotsky, *Kak vooruzhalas' revoliutsiia*, vol. 2, p. 127.

109 *Sochineniia*, vol. 15, pp. 69–70.

110 *Kak vooruzhalas' revoliutsiia*, vol. 2, p. 128. For more details of Trotsky's idea, see vol. 1, pp. 188–90.

111 *ABC of Communism*, pp. 213–14.

112 Tukhachevsky, op. cit., p. 19.

113 *Sochineniia*, vol. 15, pp. 112–13.

114 *Sochineniia*, vol. 36, p. 420. One of the most widespread propaganda posters in the Civil War proclaimed 'The press is our weapon'.

115 See pp. 160–2 infra. M. N. Pokrovsky, a member of the collegium of the Commissariat for Education, went so far as to suggest in 1920 that the universities should be taken over by persons entrusted with military powers, but this was not carried out. See *Narodnoe prosveshchenie*, no. 18–20 (1920) p. 7.

116 Shatagin, op. cit., pp. 151–2.

117 A. M. Bol'shakov, *Derevnia* (Moscow, 1927) p. 280.

118 See Erickson, op. cit. See also R. Kolkowicz, *The Soviet Military and the Communist Party* (Princeton, 1967).

119 Erickson, op. cit., p. 175.

120 Berkhin, op. cit., p. 285.

121 See B. Souvarine, *Stalin, A Critical Survey of Bolshevism* (New York, 1939) p. 289.

122 See Carr, *The Bolshevik Revolution, The Interregnum, 1923–1924* (London, 1954) pp. 286–9.

123 Even at the time, the Voluntary Organisations were fully aware of their unique role. See *Zemgor. Poltora goda raboty glavnogo po snabzheniiu armii komiteta vserossiiskikh zemnogo i gorodskogo soiuzov, iun' 1915 g.–fevral' 1917* (Moscow, 1917) p. 73 ff.

124 Trotsky, *Kak vooruzhalas' revoliutsiia*, vol 3, p. 77.

125 *Deviatyi s"ezd Rossiiskoi kommunisticheskoi partii*, pp. 101–2.

126 Trotsky, *Kak vooruzhalas' revoliutsiia*, vol. 3, pt. 2, p. 241.

127 See *Pravda*, 29 December 1923.

128 Trotsky, *The Revolution Betrayed* (New York, 1937), pp. 89–90.

129 Berkhin, op. cit., p. 154.

130 A. Berkman, *The Bolshevik Myth (Diary 1920–1922)* (New York, 1925) p. vii.

131 For details of the role of ex-servicemen in this way, see S. Singleton, 'The Tambov Revolt (1920–1921)', in the *Slavic Review* (September 1966) pp. 497–512.

132 A. Divil'kovskii, *Pomogai stroit' sovetskuiu vlast'–naputstvie otpusknomu krasnoarmeitsu* (Moscow, 1921) pp. 8–13.

133 Ibid., p. 2.

134 Ia. Iakovlev, *Derevnia kak ona est'* (Moscow, 1923) p. 74.

135 *KPSS v resoliutsiiakh* (Moscow, 1953) p. 751.

136 *Izvestiia*, 25 October 1924.

137 *Perevybory v Sovety RSFSR v 1925–26 g.* (Moscow, 1926) p. 35.

138 Berkhin, op. cit., p. 86.

139 See M. Moskvine, *Ma jeunesse en URSS* (Paris, 1934) pp. 52–3, for evidence of this preference.

140 Militarism is understood as the glorification of the armed forces *per se*, either by themselves or by others, and the depiction of military values as being the *embodiment* of society.

141 E. Gibbon, *The Decline and Fall of the Roman Empire* (London, 1963) p. 78.

142 There are exceptions. For some examples in this century, see W. Gutteridge, *The Military in African Politics* (London, 1969) and P. Vatikiotis (editor), *Egypt Since the Revolution* (London, 1968).

144 *Rezoliutsii III Vserossiiskogo s"ezda professional'nykh soiuzov* (Moscow, 1921), p. 55.

145 From Gorky's obituary article on Lenin in 1924. Hope springs eternal in the revolutionary mind. Lenin's words are reminiscent of the aspirations of the leaders of the Paris Commune, which became a political model for Marx and Lenin to follow. When Delescluze was appointed 'civilian war minister' on 11 May 1871, he declared, 'The horrible war . . . has already cost much generous blood . . . Nevertheless, while deploring these painful losses, when I think of the sublime future which is in store for our children, even though we may be unable to reap what we have sown, I still greet the Revolution with enthusiasm . . .'

4 Illiteracy

Maxim Gorky believed that 'the fundamental obstacle on the path of Russia to Europeanisation and culture is the fact of the overwhelming predominance of the illiterate village over the city'.[1] It is often stated that literacy is the most powerful single discriminator between what are loosely termed traditional and modern societies.[2] The political significance of widespread illiteracy in Russia from the Revolution until as late as the 1930s carries a weight that has not yet been fully recognised. Certainly it acted as one of the heaviest brakes on Bolshevik ambitions for the early realisation of their aims.

Lip-service is often paid to the importance of illiteracy in Soviet as in Tsarist Russia, but the detailed implications have not been spelt out. This lacuna is partly the result of the belief held by many highly literate writers, particularly non-Russians, that history is concerned with what people wrote and, to a lesser extent, said. By relying too heavily on documents, they fail to provide an adequate account of what actually occurred. Instead, we are given an account of what people at the time wrote and thought about what was happening, and above all what the central authorities *wanted* to happen. This lack of balance has been repeated time and again in the case of Russia. If one were to rely for evidence solely on the mass of documents[3] expressing the orders and aspirations of the Provisional Government in 1917, it would be difficult to conceive why such an industrious regime ever fell. Any responsive echo from the semi-literate and illiterate masses is apt to be ignored, because it went unrecorded. Even at the local level, the Smolensk Archives[4] represent an impressive written pile of good intentions that rarely penetrated beyond the literate towns to the recalcitrant countryside.

Illiterates tend to be ignored because they leave no documents.

Yet their presence enters every file of the Smolensk Archives like a silent backlash, creating irritation and near despair in the authorities and necessitating the endless repetition of orders from above. Source materials for the study of illiterates are of course virtually all secondhand in nature. This creates difficulties for the scholar, but even when the written archives of the early Soviet period are made available, all their wealth may add little to the solution of a problem which is better dealt with by a process of careful and imaginative deduction from what already exists. From the turn of the century until the close of NEP, we are confronted by a dearth of stored oral information. Recording techniques for the radio, gramophone and telephone were in their infancy in Russia at this time, although some verbatim minutes of political meetings in which illiterates were involved have been preserved for posterity. For lack of direct evidence from illiterates, one is thrown back on the testimony of their literate betters. In the first place there are the bald statistics on the extent of illiteracy collected locally and less frequently at national level. This was a formidable task which was only done with any measure of thoroughness in the censuses of 1897, 1920 and 1926. The fact that many illiterates and some semi-literates were also innumerate hindered the statisticians. Figures concerning the illiteracy rate are supplemented by official and unofficial comment on its incidence, evil and possible cure. There exists a great deal of evidence on the methods adopted for the eradication of illiteracy. This material is as varied as it is bulky. Besides the written word there are the films, pictures, cartoons and banners that were used as instruments in the campaign.

Two of the closest links to a lost world are conversations by and with illiterates that have been recorded, and evidence drawn from contemporary works of fiction. Living speech frozen in writing and interpreted or distorted by literates is perhaps a poor substitute for the real thing, but the style and turn of thought are often revealing. The lack of conceptual analysis, the love of rote and of laconic summary as expressed in *pogovorki* (proverbs), the need to pass on hearsay as a substitute for the written word, are all captured. Professor A. Gerschenkron has discussed the value and dangers of using fiction as a source of information.[5] Given the peculiar difficulties of assessing Soviet materials, especially with regard to the subject under review, it is doubtful whether some hypotheses can ever be finally proven, but the cumulative effect of recurring fragments of information given in fiction tend to strengthen generalisations that are also based on other kinds of evidence. As a famous student of the Russian peasants, who were nearly all illiterates, put it : 'Statistics may (and do) lie. They may be (and are) suppressed. But the picture of manners by the hand of a master outlives brass.'[6] The Russian literary intelligentsia, from its rise in the nineteenth century until its decline under Stalin, was notoriously sensitive about the dark masses. Illiterates figure in fiction with a peculiar intensity, often distorted by idealism in the case of Tolstoy or exaggerated pessimism in the case of Bunin, but nevertheless casting genuine light on their role in society.

Before we can assess the incidence, historical decline and social and political repercussions of illiteracy, the term must be defined. This is less easy than might at first appear. No clear-cut divide between literate and illiterate sections of society can be found. Many gradations of illiteracy and semi-literacy may coexist in the same society. The ability to write one's name for the purposes of a Russian census does not even mean one can write any other words, nor is the ability to write a necessary corollary of the ability to read. Copy-writing, usually the lowest form of achievement, differs greatly from creative composition. It may be possible for someone to read both a Bolshevik slogan on a banner and the works of Marx, but can he understand both? At what level does conceptual analysis come within the reader's grasp? The meaning of illiteracy also changes according to the nature of the society in which a person lives. What a society means by illiteracy depends partly upon the extent and importance of literacy in that society. The columns of the learned reviews in Britain today are full of accusations of 'illiteracy' made against professional writers of fiction. For the purposes of the 1897 census in Russia a literate person was someone who could sign his name and *claimed* to be able to read. Within a single society assessments of literacy may differ according to the levels of literary skills required for agricultural work on the one hand and entry into new industrial work on the other. Different methods of assessment succeeded one another in Russia as she went through the throes of modernisation from the 1860s on.

The nature of illiteracy changes with advances in techniques of communicating the spoken word by other means than writing it down. There is such a thing as a literacy of the spoken word. Television, which was not available to Russians in the 1920s, can be an aid towards this type of literacy. The Bolsheviks made great use of the cinema, theatre and radio in this way. Literacy of the spoken word has an obvious correlation with literacy of the written word. The correlation is not so clear between the volume of materials, whether visual or printed, that are distributed in any society and the level of spoken or written literacy, although a direct connection has sometimes been assumed. The size of readership by no means relates directly to the amount of available materials, since many variables are at work. The number of readers per copy of *Pravda* fluctuated enormously in 1917 according to the time, place, interest value and efficacy of distribution. Lenin realised that many materials might never reach their goal in any case. When the Decree on Land was distributed to soldiers after the October coup, so that they would act as unpaid carriers of propaganda on their way back to the villages, Lenin is supposed to have ordered that they each be given an old calendar as well. This was so as to deter them from using the Decree copies as cigarette papers – the calendars would do just as well.[7] It is just as hazardous to use formal education as a precise yardstick for assessing the extent and depth of literacy as it is to use publications. Informal instruction through the family or some other nexus may be just as important, but harder to trace. In the district of Bogorodsk, a province of Moscow in 1883–4, the percentage distribution of 7123 factory workers who had become literate was as follows : 38 per cent learned to read in village, town and district schools, 36 per cent learned to read outside school, 10 per cent in factory schools, 9 per cent with clergy, and 7 per cent in the course of military service.[8]

Finally, the gap between any degree of illiteracy and the literate sectors of society should not be left too wide in any definition. This is especially true where the Great Russians are concerned. Unlike many other developing countries in this century with a colonial past, literacy in the young Soviet Union was not confined to an élite educated in a foreign tongue. Behind the 1920s lay a tradition stretching back for centuries which allowed for a substantial link between illiterate and literate groups. Not only was spoken literacy by illiterates often of a very high order in Russia, as Gorky often told his readers with regard to his beloved grandmother; it was strengthened by other widespread social customs such as reading aloud to friends and neighbours, and the amazing efficiency of the bush telegraph in the rural areas. When interest in some subject was particularly strong, these ties were naturally strengthened through curiosity, and there was a glut of absorbing themes in the revolutionary period which were peculiarly attractive to the illiterate portion of the nation.

It would be a mistake to assume that in Russia, or indeed in any other country, illiterates are apolitical, a *tabula rasa* on which the prevailing regime can write what it wishes.[9] On the other hand, Lenin's vision of any peasant being capable of working at a high level in the party or government administration, as expressed in his *State and Revolution*, was too optimistic. The reality lay somewhere in between. Newly acquired literacy opened up minds that had not all been completely shackled before. The type and depth of literacy and education that Russians received in the first three decades of this century did not necessarily equip them for free enquiry : James Mill has described education of this kind as the implanting in the mind, through custom or through pain or pleasure, of an invariable sequence and association of ideas. Mill had higher hopes than this, but realised that only so much time could be devoted to acquiring intelligence as could be abstracted from labour. Working life in Victorian Britain as in the transitional stage from Tsarist to Soviet society, began at a very early age, and most schools could teach little more than the elements.

Keeping in mind the breadth and intricacies of any definition of illiteracy, let us now examine the social and political history of its extent and decline in modern Russia. Detailed studies of illiteracy for its own sake have already been undertaken by Soviet and Western scholars. For this reason no systematic analysis of the original census materials relating to illiteracy for 1897, 1926 and 1939 is given in this chapter. Analyses dealing with different age groups, regions, classes, nationalities, and with literacy growth rates correlated with population size may be found in the work of these authors.[10] We are more concerned here with the political repercussions of illiteracy. For practical purposes the term 'illiterate' is used in this chapter in the humblest sense of meaning someone unable to read a text but perhaps able to sign his name. In the period before the first general census of 1897, there exists slim and incomplete evidence concerning the incidence of illiteracy. In rural Russia at the turn of the half-century, one of every six boys and one in fourteen girls, at the most optimistic estimate, were acquiring literacy to a level that enabled them to retain it as adults. This estimate is based on data concerning literacy rates among men and women over sixty years of age by the time of the 1897 census.[11] A survey of the Saratov *guberniia* in 1844 revealed that the percentage of town dwellers who could read and write was 30 per cent, but only 2.1 per cent of the peasants were literate in this sense. In 1869 the rate for the Moscow *guberniia* as a whole was 7.5 per cent. Rural literacy rose quite rapidly in the second half of the century, but in scales of great diversity. The incidence of literacy both between and within geographical areas varied with the characteristics of subpopulations.

An important change of balance between government administration and other salaried white-collar workers, particularly those in education, occurred between the middle and the end of the century, which in the long run was bound to have an accelerating effect on the literacy rate. Until about 1850 the government bureaucracy was the chief source of demand for educated manpower. Approximate data given below from the 1897 census show that by the end of the century the total number of those employed as salaried white-collar workers in the non-agricultural sector of the economy exceeded the number of those with jobs in the government apparatus, and that employment in the educational system exceeded the civilian government civil service.

Number of Employed White-Collar Workers
Based Upon the 1897 Population Census (in thousands).

Branch		Employment
Government bureaucracy : armed forces	52,471 ⎫	203,816
Civilian bureaucracy	151,345 ⎭	
Education		172,842
Medicine, law and other free professions		52,825

According to the 1897 census, 21.1 per cent of the total population of the Russian Empire, excluding Finland, could read and write. Children below school age are for the most part illiterate, and their inclusion in the 1897 figures unduly inflates the rate of illiteracy. 35.8 per cent of all males over the age of eight were literate, compared to 12.4 per cent females. Town dwellers over eight were 54.3 per cent literate, rural inhabitants 19.6 per cent.

Like many investigations of literacy, these figures, apart from the proof of written signatures, were often no more than measurements of people's views of their abilities, as given to strangers, rather than direct evidence of any capacity to write or read with reasonable fluency.

On the basis of a study of twenty-two countries in the process of rapid modernisation, Daniel Lerner has pointed out the close relationship between urbanisation and literacy. He finds that only after these countries reached a critical minimum of urbanisation, between 7 and 17 per cent of the total population, did their literacy rates begin to rise significantly. Beyond the critical optimum of 25 per cent urbanisation, literacy continued to rise independently of the growth of cities.[12] Cities need a largely literate population to function properly. By drawing people from rural communities, cities create a demand for impersonal communication. In promoting literacy and communications media, cities supply this demand. By the middle of the nineteenth century Russia still had only two cities of over 100,000 inhabitants, but she had reached the take-off position of one in ten persons living in towns of some sort.[13] Even by 1926, however, more than 80 per cent of the people of Russia were living in rural areas, so that the critical optimal point as far as literacy was concerned only occurred during the 1930s, under the impact of rapid industrialisation and Stalin's political hegemony.

At the start of this century the gulf set between Russia and Britain, the most industrialised power in the world, was enormous with regard to literacy. In the General Election of 1910 only 17,151 illiterate voters were recorded for the whole of England and Wales, though it must be remembered that illiterates would figure more prominently among those unwilling or unable to vote.[14] By 1913 the literacy rate (reading and writing) had risen to a mere 28.4 per cent for Russia excluding Finland.[15] As early as about 1850 only 30–33 per cent of the adult population of England and Wales could neither read nor write. Even in the eighteenth century in England political literature like Thomas Paine's *Rights of Man* had sold 200,000 copies in cheap editions by 1793. That it reached the lowest classes is borne out by the comment that 'its success in making proselytes would have been a truly formidable circumstance, had their rank in society borne a proportion to their numbers'.[16] In fact England was scarcely more literate in 1850 than she had been a century earlier. The lack of any necessarily direct relationship between a reading public and political awareness should be stressed, however. Chapbooks, ballads, execution broadsheets were the gingerbread of the poorer classes, who fed on a less refined and puritanical political diet than their Russian heirs were to do after 1917.

The table [17] given below gives a comparative survey of estimates of adult literacy, meaning ability to read, in Europe and Russia at the half-century mark.

	Census Year	Total population (thousands)	Population of 10 years of age and more (thousands)	Estimated approx. rate of adult illiteracy (percentage)	Approx. number of adult illiterates (thousands)
Sweden	1850	3,483	2,673	10	267
Austrian Empire	1851	17,526	13,145	40–45	5,587
France	1851	35,754	29,166	40–45	12,396
Spain	1857	15,455	11,591	75	8,693
Russian Empire	1850	56,882	42,662	90–95	39,462
England and Wales	1851	17,928	13,487	30–33	4,248
Scotland	1851	2,889	2,177	20	435

As a rule the peripheries of Europe, especially in the south and east, were more backward (Spain and Russia), but Sweden and Scotland provided significant exceptions. The latter were also exceptional in that although much less developed industrially than England, they had higher rates of literacy. This was partly because their small populations entailed less effort in terms of education than England's (and Russia's) masses. Of the areas named in the table, the Russian and Austrian empires were similar since they both had to contend with high illiteracy rates among their heterogeneous national minorities.

The growth in Russia's literacy between 1897 and the Revolution is best measured from the data of the population census taken in 1920 (for European Russia only).

Literacy Rates for the Population of European Russia
(1897 and 1920)

	Males	Females	Total
1897	32.6	13.6	22.9
1920	42.2	25.5	33.0

Rates increased by almost 50 per cent for women, and by about 25 per cent for men. Such a rise must have had a considerable effect on the industrial labour force involved in the problem of trying to understand the events of the Revolution.[18] Despite this increase, not much was done on an official basis between the census of 1897 and 1917 to improve the situation of the illiterates. Serious thinking on the need to reform Russian spelling began in 1901, but it took a political revolution to achieve anything concrete. When the orthographic reform went through in 1917, a liberal newspaper claimed that 'it was no secret to anyone that reactionary Ministers of Education – and other ministers, too – would not support this reform, as they did not support anything that tended to benefit the common people'.[19]

The low level of literacy in Russia acted as an informal censor that was far more efficient than the official Tsarist censorship, which was aimed at the small reading public. Even many of the so-called literates suffered from insufficient knowledge. For instance, General A. Knox observed at the outbreak of the World War that although 50 per cent of the Russian reservists were classed as literates, many of them had had one or two years at school at the age of eight or ten, but had never seen a book or newspaper since : so that when they wanted to communicate with their families, their letters were usually written for them by non-commissioned officers and junior officers. It was widely known that letters went through a double censorship, first by the regimental officer, and then by the official censor.[20]

The extent of illiteracy was so great in Russia that it penetrated well into the ranks of the élite. In 1897 28 per cent of the combined numbers of the nobility, civil service and clergy were classified as illiterates.[21] This situation was to be far more acute for the postrevolutionary élite, since the Bolsheviks intended to reverse the social pyramid overnight. Even at the political centre there was a shortage of educated talent. S. V. Malyshev, who was the secretary of *Pravda* in 1914 before his arrest, stressed how difficult it was to 'know how to organize and manage a working class newspaper ... We had never been able to go to school. We were all semi-literate Bolsheviks – we all put off studying until we were imprisoned, as we nearly always were. There, day after day, we wrote out declensions, verbs, subordinate clauses and participles. When we were released from prison, we sat down at a secretary's or editor's desk on party orders.' [22]

Bolshevik attention to the political needs of the illiterate masses in 1917 was brilliantly organised on an impromptu basis and presaged later successes during the Civil War and NEP. Before his tumultuous reception at the Finland station in April, Lenin had probably never addressed in person an audience of more than a few hundred. From then on Russia's millions were accessible to Bolshevik propaganda. For those who could read, or be read to, seventy Bolshevik newspapers and journals were appearing by the time of the October coup.[23] This was a remarkable feat, yet even *Pravda* cannot have reached a wide geographical area. Of the supposed total circulation of 200,000 in March and April 1917, between 85,000 and 100,000 copies did not get beyond the confines of Petrograd.[24] In May the Bolshevik committee in the capital clamoured for a separate press organ besides *Pravda* that would represent local city interests. Lenin's sharp reply heralded the monolithic centralised attitude that was to characterise the majority of subsequent Bolshevik exercises in communication and illiteracy eradication schemes. He said 'I believe that the decision of the Petrograd Committee's Executive to establish a special newspaper in Petrograd is utterly wrong and undesirable, because it splits up our forces and introduces into our Party the elements of conflict.' [25] That was the first thought to come into his head. Apparently it did not occur to him that a new party press organ might bolster the Bolshevik cause in the capital.

In so many ways the hastily contrived methods of 1917 became enshrined in subsequent Bolshevik governmental organisation. The methods used to appeal to illiterates in the revolutionary year proved no exception to this rule. Great stress was laid on the powers of oratory, and it is no coincidence that the most eminent figures of the Revolution were also its greatest orators – Lenin, Trotsky, and Kerensky. Visually attractive banners and slogans catch the eye of anyone looking at documentary films on 1917, just as they were intended to do for illiterate and semi-literate Russian audiences at the time. The small central Bolshevik apparatus relied heavily on unpaid voluntary agents to spread political information by word of mouth beyond the industrial cities of European Russia, just as it was to continue to do so when in power. Soldiers and sailors returning to the village, members of *zemliachestva*[26] doing likewise, postmen, telephonists, elements among the million-strong railway workers, all served as grist to the Bolshevik mill.[27]

The success of Lenin's party in October 1917 made no difference to the mental gulf that still separated a literate élite from the illiterate masses. Before turning to survey the Bolshevik drive to stamp out illiteracy over the decade following the Revolution, the herculean nature of their achievement should be examined in the light of the leading Bolsheviks' intellectual position, mainly on the literate shore of the gulf. This position had a profound effect on their campaign.

Although it is true that bridges of communication did exist between the two shores (some of them have been mentioned above), the total range between the Russian intelligentsia on the one hand and the illiterate peasant on the other was extremely wide for reasons set deep in history which could not be expunged in a matter of a few years. The peculiar development of nineteenth century Russia tended to perpetuate rather than to diminish cultural differences that were narrowing in other countries. The results of political and industrial backwardness combined with vast size and heterogeneous ethnic make-up were reflected in the low literacy rates given in the 1897 census. The prerevolutionary intelligentsia was acutely aware of its isolation. Tolstoy described the situation in *War and Peace* through the characters of the illiterate peasant Platon Karataev and the cultured Pierre. Tolstoy, Dostoevsky and others struggled to find a satisfactory conception of the peasant, and in the process built up a mythical idealised image of the illiterate that culminated in Dostoevsky's 'kitchen idiot' who could teach the cultured section 'everything, everything, everything'.[28] The truth was that peasant life was virtually never depicted realistically from the inside before the

Revolution; the main validity the fictional descriptions of illiterates by literates had was an artistic one.[29]

This lack of comprehension was even more acute from the other side of the gulf. Alexander Herzen's description of an illiterate peasant appearing in a law court sums up the reaction from below to Tsarist and to early Soviet bureaucracy as well, since the role of officialdom as the scribe of the inarticulate did not change radically with the Revolution. When the peasant speaks, Herzen notes that 'he uses a somewhat antiquated Russian : whereas the judge and his clerks use the modern bureaucratic language which is so garbled an affair as to be barely intelligible ... What (*the peasant*) hears is an undifferentiated flux of noise, of which he must, if he is to preserve his skin, make as much sense as he can. He is sparing in his use of words, tries hard to cover up his nervousness, and the result is that he stands there with an asinine look on his face, like a great booby, like someone who has lost the power of speech.'[30]

The majority of first generation Bolshevik leaders (Stalin was a significant exception) stemmed from the prerevolutionary intelligentsia, as has already been pointed out.[31] In one important respect, however, they drew apart from the intelligentsia, urged on by Lenin's open scorn for its feckless attributes as many of its members drifted away from an earlier interest in public events into a *fin-de-siècle* obsession with esoteric forms of personal mysticism and aestheticism. The Bolsheviks continued to devote their attention primarily to central political issues. Yet when Lenin was faced with problems caused by illiteracy and lack of education, his views were typical in many ways of the old cultural élite. As Gorky said of the man whose views he knew well on these matters, 'Lenin is a leader and a Russian nobleman who does not lack the spiritual traits of that disappearing caste ... He does not know the popular masses, for he has never lived among them. Out of books he has learned ... by what means to whip up their instincts most easily to a fury.'[32] The cultural differences that separated Lenin from the masses made him more rather than less aware of the dangers of trying to eradicate these differences by superficial means. As the son of a Tsarist school inspector, he combined respect for the profound culture of the old intelligentsia with a realisation of the snares involved in carrying out a crash programme of popular education.

During the years from October 1917 until his death, Lenin was torn between the conflicting needs of creating a politically conscious nation as fast as possible and at the same time ensuring that vulgarised agitation did not become a substitute for thoroughgoing education on a broad base. The elimination of mass illiteracy lay at the root of the whole problem. Lenin stated the dilemma with his usual clarity, but with undue exaggeration : 'An illiterate person stands outside politics, and must first learn the alphabet. Without this there can be no politics.'[33] The proletariat could not dictate until it could read and write. Until this was achieved the Bolshevik party, with the aid of a literate, skilled bureaucracy, had to act as temporary guardian. Lenin had another urgent motive for eradicating illiteracy. As he became more closely acquainted with the organisational problems of the Russian worker and peasant in the course of his life, Lenin drew a line of increasing rigidity between what he termed *stikhiia* (spontaneity) and *soznatel'nost'* (consciousness) in their mental make-up and political attitudes. This distinction is a well-known one and does not need to be outlined again here.[34] The pertinence of these concepts to illiteracy is evident, for the quotation from Lenin above shows how he rightly considered literacy to be a *sine qua non* standing between blind spontaneity and political consciousness. The unanalytic spontaneity that comes with an attitude to the world that is one of absorbed and uncritical immersion is the hallmark of a pre-literate society. It is a quality that Tolstoy admired in Platon Karataev. Tolstoy was heir to a long line of romantics in the Rousseauist tradition who have lauded the Noble Savage. Lenin's materialist philosophy alone would have excluded him from this tradition, but his practical experience of the devasting effects of peasant spontaneity during the Civil War served to reinforce his fear of *stikhiia*.

Lenin thus saw the need for urgency in the campaign against illiteracy. When Gorky suggested shortly after the Revolution that a history of literature should be published for the workers' self-education, Lenin replied curtly, 'there is no time for writing thick books, a thick book would be read only by the intelligentsia . . .'[35] This sense of urgency prevailed in Lenin's mind in 1917 and up until the end of the Civil War. During the revolutionary year any means of influencing the illiterate population, however crude and hasty, were preferable in order to gain short-term political advantages over political opponents. Fast and facile agitation rather than sound political education was essential to the survival of Lenin's party. Political revolution from above had to precede cultural development from below.[36] In the Civil War this trend was reinforced by the crash programmes of a utopian kind for mass education and literacy that were promoted by leading Bolsheviks.

Towards the end of the Civil War, Lenin reverted to his deeper seated preference for carefully implemented long-term plans for the wider education of the Russian people which would instil much more than narrow political indoctrination. Even during the pre-NEP period his writings and speeches reveal a decided ambivalence on the twin topics of political propaganda and general, non-applied education. The problem teased his mind with great frequency.[37] Whilst continually advocating the rapid eradication of iliteracy, he did not condone the wilder methods of experimentation that were prevalent. When Bolshevik extremists wished to dismiss schoolteachers of 'bourgeois' origin from their posts, Lenin stressed that without the teachers' expertise the country would find it even harder to educate the masses.[38] The traditional side of Lenin's thought came to the fore in his dispute with A. A. Bogdanov, resulting in a decree of the Central Committee of the party published on 1 December 1920. By it the literary movement of *Proletkult* and its associated organisations were placed under the supervision of the Commissariat of Education. It is necessary at this point to outline some of the features of the Lenin-Bogdanov debate concerning the term 'proletarian culture', since they throw considerable light on Lenin's final position before his decline and death on the relationship between political consciousness and literacy.

For Bogdanov the conquest of political and economic power by a party in the name of the proletariat was secondary to the development of an independent proletarian culture, which would throw up its own ideology. Thus Bogdanov saw the attainment of literacy and education by the masses as a comparatively easy spontaneous process which would be inherently self-regulating. The idea of spontaneity in this development was as distasteful to Lenin as the uncontrolled spontaneity of the illiterate, who was to be allowed to discipline himself according to Bogdanov. Lenin always thought of mass education as something to be organised and directed from above. On another count the two men were opposed. Bogdanov did not want the proletariat to accept passively the cultural heritage of Western Europe and Tsarist Russia. Since for him culture was not a store of values, but the organising principle of social life, the wholesale adoption of previous cultures might undermine the revolutionary thought and feeling of the working masses. Lenin fought for the selective takeover of pre-Soviet culture, although the party rather than the proletariat would decide initially what to accept and what to reject. Here again Lenin adopted a conservative position in defence of the principles and products of the prerevolutionary intelligentsia. Having been the main advocate of the destruction of so many institutions of the old regime, he reacted strongly in the opposite sense on a subject near to his heart. He had himself been a model pupil at school, graduating from the classical gymnasium at Simbirsk with a gold medal. After 1917, as in his own childhood, he believed that schools should teach fundamental matters, and that low-level political indoctrination should be excluded from their curricula, despite the desperate need to make the masses aware of Bolshevik goals. He knew that quick but scanty education-cum-indoctrination of the peasants would have a dangerous boomerang effect in the long run. Believing up to the time of his death that NEP would survive for a considerable period, he envisaged a slow but thorough process of turning all sectors of Soviet society into a literate, self-conscious whole. He would not tolerate an independent proletarian culture, but as a true heir of the Russian intelligentsia insisted on humane, broad educational principles laid down with some degree of autonomy, so long as they did not conflict with Bolshevik aims.

This was a far cry from Stalin's approach to the cultural problem, as will become apparent later. Caught on the horns of a dilemma, Lenin eventually sacrificed speed to thoroughness in the drive for literacy. It was therefore left to Stalin and his supporters, for the most part having fewer links with the prerevolutionary intelligentsia, to put through the final and politically crucial stages of the literacy programme. They willingly took from Lenin the notion that political control over education was paramount, and ignored his velvet-gloved handling of that control. In their hands *soznatel'nost'* and *ideinost'* (ideological reliability), acquired through the capacity to read and write, became debased to mean something altogether less critical and free than Lenin had ever hoped to see in the future. It is significant that Bogdanov's intellectual heirs, especially the historian M. N. Pokrovsky, aided Stalin after the close of NEP to impose tight controls over culture in the name of the proletariat. The influence of the cultural Left was short-lived. By the mid-1930s Stalin purged them and replaced them with men who would enforce conservative intellectual standards.

Lenin's view of the need for patience and practical common sense in the campaign to bridge the gulf between the literates and the illiterates was based on firm ground when viewed in the light of the harsh realities of Soviet society at the end of the Civil War. Commenting on the provisional census of 1920, which showed that only 319 out of every 1000 Soviet citizens could read and write, Lenin declared 'This shows how much urgent, laborious work we have to do in order to reach the level of a normal, civilised West European state.' [39] Trotsky entered the lists on Lenin's side against Lunacharsky and Bukharin, who tended like Bogdanov to underestimate the lack of understanding between the *literati* and the general population. Lunacharsky had a brilliant mind but suffered from a vice commonly found among the old intelligentsia. He would spend long hours in conversation or writing *belles lettres* but found it difficult to concentrate on the administrative tasks Lenin thought to be most pressing, such as the liquidation of illiteracy or the formulation of sensible educational programmes. Trotsky was well aware that the literary movements thrown up by the Revolution which claimed to be voicing the cultural aspirations of the lower classes were hypocritical to a degree. In *Literature and Revolution* he attacked *Proletkult* on orthodox Marxist grounds for trying to introduce the superstructure of proletarian literature before the new socialist substructure had been given the time to evolve. Futurism was likewise criticised by Trotsky for attempting to forge artificially premature ties with the semi-literate workers : he scoffingly declared that only a nation as economically backward as Russia could be so thrilled by the claims of technology as portrayed naively by the Futurists.

Scholars within and outside the Soviet Union who have written about the literary and artistic movements of the 1920s sometimes ignore the meagre extent of the impact these élites had on the population at large. In actuality the position was not unlike that of the Tsarist period. The major difference lay in the fact that most of the new movements acted as banners for promoting revolutionary political, social and aesthetic ideas. Thus they attracted the interest and concern of the Bolshevik party, and so were in the limelight, but then the masses were as little aware of high politics as they were of the activities of Bohemian literary groups concentrated on Moscow and Leningrad. Gorky and Esenin, the two geniuses who were reputed to stem from the proletariat and the peasantry respectively, and whose writings were claimed as the true voice of these mute classes, were used as a convenient popular myth by the Bolsheviks, despite the personal and political waywardness of the two men. In reality, Gorky was neither proletarian nor unlettered in his early youth. On both sides of the family, parents and grandparents were *meshchane* (lower middle class).

Esenin is a subtler and more interesting case. It is tue that he spent the first sixteen years of his life among illiterates in the countryside, but he lived with his affluent grandfather, a miller, and so avoided the daily toil of the Russian peasant. He dwelt mentally in a private dream world, affected by the aesthetics of religion. In 1912 Esenin went to Moscow, where he spent three years as a type-corrector before moving to St. Petersburg. Here he rapidly became the white-smocked, golden-belted idol of the literary salons which believed they had within their grasp a typical peasant who was also a poetic genius. Esenin at the time, and later his biographers, ignored the period he spent in Moscow between leaving the countryside and going to the capital. On returning for a brief visit to the village in 1923, Esenin found himself to be out of touch with peasant life, and the lack of strong ties between his poetry and the cruel realities of rural Russia worried him until his suicide in 1925.

The low circulation and poor distribution of leading literary journals in NEP provide concrete evidence of the élitist nature of the cultured few. *Young Guard*, one of the most popular journals, had a circulation of 9000 in 1922 and dropped to between 5000 and 6000 an issue by 1926.[40] Many copies of journals of this kind were sent to public libraries and thus reached a slightly wider public, but on the whole distribution methods were badly organised. Most of the circulation was confined to the large cities. As of mid-1923, Moscow and Petrograd published only 30 per cent of all the journals in the Soviet Union, but had 90 per cent of all the circulation.[41] The procedures for distributing periodicals and books to the provinces were chaotic, so that the wide readership networks which were claimed often only existed on paper. By the late 1920s the heirs to the 'thick journals' of the nineteenth century were declining fast, due to political intervention, financial hardship, and the rise of more specialised publications. A survey of the reading tastes of workers based on books lent out by Moscow Trade Union libraries in the winter of 1926–7 showed that 64 per cent of the workers read at least one literary work during the period. Strong preference was expressed for contemporary novels, and 50 per cent took out books written by so-called 'proletarian' writers. The high percentages are impressive, but we are dealing here with the cream of the country's and the capital's workers, who were as far removed in their intellectual capacities from the mass of the Soviet labour force as they in turn were poles apart from the 'proletarian' leaders of the literary world. The three works most commonly read in these libraries were *Cement* by F. Gladkov, *The Artamanov Affair* and *Mother* by Gorky, in that order.[42] All three novels describe in artless detail the daily life of factory workers, holding up a factual mirror for their working class readers to admire. The more avant-garde and esoteric achievements of the literary world apparently held no interest even for such paragons of the proletariat. The conclusion drawn here seems self-evident for most societies and not just for early Soviet Russia, but it should be constrasted with the extravagant hopes of movements like *Proletkult*. This raises a more general hypothesis, one that we are perhaps reluctant to face, but which nevertheless may contain some truth. By the end of the 1920s the hermetic cultural groups which arose after the Revolution with such vigour and in such variety were still striking no firm roots in Soviet society as a whole. Some of their adherents produced work of artistic genius, but few if any achieved their broader political and social aims. For the most part the movements may well have run out of steam before the last great onslaught against illiteracy under Stalin, which coincided in time with the imposition of firm political controls over the intelligentsia and its products.

Having noted the continuing gulf between the most articulate and the least, and Lenin's views on the problems involved in bridging it, let us now turn to examine Bolshevik methods and progress after 1917 in the campaign against illiteracy. The achievement was remarkable, particularly in the unstable early period. Three stages of the campaign can be discerned. The first coincided roughly with the term of the Civil War, the second with

NEP. 1923 witnessed changes in policy and administration that were to receive a sharp jolt from the results of the population census of 1926, which revealed an actual increase in illiteracy. From May 1929 Stalin initiated the third stage with a long-term drive based on different principles which in the end finally eliminated the problem of widespread illiteracy.

The eradication campaign covered two main sectors of the population. In the first place it was vital to provide all children with elementary schooling in order to get at the root of illiteracy. The main efforts of the Tsarist Duma and Ministry of Education had been directed towards building up a complete network of primary schools throughout Russia.[43] In the second place the problem of adult illiteracy had to be faced. The Tsarist government had left this for the most part to private initiative, hoping that adult illiteracy would die out of its own accord over the decades. Lenin was not content with this time-scale. Convinced that the success of the socialist revolution hung to a great extent on the raising of labour productivity, which in turn depended on improving the national level of culture, he pointed to universal literacy as an essential prerequisite.[44] On the basis of these considerations it was announced at the first All-Russian Congress of Education in August 1918 that the whole country would have to be provided with elementary schools for adult illiterates and semi-literates.[45] The Bolshevik party was not slow in realising the potential value of the campaign as a thorough way of indoctrinating the masses at the same time as teaching them to read and write. At the first Congress for extra-mural education in May 1919 both formal and informal instruction for illiterates was brought under the aegis of the party. As Krupskaia bluntly put it, 'Cultural work must be closely combined with political tasks.'[46] She believed that the peasant's interest would be stirred if he could appreciate that by learning to read he would be able to better his own political and, above all, economic position in society. The decree on the organisation of teaching outside the school system in the RSFSR, which was promulgated on 14 June 1919, promised that the new institutions would be under the direct control of the proletariat and the peasantry. As of 1919 the notion of the dictatorship of the proletariat, let alone the peasantry, was already an idle dream.

By this decree the first opportunity was given to the Bolshevik party to assert a strong hold over men's minds by engraving on them its own exclusive view of the world. At the time and ever afterwards the Bolsheviks claimed that they acted in this way in order to counteract earlier White propaganda directed towards illiterates. If one looks at a typical Soviet primer for adult illiterates published during the Civil War, the implication is clear. Within the brief purview of thirty-two large-type pages an introduction to the alphabet is merged with the crudest exposition of Bolshevik political and socio-economic tenets. For the completely illiterate, the coloured jacket portrays a proud worker and a peasant standing on torn fetters, a shattered crown and severed double-headed eagle. Over the horizon dotted with factory chimneys and hayricks a livid red sun rises, beaming enormous rays over the landscape. Pages one to thirteen go on to display the letters of the alphabet with visual aids, and from page fourteen onwards a fairytale narrative of the naivest simplicity tells of the kulak, the bourgeoisie and the evils of the Tsarist regime.[47] The transition from illiterate ignorance to a knowledge of given half-truths is breathtaking in its curtness.

The party's crash programme of combined agitation and illiteracy eradication survived until 1920, coinciding in duration with other hastily arranged social projects, some of which have been mentioned in Chapter 2. The first and basic decree on the liquidation of illiteracy, issued on 29 December 1919, had laid down compulsory schooling for all those between the ages of eight and fifty who were unable to read or write. Ten years later Krupskaia admitted that not a single article of the decree was enforced during the Civil War.[48] On financial grounds alone the programme would have collapsed, since there was no mention of funds in the decree. Other projects that remained largely on paper included an outline plan of the Commissariat for Education for the instruction of illiterates, and the exhortations by the Teachers' Trade Union and the *Komsomol* (The Young Communist League) to their members to participate in the eradication campaign.[49] In June 1920 the Extraordinary Commission for the Struggle against Illiteracy was set up to act as an overall coordinating body. By the winter of 1920–1 it was claimed that a total of 124,000 people were engaged throughout the country in giving instruction to 1,157,600 illiterates.[50] Despite an excess of haste and optimism, the achievement of this first period was substantial, since according to provisional census results approximately five million illiterates were taught to read and write between October 1917 and the end of the Civil War.

The second stage of the long struggle against illiteracy started off badly. With the implementation of NEP, funds for adult education were transferred to local budgets. By 1922–3 the number of literacy centres and of those attending them fell to one-tenth of what they had risen to in 1921.[51] The city proletariat was exhausted by the strain of the Civil War, whilst the peasantry sank back into immemorial mental lethargy or was ravaged by the series of famines which swept the country. As Lenin warned, the dose of superficial Bolshevik propaganda, directly linked with the teaching of the alphabet, had a boomerang effect on many peasants who could not stomach the anti-religious agitation included in the courses. Menshevik critics of the regime claimed that compared with the prerevolutionary period Russia in 1922 had 30 per cent fewer schools overall and that 70 per cent of all children between eight and eleven years of age were illiterate.[52]

In the same year Lenin called for an end to the earlier policy of using the literacy campaign as a convenient instrument for quick indoctrination. Here he was reverting to his real preference for an intellectually respectable system of general education. In the draft for a speech at the Eleventh Congress of the Bolshevik Party, Lenin declared that 'the time for propaganda by decrees is past'.[53] His exhortations were accepted, and during the period 1923–9, until Stalin turned his attention to the problem, the campaign was far more loosely connected with official agitation than it had been in the first years after the Revolution. The Commissariat for Education encouraged non-party organisations to help in the fight. In 1923 a semi-independent body called 'Down with Illiteracy' (*Doloi negramotnost'*) was allowed to undertake its own campaign. Under the chairmanship of M. I. Kalinin it attracted a large membership and maintained 12,000 'liquidation centres' from its own funds, but as Lunacharsky stated in October 1924, 'the society for the liquidation of illiteracy passes wonderful resolutions, but the concrete results of its work are despicable'.[54] By the beginning of the same year the cultural interests of the literate sector of the nation remained at a low ebb, if one can judge this by knowing the numbers of books in private possession. A series of surveys carried out by the famous statistician S. G. Strumilin in 1924 show that the great majority of workers and half of the white-collar employees living in the capital had no books of their own, although some of them resorted to public libraries. On the bright side Strumilin found that the number of workers who obtained books of their own had doubled since the Revolution, though white-collar employees were actually buying fewer than they had done prior to 1917.[55]

Although some of the cruder political aspects of the first stage of the illiteracy campaign were now abandoned, the party still kept an eye on its own interests in other ways. From 1923 onwards special key categories of the population were singled out for attention, as opposed to the previous blanket approach to illiterates of whatever kind. The categories included trade union and *Komsomol* members, women deputies to the Soviets and Red Army men : all of these groups formed vital chains of communication between the party and the masses. If their cultural level could be lifted fast, they would provide the political centre with able articulators of its views among the population at large.

A similar process was going on in this period at lower political levels, as might be expected of a nationwide project that was tightly controlled from Moscow despite some relaxation due to the peculiar characteristics of NEP. In 1924 communist organisers in the Smolensk *guberniia* (a vast administrative area) were concentrating especially on the elementary education of youths of pre-military age and trade union members.[56] For lack of sufficient personnel they could not yet tackle the problem of liquidating illiteracy among the more influential of the peasant women, like delegates to town meetings (a sector with a very high illiteracy rate), but in 1926 we find the Belyi *uezd* (district) encouraging rural female schoolteachers to work on this task.[57] There is no doubting the keenness and industry with which the Bolsheviks handled the complicated problems of illiteracy at the grass roots, as a reading of the Smolensk Archives on this topic proves. The organisation was nearly always split into the two rigidly segregated categories of town and country areas, with far more energy devoted to the former by the literate, town-dwelling Bolshevik party workers.[58]

For March 1924 we have a complete list of all types of institutions in the Smolensk area dealing with illiterates, semi-literates and elementary political agitation (see table).[59] The latter category

	In the city of Smolensk	In the town of Iartsevo	12 other uezdy	Total	Number of those attending, where known
Likpunkty ('Liquidation Centres') for illiterates	9	7	190	206	4594
Schools for semi-literates	5	2	14	21	—
Reading rooms	—	—	274	274	—
Clubs	8	1	11	20	—
Libraries	4	1	113	118	—
Schools for political literacy (politgramota)	6	1	12	19	260

was now kept distinct from the others, in line with Lenin's change of policy in 1923. The compilers of this information observed that all the institutions had been fully developed according to plan, except for the *likpunkty* (liquidation centres), which had only attained 72 per cent of the number laid down as a target. Thus the most essential part of the plan, without which the other parts would be rendered superfluous, was not being fulfilled. The concentration of effort on the two main industrial centres of the Western *oblast'* (province), Smolensk and Iartsevo, was remarkable, though it was in line with contemporary central policy regarding a selective approach to the campaign. In the rural areas of the *uezdy* there was a waste of effort due to an overstretched organisational network. On average only twenty or so persons attended each *likpunkt* and twenty-six every school for political literacy. Even when such factors as the enormous size of the areas concerned and the lack of transport are taken into account, the dispersal seems exaggerated. Certainly it serves to show what a time-consuming affair the literacy campaign was, as many officials lamented in their written reports contained in the Smolensk Archives. In 1926 'self-instruction circles' were set up in the Smolensk *guberniia* in an effort to relieve the party authorities and their agents, but nothing was left to chance nor to unorthodoxy, and detailed party orders on curricula, reading lists, etc. were produced for the circles, which were frequently inspected as well.[60]

A report of the Belyi *uezd* party committee for March 1926 stated that although a total of 1870 persons were being taught to read and write in *uezd likpunkty* and in other less formal groups, illiteracy as a whole actually appeared to be on the increase.[61] In due course this startling opinion was corroborated on a national scale. After the slump in the number of local *likpunkty* in the winter of 1922–3, the situation improved gradually until 1925, but in the following year a new decline was perceptible.[62] Lunacharsky ascribed it to two main causes – waning energy among the ranks of the campaigners and bad distribution of reading materials. 'A man may have learnt the alphabet, but he gets no newspapers, he possesses no books, so there is no particular need for him to read and write, and soon he has forgotten everything.'[63] Bolshevik and peasant conceptions of the good life differed widely. For many aspects of the peasant world literacy was not particularly important. Conclusive and shattering evidence on the continuing high level and actual increase of illiteracy was provided by the population census of December 1926. This showed that illiteracy in the whole population had decreased by 17.3 per cent compared with the 1897 census and by 7.7 per cent compared with the partial census of 1920.[64] These figures on their own were reasonably encouraging, although they meant that one in two persons over the age of eight was still illiterate. Other assessments showed that the rate of illiteracy was especially high in the school-age group : in fact illiteracy was on the increase from the lower age levels upwards.[65]

This serious reversal of all previous efforts was due to a third factor, not mentioned by Lunacharsky. Approximately half of all Soviet children were growing up illiterate at the time of the census. The decree of October 1918 ordaining obligatory schooling for all children up to the age of seventeen had never been fulfilled. Even a four-year period of schooling was not enforced between 1918 and 1926, so that in many cases it was impossible to give a basic course in reading and writing. The worst hit sectors as a result were the peasants and women. The 1926 census showed that while 76.3 per cent of urban dwellers over the age of nine were literate, only 45.2 per cent of the rural population could read and write. 66.5 per cent of all men were literate, compared with 37.1 per cent of all women.[66] As in the earlier censuses, significant regional and ethnic differences still prevailed.

By the winter of 1926 the Soviet Union was on the eve of cataclysmic agricultural and industrial changes, although this was not as yet apparent to her leaders, still less to the masses. A country where every second adult was illiterate was about to embark on an ill-premeditated course which would require skilled minds to organise and run it at all levels. More important from the purely political point of view, Stalin would soon be attempting with a considerable degree of success to turn an authoritarian system into a totalitarian state. He would be dealing with a highly malleable population, at least half of which was only to attain basic, let alone political, literacy during his hegemony.

The social and above all political implications of this co-incidence will be considered when we come to discuss this third and final stage of the literacy campaign which began in May 1929. But first we must examine other factors involved in the period from 1917 to 1927. Frequently they will be found to be inter-woven closely with themes treated elsewhere in this book. It was partly for lack of a reasonable literacy rate that the dictatorship of the proletariat through such instruments as workers' control became an idle dream, and that an articulate bureaucracy to cater for the needs of the masses sprang up again so quickly after the Revolution. The small-scale structure of Soviet society, discussed in the next chapter, also had its effect on the eradication campaign.

The immensity of the task compared with the slender re-sources of the Bolshevik party created a variety of problems. Only in 1928 did the number of full party members pass the million mark, by which time they were dealing with over 150 million people. In 1926 we know from the population census that there were at least 85 million illiterates. The number of full party members then stood at 639,652.[67] Illiteracy was merely one among a multitude of social and other tasks which confronted party members, who had to become Jacks-of-all-trades if they were to cope with all of them. Many Bolsheviks were particularly ill-suited to organise the literacy campaign. In 1922 92.7 per cent of all party members including candidates had received only primary education or less. A mere 0.6 per cent had studied in institutions of higher education. By 1927 the position had scarcely changed, when the percentages stood at 91.3 and 0.8, respectively.[68] The shortage of numbers and expertise was rendered even more crippling by the lack of money. As was mentioned earlier, the basic decree of 1919 on the eradication of illiteracy made no mention of any funds that might be available for the campaign. Financial stringency was a feature of the movement as a whole, and the burden of finding resources usually fell on the local authorities concerned.

The party came to rely heavily on extraneous agents in the need to recruit large numbers of suitable personnel at the lowest possible cost. An obvious source of aid appeared to be the literary intelligentsia, but the combined effect of Lenin's aversion to some of their leaders' eccentricities and their own lack of contact with the masses circumscribed their value. Maiakovsky's efforts to popularise propaganda and extend the benefits of literature to at least the semi-literate level were received with mistrust by Lenin. 'Pushkin I understand and enjoy,' he said, 'Nekrasov I acknowledge, but Maiakovsky – excuse me, I can't understand him.'[69] Lenin's concern for preserving Russia's cultural heritage led him to disapprove of the Futurist attack on the art of the past. The 'proletarians' in literary circles also tended to favour the classics and attacked Maiakovsky. More important, it was clear that the masses were not reading Maiakovsky. In 1923 he organised the Left Front of Art in a new attempt to reach a wider public. As he said later, 'the question of a clear meaning for everybody rose before me, and I started to write more for the masses'.[70] Yet even the circulation of the journal *Lef* remained small.

One obvious technical reason for Maiakovsky's failures in this respect was his heavy reliance, despite numerous experiments in other media, on the printed word. In the Civil War years the shortage of paper was as much a problem as illiteracy in carrying out agitation programmes. It is true that in the long run the publication and circulation of newspapers and books increased substantially between the First World War and the end of NEP. Whereas the number of newspapers issued in 1913 was 859 with a single printing circulation of 2.7 million copies, the corresponding figures for 1928 were 1,197 and 9.4 millions.[71] But this growth was far more rapid than the rate at which the level of literacy rose. For a time Russia slipped back at least half a century into a predominantly oral tradition. It is significant that very few novels were produced in this period. Paper was in such short supply that Esenin could not even get his brief poems printed, and ostentatiously took to writing them on a monastery wall.[72] Vivid evidence of the dearth of paper can be seen visually by scanning on microfilm the early Smolensk Archives after 1917. For the most part they are written on ragged scraps of official Tsarist notepaper.[73] The party as well as the writers and the educators had to make keen economies.

Another barrier to literacy was the Cyrillic script. A few logical reforms were made at the time of the Revolution, but the script still presented special difficulties to someone learning to read and write, despite its phonetic character. There are thirty-one letters to master instead of the twenty-six in the Latin alphabet, and a wide discrepancy in form exists between the handwritten and printed letters.[74] The Soviet regime complicated matters by introducing a vast quantity of new abbreviations which ran riot in NEP. Handbooks for sophisticated trade union members for the year 1922 included long lists of abbreviations and their meaning. Even such simple and common ones as *Gosplan* (the central planning agency) and *VUZ* (Institution for Higher Education) are set out with careful explanations.[75]

The Commissariat for Education was not slow in resorting to audio-visual media in order to reach illiterates. Writers and artists who collaborated with central and local authorities in this way were of more practical use than the high priests of the literary movements. The range of communications media available in the 1920s was much more limited technologically than it was to become later. Even in Germany prior to 1930 almost none of the propaganda methods which Goebbels was to develop were in use. Until Alfred Hugenberg's time the main technical means on which the Nazis relied were lorries for transporting supporters quickly from place to place.[76] In the Soviet Union expert use was made of the media which could be applied to mass audiences at the time, like the theatre, films, the visual arts, and to a much lesser extent the radio. On coming to power the Bolsheviks immediately took control over the theatre (it took six years to do the same thing after the French Revolution).[77] During the Civil War large numbers of productions by amateur groups were given, mainly to military audiences, thus attracting the illiterate peasant in uniform. In contrast the city-centred literary movements theorised a great deal on the need to reach the wider population, but except for Maiakovsy's *LEF* group they rarely took their art to the provinces.

Proletkult's projects for mass productions did not often material-
ise, and V. Meyerhold's visionary schemes were too unwieldy and
expensive to repeat on a large scale. The Cubo-Futurists frankly
admitted that they were not interested in the stagnant countryside.
Yet between 1918 and 1924 amateur theatre at least did have a
real impact on the masses. There were thousands of performing
groups, many of which travelled widely round the provinces.
Tickets were often issued free, and large interested audiences
attended productions.[78]

As an instrument in the fight against illiteracy the film got off
to a slower start than the theatre. By 1920–1 less than half of the
thousand or so cinemas that existed in 1917 remained open. The
low number of films that were shown in the first two years of NEP
were neither of instructional nor ideological use to the regime, since
they were chiefly pre-1917 or foreign in origin. In 1924 the Association of Revolutionary Cinematography was founded with the
slogan : 'The film is the most powerful weapon in the struggle for
communist culture.'[79] A new film trust, *Sovkino*, helped to continue the golden age of the silent film in the USSR. But it was at
the local level, among the peasantry, that the film could have the
most valuable effect as a substitute for the written word. By April
1926 it was claimed that 976 itinerant film groups were each visit-
ing twenty villages a month. Literate peasants introduced the films
and used them as stimuli to create a demand for further information through books. In 1925 there were only fifty permanent
village cinemas in the whole of the Soviet Union, although the
Red Army reached the peasant through its 2562 establishments.[80]
We know something of the detailed rural distribution of media for
use in the literacy campaign from the Smolensk Archives. In 1926,
for instance, the party committee of one *uezd* was complaining
about the poor distribution of cinemas and films. There was only
one cinema in the whole *uezd*, and it was not supplied with reels
because they were too expensive.[81]

The report stated that in one *volost'*, a sub-district of the same
uezd, four radio points served all the community, consisting of
about 14,000 souls. In the 1920s the national radio network was
not sufficiently developed to serve as a tool in the eradication of
illiteracy. It was a heavy social and political price to pay for
technological backwardness, as Nasser by contrast makes clear
with reference to Egyptian peasants in more recent times. 'It is

true that most of our people are still illiterate. But politically that counts for far less than it did twenty years ago. Literacy and intelligence are not the same thing. Radio has changed everything. Once the villagers had no knowledge of what was happening in the capital. Government was run by small coteries of people who did not need to take account of the reactions of the people, who never saw a newspaper or could not read it if they did. Today people in the most remote villages hear of what is happening everywhere and form their opinions. Leaders cannot govern as they once did. We live in a new world.' [82] What the Soviet Union lacked in technology in the years following on the Revolution, she tried to make up for by other means. Banners and above all posters in vast numbers provided visual information with a minimum of words for illiterates and the newly literate. Walls, vehicles, shop-windows covered with them made the streets a kind of semi-literate's library. The artistic standard of many posters reached a zenith during NEP that has never been surpassed. [83] Their influence was ubiquitous. Theodore Dreiser discovered when he visited the Soviet Union towards the close of NEP 'in every station, hotel, government post office, government or cooperative store, factory, office building, theatre, home, even, the endless posters of this most ambitious of governments urging (never commanding really) the people to do this and that, from combing their hair to swatting flies, washing out the stables and milk pails, cleaning the babies' milk bottles, opening the windows of sick-rooms, ploughing with tractors, fertilizing with the right fertilizers, building with the right lumber, eating the right food – Oh Lord, hold me ! I feel myself spinning round.' [84]

The military proved to be a far more practical and effective agent in the drive for literacy than the writers ever were. The Russian army was the most accurate assessor of literacy rates in the Empire before the census of 1897. This was because when the compulsory annual drafts took place recruits were regularly tested in regard to their degree of education. The figures are especially useful in that they date from well back into the nineteenth century and refer to a precisely defined age group. The table on page 161 gives the percentage of literacy among males taken into military service in the Russian Empire between 1880 and 1913. [85]

Literacy rates rose from one-fifth in 1870 to two-fifths in the

Year	Percentage
1880	22
1885	27
1890	32
1895	39 (estimated)
1900	49
1905	56
1910	65
1913	68

mid-1890s and to two-thirds in 1913. Standards were far higher than the national overall rate, but it must be remembered that we are dealing here with able-bodied men only, thus excluding all women and unfit males. Nevertheless some element of mystery still surrounds the apparent discrepancy between these figures and the much less optimistic scattered evidence from other sources. Also it is often said that the Tsarist army was a great elementary educator of the peasantry, but this should be qualified in the light of these rates, which prove the relatively high literacy rate of recruits just *before* they submitted to military service.

Figures taken from military sources after the start of the First World War are incomplete and unreliable, but it does seem that the role of the military as an educator increased, especially after the establishment of the political commissar system and the decree of April 1918 providing for compulsory education in the ranks. A devastating war followed by Civil War wiped out huge numbers of newly literate men, so that ground gained was quickly lost again, but there were some permanent advantages. The number of peasants in the ranks ran into many millions. Uprooted from their place of origin, they could no longer rely on their usual channels of oral information filtered down to them from the literate level, so they had more incentive to learn to read and write in order to cope with their new mobile way of life. At the end of the Civil War tens of thousands of young peasants who had become both literate and party members while serving in the Red Army were dispersed to their villages. Just as military deserters and demobilised men towards the close of 1917 served as cultural and political leaven in the countryside, so this new wave played a valuable role in spreading literacy, and with it the prestige of the party.[86] It is not by pure chance, nor entirely through the military impact on the political scene in the Civil War, that Bolshevik journalism today remains impregnated with military jargon. After 1921 the army continued to play a useful though diminished part in the fight for literacy. The standing army was reduced in size, and the turnover slowed down considerably. In 1924 Frunze was still complaining about the very variable standards of training in the ranks due to the backwardness of illiterates.[87] A military decree of 28 February 1922, ordering that no illiterates should be left in the army by 1 May 1922, had proved to be much too optimistic. Nevertheless by the mid-1920s it could be said, in the words of a contemporary account of barrack life, that 'a recruit knows that in the Red Army he will be taught not only military affairs : he will be taught how to read and write; he will get to know what is happening in the wide world, what is being written in books and newspapers'.[88]

In NEP the rapidly growing bureaucracy became a substitute for the military to some extent as a large-scale organisation concerned with the promotion of literacy. Much of the administration mentioned earlier in this chapter was carried out by the Commissariat for Education and other governmental bodies.[89] Like all centralised organisations in Soviet Russia, the work of the Commissariat suffered from several disadvantages in a backward, widespread and small-scale society. New elements were constantly being absorbed into the bureaucracy. By the end of 1922 an official analysis showed that two-thirds of all full party members and half the candidate members were employed in white-collar jobs.[90] In December 1923 a resolution drafted by Stalin, Trotsky and Kamenev complained that 'active worker communists, who should naturally constitute the link between the party and the non-party masses, are almost entirely absorbed in administrative and managerial work'.[91] For status reasons men with any degree of education wished to live in a city and sought a job in a government office. The mere fact that he could read and write placed even the humblest clerk above the mass of the semi-literate and illiterate masses, giving him a status apart that could not have been maintained in a more advanced society. This trend sucked up increasing numbers of educated personnel and deprived the localities of valuable agents.

The Bolsheviks became increasingly aware of the isolation of their cadres in this respect. The central authorities urged local party organisations to make better contacts with the literacy campaign at the grass roots level, but the bureaucratic trend affected the localities just as it did the centre. Regional party workers were more aware of the time-consuming nature of the campaign through hard experience. They had to rely on semi-independent agents for lack of sufficient party members and time. In the Smolensk *guberniia* in one cell alone, which was the smallest political unit, the 188 non-party individuals as well as many party men were engaged in improving literacy standards during the winter of 1925–6.[92] Many types of people were called on to undertake work : only a few of the most important groups can be mentioned here.

In December 1924 A. A. Andreev, Secretary of the Central Committee of the Party, sent a circular to all local party Secretaries, exhorting them to increase the numbers of workers and village correspondents who collected information for press organs throughout the country. At that time there were about 100,000 of them.[93] He advised not to recruit too many indiscriminately, but to find cultured and politically mature candidates who would make an admirable link between the two worlds of the written and the spoken word and would be influential formulators of opinion in local society. Village school teachers were another obvious group for the party to woo, since their whole careers were devoted primarily to instilling the three 'R's' into peasant children (and often adults). In February 1925 the *Orgburo* instructed local party authorities to treat non-party rural teachers with kid gloves, so that they would not be antagonised into quitting their jobs as the result of political harrying, and might even be persuaded to join the party.[94] Female school teachers were invaluable instruments for penetrating into the most illiterate sector of the adult community, the peasant women.[95] Teachers of all kinds had to become substitutes for the village priests, who in Tsarist Russia had preserved the religious associations of literacy, so important through the centuries. Part of that tradition had been obscurantist, as Engels noted of mid-nineteenth century England also : 'The Sunday schools of the State church ... do not teach writing because it is too worldly an employment for Sunday.'[96] Yet in some ways the decline of the priest as an educator, which was greatly accelerated by the decree of August 1918 on the separation of school instruction from the church, had debilitating effects on the rise of literacy. Prior to 1917 the Holy Synod could and did send village priests to remote areas of Russia where no other educational agents would ever go of their own accord. Prerevolutionary maps published by the Holy Synod showing the geographical distribution of church schools in the outlying parts of the Empire reveal an impressive coverage.

Another active group of agents who were well adapted to penetrate from the towns into the countryside were the railwaymen. The Smolensk Archives and other sources make frequent mention of them as valuable distributors of the tools of literacy and as agitators, though by the nature of their work they were not usually able to stay sufficiently long enough in one place to act as teachers.[97] More useful in some ways were the professional and semi-professional workers in the countryside like agronomists, doctors and *fel'dshers*. They had urgent tasks of their own to fulfil, but they sometimes devoted themselves to teaching illiterates in their spare time.[98] Doctors and *fel'dshers* who were sent by compulsion to work in rural areas by the Soviet regime at last began to approach the ideal *zemstvo* view of them as cultural leaven among the peasantry. The *fel'dshers*, semi-trained personnel somewhere between a nurse and a doctor, were typical products of an educationally backward society, and proved to be useful links between literate and illiterate sectors.[99] Despite the efforts of so many informal agents of the central policy makers, the Russian peasant was slow to hear of the literacy campaign, let alone to master the alphabet and begin the long process of learning to read and write. The positive relationship between urbanisation and literacy rates mentioned earlier in this chapter [100] suffered a setback between 1917 and the mid-1920s, when city populations declined to a remarkable degree. A huge country like the Soviet Union inevitably suffered from larger regional variations in literacy rates than a compact nation like Britain. Recently scholars have shown with some measure of precision how gradients of literacy decline in less developed countries as distances from urban nexi increase.[101] The situation was probably very similar in Russia during NEP, although it cannot be proved exactly for lack of sufficient regional statistics. A countervailing influence was the spread of electricity in the countryside. D. Vertov's short film on peasants' reactions to the arrival of the electric bulb in their village is a vivid portrayal of the connection between light and enlightenment.[102] Lenin stressed the vital tie between the spread of electrification and literacy.[103] In the long Russian winter many idle peasant hours could be put to better use than drinking and stove-lazing once a good source of light was available in the villages.

Let us now turn to the third stage in the struggle for national literacy before attempting to assess the social and political repercussions of the campaign as a whole.

The disappointing results of the 1926 population census, which became known in the winter of 1927–8 only, were followed by other depressing surveys on the state of literacy. Figures published in 1928 and 1929 showed that in the age group 16–35 there were about 16 million illiterates and between 30 to 40 million semi-literates. After them were growing up another 5 million illiterate children between twelve and sixteen years old.[104] The implication of these figures for the type of labour force on which the First and Second Five-Year Plans would have to rely was serious indeed. In the Moscow area alone, which was to be one of the key centres in the First Five-Year Plan, 45 per cent of all those between the ages of sixteen and fifty were illiterate.[105] The problem would become far more acute as new waves of illiterates streamed into the cities when industrialisation got under way. In an entirely new centre like Magnitogorsk, in the middle of a vast rural area, the illiteracy level might become the primary cause of failure.

A gigantic effort inscribed in the control figures of the First Five-Year Plan was the party's answer to the crisis. Whereas the *likpunkty* in 1928–9 gave instruction to a mere 1,648,000 illiterates, the Plan provided for 18.2 million illiterates and semi-literates to be taught by 1932–3.[106] A special resolution of the Central Committee of the Party issued on 17 May 1929 called on all the agencies involved in the campaign to ensure that within one year every industrial worker would be literate and within two every *sovkhoz* (state farm) and *kolkhoz* (collective farm) peasant.[107] By July 1930 it was found that these targets were far too optimistic. Only 75 per cent of the illiterate proletariat had been enrolled for instruction and only 30 per cent of them were actually following courses.[108] In September 1930, therefore, a newly constituted all-Russian organisation for the liquidation of illiteracy asserted tight central control over the various bodies engaged in the campaign. Once again, as in the Civil War, political agitation was very closely linked with teaching: illiterates were now indoctrinated on the need for collectivisation and higher industrial production. Even Krupskaia, who had always favoured such a link more than Lenin, felt compelled to warn the party against taking this trend too far.[109]

The party's combined programme of enlightenment and political control prompted more direct criticism from the grass roots. As the chairman of a Siberian village Soviet put it to a local Bolshevik, 'What kind of party man are you? Is it really your job to busy yourself with the liquidation of illiteracy? Let the teacher do this work.'[110] Soviet historians have justified political intrusion after the end of NEP, using arguments similar to those wielded in the Civil War. In the earlier period initial White influence over illiterate minds had to be countered by Bolshevik intervention. In the latter, so historians claim, the kulaks and the priesthood became the internal opponents of the spread of literacy, since both groups stood to profit from their economic and mental hold over untutored peasants.[111] It is certainly true that many of the victims of anti-Bolshevik riots in 1929–30 happened to be engaged in the literacy campaign. One source states that more than 40 per cent of all literacy workers in the country areas were attacked within a period of nine months in 1929.[112] Perhaps they were unpopular simply because they were educators, but it is more likely that they were hated because they represented the party in the eyes of the local inhabitants.

An order of the RSFSR Council of People's Commissars issued on 15 August 1931, just twelve years after Lenin's similar decree of 1919, laid down that all illiterates between the ages of sixteen and fifty were obliged to take instruction.[113] This time peacetime conditions, greater financial resources and more stringent central control and enforcement had their effect. Already in his report on the results of the First Five-Year Plan, A. S. Bubnov claimed that in four years and three months 29 million illiterates and 17.7 million semi-literates had learnt to read and write.[114] Another set of official figures of the illiteracy campaign gave a somewhat less rosy picture. According to them, not less than 40 million illiterates and semi-literates had been won over between 1928 and 1932.[115] The exact numbers will never be known, but it is certain that the years 1929–33 mark the greatest achievement in the whole of the campaign under Soviet rule. The population census of January

1939 revealed that 81.2 per cent of the population over nine years of age and 89.1 per cent of the 9–49 age group could read and write. Thus roughly only 1 in 5 persons was now illiterate. In twenty-two years the Soviet government had dragged its peoples up to the literacy level prevailing in most West European countries at the close of the nineteenth century. A similiar feat had taken at least a hundred years to accomplish in Britain, France and Germany.

What were the socio-economic and political implications that lay behind these bald figures? The quick, explosive nature of political revolution and in particular of a political *coup d'état* like that of October 1917 has always contrasted in historical development with the far slower process of revolutionary social change. This contrast is nowhere better to be seen than in the social process of education. No political *fiat* like Lenin's decree of 1919 on illiteracy will in itself produce the desired social results. For social results, if not for a political change of regime at the centre, the willing co-operation of millions is needed. Education is a desirable attribute, yet even if both the political regime and the illiterate masses are eager to acquire it for the nation, the path to it must be long, since slow thoroughness is one of the chief characteristics of true education as opposed to superficial propaganda and indoctrination. It is not surprising that the aftermath of illiteracy is still apparent in Soviet mass media today. The tradition of radio readings still persists as one of the major types of broadcast, although the original reason for them has disappeared.

Special problems relating to Soviet education in the Civil War and NEP tended to put further brakes on schemes which in any case ideally should be slow. A rash of experimental educational systems broke out after the Revolution, causing havoc in the pre-existing structure. Instead of introducing them gradually over a fifteen to twenty year period, the pedagogues concerned could not wait even for a year to see the beneficial results of their utopias. There was not enough money to implement them properly, but there was more than enough inanity. One primary school headmistress proudly told a visitor in 1925, 'We are trying to relate the work of the school to the life of the city. We no longer teach subjects such as arithmetic, spelling, geography. That type of specialization has been given up.'[116] So much for numeracy and literacy. On both sides of the classroom there were human problems too. Many teachers fled after the Revolution, and others refused to cooperate with the new regime. The World War, Civil War, famines and the refugee crisis threw up hundreds of thousands of orphans in their wake, creating a major social and educational problem for the Soviet regime. In view of so many difficulties, it was not until 1930 that a practicable timetable was drawn up for obligatory and universal four-year schooling.[117] Long after that date a cultural gap remained between the public literate world of the school and the often directly contradictory private oral tradition of the pupil's parents and family elders.

As the revolution in literacy progressed, changes in social status resulting from the acquisition of the three 'R's' slowly became apparent. This was true in a few restricted spheres even in the nineteenth century. For instance, between 1880 and 1911 the number of teachers of peasant descent in rural elementary schools rose from 7369 to 44,607.[118] Thus an indigenous group carrying local prestige and heavily committed to the task of educational progress was growing quite rapidly. In the early Soviet era changes in social status due to freshly won literacy were most apparent in the lower ranks of the bureaucracy. The whole concept of the *kul'turnyi chelovek* (cultured person) in Soviet Russia is redolent of a society emerging into literacy, a society which claims to despise status won by money but sets great store by hard and newly won education. Literary and social polish went together. Mid-1920s pamphlets on workers' self-education remind one strongly of mid-Victorian primers on etiquette for the rising but still lower orders.[119]

The regime's propagandists used improved social status as a bait with which to attract illiterates into the ranks of the *kul'turnye*. They portrayed the immediate benefits available to the newly literate in many walks of life. Factory workers in their forties or fifties would shed their loneliness by undergoing a course of instruction in the *likpunkt*. Then they could read the literature in the workers' club, join in meetings where written documents were needed, acquire new prestige among their colleagues, and even get elected to the factory committee.[120] Soldiers in the barracks, who had been ashamed because they could not write to their wives, were attracted by illustrated materials to master the script underneath the pictures. Having learnt to read and write, they would, so it was claimed, threaten never to return home unless their families in turn became able to read and reply to the letters sent to them.[121]

As the Soviet Union improved its literacy rates, the old pre-revolutionary gulf between a small literate élite and the masses narrowed. In the 1920s many of the leading Old Bolsheviks, the *spetsy* and social remnants from the previous regime must have experienced the same kind of alienation that the Tsarist intelli-gentsia felt when dealing with illiterates. This tension found ex-pression in NEP through the novels of K. K. Vaginov. By the mid-1930s at least Soviet society was acquiring a new unity in this sense. The old social pyramid was gradually being flattened, sometimes to the detriment of administrative order. Recall for a moment Herzen's vignette of a frightened Russian peasant facing his articulate betters in a Tsarist law court with all the disadvan-tages that accompanied his illiteracy. By the 1920s we find the Procurator-General berating semi-literate local judges and juries for their improper behaviour caused by ignorance rather than through wilful illegality.[122] Instead of leaving ignorance to breed more ignorance, as in Tsarist times, the courts were criticised in NEP for not giving enough guidance to illiterates and uneducated defendants on how to present their cases.[123]

The road to literacy, however, does not necessarily lead to greater social unity. Reading and writing are normally solitary activities which are also conducive to individual freedom of thought and expression. Soviet Russia stood at the crossroads in this sense in the late 1920s. The route she eventually took was determined by pressing economic and political considerations which should now be examined in the light of the campaign for literacy.

The correlation between literacy rates and economic develop-ment had been noted in official circles with some alarm in nine-teenth century Russia. 'Illiteracy in workers represents the main obstacle to the spread of technical skills among the people and it is also the most important cause of low labour productivity,' de-clared a resolution of a congress on professional training held in 1895.[124] Even earlier, in the 1880s, the Minister of Finance, I. A. Vyshnegradsky, had been concerned with the level of skill and literacy of the industrial labour force. He stimulated a number of theoretical and empirical studies which began to appear in the 1890s.[125] These studies showed that a rank correlation between education and wages was evident, though it could not be assumed that literacy was the major determinant of the wage level. After the turn of the century further enquiries pointed out that in some areas illiterate *kustari* (home craftsmen) earned on average two and a half times less than their literate co-workers. Incentive to education was stimulated by illiterates' clear awareness of the economic consequences of their handicap, but a vicious circle often arose. Whereas reasonably well educated German peasants were capable of forming their own unions and organising new factories for the sugar industry, the Siberian peasant dairy industry quickly fell into the hands of private capital through lack of elementary knowledge. Economic progress and profits were needed to finance general education in Russia, but profits were hard to maximise on the basis of such a backward labour force and remained largely beyond the control of the lower classes.[126]

The same kind of problem was still present at the close of NEP, as those who were directly connected with production well knew. Party spokesmen in the rural areas at harvest time drew frequent parallels between the levels of Russian and foreign culture, and the need to raise peasant literacy standards in order to improve agricultural returns.[127] After 1917 S. G. Strumilin and B. Babynin extended prerevolutionary research by trying to distinguish between the economic benefits for formal education and those derived from skills acquired on the job. Strumilin showed that each year of school attendance contributed a larger increment to the increase of manual wages than a year of factory experience.[128] During NEP the slow pace of industrial development and the actual decline at first in urban population meant that the great majority of the peasant labour force never reached the factories and towns where literacy rates and skills could be promoted at a much faster rate than in the countryside. Marx's description of the French provinces at an earlier date could equally be applied in general terms to the Russian peasantry in NEP : 'It itself directly produces the major part of its consumption and thus acquires its means of life more through exchange with nature than in intercourse with society.'[129] In such a society the benefits and rewards of non-oral communication were not readily apparent. Innumeracy too was perpetuated through sluggish economic exchange with a minimum of financial liquidity involved. During the short-lived period of workers' control in the factories, one of the main problems facing the first and second generation peasant-workers was the lack of enough numerate book-keepers. M. P. Tomsky confessed that accounts done by workers were so bad that it looked as though the plants were being sabotaged : but he added 'I do not think it is sabotage, only Rusian illiteracy.'[130] Tomsky made no distinction between innumeracy and illiteracy, but there is an important political as well as semantic difference. Unlike words, figures have no political significance in themselves; only in their application do they become marginally involved in political issues, as in the case of workers' control. Lenin had envisaged in *State and Revolution* that any worker or peasant could become a book-keeper, but the process took longer than he thought.[131]

Even very modest rises in industrial production brought with them new problems connected with the low literacy rate. Town factories now provided facilities for employing peasants and children throughout the year (although the latter were supposed in theory to be prevented from working by early Soviet legislation). Thus at first the opportunity cost of sending illiterates to school increased and probably affected attendance at *likpunkty* at the very moment when the need for more widespread literacy became more urgent. This at least had been the experience of previous industrial revolutions in Western Europe. Another deterrent against literacy as labour moved into industry was the reluctance of both trade unions and managers to employ literate women, since they commanded higher wages than illiterate females.[132] As industry slowly became more mechanised so work accidents rose in number and frequency. The most common victims were illiterates. All these problems still existed during the crucial economic experiment of the first Five-Year Plans. They continued for the obvious reason that the productivity effects of the rapid growth of literacy in the Soviet Union during NEP could only be realised as the new youth became part of the labour force in the 1930s. Also, as we have seen, the greatest advance in the illiteracy eradication campaign came from the middle of 1929 onwards.

These considerations had an important effect on the failure in NEP to get industry on to a sufficiently strong base from which it could develop without the need for drastic political intervention from above. Yet at least one retarding factor was missing which had tended to slow down progress in Russia and elsewhere prior to 1917. In the nineteenth century the notion that men are born with their given status in society was still widespread. To teach a peasant or a worker to read and write was to alter nature and create chaos in the socio-economic structure. When an attempt was made in 1807 to introduce elementary schools in England, the President of the Royal Society said that it would teach the lower classes 'to despise their lot in life, instead of making them good servants in agriculture ... instead of teaching them subordination, it would render them factious and refractory, as was evident in the manufacturing counties'.[133] A similar view prevailed until a much later date in Russia. During the reign of Alexander III (1881–94) some formulators of governmental policy, with the shining exception of Vyshnegradsky, clearly aimed at preventing economic and social advancement through education. Such a policy had detrimental effects which could still be felt after 1917. When the First Five-Year Plan was inaugurated, however, it could be declared with justice : 'A long time ago we had already arrived at the conclusion that the expenditures of the state budget to raise the cultural level of the country ought to be considered along with the expenditures on technical reconstruction of production as capital expenditures, and as equal in terms of their importance to our economy.' [134]

In spite of enlightened official policy the continuing low levels of literacy and skills prevented the quick reversal of the pre-revolutionary hierarchy of economic management. It has been estimated that only 12 per cent or even less of those employed in manual labour before 1917 acquired non-manual posts between the Revolution and 1929. Former members of the exploiting classes had seven times more chance than manual workers of getting jobs in management during this period.[135] The position did not change very much during the first two Five-Year Plans. The consequences of a poorly educated proletariat were further complicated by the stagnant situation in industry through many of the NEP years. The number of jobs open to non-manual workers remained limited, and the *Rabfak* (Workers' Faculties) courses, intended to train the proletariat for management, were often filled by men of non-proletarian origin. The party's campaign for *vydvizhen-chestvo* (promotion from the ranks) was only a partial success.

A penetrating theoretical insight into the relationship between educational, economic and political standards, which is pertinent to the problem of continuing illiteracy in Russia, was given before the Revolution by J. W. Machajski, a Pole in Soviet government service who died in 1926. Machajski did not agree with Marx that the proletariat would be emancipated by socialisation of the means of production alone. It was also essential to bring about what Machajski called the 'socialisation of knowledge'.[136] He believed that even when the Bolsheviks abolished private ownership of the means of production, 'the 'professional intelligentsia' would still maintain its ascendancy by taking over the management of production and by establishing a monopoly over the specialised knowledge needed to run a complex national economy like that of the Soviet Union.[137] Bogdanov, whose difference of opinion with Lenin on a closely related theme has been noted earlier, likewise characterised the Soviet regime as a non-working class regime of intellectual office-holders. Bukharin tried with considerable casuistry to get round the basic theoretical problem posed by Machajski, adding a new element to Marxist thought in his *Historical Materialism: A System of Sociology* (1821). He conjectured that things like books, libraries, museums, etc., were actually part of the *material* basis for the further development of the superstructure. This was because they represented culture in a 'solidified' form. *Pravda*'s vehement denial as late as 1938 [138] that the intelligentsia constituted a new class of oppressors, and its scathing attack on Machajski's almost forgotten views, revealed persisting official sensitivity on this point. It is true that the party did all in its power after 1917 to bring about the 'socialisation of knowledge', but the process was slow, and some of Machajski's earlier predictions still bore an uncomfortable similarity to the position as late as the 1930s.

Illiteracy in the Soviet Union had an extremely significant though in some ways incalculable effect on the course of the political development of the nation. Economic and social influences resulting from widespread illiteracy made an impact from 1917 onwards that was bound up inextricably with political considerations, yet in a sense the final political repercussions were left hanging in the balance until the fall of Trotsky and the consolidation of Stalin's position in 1928. This was because the avowed aim of the Bolshevik party was to permit the masses, once they became literate and politically conscious, to run the country themselves through the dictatorship of the proletariat. The aim has prevailed in theory from October 1917 until the present day. For many political reasons which have been studied by others and which cannot be reiterated here, the possibility of implementing such a programme receded swiftly after the Revolution. The social burden of illiteracy is yet another reason that remains to be weighed in the balance here.

Although the incapacity to read and write is not an impassable barrier against participation by the illiterate mass in politics, it is undeniable that the acquisition of literacy makes a people more aware of the values and aims of the privileged literate minority and of its own relative deprivation of power. If the democratic potential of the widespread literacy that was achieved in the Soviet Union by the late 1930s were extracted for a dangerous moment from the general authoritarian political mould in which it was embedded, it is legitimate to suppose that liberal forces might well have taken root in Soviet society. The reasons why they did not in fact do so should now be given.

The persistent phenomenon of illiteracy in the first decade of Soviet power had led to the entrenchment of the Bolshevik party as the articulator of the dumb masses, a role which became increasingly difficult to abandon as time went on. In the revolutionary upheaval of 1917 the Bolsheviks benefited from very real political pressures exerted by sectors of the illiterate peasantry and proletariat; indeed they had to adapt their agricultural policies to suit the elemental peasant tide. These pressures were mainly destructive in nature. They led to the fall of the Provisional Government, and the Bolsheviks profited by the ensuing chaos, which they encouraged for a period. The untutored passion of the illiterate, so useful in a revolutionary situation, can contribute far less to the gradual building of a new state and society by patient administration. Workers' control on a mass basis failed partly for lack of diffused education among the ranks of the proletariat which might have helped it to withstand central Bolshevik criticism.

The party, and particularly the growing party bureaucracy, attracted literate elements of the proletariat into their ranks. Workers with at least some education were tempted to leave the factory floor for white-collar jobs with higher status, a trend which led to ambitious careerism after 1917. In an effort to rid itself of these and other opportunists, the Bolsheviks conducted a purge of 'bureaucratized and corrupt elements' in 1921, which cost the party a quarter of its membership.[139] The pattern was repeated in later years. A related and even more troubling dilemma was the continuing preponderance of non-proletarian officials in the party bureaucracy, a situation which was similar to the domination of economic management by the *spetsy*. Both situations were due in part to the lack of sufficient educated workers rising from below to take over responsibility. In view of this, it was all the more unfortunate that the small number of workers of proletarian or peasant origin who did enter the party bureaucracy in the early years were often motivated by private ambition rather than by the desire to promote the interests of their non-literate colleagues. Furthermore, as Stalin, Trotsky and Kamenev observed in 1923, 'Active worker communists, who should naturally constitute the link between the party and the non-party masses, are almost entirely absorbed in administrative and managerial work.'[140] The gulf between a mainly literate political hierarchy and the uneducated masses was being perpetuated in the first years of Soviet rule, despite all attempts to narrow it. In 1925 Tomsky urged the trade unions that the most effective way for them to stand up against the crushing influence of the party bureaucracy was to improve the literacy level and quality of their membership rather than to rely on mere weight of numbers.[141]

Within the party itself poor standards of literacy and education at the lower levels of the hierarchy tended to perpetuate and reinforce the centralisation of authority at the higher levels. Although there were slight increases in the percentages of party members with secondary and higher education between 1922 and 1927, the educational composition of the party as a whole deteriorated during these years. The proportion of members who had completed at least four years of formal schooling (92 per cent in 1919) declined from 82 per cent in 1922 to 71 per cent in 1927. There was also an actual increase in the number of communists with bare literacy, acquired by self-instruction or through adult literacy classes. This was due to the mass intake of manual workers and peasants after the death of Lenin. The trend may even have been accentuated rather than reversed during the mass recruitment campaigns of 1927–32. Even by 1939 four out of five party members were educated to less than the secondary level.

By the close of NEP the prospects for literacy as an instrument for the liberalisation of the regime seemed dim when judged on the basis of the record up to that time. The slowness of social and economic progress before and during NEP, caused in part by illiteracy, eventually led Stalin to abandon an evolutionary policy and to impose instead a second revolution from above in the shape of collectivisation and the first Five-Year Plan. The character of the massive literacy campaign which got under way in May 1929 resembled its predecessor of the Civil War years rather than the more relaxed campaigns during NEP. It produced a sharp rise in the national literacy rate, but at the expense of true education as Lenin had understood it. The chief aim was an economic and not a cultural one – to provide a barely literate mass labour force as fast as possible for employment in the Five-Year Plans. Krupskaia's comment on the campaign was that it 'has helped millions of people to read and write, but the knowledge gained was of the most elementary kind'.[142]

The fastest process of crude elementary education the world had ever seen coincided in time with the imposition of one of the most efficient systems of censorship known in the history of man since he became a language-using animal. With one hand the Soviet regime finally removed the vestiges of a pre-literate society. With the other it created a new type of controlled literacy that has become much more familiar since the end of the 1920s in other parts of the world. Stalin's policies catch the eye more than any similar move in history by their speed, ruthlessness and enormous scope. These three qualities were seen by him to be essential to the successful outcome of the venture, which was undertaken with typical Russian maximalism. But in some ways Stalin was merely repeating on a grand and exaggerated scale a reactionary pattern that had been revealed at other times and in other places. In modern Russian history it has been the exception rather than the rule to uphold a free press. From 1792 till 1928 there were only a few months (February–July 1917) when the censor was officially absent from the political scene. One of the prime motives has always been to control the minds of the newly literate public as it emerges into political consciousness. The Procurator of the Holy Synod from 1866, K. P. Pobedonostsev (or 'Lampadonostsev' ['Lamp Carrier'] as the writer N. S. Leskov sarcastically dubbed him), was the most notorious protagonist of this view in the latter half of the nineteenth century.

Strangely enough, some aspects of Victorian Britain afford an interesting foretaste of the Soviet situation. Britain was the first country in the world to grapple with the social and political changes that accompanied industrialisation and the simultaneous arrival of mass literacy. Pobedonostsev had his counterparts in London earlier in the century, who reiterated the famous notion Peacock put into the mouth of a character in *Nightmare Abbey* : 'How can we be cheerful when we are surrounded by a *reading public*, that is growing too wise for its betters.' A large section of the confident British middle classes in the Victorian era saw history 'as a kind of Hegelian dialectic stopping providentially and inevitably with themselves, projecting their own society infinitely into the future'.[143] The wide differences that in most ways separated their ideology from that of Marx and Stalin seem to be unexpectedly bridged here. The middle classes propagated their view of the world in an attempt to make the working classes over in their own image. Like the Bolshevik party, they claimed to be progressive. Like the Bolsheviks also, they at first put forward their doctrine as a science, which was as unchangeable as the conclusions of Newton. Passionately convinced that 'political economy' was the only method of running society, some of them tried to force a knowledge of this doctrine on the lower orders. Thus James Phillips Kay could write that the 'ascertained truths of political science' should be taught to working men, together with 'correct political information'.

Britain never resorted to censorship on the scale which Stalin was to adopt, despite these single-minded and authoritarian attitudes. Unlike the position in the Soviet Union at the end of the 1920s, there were other formulators of British public opinion with sufficient power to soften the edges of the paternalist doctrine. Although the growth of literacy in Britain was quite fast between 1850 and 1900, both literacy and industrialisation came to Britain relatively slowly as a whole, so that she avoided the acute crisis facing Russia at the end of NEP.

There are many indications in the literacy campaigns of NEP, not to speak of the more stringent Civil War period, which hint at the path Stalin's censor was to take later. The struggle to learn to read and write was nearly always seen as a communal task from which it was inadvisable to separate oneself. Those on the first steps of fluency were exhorted to read their newspapers and books in an organised 'circle' and not to imbibe knowledge on their own initiative.[144] Material conditions reinforced this trend. Often only one newspaper would be available to a large group, and one electric light as well. Central organs of the communications media were already intent during NEP on forcing local offices to do no more than merely copy what they produced.[145] In December 1924 L. M. Kaganovich advised all party cells throughout the country to 'struggle most resolutely against the individualistic tendencies of separate propagandists'.[146] 'Self-instruction circles' (*Kruzhki samoobrazovaniia*) were allowed no independence in spite of their title. Detailed orders on curricula, reading materials and methods were handed down to them from above.[147] Each successive wave of newly admitted party members was checked to ensure that they had received orthodox training in literacy and *politgramota* (political education). The Party Central Control Commission was particularly worried about the large numbers of illiterate and newly literate recruits who entered the party shortly after Lenin's death. Local agencies were instructed not to allow the new men to engage in the literacy campaign until they had undergone proper training in party schools.[148]

By the time of the crucial turning point in 1930, when the intelligentsia and the rest of the nation was put into the straitjacket of the Stalinist censor, there was less potential opposition than previously in the way of the shift in policy. Intellectual ties between Russians in exile and their Soviet counterparts weakened as the 1920s advanced, and the doctrine of Socialism in One Country helped to isolate the Soviet intelligentsia. The great cultural divide between the literary groups at the centre and the mass of the population became more noticeable as 1917 receded. Earlier attempts to bring high culture to the people had petered out, and with them died the series of literary and artistic experiments which had enlivened the first stages of NEP. It is open to dispute how long the great cultural renaissance after the Revolution would have survived if it had not been brought to an end in 1930.

The actual application of Stalin's muzzle need only be described in broadest outline, since this attack on the freedom of expression in the Soviet Union has already been investigated by scholars. Until 1925 there was no major party declaration on the control of literature, although *Glavlit* had been set up in 1922 to deal with specific matters of censorship. Even when the party did express its opinion in 1925, it turned out to be a policy of non-intervention for the time being. From 1929 the Association of Proletarian

Writers (*RAPP*) was used as an instrument by the party to attack its non-political rival, the All-Russian Union of Writers. Scapegoats like E. Zamiatin and B. Pilniak were found in the Union. The purge broadened to cover other intellectuals whose ideas were more likely than those of some high literary priests to percolate to the masses. Textbooks on literature used in the schools were full of the doctrines of V. Pereverzev, who was now attacked for his 'Menshevik' ideas. Stalin had never belonged to the large group of Old Bolsheviks who had close cultural ties with the pre-revolutionary intelligentsia. Until the fall of Trotsky they still had a very strong hand in the direction of the national culture. Stalin had few qualms about the wisdom of his new policy. The autocratic streak in his character came to the fore in a situation which encouraged strong policies. The second revolution could be jeopardised by threats from abroad or just as easily by social unrest at home generated by ruthless collectivisation and industrialisation.

The effect of Stalin's imposition of rigorous controls over free speech and writing has been studied in detail as far as the leaders of the intelligentsia are concerned. Just as important, if not more so, is the fate of the millions on the verge of literacy or newly literate. It has never been pointed out that censorship was tightened up at the very moment when for the first time in history nearly the whole Russian population was on the brink of being able to make independent, though perhaps naive, judgments on political affairs based on reading. It is conceivable, even probable, that Stalin had the masses in mind more than the cultural élite when he took action. In the future a regime of the type he was in the process of consolidating would have more to fear from a fully literate and free-thinking younger generation than from a hermetic élite whose greatest achievements already lay in the recent past. By ensuring that literacy would not come to be synonymous with independence of mind at a crucial and unstable stage in Soviet history, Stalin was helping to guarantee his personal position and the paternalistic role of the party for years to come.

The definition of what comprises a literate person, let alone a *politically* literate person, must contain within it a very wide range of capabilities, as was pointed out at the beginning of this chapter. By 1930 the overwhelming majority of the Russian nation was still climbing the lower rungs of political literacy, by which is meant an elementary grasp of the nature of political organisation and above all of the meaning of political concepts. All through the available materials on semi-literates and the newly literate from 1917 up to the 1930s, there is clear evidence of the superficial notions these groups had of the world of politics. A few examples may suffice here. In 1917 active Bolshevik supporters who had learnt a little about the Second International would board or sabotage, as the need arose, all railway carriages except those with the word 'International' on their sides (part of Cooks' Sleeping Car sign).[149] Truth is stranger than fiction in this respect, although the humorous fiction of NEP constantly plays on the same theme, often using episodes observed in everyday life. In I. Il'f and E. Petrov's *Twelve Chairs* there appears a doorman whose most savoury words of abuse are party slogans, though he remains oblivious of their meaning.

In the rural areas ignorance was naturally deeper and more widespread. Organisers of *politgramota* circles in the Smolensk *guberniia* frequently remarked upon the complete lack of interest in abstract ideas and theoretical topics.[150] Peasant leaders who arranged for agitators to visit their communities from the towns believed that 'sicilism' (socialism), as they called it, and electrification were to be classed together as abstract political concepts.[151] By 1927 A. M. Bol'shakov, an astute peasant observer of provincial manners, noticed that peasants were beginning to use political terminology which ten years previously could only be heard from the lips of cultured town-dwellers. He attributed the improvement above all to the wider distribution of newspapers in the localities. At the same time he was forced to admit that peasants mispronounced the new words and placed the letters in the wrong order.[152]

Peasants emerging from illiteracy at the end of NEP still remained engrossed in commune-level rather than in nationwide politics. The significance of this will be dealt with in more detail in the next chapter.

The newly literate millions were naive where high-level politics were concerned. Before the Revolution it was noticed that illiterates and newly literate people revered books and libraries as if they were the repositories of holy information. On the other hand members of the intelligentsia marked books and even tore out pages.[153] The whole system of Tsarist education was geared to the notion that the decoding of other people's thought was taught before the encoding of one's own. One learnt by repetition, not by creation. This passive attitude to knowledge survived the pedagogical experiments of the immediate postrevolutionary period and remained a characteristic of the Soviet literacy movement until its decline. The outpouring of popular political agitation after 1917 was carefully adapted to this frame of mind, relying on crude repetition as its major weapon. Lenin's and Stalin's writings also used the same method at a higher level of sophistication. Whereas Lenin was well aware of the device, Stalin probably fell back on it subconsciously. Stalin's own education in a religious seminary had been entirely by rote, and his mature style still carried traces of the Orthodox liturgy.

It is not surprising to find that at the end of NEP and for some time afterwards even highly literate townsmen still preferred to read Gladkov's *Cement*, the popular Siberian ballads of Pavel Vasil'ev and third-rate West European novels rather than the more complicated masterpieces of Russian literature. In the political sphere they took far more easily to the lightweight ephemeral leaflets that were disseminated by their thousands than to the more serious works of party historians or propagandists. Saval'ev's vulgarised version of the history of the Revolution was much preferred to the writings of M. N. Pokrovsky. If one recalls the very low educational level of Bolshevik party members at the end of the 1920s, their grasp of the finer points of the political debates that raged at the top of the party hierarchy must have been extremely feeble. Yet at least there still remained a selection of arguments from which to choose. By the 1930s a monolithic pattern descended on party discussions. The party rank and file, and with it the rest of the nation, was subjected to a single source of political wisdom and interpretation.

Thucydides, in his history of the Peloponnesian war, lists those general changes in human society which took place after a revolution. He observes that 'the ordinary acceptation of words in their relation to things was changed as men thought fit'.[154] This was certainly the case in the Soviet Union after 1917, at least as far as some men − the rulers and ideologists of the Bolshevik party − were concerned. Isaiah Berlin among others has pointed out how political concepts took on a special meaning under the hammer of Lenin's and Stalin's minds.[155] Max Eastman, an erstwhile admirer of Soviet culture in the 1920s, unwittingly compared Lunacharsky with Plato's philosopher-king : 'And now, after 2200 years, the king's son has come. But he has come in overalls and the old clothes of the farm.' [156] The same temptation was open to the philosopher-king and the Bolshevik leaders. They could fabricate political meanings for the good of the masses and impose them with comparative ease on passive intelligences. Such a course provided a useful release from the stresses caused by the dichotomy between a Marxist-Leninist ideal political model and the realities of the Soviet situation. A nation still in its infancy as far as political sophistication went would not be able to detect the transmutations of meaning involved. In the event foreign visitors of superior intelligence like André Gide and apparently diligent observers like the Webbs were also misled by the new uses to which political concepts had been put by the 1930s.

The manipulation of political definitions could be relatively ham-fisted and yet still be subtle enough for domestic consumption. The four-volume dictionary of the Russian language published under the chief editorship of D. N. Ushakov between 1935 and 1940 provides a good example. The introduction candidly refers to 'an attempt to reflect the process of re-fashioning lexicographical material in the period of the proletarian revolution'. The dictionary bears the stamp of its time in its aggressively doctrinaire definitions of political terms. An extreme instance is provided by the phrase quoted in illustration of the word *'podruchnyi'* in its fourth sense, meaning an assistant : 'The plotter and fascist murderer Bukharin, despised assistant of the ober-bandit Judas Trotsky.' More typical is the definition of utilitarianism : 'in bourgeois ethics – an idealist tendency'. The editors took the opportunity open to them in a newly literate and politically ill-educated society to include the words for dangerous tendencies of the past and to denigrate them by means of their definitions.[157] In 1934 academic respectability was lent to this trend with the appearance of V. Vygotsky's *Thought and Language*. This psychologist's work pleased Marxist theorists since it clearly recognised the role of educators in society in giving shape to what I. Pavlov called the Second Signal System – the mediating structures through which the stimulus signals of the physical world are filtered. According to Vygotsky, the mind of a child or a newly literate person was conditioned by the interaction of spontaneous and non-spontaneous concepts. The latter could be fed in by an authoritarian educational system and served to condition and control the unruly spontaneous (*stikhiinyi*) elements.[158]

A Soviet propaganda poster widely distributed during NEP depicts a blindfolded peasant in bast shoes approaching the edge of a cliff with hands outstretched. It was used as a visual device to show the dangers of illiteracy to illiterates. By the middle of the 1930s alphabetical and grammatical illiteracy was receding fast, but political illiteracy remained as high or higher than before. In this sense the blindfold was still there. It was all the more dangerous for the future of the country's political health, because the regime now claimed that it had been torn off, and the masses were inclined to believe the regime.

In conclusion it may be useful to stand back from the details of the Russian experience and take a broad, comparative look at illiteracy and its problems in the first third of the twentieth century. There were other countries with similar problems. Turkey is probably the closest parallel. Both countries underwent revolutions after the turn of the century: like Russia Turkey was an underdeveloped area with a preponderantly peasant society. Turkey's cultural élite had been subjected to long and increasingly important influences from Western Europe which permeated its revolutionary ideals. Both nations had substantial, ignorant minority races within their borders, and both suffered from low literacy rates. Differences are always more illuminating than similarities. Even Turkey's size and large population presented Lilliputian problems compared with those of Russia, yet in terms of speed and technical efficiency the Soviet campaign far outstripped the devoted personal efforts of Attaturk, who was just as avid as Lenin to educate the peasantry and travelled round Anatolia demonstrating the new script on village blackboards. Whereas the Soviet population was only 10 per cent illiterate by 1939, 60 per cent of the Turks still could not read nor write in 1960.[159] Attaturk's death in 1938 took the wind out of the literacy campaign, which, unlike the Soviet operation, did not retain its original energy at a crucial breakthrough stage.

For the Turks the literacy campaign contained within itself a web of religious, national and political implications that were not so directly bound up with the cultural transition that took place in the Soviet Union. Islam impinged on social behaviour more than Orthodox Christianity did, so that secularisation entailed fundamental changes in social values as well as administrative alterations. In the Ottoman Empire education and nearly all cultural matters had been dominated by Islam. The switch from Arabic script to the Latin alphabet was more than a symbol of progress : it severed the bonds with religious culture and turned the whole of Turkey, not just its élite, to the West for guidance. Lenin described similar Chinese plans in favour of latinisation as 'the great revolution of the East'. Chinese ideographs, like the complicated Arabic script, enabled knowledge to be restricted to a small group of people. In Turkey, as in the USSR from the 1930s onwards, narrow cultural nationalism prevailed in spite of secularisation and the jettisoning of other traditional values. A literate nation for both Attaturk and Stalin was an undivided body fully conscious of its unity. Turkish philologists developed a con-venient though ludicrous theory that a Turk had been the first human on earth to utter a linguistic sound as he contemplated the sun. Stalin put forward the thesis that the future international language of socialism would not be an amalgam of existing languages, as postulated by the Soviet philologist N. Marr, but one pure idiom, which, it was hinted, would be Russian.

Germany in the twentieth century provides a disturbing mixture of similarity and contrast with the Soviet experience. By 1930 no more than 10 per cent of the population of Europe excluding Russia was illiterate. The picture was uneven. There was wide-spread illiteracy at the periphery of the Continent, but Germany had one of the highest standards in the world. A multi-party system survived into the early 1930s, so that in the first stages of the Nazi regime after 1933 Goebbels had to contend with rival sources of political propaganda. Before the 1930s there was no sign of the impressive technological apparatus which Goebbels later applied to the service of propaganda. After Hitler's rise to power the Ger-man censor was confronted with an infinitely better educated and more politically sophisticated audience than the Soviet population; and there had been no trend during the 1920s towards authoritar-ian control over men's minds of the type that had evolved in the Soviet Union. Goebbels found it necessary to devote considerable energy to carrying out audience research in order to test public reactions to the censor and the propaganda machine. The rapid success of the Nazi campaign in moulding political opinion demonstrates that a high rate of illiteracy in the recent past is not a *sine qua non* for producing a passive audience. It also points to the degree of control a regime like that of the Bolsheviks may come to exercise over a nation when low cultural and political levels of understanding are coexistent with and manipulated by an effective system of censorship and thought control. Postwar history has shown the relatively transitory influence of Nazi ideology on the German nation compared to the lasting hold of the official Soviet doctrine, although it is hard to say whether the position would have been at all similar if the outcome of the Second World War had been different.

The strands which together wove the pattern of Stalinist totalitarianism were many and complicated in their combined effect. The effects of illiteracy were caught up in the pattern and perhaps deserve more attention than they have been awarded. Illiteracy was one of the main brakes on the achievement of the Soviet regime's early utopian schemes, but later helped to quicken the process of Stalinisation. Catherine the Great, in some ways one of the most enlightened of Russia's rulers, admitted that 'it is easier to govern an ignorant and illiterate people'. In the 1920s and even more so in the 1930s we are confronted with the apparent paradox of a government which was intent on providing universal literacy as fast as possible (and was much more successful than other contemporary regimes with the same aim), but which came to impose draconic restrictions on the uses of literacy once it was acquired. The ultimate motive was to educate the masses, so that life could be breathed into the phrase 'the dictatorship of the proletariat' : but this ideal gave way, at least in the short term, to pressing economic and political considerations which the regime took to be paramount.

The short term is still with us. The first generation of literates which grew up in the 1930s or acquired literacy as adults was so well conditioned by Soviet controls over political knowledge that the next generation was indoctrinated by its seniors within an established and stable framework of thought. The system was so powerful that it could be applied with some measure of success, although this did not last, to foreign nations with very different cultural and historical backgrounds. In a famous book C. Milosz has described the remarkable intellectual transformation that took place in Poland after the Second World War.[160] The ferment in the Soviet intelligentsia today, though it is scarcely apparent at lower cultural levels, may presage a more general attempt to use one of the highest literacy rates and educational standards in the world for independent thought. In his prophetic vision of the future, *My*, written in 1920–21, Zamiatin believed that a thousand years of Orwellian propaganda would not be enough to transform men into mindless creatures. In the totalitarian regime he envisages, an operation on the brain becomes the final resort of the government to eliminate the imagination and thus suppress any longing for freedom.

1 'V. I. Lenin', in *Russkii sovremennik* (Moscow, 1924) no. 1.

2 See, for instance, Daniel Lerner, *The Passing of Traditional Society* (New York, 1962) p. 445.

3 R. P. Browder and A. F. Kerensky (editors), *The Russian Provisional Government: 1917*, 3 vols. (Stanford, 1961).

4 The Smolensk Archives, brought back from this city in western Russia by the Germans in the Second World War, cover local party activities in the 1920s and 1930s.

5 A. Gerschenkron, 'A Neglected Source of Economic Information on Soviet Russia', in the *American Slavic and East European Review*, vol. 9 (1950) pp. 1–19. See also E. J. Simmons (editor), *Through the Glass of Soviet Literature: Views of Russian Society* (New York, 1961).

6 Sir John Maynard, *The Russian Peasant and Other Studies* (London, 1942) p. 13.

7 V. D. Bonch-Bruevich, *Na boevykh postakh fevral'skoi i oktiabr'skoi revoliutsii* (Moscow, 1931) p. 115.

8 A. G. Rashin, *Formirovanie rabochego klassa Rossii* (Moscow, 1958) p. 588.

9 Thus the question posed by Peter Laslett in *The World We Have Lost* (London, 1965) p. 194, is naive : 'Without access to books, without always being able to write as much as their own names, how could the husbandmen [*in seventeenth century England*] of a village where the politically active gentlemen lived be expected to think at all?' Clara Zetkin made the same error of judgment when speaking to Lenin : Es [illiteracy] hat das Gehirn der Arbeiter und Bauern davor geschützt, mit bürgerlichen Begriffen und Anschauungen vollgepropft und versucht zu werden. Eure Propaganda und Agitation fällt auf jungfräulichen Boden. (*Erinnerungen an Lenin* [Berlin, 1957] p. 19).

10 The most thorough Soviet analysis is in V. A. Kumanev, *Sotsializm i vsenarodnaia gramotnost'* (Moscow, 1967), which covers all three major censuses and many regional ones between 1897 and 1939. It also contains a good bibliography. For the 1897 census alone, see note 11 infra. Rashin also gives systematic accounts. See notes 8 and 15 in this chapter and his *Naselenie Rossii za 100 let* (Moscow, 1956). The most useful Western author still remains F. Lorimer. See his *The Population of the Soviet Union* (Geneva, 1946) pp. 52–61, 67–70, 198–201.

11 For the 1897 census see A. A. Troinitsky (editor), *Pervaia vseobshchaia perepis' naseleniia rossiiskoi imperii*, vol. 1 (St. Petersburg, 1905).

12 op. cit., p. 59, where the full logic of Lerner's thesis is spelt out.

13 David J. M. Hooson, 'The Growth of Cities in Pre-Soviet Russia', in R. P. Berkinsale and J. M. Houston (editors), *Urbanization and its Problems: Essays in Honour of E. W. Gilbert* (Oxford, 1968) p. 257.

14 *Illiterate Voters* (*General Elections, 1910*) (His Majesty's Stationery Office). Women could not vote, and the shifting labour force was inadequately registered.

15 Rashin, 'Gramotnost'' i narodnoe obrazovanie v Rossii v XIX i nachale XX v.', in *Istoricheskie zapiski* (1951) pp. 39–49.

16 John Aikin, *Annals of the Reign of King George the Third*, vol. 1 (London, 1825) p. 449.

17 These figures are extracted from Table 24 in C. M. Cipolla, *Literacy and Development in the West* (London, 1969) p. 115.

18 See also Rashin, op. cit., pp. 595, 602, for statistics on the literacy rate of industrial workers based on the RSFSR census of factory labour undertaken in 1918.

19 *Russkiia vedomosti*, 2 June 1917.

20 A. Knox, *With the Russian Army 1914–1917* (London, 1921) p. 389.

21 See W. H. E. Johnson, *Russia's Educational Heritage* (New Brunswick, 1850) p. 284.

22 A high proportion of the white priests – the 'white clergy' – were illiterate. S. V. Malyshev, 'Na proletarskikh stupeniiakh', *Molodaia gvardiia* (1925) no. 2–3.

23 V. P. Budnikov, *Bolshevistkaia partiinaia pechat' v 1917 godu* (Kharkov, 1959) p. 53.

24 *Protokoly VI s"ezda RSDRP(b)* (Moscow, 1919) p. 39.

25 Lenin, *Collected Works*, vol. 24, p. 553.

26 These were societies of individuals formed in the cities and towns for persons hailing originally from the same rural areas as each other.

27 For a more detailed survey of Bolshevik press and propaganda activities in 1917, see the two essays concerned in Pethybridge, *The Spread of the Russian Revolution – Essays on 1917.*

28 For the background to this notion, see Donald Fanger, 'The Peasant in Literature', in W. S. Vucinich (editor), *The Peasant in Nineteenth-Century Russia* (Stanford, 1968) pp. 231–62, and particularly pp. 254–6.

29 See I. Z. Serman, 'Problema krest'ianskogo romana v russkoi kritike serediny XIX veka', in B. I. Bursov and I. Z. Serman (editors), *Problemy realizma russkoi literatury XIX veka* (Moscow, 1961) pp. 162–82.

30 A. Herzen, *The Russian People and Socialism* (London, 1956) p. 182.

31 See Chapter 1.

32 Quoted from Bertram D. Wolfe, *The Bridge and the Abyss: The Troubled Friendship of Maxim Gorky and V. I. Lenin* (London, 1967) p. 69.

33 Lenin, *Sochineniia*, 4th edn., vol. 33, p. 55.

34 On Lenin's general fear of *stikhiia* among the masses, see Wolfe, *An Ideology in Power: Reflections on the Russian Revolution* (London, 1969) p. 145 ff. For the political and organisational consequences of Lenin's view with regard to the Russian proletariat, see Hammond, *Lenin on Trade Unions and Revolution 1893–1917.* Only occasionally, when it suited Lenin for political convenience, did he promote *stikhiia*. See Chapter 2, p. 58.

35 Gorky, *V. I. Lenin* (Moscow, 1931).

36 Lenin had always been clear-sighted on this order of priority. When a member of the Petersburg Marxist circle in 1894 pointed to education as a means of changing the social order, Lenin broke in with a cold little laugh : 'Well, if anyone wants to save the country through the Committee for Illiteracy, we won't hinder him.' See N. K. Krupskaia, *Vospominaniia o Lenine* (Moscow, 1931) p. 5. Lenin was well aware of the value of using differing styles for different audiences. B. Eichenbaum analysed Lenin's prose style and found that it consisted of three elements – the boorish language of the Tsarist intelligentsia, the oratorical style of Cicero, and a strong colloquial ingredient, which was applied to mass audiences. See 'Osnovnye stilevye tendentsii v rechi Lenina', in *Lef*, no. 1 (Moscow, 1924) pp. 57–70.

37 For examples of his interest, see his *Collected Works*, 4th edn., vol. 28, pp. 94, 461; vol. 30, p. 298; vol. 31, pp. 177–9; vol. 32, pp. 121, 127–32, 272, 505.

38 Ibid., vol. 31, pp. 368–9.

39 Lenin, *O narodnom obrazovanii. Stat'i i rechi* (Moscow, 1957) p. 414 ff.

40 R. A. Maguire, *Red Virgin Soil: Soviet Literature in the 1920s* (Princeton, 1968) p. 366. *Red Virgin Soil (Krasnaia nov')*, another 'thick' journal, had an average sale of 11,000 in NEP, which was a very respectable figure; but this journal too was not intended for a mass audience. There was no attempt to write down to the reader, nor were any of the usual devices for building circulation employed.

41 D. Lebedev, 'Zhurnaly SSSR', in *Zhurnalist*, no. 7 (1923) pp. 35–6.

42 The information on the survey is taken from a brochure in the archives of the International Institute for Social History, Amsterdam, entitled *Chto chitaiut vzroslye rabochie i sluzhashchie po belletristike* (Moscow, 1928).

43 Throughout most of the modern Tsarist period the Russian church alone was allowed to establish parochial schools among the Orthodox. See *Svod zakonov rossiiskoi imperii*, vol. 10, pt. 1 (St. Petersburg, 1857) sections 1476 (supplement), 1699 (supplement), 1823 (supplement), 3124, 3476.

44 *Sochineniia*, vol. 27, p. 228.

45 See *Likvidatsiia bezgramotnosti* (Moscow, 1920) p. 8 ff.

46 Ibid., pp. 39–46.

47 The pamphlet described is the *Sovetskii bukvar' dlia vzroslykh*, (*Ural'skoe oblastnoe gosudarstvennoe izdatel'stvo*), (Ekaterinburg, 1919). It is to be found in the archives of the Institute for Social History, Amsterdam.

48 Krupskaia, *Pedagogicheskie sochineniia v desiati tomakh* (Moscow, 1957–62) vol. 9, pp. 404–8.

49 See *Narodnoe prosveshchenie* (1920) nos. 59–61, p. 14 ff, and nos. 65–8.

50 V. I. Bessonova, 'Lenin i bor'ba za narodnuiu gramotnost' (1919–1924 gg.)', in *Iz istorii revoliutsionnoi i gosudarstvennoi deiatel'nosti V. I. Lenina* (Moscow, 1960) p. 301.

51 The figures for 1922–3 were 3535 'liquidation centres' and 110,800 taking courses. See *Pedagogicheskaia entsiklopediia*, p. 355 ff.

52 *Nasha zhizn'* (November, 1922).

53 *Leninskii sbornik*, vol. 8 (Moscow, 1930) p. 17 ff.

54 *Narodnoe prosveshchenie* (1924) no. 9/10, p. 18.

55 S. G. Strumilin, *Izbrannye proizvedeniia v piati tomakh*, vol. 3, *problemy ekonomiki truda* (Moscow, 1964) pp. 266–7.

56 Smolensk Archives, Thirteenth Party Conference of All-Union Communist Organisations (operating in the Western *Oblast'*), file WKP 275.

57 Smolensk Archives, file WKP 26.

58 One among many examples of this method of organisation and comparative neglect for the rural area can be studied in the meetings of the *Agitprop* Collegium for the Sitshev region of the Western *Oblast'* held between April and November 1924 (file WKP 10).

59 File WKP 275. The total population of Smolensk *gubernaiia* in 1926 was over 2,300,000 (of whom 9 per cent were towndwellers).

60 File WKP 286.

61 File WKP 249.

62 In 1925–6 50,925 *likpunkty* with 1,639,000 participants were recorded : for 1926–7 the figures were 46,826 and 1,516,000 respectively. See *Pedagogicheskaia entsiklopediia*, vol. 3, p. 355 ff.

63 A. V. Lunacharsky, *O narodnom obrazovanii* (Moscow, 1958) p. 322. It was also often pointed out that many who took more than one literacy course repeatedly failed to benefit from instruction. See for example *Otchet Leningradskogo raikoma vserossiiskogo soiuza rabochikh metallistov 7-mu gubernskomu s"ezdu metallistov za 1924 g.* (Leningrad, 1925) p. 66.

64 *Vsesoiuznaia perepis' naseleniia 1926 g.* (Moscow, 1928–33).

65 See Krupskaia, op. cit., vol. 9, p. 290.

66 See I. M. Bogdanov, 'Vazhneishye itogi perepisei naseleniia i shkol'noi v prilozhenii k zaprosam prosveshcheniia', in *Narodnoe prosveshchenie*, no. 5 (1928) pp. 109–20.

67 The figures for full party membership are taken from T. H. Rigby, *Communist Party Membership in the USSR 1917–1967* (Princeton, 1968) p. 52. The figures for party members refer to 1 January 1926, whereas the population census was taken on 17 December 1926.

68 Ibid., p. 401.

69 Quoted in E. J. Brown, *Soviet Literature since the Revolution* (New York, 1963) p. 52.

70 Ibid., p. 57.

71 *Tsifry o pechati SSSR* (Moscow, 1940) p. 14.

72 F. de Graaff, *Serge Ésénine (1895–1925), Sa vie et son oeuvre* (Leiden, 1933) p. 28.

73 See files WKP 2 and WKP 3.

74 Lunacharsky entertained the notion of a gradual substitution of the Latin alphabet for the Russian, on the lines of the transitional methods then being used in Turkey for the change from Arabic to Latin : but he was opposed to a sudden change, since it would raise a temporary barrier between a new generation of readers and the as yet unrevised Russian classical writers.

75 *Sputnik professionalista. Zapisnaia knizhka na 1922 g.* (Mos-

cow, 1922), in the Archives of the Institute for Social History, Amsterdam. Foreigners in the Soviet Union found that even well-educated Russians could not understand the etymological hotch-potch of the new abbreviations. See E. J. Dillon, *Russia Today and Yesterday* (London, 1929) pp. 71–2. Once Lenin was told that the 'shkrab' was dying out. He thought the word meant an obscure sea creature, but he was informed that it was an abbreviation for 'skholnyi rabochii' (school worker). This anecdote is given in A. N. Sokolov, *Put' slova.*

76 See Z. A. B. Zeman, *Nazi Propaganda* (London, 1964) p. 28.

77 For the details of Soviet administration of the theatre, see N. A. Gorchakov, *Istoriia sovetskogo teatra* (New York, 1956) especially pp. 43–4.

78 M. Slonim, *The Russian Theatre* (London, 1963) pp. 230–96, provides interesting information on the theatre in the Civil War and NEP.

79 See N. A. Lebedev, *Ocherk istorii kino SSSR* (Moscow, 1947) pp. 86–90.

80 *Film und Filmkunst in der UDSSR 1917–1928* (Moscow, 1928) p. 30 ff.

81 File WKP 249.

82 Quoted in D. Lerner, 'Communication Systems and Social Systems. A Statistical Exploration in History and Policy', in *Behavioral Science*, vol. 2, no. 4 (1957) p. 274.

83 Faithful reproductions of some of the more outstanding examples can still be seen in *Plakate der russischen Revolution, 1917–1929* (Berlin, 1966).

84 *Dreiser Looks at Russia* (London, 1928) p. 90.

85 Taken from Rashin, op. cit., p. 582.

86 A specific example of the deliberate organisation of demobilised peasants for work in the eradication of illiteracy can be studied in File WKP 25 of the Smolensk Archives..

87 M. V. Frunze, *Izbrannye proizvedeniia*, vol. 2 (Moscow, 1957) pp. 374, 381.

88 P. Sychev, *Zhizn' krasnoi kazarmy i krasnogo lageria* (Moscow, 1927) pp. 5, 25.

89 For the work of *Narkompros*, see S. Fitzpatrick, *The Commissariat of Enlightenment* (Cambridge, 1971).

90 *Izvestiia Tsentral'nogo Komiteta*, no. 10 (October, 1922).

91 *Pravda*, 7 December 1923.

92 File WKP 249.

93 Ibid., file WKP 248.

94 Ibid.

95 See file WKP 26 for advice on this point.

96 F. Engels, *The Condition of the Working Class in England in 1844* (New York, 1887) pp. 3–4.

97 For the role of the railway workers as agitators in 1917, see the chapter on the railways in Pethybridge, op. cit., pp. 1–56.

98 For examples, see files WKP 25 and 248 in the Smolensk Archives.

99 See M. Field, *Doctor and Patient in Soviet Russia* (Cambridge, Mass., 1957) pp. 20–21, 80–81, 87.

100 See p. 138 above.

101 See, amongst others, J. P. Gibbs (editor), *Urban Research Methods* (Princeton, 1961) pp. 521–2, 546–7.

102 The film is in the series *Kinopravda*, no. 22 (1925).

103 Lenin, *Ob elektrifikatsii*, pp. 28–30.

104 S. L. Rimskii, 'Udarnaia politicheskaia zadacha', in *Narodnoe prosveshchenie*, no. 12 (1929) p. 34.

105 Ibid., p. 35.

106 *Narodnoe prosveshchenie v piatiletnem plane sotsialisticheskogo stroitel'stva* (Moscow, 1930) p. 63 ff.

107 N. I. Boldyrev (editor), *Direktivy VKP (b) i postanovleniia sovetskogo pravitel'stva o narodnom obrazovanii, Sbornik dokumentov za 1917–1947 gg.*, vol. 2 (Moscow, 1947) pp. 127–30.

108 G. Romanov, 'Likvidatsiia negramotnosti nakanune XVI parts"ezda', in *Narodnoe prosveshchenie*, no. 7/8 (1930) pp. 17–21.

109 'O metodakh obuchenii negramotnykh', Krupskaia, op. cit., vol. 9 (1930) pp. 439–47.

110 *Prosveshchenie Sibiri*, no. 1 (1930) p. 66.

111 See, for instance, V. A. Kumanev, op. cit., pp. 220–9.

112 L. Kirsanev and A. Shishkin, *Klassovaia bor'ba v derevne i politiko-prosvetitel'naia rabota*.

113 *Sobranie uzakonenii 1931*, no. 47, article 357.

114 *O kul'turnom pod"eme SSSR za gody pervoi piatiletki* (Moscow, 1933) p. 10.

115 *Postanovlenie Tsk VKP (b) i Sovnarkom, O rabote po obucheniiu negramotnykh i malogramotnykh* (Moscow, 1936).

116 Scott Nearing, *Education in Soviet Russia* (London, 1926) p. 41.

117 *Direktivy i postanovleniia, O vseobshchem obiazatel'nom nachal'nom obuchenii*, vol. 1, pp. 97–100.

118 A. Kahan, 'Determinants of the Incidence of Literacy in Rural Nineteenth-Century Russia', in C. A. Anderson (editor), *Education and Economic Development* (London 1965) p. 302.

119 See A. A. Petrov, *Pamiatka rabochego samoobrazovaniia*

(Moscow, 1924) with its odd mixture of educational and moral advice, including how to avoid prostitutes and swearing. For a direct Tsarist link with Victorian England in this respect, see V. Gabbe, *Kak nado zhit' chtoby shchastlivym byt'. Sostavleno po Smail'su* (St. Petersburg, 1882).

120 V. Anan'in and S. Dmitriev (editors). *Po fabrikam i zavodam: ocherki proizvodstva i byta* (Moscow, 1926) pp. 162–3. The account is followed by a naïve moral tale in verse :

Po tserkvam khodili ran'she
Za nebesnym tsarstvom,
A seichas vot privykaet,
Pravit' gosudarstvom.

Once they went to church
In search of the heavenly kingdom,
But now they are getting used to
Running the government.

121 P. Sychev, op. cit., p. 26. This familiar situation in the 1920s is depicted with humorous touches in M. Zoshchenko's story, *The Patient.*

122 *Otchet prokuratory RSFSR prezidiumu VTsIK za 1926 g.* (Moscow) pp. 61–7.

123 See E. Dombrovsky, 'Deistviia suda po priniatiiu k proizvodstvu i naznacheniiu k razboru del po grazh. kodeksu', in *Ezhegodnik sovetskoi iustitsii,* no. 49 (1923) pp. 1137–8.

124 Quoted in A. N. Veselov, 'Nizshee professional'no-tekhnicheskoe obrazovanie v Rossii v kontse XIX i nachale XX veka', in *Sovetskaia pedagogika,* no. 1 (1953) p. 80.

125 A representative example is the series of essays entitled *Ekonomicheskaia otsenka narodnogo obrazovanii,* published in St. Petersburg in 1896.

126 I. Ozerov, *Na bor'bu s narodnoi t'moi* (Moscow, 1967) pp. 10, 11, 15.

127 See for instance the Smolensk Archives, file WKP 23, for speeches by itinerant agitators campaigning in rural areas containing very few party members.

128 See 'Kvalifikatsiia truda i vyuchka rabochikh' in *Materialy po statistike truda,* vol. 6 (Petrograd, 1919) and 'Khoziaistvennoe znachenie narodnogo obrazovania', in *Planovoe khoziaistvo,* nos. 9–10 (1924).

129 Karl Marx, *The Eighteenth Brumaire of Louis Bonaparte.*

130 *Pervy s"ezd profsoiuzov* (January, 1918) p. 119.

131 In *Bronepoezd* (The Armoured Train), a novel of the Civil War, V. Ivanov depicts one of his characters learning multiplication under conditions of harassment.

132 See E. H. Carr and R. W. Davies, *The Foundations of a Planned Economy 1926–1929*, vol. 1, part 2, pp. 470–4. Cf. N. T. Dodge, *Women in the Soviet Economy* (Baltimore, 1966) pp. 32–3, 140–2.

133 J. L. and B. Hammond, *Town Labourer* (London, 1918) p. 57.

134 *Planovoe khoziaistvo*, no. 7 (1929).

135 See R. A. Feldmesser, 'The persistence of status advantages in Soviet Russia', in the *American Journal of Sociology* (1953) pp. 21–6.

136 *Umstvennyi rabochii*, part 2 (Geneva) 1904–5, p. 55. See also E. Lozinsky, *Chto zhe takoe, nakonets, intelligentsiia* (St. Petersburg, 1907) for the expression of similar views to those of Machajski.

137 'An Unfinished Essay in the Nature of a Critique of Socialism', unpublished (Paris, 1911) pp. 16–17.

138 In a decree emphasising the role of the intelligentsia in the Five-Year Plans, *Pravda*, 15 November 1938. See another article in *Pravda*, 18 November 1938.

139 On the careerist attitude of new party members, see Rigby, op. cit., especially chaps. 1 to 3.

140 Quoted in Rigby, op. cit., p. 121.

141 Ibid., pp. 402–6. For Tomsky's observations, see *XIV s"ezd vsesoiuznoi kommunisticheskoi partii (b), stenograficheskii otchet* (Moscow, 1926) pp. 722–48

142 Krupskaia, op. cit., vol. 9, p. 540.

143 R. K. Webb, *The British Working Class Reader 1790–1848; Literacy and Social Tension* (London, 1955) p. 161.

144 See A. A. Petrov, op. cit.

145 See *Kak naladit' rabotu stennoi gazety*, published by *Gudok*, the central organ of the Railwaymen's Trade Union (Moscow, 1926) p. 7.

146 Smolensk Archives, file WKP 248.

147 Ibid., file WKP 286 (1926).

148 Ibid., file WKP 126 (1924).

149 P. A. Polovtsev, *Glory and Downfall: Reminiscences of a Russian General Staff Officer* (London, 1935) p. 206.

150 Smolensk Archives, file WKP 25.

151 *Novaia zhizn'*, no. 117 (1918).

152 A. M. Bol'shakov, *Derevnia 1917–27* (Moscow, 1927) p. 278.

153 A. Smiriagin, *Intelligentsiia i narod* (St. Petersburg, 1903) pp. 112–13

154 Book 3, LXXXII.

155 Isaiah Berlin, 'Political Ideas in the Twentieth Century', in *Foreign Affairs* (April 1950) pp. 351–85.

156 *Education and Art in Soviet Russia* (New York, n.d.) p. 5.

157 The information relating to Ushakov's *Tolkovyi slovar' russkogo iazyka* is taken from an interesting article by M. Waller, 'The -Isms of Stalinism', in *Soviet Studies* (October 1968) pp. 229–34.

158 See L. Vygotsky, *Thought and Language* (Boston, 1962) and J. Piaget, *Comments on Vygotsky's Critical Remarks Concerning the Language and Thought of the Child, and Judgment and Reasoning in the Child* (Boston, 1962).

159 A. M. Kazamias, *Education and the Quest for Modernity in Turkey* (London, 1966) pp. 174–5.

160 *The Captive Mind* (London, 1953).

5 Large-scale Theories versus Small-scale Realities

The study of small social groups is for the most part a twentieth century occupation. Nineteenth century social historians were captivated by the formation in their time of broader class structures and burgeoning capitalist and bureaucratic systems. They tended to neglect the rapid dissolution of many intimate groupings that was taking place. It is true that scholars like E. Durkheim and G. Simmel realised the influence of primary groups on methods of social and political control, and examined the web of their affiliations, but these men were exceptions. In recent years this gap in our knowledge has been more than compensated for, but Soviet history has not been subjected to the same type of analysis. As is so often the case, modern research methods have been applied to Western political systems, but not as yet to the USSR.

The nature of persisting small-scale social units in Soviet life through the 1920s is of especial interest, because in a sense they represent the overflow of nineteenth century forms into the post-revolutionary period. Moreover they were in sharp contrast to the more modern large-scale social and political structures that existed in Russia and, *a fortiori*, to the large-scale plans for future Soviet society cherished by the Bolsheviks. The ensuing tensions between traditional features on the one hand and, on the other, traits more frequently to be found in advanced West European systems by this time, had political repercussions that opened the way to the Stalinist regime of the 1930s. Whereas the problem of illiteracy affected the individual mind grappling with the intricacies of the changing political scene, the fragmented character of early Soviet society influenced the ways in which small groups of men either tried to link together and come to organisational terms with the central authorities, or else failed and became submerged below the level of serious political consideration.

One does not need to be a Marxist to realise the importance of the economic foundations which underpinned the small-scale structure of the overwhelming part of Soviet society. The two almost indissoluble economic and social strands were also closely connected with the factional political struggles at the peak of the Bolshevik party. As Alec Nove has written, 'This was "political economy" *par excellence*, and both the objective issues and the struggle for power were realities, which interpenetrated each other.'[1] The economic reality over the revolutionary period was that by 1921 the output by value of large-scale industry actually declined to little more than one-eighth of what it had been in 1913,[2] yet between 1920 and 1924 it increased more than three-fold. At the root of economic life in the first years of NEP the individual small-scale peasant holding was still the controlling factor. A slowly increasing supply of foodstuffs and raw materials began to flow from them into the large-scale industrial sector, set idle wheels turning, encouraged the counterflow of manufactured goods, and put in motion a process of cumulative large-scale growth. This development was mainly touched off by the agricultural revival created by households of which the vast majority, as A. Chaianov showed,[3] used no externally hired labour in these years. The vast gulf between small-scale economic realities and large-scale industrial ambitions could not be bridged fast enough for what were judged to be Soviet needs, and a violent economic revolution followed NEP. This change, and the political arguments which preceded it, have been traced in great detail, but some of the social implications have been somewhat neglected. The main focus of this chapter centres on these implications, although it is taken for granted that they cannot be arbitrarily divorced from other themes.

The vexed question of class structure scarcely enters into play here. All classes, however defined, were deeply influenced by external forces like the size of the country and the poor state of transport, cutting one community off from another. Those small-scale political and economic groups which made the effort to turn themselves into larger-scale entities on a nationwide basis, like the local soviets or the *kustari* (home craftsmen), embraced within themselves a cross-section of mixed class interests. The human agents who effected links of one kind or another between town and country, which very roughly reflected the division between large and small-scale social activities, became, often by virtue of their mobility, *déclassés* or Soviet *raznochintsy*. The Nepman and the Bolshevik agitator often could not be contained in any clearly definable class compartment.

In a transitional, unstable era like NEP, it was virtually impossible to draw hard and fast class lines. The revolutionary turmoil had thrown up new subtleties like the *spetsy*, but even more enduring social categories were often spuriously labelled. Class differentiation among the peasantry was notoriously confusing. The kulak, or so-called rich peasant, who was partly the product of the Stolypin reforms of 1906, appeared to be relatively easy to detect, but in fact this was not the case. In a generally impoverished rural society the material goods which set him apart from the so-called *seredniak*, or middle peasant, were so negligible that they could be swept away by a slight change in fortune, such as bad weather, the loss of one labourer or even a horse. Strangely enough, the most reliable defining rule had nothing to do with agriculture, since a kulak's small capital acquired through a trade or craft, or the sale of liquor, was what often set him apart from the *seredniak*.

There is almost no internal evidence of the subjective views of the peasants themselves with regard to their own prestige and status. We are left with the arbitrary categories imposed on them by the Bolshevik leaders and their advisors, most of whom during NEP had originated from towns and remained in them.[4] Their tool was Marxist doctrine. It is true, though astonishing, that the role of the class concept is nowhere exposed in the works of either Marx or Engels, despite the fact that the notion is used very frequently. It is virtually an undefined concept of which the meaning is explained contextually, yet in highly abstract terms. The Bolsheviks adopted the very broad class divisions discussed by Marx and tried to apply them to a society in which Marx had taken no particular interest. As far as the proletariat was concerned, Lenin eventually divorced its 'class consciousness', which became embodied in the authority of the Communist Party, from the empirically observed thoughts of real Soviet proletarians. To a slightly lesser degree the same thing happened with the peasantry. The reified Bolshevik concept of the kulak had little to do with the infinite subtleties of the actual class position of the richer peasant. Thus the *batraks*, men usually living solely from paid agricultural labour, were naively and confusingly held to be like proletarians by the Bolsheviks, who thought (wrongly) that official aid to the *batraks* and the *bedniaks* ('poor peasants') would encourage the 'middle' peasants to side with them against the kulaks.

The whole issue of class was clouded further by the changing party line during NEP, which meant that the diagnosis of peasant stratification altered according to the shifting arguments of political theorists.[5] Finally, it is doubtful whether Marx's economic postulates were of much use in a largely non-monetised peasant world, where barter prevailed in casual exchanges between acquaintances on a basis of good will. This was a far cry from the impersonal forces of the market as seen by Marx. The Russian peasant was not often interested in maximising output, and the family unit could not be described by applying standard theories of the main factors of production. In the world's storehouse of thought, it might be less absurd, despite the gross anachronism, to apply Aristotle's teleological scheme originating in the economic, social and embryonic political structure of the peasant household, rather than to try to adapt Marx to early Soviet conditions.

Even if an observer could disentangle himself from the morass of theory and get at the real situation, which in any case is impossible to do for lack of detailed information,[6] it is very doubtful whether a scholarly excursus into the intricacies of class structure would add much to our understanding of the social background to Stalinism. The general weakness of the Russian working class as a whole is what we need to know in order to follow, for example, the demise of workers' control. The almost universal apolitical characteristics of the peasantry cut across the somewhat arbitrary divisions of poor, middle and rich. *Sub specie aeternitatis*, the Bolshevik class jargon of the 1920s, although of interest as a symbolical political weapon, will probably seem ephemeral and superficial as a tool of social diagnosis.

A more useful method of approaching the study of small-scale social groups and their possible representation in larger bodies is to keep in mind the relationship between town and country in the first decade of the Soviet regime. This geographical demarcation can be too facile, but it contains less hazards than the definition of class, and it marks the broad division between small-scale and large-scale entities.[7] The slow but continuous process of urbanisation set up a continuum in society that cut across class differences and location in town or country. In NEP the few Soviet cities of any size were also economic parasites, still dependent on food supplies from thousands of remote villages. Yet in many other ways a dichotomy prevailed. The age-long suspicion by the peasants of central authority was reciprocated by the second-rate role ascribed to the peasantry in Bolshevik ideology and increasing bureaucratic mistrust, as the party took on administrative tasks like tax collecting in the countryside. Even when peasants moved into the towns and became first generation proletarians, they still depended heavily on their *zemliachestva* connections (societies of people hailing from the same rural area) in the towns, and were cold-shouldered by workers of longer standing, who resented competition for scarce jobs as unemployment grew, and feared the gradual dilution of their status as second or third generation proletarians.[8]

One final word of caution is needed with regard to method before turning to survey Marxist-Leninist doctrine on large-scale systems. It is impossible to make broad generalisations about small-scale social units in a country endowed with the size and ethnic complexity of Russia. As far as the social history of the peasantry is concerned, scholars have long been aware that one can prove black to be white, merely by referring to different parts of the country.[9] The minute scale of social and economic contact between peasants meant that each local community went through a different sequence of internal history largely unrelated to national trends. A scholar who has made a detailed study of the *skhod*, or peasant gathering, at the grass-roots level in the mid-1920s, concludes that of the three aspects of its affairs, agricultural business was almost entirely self-enclosed. Public services were largely self-regulated, since although the Bolsheviks wished to intervene, financial stringencies curtailed their efforts. Administrative matters where higher authorities were directly concerned, such as tax collecting, legal affairs, etc., were the only area of substantial infiltration from the outside world.[10] It is possible to generalise on central, large-scale institutions like the military or the bureaucracy, but again only with respect to their all-Russian functions, not on their dealings with local agencies at all levels. Until Soviet archives are as open to investigation as French rural materials, one cannot carry out work of the kind that has transformed the social interpretation of the French Revolution; but one must avoid the trap of drawing broad conclusions simply because there is not enough detailed evidence to nullify them. Certainly Marxist-Leninist historians, in reducing social conflicts to stereotypes, have been apt to underestimate heterogeneity.

Lenin was firmly convinced that large-scale social structures were superior to small-scale groupings. His theoretical predilections derived from the ideas of Marx and Engels on this subject. These ideas are elaborated in their most detailed and explicit form in *The German Ideology.* In their basic definition of social affairs, the authors refer at once to the mesh of relations on one scale or another which binds men together : 'By social we understand the cooperation of several individuals, no matter under what conditions, in what manner and to what end.' [11] Even prior to their discussion of the original small-scale social unit of the family comes the premise that man must eat and clothe himself in order to be able to make history. The economic factor thus dominates this most primitive type of social unit, as it does the eventual division of labour beyond that of man, wife and children. Increased productivity, the increase of the population and of family needs lead, in addition, to the unequal distribution of labour and its products, including property.[12]

Small-scale economic and social functions slowly enlarge in time to include wider interests, such as those of tribe and class. In due course destructive rather than productive socio-economic forces come into play, like machinery, money, and above all the difference between urban and rural man. For Marx and Engels the separation, on the basis of private property, of town and country is the chief manifestation of the social division of labour. The typical peasant is narrow-minded in social terms and has a small-owner economic point of view. The proletariat and the owners of larger amounts of capital are both town-dwellers, but all three groups have divergent interests which tend to split up society and degrade the quality of life. In *The German Ideology* the division of labour is treated in rather a confused way, with uncoordinated references to several relationships, such as mental and physical differences, the interests of the individual versus those of the community, as well as the economic, geographical and class contexts. However, through all these considerations runs the unifying theme of social fragmentation and the historical necessity to overcome it in some way.

The answer to this problem for Marx and Engels is not to

arrest society at the primitive, small-scale stage, which in any case they believe impossible to do for predetermined reasons, but to proceed with the larger-scale system of capitalism. Yet only the disappearance of private property can make way for the unification of all society into one enterprise, one factory, one association. The human catalyst for this final resolution cannot be the bourgeoisie, the first manipulators of large-scale capital and social units, since, as Engels says, it 'has its own special interest in each country, and since this interest is always supreme, they can never go beyond the limitations of nationalism'.[13] Only the proletariat can enter into an effective, supranational society. In Marx's words, 'Only with this universal development of productive forces is a *universal* intercourse between men established, which produces in all nations simultaneously the phenomenon of the "propertyless" mass (universal competition), makes each nation dependent on the revolutions of others, and finally has put *world-historical*, empirically universal individuals in place of local ones.'[14] The decline of the division of labour in universal society would lead to the end of small-scale specialisation in both economic and social activities. The proletarian equivalent of B. Jowett's gilded Balliol amateur would emerge, 'ein total entwickeltes Individuum', as Marx put it, who could 'hunt in the morning, fish in the afternoon, rear cattle in the evening, criticize after dinner'.

This visionary social goal is not achieved simultaneously all over the world: neither does the historical process fall into neatly divided stages. Evolution 'takes place only very slowly; the various stages and interests are never completely overcome, but only subordinated to the prevailing interest and trail along beside the latter for centuries afterwards'.[15] As an instance of this Marx and Engels noted the coexistence in their own age of peasants weaving for their own use with the new town factories producing for foreign markets.[16] Russia since the middle of the nineteenth century contained in an exaggerated form a similar combination of large industrial units and a widely scattered, fissiparous peasant society. The width of the gulf between the two aspects first became apparent in textile production.

Lenin's views of Russia's society and economy in the revolutionary period were coloured by Marxist theory on the division of labour to an extent that has been subsequently underestimated by foreign scholars. Lenin applied the stages of the development of capitalism, as described by Marx in *Das Kapital*, to the Russian situation at the turn of the century. Like Marx he stressed that the contradictions of advanced industrial capitalism need not be apparent, but merely immanent, for capitalism to be present in any given society. He therefore contested the Populist view that capitalism could not exist without a strong, large-scale machine industry, and went on to outline the organic process of capitalism through small-scale to larger-scale units that was taking place in Russia. He saw it as a teleological process, working up from the peasantry to the proletariat and endowing both of them, incidentally, with a gradually widening consciousness of their political role, although a nation-wide political party was required in order to bring the development to a head. Lenin admitted with the Populists that Russian peasants for the most part lived in tiny, isolated units of production which severely limited their social and political horizons. Taking another leaf out of Marx, Lenin pointed to the dual role played by usury capital among the peasantry.[17] On the one hand it accentuated immobility and small-scale dependence on money-lenders: on the other, it triggered off the process whereby peasants gradually became wage-labourers – a vital precondition for the evolution of capitalism. Lenin realised at an early stage how the influx of peasants into the towns would help to loosen the fetters of local relationships that had enchained them for centuries.[18]

Lenin's ambivalent stance on usury capital was repeated in his view of Russia's influential small-scale handicraft (*kustarnyi*) industry. When he wished to epitomise socio-economic and political backwardness in his early writings, he often cited the *kustarnyi* system. Yet he did not deny that it provided one of the best links between rural and urban types of production, and to that extent improved ties between the peasantry and the more progressive proletariat. Russian town labourers lived in large groups and worked in some of the world's biggest factories. In terms of scale, with all that this meant in terms of potential economic, social and political power, they were in an advantageous position. Of their own accord they had already organised themselves into agitational units based on the workers' funds, or *kassy*. In the light of Lenin's early analyses it is clear that his eventual call, following on the risings of 1905, for the alliance of the proletariat with the peasantry was not an opportunist move, but was the culminating point of a theory based on factual analysis that had been almost fully worked out by 1899.

Lenin's teleological ideas concerning the development of large-scale entities did not stop here. The crucial political deduction he drew from the socio-economic developments described above was that a tightly organised party was needed to represent the workers and their political relations with all other sectors of the population in a way which the *kassy* could never achieve. Only a compact party nexus with extensions on a national scale could encompass all the activities of the proletariat and the peasantry and arrange them to good effect. Hence Lenin's absorbed interest in *Pravda*. A national newspaper could bring into contact with each other all the local fragments of opposition and unify them. At this vital point in his argument Lenin drew a hopeful conclusion that was to be negated by a combination of ruthless political development and socio-economic backwardness after 1917. He believed that the Bolshevik party could not possibly supplant the historic role of the masses. On the contrary, only with the aid of a party of this stature would the masses be able to act on a large scale in the political sense. Lenin never jettisoned this belief, despite growing evidence that it was not being fulfilled towards the end of his life. After his death, the bridge was never built between the uncoordinated aspirations of the masses and the large-scale activities of the party. The resulting gulf led directly to the totalitarian conditions of the 1930s.

In the utopian euphoria of the early phase of the Revolution Lenin genuinely believed, as was seen in Chapter 2, in the immediate implementation of the direct exchange of products in a community freed from the dichotomy between town and country, large-scale and small-scale socio-economic structures. This was the experiment of War Communism. He acknowledged the Tsarist inheritance of certain large-scale industrial and bureaucratic developments in his *State and Revolution*, and thought that in the technical sense they were a necessary stepping-stone towards the imminent international socialist community. Their functions were simple enough for the proletariat in league with the peasantry to take over and run in their own name.

The continuing success of such an advanced socio-economic system within Russia could only be ensured so long as 'each nation is dependent on the revolutions of others', as Lenin agreed with

Marx. Despite Russia's temporary forced withdrawal into national isolation shortly after 1917, Lenin never abandoned this chiliastic vision of the immediate future, first expressed in his declaration of August 1915 that 'the United States of the World . . . coincides with socialism'.[19] To this end the Comintern was founded in March 1919. During this year there is hardly a public statement by Lenin on any subject which does not contain some reference to a universal society. On 30 December 1922 Stalin, like Lenin, viewed the creation of the USSR on that day as the prototype of the future World Soviet Socialist Republic.[20]

Lenin's main motive for looking to permanent revolution is usually given as the need to gain international support for Russia's underdeveloped capitalist system and proletariat, but beyond this, and more fundamental, was the desire to put an end to the division of labour and to create the universal man. This idea reappeared in many of his projects, even when they were not primarily connected with internationalism. For instance, as we have seen, he was confident that the electrification of Russia would break up the small-scale agricultural economy and the peasants' narrow psychological outlook. If electrification could be extended to neighbouring countries, he thought it would serve to replace national prejudices by broader international cooperation.[21] Bukharin and Bogdanov re-echoed the social and cultural aspects of Marx's forecast regarding the breakdown of divisive specialisations. *The ABC of Communism* declares that 'under communism people receive a many-sided culture, and find themselves at home in many branches of production'. Bogdanov saw *Proletkult* as the fruit of the new, unrestricted civilisation.[22]

Visions of this nature were typical of the early revolutionary years, and particularly of the Left Communists. As in other spheres of thought, the latter went so far as to ignore Marx's later pessimism which was not yet apparent in *The German Ideology*. Both Marx and Engels retreated from their prophecy that the division of labour would disappear completely. In 1868 Marx revived the phrase 'distribution of labour' and admitted that it was absolutely necessary and self-evident.[23] In this sense he showed more foresight than his Bolshevik disciples. The technological developments of the twentieth century have in fact created greater specialisation and more differentiation rather than less, in communist and capitalist countries alike.

The actual character of early Soviet society contrasted acutely with the aims of Marx and Lenin. The idea of throwing up a homogeneous national community overnight, let alone of fusing it with an international proletariat, was even more utopian than any of the schemes that were mentioned earlier in this book. A great gulf lay between approximately one-fifth of the nation which lived in towns and the remaining 80 per cent. This division corresponded almost exactly on the one hand with those who had reasonably widespread social contacts, and were more often than not employed in large-scale industrial or bureaucratic institutions, and on the other with the peasantry, geared almost exclusively for a variety of reasons to a small-scale existence that had little to do in social terms with the other one-fifth of the population. The *political* revolution of 1917 did almost nothing to heal this great divide; in fact, as we shall see, it made it wider in some ways. At first the Bolsheviks from the towns merely took over and nationalised those large-scale institutions, Lenin's 'commanding heights' of the economy, which had already become subject to central direction and organisation in the late Tsarist period. The peasant economy remained scarcely affected. Indeed, it stood in passive revolt against the town by refusing to supply grain. To this extent Marx was right in stressing the crucial role of the distribution of labour and of goods.

This ongoing economic dilemma of town and country affected the whole of the period from 1917 to 1928 and has been widely discussed. The social aspects of the dichotomy and its eventual political repercussions still need further investigation. In order to grasp the disseminated and small-scale nature of social life in NEP, we must first look at certain permanent geographical features which governed it. Russia in the 1920s was in some ways so backward that L. Namier's general statement referring to the second half of eighteenth century Britain could equally apply to NEP : 'The relations of groups of men to plots of land, of organized communities to units of territory, form the basic content of political history; social stratifications and convulsions, primarily arising from the relationship of men to land, make the greater, not always fully conscious, part of the domestic history of nations.' [24]

The territory of the infant Soviet Union formed 17 per cent of the inhabited surface of the earth. Mere vastness tells us nothing on its own. The relationship of human population to size is all-important. The natural resources of modern Russia, including iron ore, coal, gas, oil, etc., as well as purely agricultural resources, are scattered over huge and often remote areas. Paradoxically, the faster Russia modernised in the nineteenth century, the more she needed her population dispersed in order to extract newly developed wealth. Her accelerated pace of territorial expansion, approximately fifty square miles on average per day over the last four hundred years, also required the expedition of men over immense distances for strategic purposes. Travelling through Siberia not long before the Revolution, F. Nansen noted with surprise that its total population was under 50 per cent of that of the Scandinavian peninsula, which itself was one of the most thinly inhabited areas of the globe.[25] Virtual economic autarchy after 1917 meant that unprofitable crops and industries, often dependent on far-flung climatic regions, had still to be developed by local labour forces.

The massive preponderance of peasants up to the end of the 1920s in itself ensured a widely disseminated population, apart from the other factors just mentioned. The economic and geographical problem can be re-stated in social and political terms. At the beginning of January 1924 the membership of the Bolshevik party stood at 472,000,[26] out of a national population of 137,674,000.[27] Party workers realised the difficulties in injecting elements from the centre into every outlying region. Even in European Russia there were usually only one or two party cells to a *volost'*, an administrative unit often larger than a British county. As it was rare for all the members of a cell to hail from the same settlement, they might have to walk nine or more miles in order to meet another communist at the cell. As a result, most peasant party members worked alone and tended to lose touch with central orthodoxies.[28] In an attempt to counteract this, the central party secretariat in Moscow concentrated its courses of political instruction for peasant members on *guberniia* towns, thus ensuring that well-instructed teachers were involved : but this in turn meant that few peasants could find the time or money to travel the even greater distances involved.[29] A vicious circle was in operation.

The methods by which this fragmented society had to transport itself and communicate messages across the land continent served to reinforce isolation and immobility. Petrograd was notoriously out of touch with the provinces. Their large number, remoteness and dissimilar conditions all contributed to the communications problem.[30] The transfer of the capital to Moscow after the Revolution moved it away from the extreme edge of the continent and made the political and administrative centre coincide with the communications hub of the country, represented graphically by Moscow's nine railway stations pointing all round the compass. Yet many permanent natural features remained unaffected. The country's perimeter was very long, and most regions were remote from the sea coast, or bordered on the inclement Arctic. The Soviet Union was still practically bereft of aeroplanes and cars due to her economic backwardness. Messages and people moved chiefly by foot, sledge or horse-cart. Only a relatively small percentage of the population used the railway or river transport to any extent.

Railway construction, together with textiles, had provided the impetus for large-scale industrial projects in Russia. For long distance hauls the public, the economy, and virtually all messages in the form of letters, newspapers, telephone and telegraph,[31] continued to rely heavily on railway communications in the 1920s. Railways are a type of transport that fall easily under central control, and whose construction may even intensify political centralism, because of the rationality of disposing lines so as to converge at a central point. Like the absence of useful maritime peripheries, however, they can only serve as a secondary reinforcement of pre-existing leanings to political centralism. Canada similarly depends greatly on railways, has widely separated confines and high latitudes, but possesses a very different socio-economic and political system.[32]

It was precisely the all-important Russian railway network which suffered the most of all types of transport in the Revolution and the Civil War. The social and political effects of this in 1917 are discussed elsewhere by the present author.[33] Here it is sufficient to point out that by October 1917 the average daily wagon-loadings had declined to two-thirds of what they had been two years before. During the Civil War years they shrank by eight times more.[34] The loss of the Donbas coal region and the stoppage of oil supplies from Baku and Groznyi meant that locomotives had to use wood fuel almost exclusively. Difficulties in repairs[35] and direct physical destruction cut down efficiency so much that the few lines operating efficiently were mainly reserved for the urgent military needs of the widespread fronts. The authorities tried to get this information across to the peasantry in 1919 through the medium of propaganda posters, since they were compelled to raise the price of railway tickets, partly to provide more money for repairs, partly to inhibit travel by the public; as one of the posters implied, 'there is no end to the waves of people – and they carry a cucumber and a half with them'.[36]

It was realised at the time that the railway chaos cut the peasants off from town connections and one agricultural area from another. The rift between large and small-scale social units was increasing. The Soviet government calculated that 3600 railway bridges, 1200 miles of track, 380 engine depots and railway shops, as well as 3600 other bridges and over 50,000 miles of telegraph were destroyed by belligerents.[37] Estimates made in 1922 showed that at least £75 million were needed for the restoration of the main railway lines, and a further £100 million to rebuild the secondary tracks and seaports.[38] Such sums were not available. Over 1400 *subbotniki* (voluntary workers) laboured on the reconstruction of the Petrograd railway network alone in 1921. Only in the autumn of 1921 was a section of Petrograd's port reopened.[39]

Other forms of communication remained pitifully poor throughout NEP. Many of the great Russian rivers flow to the Arctic and are frozen for a large part of the year. However the productivity of river transport rose much faster after 1921 than that of the railways.[40] It is not so easy to destroy a waterway. Metalled roads and the motor vehicles to use them remained extremely scarce in the first decade of Soviet rule. Horses were still the most useful type of power outside the cities. Yet in Tver *guberniia*, not so far from Moscow by Russian standards (111 miles), only 66.5 per cent of all households in a *volost'* possessed a horse, and a mere .8 per cent had two horses or more, leaving one free for travel during work periods.[41]

The postal system varied considerably in efficiency according to which part of the country one lived in. In Tver *guberniia* it was as good as anywhere outside a few industrial regions. Before the Revolution letters arrived in the *volost'* mentioned above twice a week, although post could only be sent off and stamps obtained from the main *volost'* community, Goritskaia, which was ten miles and more from some villages. By November 1927 the situation had not improved much. Letters were still delivered twice a week. They were handed direct to the addressees by means of one horse and two pedestrian circuits, which also sold stamps and took in letters *en route*.[42] Given the disruption of all communications by the Revolution, and continuing illiteracy, the figures for any year during NEP, had they been recorded, might not have been significantly higher than those for the year 1913, when it was found that on average each inhabitant of the Empire posted four letters, received 2.6 newspapers or journals of any kind, and despatched .26 telegrams.[43] Certainly in Goritskaia *volost'* people received fewer letters in 1926 than they had done in 1913. The number dropped drastically after 1920 when Soviet citizens were no longer allowed to send letters free of charge.[44] Telephone connections did not exist in Goritskaia *volost'* before the Revolution, but by 1927 there were single instruments in one or two villages. It was too expensive for most private individuals to send telegrams, so the network was used almost entirely by the authorities. Whereas 577 telegrams had been sent off and 1158 received in the *volost'* in 1913, the figures for 1926 were 672 and 785 respectively.[45]

The impact of poor communications was felt all the more keenly when the *volost'* areas were enlarged in 1923–4.[46] In 1925 some rural soviets were still not aware of the laws concerning them which had been issued in 1924. M. Kalinin, the peasants' spokesman, declared that the villages in general were cut off from the centre and left to their own devices.[47] The social and political implications were alarming. The secretaries of the *volost'* executive committees, who were supposed to be the chief link in administration at the lower levels, were said to be unable to fulfil this role because of bad communications and the plethora of paperwork arriving all too slowly on their desks.[48] In April 1925 the Second Conference of Soviet Construction passed a resolution intended to deal with the problem of communications in administrative work,[49] but in fact little was achieved in this sphere during the following years. Lack of coordination persisted between the localities and the centre, providing grist to the mill of increasing Bolshevik centralisation. At the close of the nineteenth century the reactionary K. Pobedonostsev was said to have seen 'the works of the devil everywhere, in telegraphs, telephones and railways'.[50] Although some progress in communications had been made since his time, there were still few signs of that type of organised social and political decentralisation which Pobedonostsev had feared.

How did these conditions affect the millions of peasant family units scattered throughout Russia's vastness? This was the smallest and most typical social unit. If revolution is intended to cure unendurable social conflict by reshaping society as a whole, then revolution in this sense had scarcely brushed the Soviet village family by the mid-1920s. Embedded in pre-industrial surroundings for the most part, having sparse contacts with similar families living within a comparatively small radius, and even fewer contacts with the country's economic and political mainsprings, peasant households had largely escaped the influence of those central reformist theories on the family that were surveyed in Chapter 2.[51] Following on early attempts to break down the family nexus entirely, the prevailing Bolshevik view during NEP was that the family structure was passing through a transitional stage, since it was admitted that pre-socialist relationships still survived, that the central state was weak, and new social forms had hardly developed. The family could not as yet be abolished. Soviet citizens were advised not to 'shut oneself off in the family, but rather to grow out of the family shell into the new Socialist Society . . . to carry the entire family over into the public organisations'.[52]

The economic preconditions for the merging of the peasant family into broader social relationships were not apparent in NEP. Perhaps the most crucial phase was the entrance of women into social production, but this was impossible to do on a wide basis in the 1920s. Peasant women in particular lacked the skills and the literacy level required to take up jobs away from home, even if work was available. Male unemployment, and reluctance on the part of economic managers to invest in crèches and public dining rooms, meant that women were squeezed out of the labour market. *Zhenotdel*, a special section of the party, was responsible for drawing women into broader public activities, both cultural and political, but its impact on the peasantry was minimal.

It was not possible, for socio-economic and also for psychological reasons, to split peasant families up into individual persons, and to deal with them as such. For the Great Russian peasants all affairs revolved around the household or *dvor*.[53] This was a survival in modified form of the kinship group which had been familiar in feudal Europe. The extended family must not be seen romantically as the potential basis for an ideal socio-political system. It lived on in Russia because it was still useful in a backward country which had not yet discarded vestiges from previous centuries such as illiteracy, a non-monetary agricultural economy, and a paucity of written laws and contracts. The *dvor* could preserve what the individual could not. Thus the democratic concept of the right to a personal vote or to civic protection was alien to peasant life. Heads of households still represented other members of the family, despite Soviet attempts to ensure the election of village soviets by individual choice.

The *dvor* was imprisoned within a network of restrictive and inward-looking socio-economic institutions. The *mir*, or peasant commune, regulated the collective tenure of a small number of households, although it was not concerned with collective cultivation. Local government of this kind, based solely on ties of kinship, was incapable of solving wider problems of ownership. The *mir* survived from prerevolutionary times, and remained the almost universal controller of peasant relations. In 1926 it was claimed by the Commissar for Agriculture that 90 per cent of the peasantry still belonged to one.[54] Even by 1928, on the verge of collectivisation, the *skhod*, or village assembly, usually had considerably more influence over the affairs of the *mir* and the households than more recently established Soviet institutions. The tenacious grip of the *mir* and the *skhod*, and their importance in promoting parochial views and obstructing the forging of links with the town-centred Bolsheviks, only dawned slowly on the party. At the Fifteenth Party Congress held in December 1927, it was observed that the *mir* played an extremely vital role, to which 'not enough attention has so far been paid by us'.[55]

The *mir*'s methods of cultivating scattered strips and joint crop rotation, amongst other devices, made it difficult for households, let alone individuals, to opt out of the system and strike out on their own. Those that managed to escape to the *khutora*, or single farms, were usually the most progressive, thus rendering the *mir* even more traditional and introspective. Both for those households inside the *mir* and for those outside it, the mesh of social and economic relationships was compact and on a tiny scale. Many of the possible social connections leading away from a certain household led back to it again after a few links. It would have been extremely difficult for a central government with a far closer awareness of peasant realities than the Bolsheviks to build effective administrative bridges between town and country, to interest recalcitrant small-scale agricultural society in progressive ideas emanating from the cities.[56]

There was no real wish from the peasants' side to share in the wider awareness of the town-dwellers. Whereas the all-important concept of nationalisation was understood to be state ownership by the educated, the peasants took it to mean that the land belonged first of all to God and then, jointly, to those who worked it. For them the economic arrangement of NEP was not an artificial breathing-space after the exhausting Revolution and Civil War, but the preliminary move towards their view of 'nationalisation', which virtually excluded interference in agricultural affairs by those who did not till the earth.[57] In the course of Russian history the peasantry had often sublimated its hostility to central government by evasion or even by flight through enormous land masses, thus avoiding head-on confrontations. Gorky found that the peasants' obsessive wish for seclusion in small communities extended as far as the factory system, which annually drew in thousands of new recruits from the land into some of the largest single industrial units in the world. Gorky was told by peasants that the new proletarians were 'restless when they are in a big heap. They should be split up into small *artels*, with a few hundreds here and a few hundreds there.' Gorky was advised that diminutive, self-sufficient factories should be set up in every province with lots of space between them.[58]

The peasants had learnt through centuries of ill-treatment to mistrust all authorities beyond those they could observe at close hand in day-to-day transactions. In an age of particular unrest and suspicion they leant more heavily than ever on the lasting loyalties of the family nexus. This held good for the so-called *bedniaki* or poor peasants also, despite the fact that they were wooed by the Bolsheviks to form an alliance with the proletariat. The *bedniaki* received some material benefits from the regime during the Civil War and NEP, but like the rest of the peasantry they became disillusioned by the sudden turns in Soviet social and economic policies. Moreover, in their hearts the poorer peasants often preferred to emulate the richer elements of their class rather than to remain the foil of abstract and often ill-founded Bolshevik theories of class conflict.

Perhaps the greatest barrier to liberation from parochialism, greater than lack of communications and the peasant family and *mir*, was ignorance and lack of education. The social and political significance of illiteracy was assessed in the preceding chapter. Despite the amazing travelling powers of rumour in rural society, the oral culture to which the vast majority of peasants were bound curtailed the spread of information on all topics and reduced the scope of many activities. Rumour was a notoriously unreliable method of passing on knowledge.[59] The few who could read made scant use of their skill. If the figures for newspaper circulation in Tver *guberniia* are anything to go by, fewer journals were subscribed for in 1924 than in 1913, and these were mainly local newspapers.[60] However, news contained in them probably reached a wider peasant audience in the latter period. The local clergy, traders and government employees had been the main subscribers before 1917, and prior to the Revolution there was no organised procedure for reading out the contents aloud to illiterate audiences.[61] Tver was relatively close to Moscow and literate peasants could at least read centrally inspired news in their own language. The remote minority nationalities were even more benighted. In Soviet Central Asia both the language and the Cyrillic script were alien to the indigenous and largely illiterate Moslem population at this time. The Civil War only subsided in this part of the Soviet Union in 1924.

The attitude of the peasants to the workings of the central law, which in modern times is generally supposed to be applicable throughout the state for which it holds, may serve as another illustration of their parochial mental view. Before the Revolution very few cases were transferred from the local *volost'* courts to the towns.[62] In fact before 1917 and throughout NEP the *mir* usually did not feel bound by legal procedure nor even by the *mir*'s own informal precedents. Local justice was utilitarian and practical, directed to the maintenance of ordained relations within a restricted circle of peasants with scant regard for external pressures. Thus Soviet writers on NEP have noted the considerable discrepancy between sentences passed for several types of crime in town and country. The separatism that had characterised these legal or quasi-legal processes long before 1917 was in some ways enhanced as a result of the Revolution. The central authorities issued general directives after 1917, but individual communities more often than not ignored them. A whole gamut of different kinds of informal 'revolutionary people's courts', 'investigation committees' and 'tribunals' were set up at local levels, and un-licensed legal practitioners sprang up everywhere. P. Stuchka, the acting Commissar of Justice, had to admit that 'from November 1917 to 1922 law was formally lacking'.[63] Even after this period, central legal procedures barely intruded on peasant affairs. Very few court sessions were held away from the towns, which served large agricultural hinterlands. In 1923 it could still take fifteen days for legal documents to be sent by post from a *volost'* court to the nearest higher legal authority.[64]

The emphasis that has been laid in the last few pages on such subjective matters as the psychological attitude of the peasantry to external affairs by no means implies a belittling of the signifi-cance of those other, more objective factors, such as geographical and economic pressures which were discussed earlier. An interact-ing amalgam of them all affected peasant sensibilities. The Bol-sheviks reflected their view of the peasantry through a Marxist prism and exaggerated the economic aspects of the problem. The unorthodox Bogdanov went so far as to claim that the collective ideal of comradely collaboration amongst the proletariat had arisen directly on the foundation of large-scale machine production in the era of bourgeois capitalism.[65] Similar short cuts and *non sequiturs* were expected to arise from the collectivisation of the Soviet peasantry after NEP. Some Western historians, on the other hand, have tended to lay too much stress on mental attitudes. P. Laslett, writing on the small-scale web of social and political relationships in seventeenth century England, appears to maintain that the chief difference between the patriarchal society and industrial society is basically a psychological and emotional difference. He under-estimates the importance of the wage relation between master and servant and other incipient signs of new economic developments.[66] In any case it is not possible to divorce the two general influences which are often inextricably fused. An example of this is the social and political tension between town and country in the early Soviet period which arose partly from the mental illusion that each sec-tor was trying to impoverish the other all the time. The workers contrasted their lack of food and fuel with the relative abundance of these in the rural areas. The peasants were embittered in NEP because they had to pay twice the price for industrial goods that they paid before 1914. Economic shortages were thus exacerbated by psychological prejudices. In reality both sectors suffered above all from the nation's poverty and size, and only in the second place from the results of mutual antagonism.

The discrepancy between Marxist-Leninist large-scale ambitions and the real character of the overwhelming sector of the nation's social and economic life was very striking. More than this, small-scale features appeared actually to be gaining ground from the Revolution to about the middle of the 1920s. Instead of being 'subordinated to the prevailing interest' of Marx's large-scale progress,[67] they threatened to overwhelm and even wipe out central administration and control.

It is hardly an exaggeration to say that during 1917 two distinct though almost simultaneous revolutions took place. The struggle in the towns had few connections with the peasant *jacqueries* in the countryside. The urban Bolsheviks eventually tried to subsume peasant interests by taking over the agricultural programme of the Socialist Revolutionaries, which had met with some success in the rural areas. Lenin's long-term plans for land did not coincide with peasant opinion, although this did not become plain to the peasantry until some time after 1917. The outbreak of the Civil War and the different social alignments behind conflicting military camps gave clear evidence of the fragmentation of social unity. The Bolshevik-controlled areas of Russia were reduced to the size of medieval Muscovy at one stage of the War, and whole minority nationalities in addition to segments of the Great Russian population attempted to break off all relations with Moscow.

Bukharin, in a gloss on Marx, admitted that 'under certain conditions, society may dissolve into a number of societies (usually under conditions of decline)'.[68] He also claimed that the basic criterion for a single society was a united geographical network of what he called 'social technology', or system of tools of labour. 'In some places they are crowded close together (for instance, in the great industrial centres), in other places, *other* tools are *scattered*;' but so long as the whole population was connected by an adequate labour relation, social unity would survive. As an example, Bukharin claimed that if all the machines serving the purposes of coal mining in contemporary Germany should miraculously ascend to heaven, the entire socio-economic process would be disrupted.[69] Making allowances for the crude causal relationship between social and economic factors in Bukharin's line of thought, it seems clear that according to his definition of society as 'the broadest system of mutually interacting persons, embracing all their permanent mutual interactions, and based upon their labour relations',[70] a united society did not exist in Russia from February 1917. Nor was it fully reconstituted by non-coercive means thereafter. The widely divergent interests of town and country continued to be in conflict until the large-scale collectivisation of agriculture finally harnessed one sector to the other by force.

The process of social, economic and even occasional political self-sufficiency accelerated in the immediate postrevolutionary period. We have seen how communications between town and country were severed in the Civil War. Within each of these quasi-autarchic sectors, moreover, a trend towards disintegration rapidly developed. In the dominating peasant sector most of the large peasant holdings established as a result of the Stolypin reform were broken up and distributed. The Bolshevik decree on land gave sanction to the peasants' seizure and decimation of the landlords' estates which had already begun between the February and October Revolutions. The number of *dvors* rose from 16 million in 1917 to 24 million in 1924. If one surveys the long, troubled history of agriculture from the emancipation of the serfs to the present day, the overall social effect of land fragmentation probably remains greater than the impact of Stalin's collectivisation. At the outset of this period, in 1859, P. O. Kiselev, the Tsarist Minister for Agriculture, prophesied that fragmentation would have long-term social repercussions and would be harmful to any fundamental improvements in agriculture.[71] At the present time, forty years after collectivisation, the legacy from the days of separate homesteads lives on in the *kolkhozy*. Fields are still restricted to their original size, and the methods of running these large units are often more appropriate to a small family farm.[72]

After 1917 the decline in size of the most concentrated social units, the towns, had even more serious implications for the cohesiveness of the country as a whole. The big drop in large-scale industrial production at this time has already been mentioned.[73] The total population also fell during the Civil War, but the decrease in town-dwellers was far greater in proportion to the depopulation of the rural areas. Urban inhabitants, who numbered 29 million (20.4 per cent of the total) on 1 January 1917, were reduced to 21.1 million (15.7 per cent) by 28 August 1920.[74] It was estimated that the population of Petrograd dropped from 2.25

million in 1917 to 700,000 in 1920.[75] The distribution of the national population between town and country regained the 1914 pattern (cities equalling 18.5 per cent of the total) by the end of 1928 only.[76] The reasons for the decline of the towns were numerous and interlocking. The upper and middle classes forsook their town houses, followed by many of their ex-servants. The vast Tsarist bureaucracy, centred on the old capital, dissolved. Foreign trade dried up and vital domestic raw materials for factory processing no longer reached the towns. Disease, cold and hunger drove out thousands more.[77]

The crucial point about this general decline was the flight of the workers from the cities. Only 2.5 million were left in industry at the start of 1918, representing a fall of half a million since the beginning of 1917. Unemployment alone could not account for these figures, because many factories continued to function until the summer of 1918. A million workers joined the Red Army and so left the towns. Another 300,000 or so, many of them first generation proletarians, went to the villages, hoping that they would benefit from the redistribution of the land. Here at last was a strong link between town and country, but it was socially and economically retrogressive. The dissolution of the proletariat weakened the social influence of the towns as it did the efficiency of large-scale industry. More important still, it widened the gap between Lenin's aspirations for political leadership by the proletariat and the tragic reality. The Bolshevik party, as we have seen, could not tolerate the notion at this time that workers' control, or even the trade unions, might vie with it as the political vanguard of the nation.

When H. G. Wells asked Lenin in September 1920 how far he contemplated the dying out of towns in Russia, Lenin replied: 'The towns will get very much smaller ... They will be different. Yes, quite different.' Wells then implied that the existing towns would have to be scrapped. The great buildings of Petrograd might become like those of Novgorod the Great or the temples at Paestum. Lenin 'agreed quite cheerfully',[78] without giving his reasons. Either he was pulling Wells's leg, or, more likely, he optimistically viewed such a development as a kind of *smychka* or blending of town and country on a grand scale. Time showed that this was not to be the case. Urban depopulation was a temporary phenomenon, and it did not promote *smychka*.

Russia was faced with the real threat of complete social disintegration under the impact of the Revolution. The linchpin of the autocrat was removed in February 1917 together with the top-heavy bureaucracy which had contrived to maintain some kind of social cohesion in the Empire. The influence of the gentry and the middle strata of society collapsed in the course of the next few months. This was more crucial for the social future of the state than the end of the Romanovs. The liberal wing of the gentry and professional men had slowly begun to build administrative bridges between the over-centralised bureaucracy and small-scale society. The *zemstvo* system, if it had been allowed to develop, might have provided an essential buffer between the polarised elements in society. The political *coup* of the far left wing in October 1917 set the seal on the fate of the liberals. The social vacuum caused by the emigration was enormous. This theme remains a question for speculation rather than for scholarship, since only vague hypotheses can be made as to the amount of talent wasted. The numbers involved were very high. Estimates vary from less than one million to nearly three,[79] but even the lowest figure must have included a great part of the nation's human capability.

It is true that the economic influence of the gentry in particular had declined steeply since the Emancipation of the Serfs. It was poorly adapted to a society in the process of fast industrialisation.[80] Yet as a class, together with recruits from lower social layers, it still formed the backbone of the two main instruments approved by the Autocracy for manipulating the masses, i.e. the state bureaucracy and the armed forces. More important than this, the gentry, professional people and the merchants represented the best-informed, most mobile and widespread informal social network in the provinces, whilst at the same time keeping up close contacts with the political mainsprings of the country. During the English Civil War the rural gentry, which comprised one-twentieth of the total population and pervaded two-thirds of English territory with its influence at the grass-roots level, successfully took over the administration of the country when the Crown lost touch. Both continuity *and* political progress were thus ensured. The loss of the Russian landlord, the local lawyer, doctor and even the reactionary priest had an incalculable effect on the future relations, or lack of them, between the Bolsheviks and the masses.

The gap left by the departure of the monarchy was eventually filled by the Bolshevik party, which proved to be the only central authority capable of wielding adequate control over the whole of the country. It struggled against great odds. Small in numbers, hindered by a Civil War and a ruined economy, blinkered by its atypical Marxist and urban viewpoint, it only grasped the nettle of how to make effective radical changes in society at the close of NEP. The method of carrying out these changes was greatly influenced not only by the recalcitrant nature of Soviety society, but also by the party's previous experience of trying to control its own scattered local organisations from one centre. This experience in turn was preconditioned by Lenin's authoritarian view of party hierarchy as expounded in *What is To Be Done?* before the Revolution.

The general trend towards a highly centralised party autocracy has often been described,[81] and it may be taken for granted here. The first five years of Bolshevik power were threatened by continual factional struggles in the local party organisations. Many of these fights typically had nothing to do with central aims and everything to do with separate local affairs. The danger of complete breaks between the centre and the provincial cells in the middle of a Civil War was such that the party was able to apply draconic measures to bring its members to heel without stirring up very much high-level opposition. By 1923 only the central Bolshevik *apparat* counted : the mass of party members, particularly in the localities, merely obeyed. It had not been possible to link them up into a well-balanced system with due weight apportioned to both the provinces and the capital. In the words of Trotsky, addressing the party Central Committee in October 1923 :

> There has been created a very broad stratum of party workers, entering into the apparatus of the government of the party, who completely renounce their own party opinion, at least the open expression of it, as though assuming that the secretarial hierarchy is the apparatus which creates party opinion and party decisions. Beneath this stratum, there lies the broad mass of the party, before whom every decision stands in the form of a summons or a command.[82]

Just ten years later, other party leaders were noticing belatedly how this command structure had a cumulative and adverse effect on the geographical location of good party workers. As I. Skvortsov-Stepanov remarked, 'The provinces have become deserted. It is often noticed that the countryside is afraid to send somebody to the centre, for as soon as this happens the comrade in question goes to the Central Committee, gives his views there on how necessary it is for him to stay at the centre, and stays there. In this way the centre pumps the living forces out of the countryside. It cannot go on like this.'[83] In fact the position had been acute for at least six years prior to this statement of 1933.[84]

From October 1917 to the end of NEP the Bolsheviks made genuine attempts to narrow the socio-economic gap between themselves at the centre and the rest of society. Continual failures finally led to the abandonment of careful bridge-building. The party eventually resorted to the same coercive, arbitrary procedures with regard to social institutions that it had already applied to its own internal organisation. The painfully slow emergence of auxiliary socio-political bodies with a slight measure of autonomy was halted before they had a fighting chance of survival. In different contexts we have already seen this abortive process in action in workers' control and the idea of a national militia. The former failed because the proletariat was not competent to take on an advisory role in industry. No less formidable a reason, however, was Lenin's determination that it should fail.[85] A large number of diverse opinions on factory management, such as might be created by the notion of ownership-sharing, could lead to renewed economic struggles. As Bukharin put it, 'If, by our division, we would produce small owners, the following would occur – the richer would overcome the poorer ... They would ensnare the workers and would thus gradually become true capitalists.'[86] Lenin explained in 1918 that one-man management was vital in order to make the transition from small-scale production to large-scale trusts. To build these trusts, he believed that the advice of former capitalists was needed. Those who had participated in workers' control should now learn from the experience of capitalist technicians how to manage industry. The introduction of NEP should in theory have helped the workers through the trade unions to regain part of their independence, but this did not come about, since the few large-scale industries which employed the vast majority of trade union members stayed mainly under state ownership and close party supervision.

The hope of replacing a centralised standing army by a network of local militias suffered a similar fast eclipse. Here again Lenin's and Trotsky's determination to maintain a regular army to defend the party in time of peril was of cardinal importance, but external influences stemming from the diffuse nature of Russian society also weighed heavily. I. Smilga pointed out [87] that it would be technically impossible for a scattered militia to concentrate quickly in time of war on account of the poor state of communications.[88] The territorial principle of recruiting a militia would mean that a small number of townsmen and proletarians would be swamped by massive peasant numbers. Correct social and political guidance would be dimmed, and widespread desertions might take place in the remote localities.[89] The militia persisted in a much diluted form until the 1930s. Overshadowed by a large regular army, it presented no disintegrating challenge to the political leadership.

Neither did the Soviet network, another survival of revolutionary idealism, which was supposed to provide the instance *par excellence* of an intricate network which could in time link the party to the people, the town to the countryside. The functions of the Soviets in this respect, as ascribed to them by the Bolsheviks, have been interpreted too literally by non-communist scholars. The atrophy of the Soviet system after 1917 and its strict subordination to the centralised party have been described in considerable detail.[90] What is of interest to us here is the contrast between the somewhat naive trust Lenin and others put in it before and during 1917 as an alternative to hierarchical administration, and the failure of the system to live up to this ideal after the Revolution. Both Lenin and Bukharin saw the Soviets as the 'fundamental organisations'[91] of the new social system. They were to serve as the antidote to prerevolutionary large-scale bureaucracy. Their structure seemed well adapted to this purpose, since during 1917 their numbers proliferated throughout the localities, throwing up a spontaneously formed network that might have allowed a more permanent type of mass social influence to percolate from the periphery to the political centre. The local Soviets did in fact become the main formal agents during 1917–18 for the organisation of workers' control and the confiscation of land, which were the two main fissiparous social processes at work among the proletariat and peasantry respectively. In theory the vertical Tsarist bureaucracy, supplemented by the semi-autonomous horizontal *zemstvo* administration on a territorial basis, was to be replaced by the unified Soviet network, which was the architectural expression of democratic centralism, a kind of spatial projection of political and social power at all levels. As Lenin put it in *State and Revolution*, there was to be an 'immediate introduction of control and supervision by *all*, so that *all* may become bureaucrats for a time and that, therefore, nobody may be able to become a bureaucrat'.[92]

It is striking that in his earliest practical efforts during 1917 and shortly afterwards to stamp out Russia's traditional dichotomies between large-scale and small-scale entities, Lenin tended to sacrifice the centre, the town, the large group to their opposites. We have seen this leaning in his original attitude to workers' control, to the militia, and even to the precipitous decline of city populations. It also coloured the first stages of his strategy for winning a Bolshevik victory in 1917. Lenin relied (ill-advisedly as it turned out) on initial support from the localities, which he hoped would swamp the industrial centres with left-wing influences.[93] But as in all other spheres, Lenin rapidly changed his mind when the full anarchic implications of these tactics became clear. The Soviet system declined, like workers' control, under the dual constraint of Bolshevik mistrust and the inability of local bodies to run themselves efficiently and link up with the centre.

Just as the establishment of local Soviets often preceded the formation of Bolshevik party cells in the provinces during 1917, so the subsequent loss of authority to the All-Russian Congress of Soviets from the local organs developed prior to the corresponding centralisation of party organisation in the period 1917–21.[94] Once the party had set its own house in order, it went on to suck out all the remaining vestiges of independence still left in local Soviet administration. As early as March 1919 this was made crystal clear at the Eighth Party Congress: '... The Russian Communist Party must win for itself undivided political mastery in the Soviets and practical control over all their work.'[95] Lenin gave in to the trend, declaring by 1921, 'We could not help fusing the Soviet "authorities" with the party "authorities" – with us they are fused and they will be.'[96] The ideal vision of the Soviets as the conciliator between the centre and the masses was largely abandoned. The huge local network was left intact but reduced to an educational machine under the thumb of the party. Lenin now stressed that 'Only in the Soviets does the mass of the exploited begin really to learn, not from books, but from their own practical experience, the business of socialist construction ...'[97] Yet even the independence of this essential privilege was suspect. When Lunacharsky and Krupskaia advocated the establishment of educational Soviets elected by the masses themselves at the lowest administrative levels, the scheme was rejected out of hand by the party leaders. Krupskaia grumbled, in an indirect attack on her husband's policy, that the party opponents of the educational Soviets 'still cannot throw off the old view of the mass as an object of the intelligentsia's care, like a small and unreasonable child ...'.[98] This was an acute stroke of criticism. We have seen with regard to the problem of illiteracy that many of the Old Bolsheviks inherited the prejudices of the Tsarist intelligentsia.

The rural Soviets lost their potential influence partly through the incompetence or unwillingness of the masses to enter into the spirit of them. The All-Russian Congress of Soviets, on account of its unwieldy nature, was also a non-starter. A mass meeting of more than a thousand delegates, representing the vast areas of the country, was bound to prove unwieldy. The city Soviets very soon became little more than large city councils. The rural Soviets were potentially the best instruments for involving the peasants in wider affairs than their own farms, but very few peasants were interested in or able to understand the notion of social and political integration into an all-Russian system. Yet the percentage of peasants voting for the rural Soviets reached as high as 30 per cent by 1923.[99] Some peasants probably stood for office in the Soviets as a sign of protest against the hermetic family structure in which they had hitherto been enclosed. The mere fact of their adherence, however, in no way ensured the health of the system. From the start many local Soviets of their own accord sent the minutes of their meetings to the *guberniia* Soviet, thus perpetuating a centralist Tsarist feature. Decrees enacted by the centre, including attempts to resuscitate the Soviets, became a dead letter in the localities. The intellectual and frequently the geographical distance of the rural Soviets from the population, coupled with the fact that the peasant *skhod* offered a rival interpretation of far greater vitality, prevented any measure of genuine effectiveness.

The failure of the Soviets to forge living links between the peasantry and the centre was repeated in a number of other institutions which were supposed to wipe out the small-scale/large-scale dichotomy. The experiment of agricultural cooperation between 1923 and the close of NEP has been studied from the economic angle,[100] but the social implications are also of interest. In social terms, the problem of amalgamating peasant units into larger organisations presented a far greater problem for the Bolsheviks than did proletarian institutions. Industrial workers were far fewer in number, infinitely more concentrated geographically, and by the end of the Civil War less of a threat to Lenin's autocracy. Potentially independent proletarian movements like workers' control and the trade unions could therefore be subjugated and reorganised at a much earlier stage of Soviet history than peasant social units like the *mir* and the *skhod*. The revival of peasant cooperation after 1923 was an abortive attempt to integrate these two units into the nation's economic plans for the future. A direct transition to communism was abandoned after the Civil War. The proper road was now seen to be via small-scale exchange and production to state capitalism, and thereafter to socialism and communism. The initial shape of peasant cooperation would consist of trade and credit, the second of cooperative plants for processing of agricultural goods, and the final one of collective production. Socialism would develop with the expansion of large-scale industry, which would be nourished chiefly by collective peasant production. This last hypothesis was the cornerstone of all the economic theories which circulated during NEP. In December 1927 the Fifteenth Party Congress eventually decided to build the industrialisation of the Five-Year Plans on the basis of large-scale cooperative farming. But the coercive methods subsequently applied revealed the extent to which even cooperation in trade and credit, the very first stage on the road, had failed to act as a gradual, non-violent link between Lenin's aspirations and Stalin's actions.

In January 1923, shortly before his death, Lenin changed his mind on cooperatives. Their activities had been severely curtailed during the Civil War, but now he envisaged them as belonging to the nascent socialist, and not as formerly to the state capitalist, sector. For him they were becoming collective and so anti-capitalist in nature. They were veering to the socialist sector, since the land belonged to the state under the control of the working class.[101] There was no hint in all this of agricultural collectivisation as carried out later by Stalin, nor of the need for violence of any kind. A secondary and more practical motive lay behind Lenin's reasoning. The chaotic condition of distribution and supply left in the wake of the Civil War meant that the unwieldy central state organs were unable to cope with the problem. The distribution of food and textiles in particular could be delegated to cooperatives. Lenin declared that the cooperative system would teach communists how to trade and peasants how to engage in socialist exchange with the towns.[102] Thus he still kept clearly in his mind the theoretical significance ascribed by Marx to the proper distribution of labour and its products as a preliminary to large-scale economic and social life. Lenin's highly optimistic *volte-face* had no reflection in socio-economic reality at the time. It represented an instant strength of mind over matter that is strange to observe in a Marxist thinker.

Nevertheless his *fiat* of 1923 did in fact lead to a fairly rapid growth in the numbers and influence of trading cooperatives. In the first year or two of NEP private traders held about half of the market for the products of industrial trusts, whereas the wholesale cooperative system provided no more than one-fifth of this market.[103] In 1924 the membership of the agricultural cooperatives was given as about 10 per cent of all peasant households. By 1928 nearly a half of them were involved.[104] 28,600 consumers' cooperatives were functioning in the same year.[105]

The development of cooperation among the peasantry was undeniable, but it did not act as a social bridge for the collectivisation that was soon to follow. The bald statistics conceal fundamental reasons for the failure of the cooperatives' objectives. From the start of the Soviet period they were infiltrated at all levels by political and social foes of the Bolsheviks. In the first half of the period 1917–28, the main danger came from Socialist Revolutionary managerial connections with the rural cooperatives and Menshevik influence in the more urban-based consumers' cooperatives: both of these connections dated back to well before 1917. During the Civil War S.R.-dominated cooperatives aided General A. I. Denikin against the Red Army, and the Czech Whites received considerable support from Siberian cooperatives.[106] With the revival of the economy in NEP, another corrupting agent appeared at the lower levels. Kulaks were attracted to the cooperatives in ever-increasing numbers. Lenin did not foresee this complication, but in 1923 N. Meshcheriakov warned that the cooperative system was a Janus-headed organism which tended to oppress the poor peasant as well as offering healthy resistance to traditional forms of capitalism. He observed that in periods of political disillusionment with the revolutionary struggle cooperatives would normally flourish (the formation of the Rochdale cooperative society after the failure of the textile workers' strike was given as an example). Meshcheriakov stressed that the prerevolutionary form of cooperative which had survived into NEP would have to be run by men with a completely altered mental attitude to the business in hand.[107]

A change of this kind did not come about, due to ingrained peasant characteristics. Kulaks and middle peasants were less parochial in their economic and social habits than the poor peasants, and took greater advantage of the cooperatives in the second half of NEP. Bukharin's optimistic view that the kulaks would be outweighed in influence by cooperatives run by other rural peasants, who would in turn be allied to the state industrial sector, held no water. The more liberal treatment of the cooperatives by the party after 1923 only gave them limited independence. Continued control from above was self-defeating in that the link in the chain between urban bureaucracy and genuine rural participation became weak or even severed. It had been realised well before the Revolution that trading cooperation, whether capitalist or socialist, could only thrive if it relied on local initiative.[108] Yet by 1921 most of the 36,000 employees of the Petrograd united consumers' cooperative hailed from the city itself rather than from the rural area it was intended to serve.[109] Just prior to October 1917 some 27,000 agricultural cooperatives flourished in Russia, with about 11 million members. By 1928 the number rose to 34,300 but membership declined to just over 8 million.[110] There were increasingly fewer beneficiaries, and they were being managed by more white-collar employees. In 1930 a survey of 477 *raiony* (regions) of the RSFSR revealed a surplus of 1500 local organs of agricultural cooperatives, all of which were said to be quite useless.[111] Those that still had some purpose, however moribund, were flooded by forms and documents which slowed up business and were incomprehensible to the average peasant.

Instead of helping to mould peasant organisations into larger groupings, the agricultural cooperatives were themselves split up in order to suit isolationist rural conditions. At the close of NEP there was on average one distribution point for every 500 peasants, necessitating an infinitely fragmented structure at the grass roots. This merely reflected the scattered character of Russia's agricultural population. The trend towards increasingly small-scale activity had been forecast two years before the Revolution, when it was realised that 'consumer cooperation still stands at the very start of its development ... the sphere of the individual, domestic use of it has scarcely been broached up to the present times'.[112] An even clearer general warning, surprisingly enough, can be found in the *Manifesto of the Communist Party*, at the point where Marx is attacking the small-scale cooperative ventures of Robert Owen : 'They continue to dream of the experimental realization of their social utopias – the establishment of isolated phalansteries; the founding of home colonies; the setting up of little Icarias – pocket editions of the New Jerusalem.' [113]

It was a typically Marxist error to believe that the economic development of cooperation would *ipso facto* refashion the mental attitudes and social habits of the Russian peasant. The Bolsheviks were putting the cart before the horse. The trend towards individual methods of farming and trade which developed before 1917 could not be thwarted from the centre by the mere imposition of artificially stimulated organisations. On the other hand it proved impossible over a short period of time to reform peasant social life from below, to eradicate illiteracy, and to improve communications. The final alternative was Stalin's hurried imposition of force on an unprecedented scale.

Besides distorting the arrangements of the officially approved cooperatives to their own parochial uses, the peasants learnt how to bypass them altogether, though at the same time working out an informal type of cooperation of their own. Near the end of NEP thousands of tiny *prostye*, or simple, associations sprang up, engaged in communal activity on some sectors of production. Predictably, they covered a much smaller area and number of people than the official cooperatives. Better geared to the restricted activity of the *mir*, they were so small that a law was passed fixing the minimum membership at ten.[114] Most of them had no ties with the main cooperative movement. It is significant that these spontaneously instigated forms of cooperation, so well adapted to peasant needs, were wiped out altogether in the collectivisation campaign. There was no amalgamation of any kind with the new system.

The weakness of the state-sponsored cooperative movement eventually impressed itself on Stalin. In 1924 his practical programme for the countryside was still borrowed straight from Bukharin. It is often said that Bukharin's career reached a watershed towards the end of the Civil War, and that he changed abruptly from his Leftist phase, reviewed in Chapter 2, to a 'right-wing', gradualist point of view. This may be true in general, but in the sphere of agriculture at least he merely abandoned an instant utopia for a gradualist one. His vision of NEP as a healing interval, which would painlessly bring together via cooperation the peasant and the townsman, and result in a unified, planned cooperative and industrial society, was unrealistic. Above all, he underestimated the strength of the traditional social characteristics of the peasantry. His ideas were also unclear as to exactly how industry was to be developed. Once again, as with the social utopias of War Communism, Maiakovsky's dreaded *byt* (Russia's customary daily social existence) prohibited the early realisation of abstract schemes imposed from above, unless they were backed up by coercion. The long step from a relatively unsuccessful form of cooperative trade and credit to forced cooperative agricultural production in collective farms entailed a gigantic social upheaval when Stalin changed his mind at the end of NEP.

The cooperative experiment foundered on the same rock as the Soviets. Another victim of the chasm between town and country which has received scant attention, despite the existence of a considerable amount of information on it,[115] was the *kustarnyi* industry. This was defined by Soviet terminology in the 1920s as all industrial establishments producing goods for more than one household but employing thirty wage earners or less; or if motive power was used, fifteen wage earners or less.[116] The importance of this sector of society can be seen at a glance from the population figures for the first all-Union census of 1926. The rural-urban break in population was shown to correspond pretty rigidly between those dependent on agriculture and related occupations, and those dependent on industry, trade and administration. The sole category that was clearly spread over urban and rural areas consisted of persons chiefly dependent on small-scale handicraft industry, the *kustari*.[117] This branch of the population seemed admirably placed to act as a link between town and country, poised as it was geographically between the two and economically serving and employing both peasants and town-dwellers alike. Viewed in this way, the *kustari* were an advance on agricultural cooperation, which, in the 1920s at least, only helped to unite peasants alone in larger social and economic groups.

Since the *kustarnyi* system, like the *mir*, was a direct inheritance from Tsarist Russia, its development before 1917 must be examined in order to understand its character and tenacity in NEP. Capitalist industry in Russia had started out in the 1830s and 1840s on the basis of handicrafts, but the relationship between the two diverged from the British prototype thereafter. *Kustarnyi* industries survived for a much longer period in Russia. Most of the peasants engaged in them remained attached to the villages because of restrictions on their movements and on the sale of land by a peasant household, despite the Emancipation of the Serfs in 1861. Even by 1917 Russian capitalists still resorted widely to the 'putting-out' system, by which part-time work was handed out to domestic artisans or to small sub-contractors. The immense size of Russia also contributed to the prolonged vitality of handicraft work, which could prosper while huge distances and poor means of transport separated one industrial centre from another. The *kustari* fell into two main types. The first consisted of producers such as blacksmiths and shoemakers who provided for a small, local market and carried out orders for individual customers; the second concentrated on the output of specific items for a far wider market and was centred in particular regions, each region being known for the high quality of the goods it specialised in. These nexi were called 'nests' (*gnezda*). Articles produced by the *kustari* of the second type were sold throughout the Empire and were also exported. *Kustari* were active not only in Russian Central Asia, Siberia and the Caucasus, but above all in the northern central zone of European Russia, the hub of the large-scale factory network. The traditional artisan areas of the Moscow region were injected with renewed vigour after the Emancipation, since peasants were forced to seek means of supplementing their earnings. Redemption payments were heavy relatively to the productivity of the land in this region, and the relationship of arable earth to meadows was adversely affected.

The goods made by *kustari* even included quite heavy metalwork as well as articles made from wood, leather, cloth, etc. The consumer needs of the Russian people were largely met by these artisans, and most townships were supplied by them. As these small-scale industries grew, control over them gradually passed to wholesale traders. Selling at a distance had to be carried out by middlemen who determined prices. After 1917 these agents were to be replaced by the Nepmen of the 1920s. By 1915 small-scale manufacturers of all kinds employed roughly 67 per cent of all persons engaged in Russian industry and produced 33 per cent of industrial output.[118] Under the impact of war and revolution all forms of trade declined. By 1920 the number of those employed as *kustari* was estimated at 1,611,000.[119] On the whole, small-scale enterprise suffered less than large-scale industries. The former thrived where they still had access to local raw materials and fuel, and those which supplied the Red Army naturally flourished.[120] With the recovery of the economy in NEP and the resuscitation of a consumer market, the number of *kustari* rose again to 2,715,000 in 1925; of these, 2,072,000 worked in the countryside and 643,000 in the towns.[121] A new incentive for the growth of small-scale industry in NEP was supplied by the operation of the 'price scissors'. As the price level for goods produced by state factories rose faster than for those turned out in rural areas, the *kustari* could compete successfully with the state-run factories in many activities. By 1926–7 over half of all industrial workers were still engaged in small-scale units (under thirty persons) and produced about 20 per cent of industrial output.[122] The general situation was reverting to that of 1915 (67 per cent of all employees producing 33 per cent). Moreover, a strikingly large proportion of business was conducted on an individual or family basis. According to another Soviet source, which gives the total number employed in small-scale industry in 1925 as 2,713,790 (slightly less than the figure given above), 2,285,161 of them were private craftsmen not dependent on labour outside the family nexus.[123] At the apogee of their power in 1929, the *kustari* comprised roughly 4,500,000 people.[124]

This figure is to some extent misleading, as on average the *kustar'*, who was more often than not engaged in agriculture as well, worked in handicrafts for only one-third as long in the course of a year as a worker in large-scale industry. Nevertheless the continuing success of artisan units on a minute scale showed in several ways how well they were adapted to Soviet needs, which had altered little since Tsarist times in this respect. The eternal factor of the long Russian winter, prohibiting work in the fields, left ample free time for peasants to make extra money by staying in the *kustarnyi* industry. Just as in the late nineteenth century, there were virtually no great modern factories producing consumer goods. In the latter half of NEP there arose a sufficiently wide stratum of prosperous peasants and town-dwellers to keep the traditional craftsmen occupied with their demands. Like their Tsarist counterparts, the *kustari* were still inhibited from leaving the land altogether, not now so much because of deliberate restriction on their movements, but because large-scale industry was not expanding fast enough to employ them in large numbers. The size of Russia had not altered much since 1917, nor had communications, so that consumer supply had still to be geared far more to spatially flexible industries, like domestic handicrafts, rather than to intensive industries centred on the widely separated towns. Thus, to give but one example among hundreds, right up to the close of NEP the whole of European Russia and beyond was provided with hand-turned spinning wheels (which in turn were used for producing other textile handicrafts) by the *kustari* of a single rural area not far from Kaluga. The local master sent off his share of spinning wheels by slow train from the nearest railhead, which was often a day's journey or more by sledge or cart from the production points. Wheels were despatched by goods trains to 700 other railway stations. The masters followed by faster trains, moving from one market to another, selling off at the most 20 to 30 wheels in one batch to local merchants. They still deigned to sell individual wheels and repaired old ones which had originally come from their region.[125]

The Bolsheviks' view of the *kustarnyi* industry, particularly the 'nest' system, as a possible social and economic link that could convert itself and its workers to large-scale methods and promote *smychka*, changed considerably during the years 1917–28. A pattern that should by now be familiar to the reader emerged. During War Communism the notion that such a traditional and semi-capitalist institution could be harnessed to Soviet idealism was completely discounted. After all, since the 1890s kulaks had begun to control the *kustarnyi* industries by employing casual peasant wage labour in them.[126] The Bolshevik Left was especially vociferous in its condemnation of the handicraft system. Bogdanov claimed that it was quite impossible to create an atmosphere of what he called 'collective collaboration' on the basis of the master-apprentice relationship of the *kustari*.[127] Trotsky concurred at this time. In a speech to the Eighth Party Congress in March 1919, he drew an interesting analogy between the militia and the *kustarnyi* systems, two small-scale social structures which he rejected with equal vigour : 'To preach partisan warfare as a military pro-gramme is just the same as recommending a return to handicrafts from large-scale industry.' [128]

Typically, it was Bukharin who converted himself and some of his colleagues to taking a different view. He foresaw with perci-pience that the *kustari* would probably increase in power and in numbers after the end of the Civil War. Instead of jettisoning such a formidable and potentially dangerous organisation, he thought that his party would be wiser to incorporate the *kustarnyi* industry in their own plans for the future.[129] Bukharin found him-self in strange company with others who had adopted this view before his time. Baron von Haxthausen, the German admirer of the *mir* in the 1850s, also praised Russian handicrafts and wanted the Tsarist government to promote their 'natural' virtues in pre-ference to artificial, capitalist large-scale industries copied from Western Europe.[130] Economic experts in the last decade of Tsarist rule no longer wanted to do away with these established heavy industries, but they agreed that 'the success of large-scale industry in many of its sectors feeds on the talents of the handicraft workers'.[131]

Lenin upheld Bukharin's view that the *kustarnyi* industry should not be smashed. Like agricultural cooperation, it wavered in his estimation between semi-capitalist and proto-socialist methods. Under the careful guidance of the Bolshevik party it could be persuaded without coercion into the right path. In the words of the official resolution, the party would 'paralyse the efforts of the *kustari* to turn themselves into petty industrialists and effect a painless transition of these outdated forms of production into a higher type of large-scale machine industry.' [132] There was also a sound practical reason for encouraging handicrafts at the close of the Civil War, as Lenin realised. Since they did not rely on large machines, they could help to set the economy on its feet before large-scale industry was in a position to do so.[133] It appeared to be relatively easy during NEP for the political centre to control the *kustarnyi* industry, for most of the privately run handicrafts were largely dependent on supplies of materials from state industry, and the majority of their workshops were leased from the state. Furthermore, relatively concentrated 'nests' of *kustari*, possessing strong economic ties with the nearby industrial cities of northern central Russia, proved to be of considerable use in reviving the hub of the economy. Although the *kustarnyi* tail still wagged the dog of large-scale consumer industry by the end of NEP, a partial *rapprochement* process did appear to be at work in the Moscow region.[134]

In his enthusiasm for handicrafts, Bukharin suggested four practical ways of harnessing them to progressive methods. They should be requested to gather fuel and raw materials for large-scale factories. The state should hand out credit to them, as well as placing large orders for goods from them. Most important of all, the *kustari* should be invited to join trade unions and slowly come into line with the factory proletariat. None of these aims materialised to any extent. The private sector remained dominant, and the overwhelming preponderance of single family units rendered negotiations of the kind suggested by Bukharin totally unsuitable. Like the cooperatives, the *kustarnyi* industry slipped from the Bolsheviks' tenuous grasp. It too became infiltrated by an increasing number of semi-capitalist manipulators in the guise of kulaks and Nepmen. Profiting from the gradual improvement of trade and financial liquidity in NEP, these agents began to monopolise the distribution of handicraft products. They could run individual craftsmen into debt, since the *kustari* were still cut off by the nature of small-scale society both from the market for their products and from personal access to the raw materials they needed. The evils of Tsarist semi-capitalist methods in the countryside returned once again.

The failure of the *kustarnyi* industry to link up on a healthy socialist basis with large-scale industry coincided with the similar lack of success on the part of the agricultural cooperatives. Both systems belonged mainly to the peasant social world, and they resisted Bolshevik blandishments for similar reasons. Bukharin was telling the truth better than he knew when he wrote in *Historical Materialism*, 'Is it possible that the technological system of society should be based on machines, while the productive relation, the actual labour relation, should be based on petty industry working with hand tools? Of course, this is an impossibility; wherever a society exists, there must be a certain equilibrium between its technology and its economy ...'[135] Soviet society, on his own evidence, did not exist as a unified whole by the end of NEP. Both types of technology did in fact coexist in a strained relationship, or rather lack of one, which was only to be solved by violent socio-economic revolution. In the course of the First Five-Year Plan over 1,600,000 *kustari* were forced into cooperative unions. During the same period the output of small-scale industry fell to one-tenth of total production.[136]

One cannot simply blame organisations *per se* for not forming adequate contacts between different branches of production and society. Organisations are run by men and designed for them, and in the last resort the human element decides the outcome of any project. This truism was very pertinent to the Soviet context. The Russian peasant was suspicious of all new systems, and needed careful face-to-face persuasion in order to induce him to collaborate. It is worth taking a look at those agents who were instrumental in trying to get the countryside to work more closely with the towns.

It has already been seen how the demise of the gentry, and also of the merchant class and the priests, left a rural vacuum in human relationships. They were replaced in some degree by the Bolsheviks' local network, but party numbers were for some years far lower than those of the gentry alone had been before 1917. The party emanated from the towns and had to establish new roots in the countryside after the hiatus of the Civil War, whereas the gentry had been there for centuries, at least in European Russia. The Bolsheviks brought with them Marxist prejudices against the peasantry and often relied on preconceived abstract theories without really trying to study the actual characteristics of the rural areas, if indeed they could be known in their multifarious entirety. Those Bolsheviks who hailed from the intelligentsia sometimes inherited the condescension of their nineteenth-century forebears towards the 'dark people', adding to it a new contempt derived from increasing impatience at the slow rate of social progress in the countryside. They were professed atheists, which was still a repugnant trait for most religious-minded peasants.

The proletarian element in the party had also experienced

direct peasant antagonism to all urban dwellers in the Revolution and the Civil War, when the cities were starved of food, and messengers from the 'Centre', as the peasants dubbed the whole outside world, were reviled. It might be thought that the many workers of recent peasant origin would make the best ambassadors in the rural areas, and indeed they were often sent there on this assumption, but in fact they frequently turned out to be more disdainful towards the true peasants than other party men, simply because they still felt socially and intellectually insecure. They also tended to become bureaucratic in their attitudes as they became immersed in administration. Sometimes they were selected just because they knew how to pull the strings, rather than because they were good Bolsheviks. Such men had little or no real knowledge of the finer points of Marxist-Leninst theory concerning small-scale socio-economic life. They also frequently became tainted by local influences and lost touch with the central aims of the party.

An example of this were the activists in the *Komsomol* movement, who were continuously criticised by the party leadership for taking too independent a line in the rural areas.[137] They fell between two stools, since they were not popular with the peasantry either, having taken an important part in food requisitioning during War Communism. Less formal attempts at contact between town and country looked well on paper but were ineffectual in reality. The *Agitprop* (agitation and propaganda) section of the Smolensk *guberniia* party committee declared that *smychka* was a farce, as all it amounted to was a mass outing by hundreds of town workers to the fields, armed with *kvas* and beer. They spent their time hunting out illicit peasant stills instead of discussing communism. Then they would 'arrange drinking bouts ... This kind of *smychka* produces nothing but harm'.[138]

The parallel system of patronage (*shefstvo*) by workers over selected parts of the countryside was encouraged by Lenin, and a resolution on its advancement was passed at the Twelfth Party Congress in 1923. Yet Krupskaia had to confess at the next Congress that few campaigns had been carried out, and with scant success.[139] The human gulf between town and country was satirised in NEP by writers like Zoshchenko, for the situation had its touches of humour. In a story entitled *A Metropolitan Deal*, a party *shefstvo* agent tries to restrain a peasant mob which is bent on electing as village chairman the only local man who has actually spent two years in a town. The party agent's verbose speech is 'interpreted' into simple rustic jargon by the leader of the poor peasant section for the benefit of the assembly. Only when it turns out that the favourite spent his two years in the town gaol for embezzlement do his backers give up their naive request.[140] But at least some peasants realised the advantages of having a sophisticated 'metropolitan' in their midst.

It was observed in the foregoing chapter with regard to the drive for literacy how non-party professional people, who were nevertheless sympathetic to communst aims, made useful contacts in the countryside.[141] These people were cultural and administrative intermediaries between local life and party circles. The Russian word 'intelligentsia' has subsequently been applied by social anthropologists to similar situations throughout the world.[142] Whereas Bolshevik agitators and functionaries represented naked political power to the peasantry, teachers, agronomists and *fel'dshers* upheld their superior status due to the fact that they were educated (often much better than the party men). The peasants were sometimes more amenable to these subtler influences. However there were problems with this cultural group as well. Shortly after the Revolution thousands of teachers and doctors either fled the country, refused to collaborate with the new regime, or continued to instil the liberal attitudes of the *zemstva* into their audiences. Thousands more eventually drifted to the towns when the urban centres took on a more civilised form of life in NEP.

Tomsky criticised the intelligentsia for clinging on to opportunities for staying in city jobs.[143] Leading labour journals joined in : 'Cultural workers receive such low pay in the countryside that they are unable to reside long in one place and move away to urban centres. As a result of this flight there is a colossal piling-up of unemployed persons in these centres.'[144] At the lower end of the cultural hierarchy, village school-teachers tended to stay on in the rural areas, but like the local Bolsheviks they were often swallowed up by peasant inertia and ceased to be an active progressive irritant. There was an economic as well as a social reason for this — their salaries and their schools were largely paid for by the *mir*.[145]

A critical point concerning human contacts in the polarised society of NEP was that the more the semi-capitalist economy flourished, the more town-country relationships came under the control of the Nepmen and the kulaks. These happened to be the two social excrescences of the 1920s that the Bolsheviks despised and feared the most for obvious reasons. We have already noted the pervasive influence of the kulaks in the Soviets, in the cooperatives and the *kustarnyi* industry. Strangely enough, the *social* as opposed to the economic effects of the Nepmen's position as a bridge between town and country have not been studied in much detail.[146] They held a commanding stance which embraced far wider circles than the microcosmic world of the kulak. For a few years they dominated internal trade, particularly retail trade. They bought the peasants' grain in the villages and took it to the towns. They set up shops in suburban areas and supplied them with other peasant products. Although their *forte* was retail trade, they also engaged in wholesaling. In 1923 a fifth of the total turnover in wholesale trade was in their hands. Nepmen acquired from the new state trusts that part of their products which they could not dispose of through lack of centrally managed channels. They also supplied the trusts with raw materials. Reinterpreted in social terms, these widespread contacts must have had great though incalculable effects. In the main they must also have been adverse influences for a regime which openly hated usurers, and which knew only too well that the majority of Nepmen were hostile to Bolshevik rule.[147]

The efforts to improve contacts between the peasants and the more concentrated and advanced sectors of society did not all originate from above. The autonomy of peasant life should not be exaggerated. The village is in some ways incomplete culturally and politically. Its life depends in part on communications with external authorities. This distinguishes it from isolated primitive groups, which are more properly a subject of inquiry for the anthropologist. The human links between local peasant communities and the state consisted chiefly of the administrative officers sent down from the towns; yet the peasants themselves made positive contributions in this respect, despite the enormous difficulties that inhibited them.

They were usually too busy or too poor to travel. S. Strumilin calculated in 1923 that the average working day of a peasant lasted between fourteen and fifteen hours in the months of better weather. Approximately thirty-eight minutes a day were also spent in getting to and from work. In winter the burden was far lighter, but long-distance travel, except by sledge, was a daunting prospect.[148] If peasants did succeed in getting to the provincial towns, they encountered a large pool of unemployed fellow-peasants there in the later years of NEP. In many ways the provincial centres were as resistant to change as the villages, although they should have been of signal importance to the Bolsheviks as the geographical link between national leadership and the masses. Kemal Atatürk came up against a similar problem in Turkey, where the small town 'middle class' actually provided the hard core of reaction to his social innovations.[149]

More often than not peasants who did move were pushed by superior political and economic forces out of their home surroundings. Recruitment and dislocation during the World War and the Civil War were the most significant political forces here. Thousands of deserters never returned to their original place of residence. Vagrancy and wandering bands of orphans on a massive scale remained major problems during NEP. The famine of 1921–2 in the lower and middle Volga areas caused the flight of approximately 800,000 people between July 1921 and April 1922.[150]

Most of these movements were chaotic in nature and consisted of sideways shifts from one rural area to another. The steady depopulation of urban centres in the postrevolutionary period hardly allowed newcomers to the towns to cling on there, even if they wished to do so. When the economy began to recover in the mid-1920s, the traditional prerevolutionary flow of peasants to the cities in search of industrial employment began once again. This was the main way in which the peasants themselves contributed to the strengthening of town-country ties. But the movement was not so large in volume as it had been before 1917, nor at first did it become as well integrated socially as it had been in the past. The urban proletariat, decimated by the Civil War and increasingly subject to the control of the trade unions, was uncertain about its status and reacted against the new arrivals who threatened to lower its educational and work standards. Even when they lived side by side, generational differences continued to separate the proletarian from the peasant-worker.

By the end of NEP no solid bridges, whether in terms of individual human collaboration or of institutions, had been constructed between the central regime and the masses, the town and the country. This failure had deep, cumulative roots. Some of them, like the social isolation of the peasantry and the lack of viable auxiliary social and political organs, long predated the Revolution. The frenetic attempts in the Civil War period to throw up instant, jerry-built utopian social edifices led to disillusionment at high party levels. Energies might have been better directed in the first place towards the long-term task of slowly narrowing the small-scale large-scale dichotomy, working on a more pragmatic basis than that provided by the idealist streak in Marxist-Leninist social thought. Solid gradualness was all the more imperative, given the adverse social conditions created by war chaos and the long period of militarisation from 1914 to 1921. Within the years of NEP an actual broadening of the gap between large- and small-scale activities occurred at the start, adding to the difficulties of the Bolshevik party. The instruments used by the party to link up the two sectors proved to be ineffective : they were not strong enough to overcome the multiple barriers put in their way by earlier developments. The authoritarian methods resorted to by the central party hierarchy to put its own internal local administration in order at the beginning of the 1920s augured ill for the future of far more diffuse systems like the Soviets, the cooperatives and the *kustarnyi* network. At the end of Zamiatin's anti-utopian novel, *My*, each city in the final 'ideal' state is surrounded by a high green wall, and none of the townsmen living in the supposedly perfect urban society are let out beyond the wall. The no-man's land between cities is roamed by a dying rural people belonging to the old civilisation, survivors of the free, instinctive (*stikhiinyi*) era.

For social reasons alone, leaving aside pressing political and economic considerations, Bukharin's strategy in the middle 1920s of waiting hopefully for the slow *rapprochement* of the different sectors of society was certainly doomed to failure. The economic and high political motives for embarking on forced collectivisation and industrialisation have been weighed in great detail by non-Russian scholars and so have been given scant emphasis here. Not enough stress has generally been laid on the turn of events in international affairs, which cut short hopes that foreign capital might be used to modernise the peasant economy. That, however, is beyond the scope of this book. What has been attempted here is to show how deeply embedded social forces also had an impact on Bolshevik theories and experiments. In some ways they were more tenacious and influential than economic and political arrangements, which could be manipulated with rather more speed and flexibility, although in the last resort the three strands had to be tackled together.

The political repercussions of these incoherent social developments, or rather lack of them, should also be stressed. The massive social and economic centralisation generated by the First Five-Year Plan was a direct, impatient reply to years of frustrated effort to use less violent means to bridge gaps. Instead of remaining largely in the realm of speculative theory, as was the case with the first utopian period during the Civil War, the typically Russian maximalist solution was now firmly fixed in actuality, with devastating effects for the whole population. Some of the earlier utopian ideas lingered on in the second period, but they were now shorn of libertarian elements.[151] The palimpsest of the writings of Marx and Engels was invoked again in order to advocate tight centralisation or what was virtually the reverse of the original aims of War Communism.[152]

Under Stalin the effort to promote the gradual evolution of lower-level social organs for state purposes was abandoned. Rural culture was overrun by the towns with scant regard for indigenous traditions of long standing. The fact that town workers had to play the major role in the task of enforcing collectivisation illustrates in social terms the complete failure of *smychka* in NEP. The buffers between town and country, the all-powerful centre and the masses, collapsed, revealing the clear outlines of a totalitarian political regime. Here was the classic social basis for a modern government of this type, as described by R. Aron, H. Arendt and W. Kornhauser,[153] in which the atomised masses face their ruler without the protection of adequate intermediary institutions. Aron maintains that a kind of classless society existed in the Stalinist period. It was not the classless society envisaged by Marx, but one in which an élite controls a fragmented mass. At the beginning of this chapter it was argued that it would be a difficult and unrewarding task to analyse social stratification in NEP for the purposes of studying the social foundations of Stalinism. The irrelevance of class in the 1930s as well is pointed out in the concluding chapter.[154] To this extent there is agreement with Aron's thesis. Arendt holds that Stalin 'had first to create artificially ...

atomised society.' [155] Kornhauser concurs: 'Repression of spontaneous behaviour in all spheres of Soviet life prevents the formation of mass movements, despite the fact that all legitimate
independent group life has been destroyed.' [156] Kornhauser is not
precise in terms of time, but presumably the last phrase refers to
the Stalinist period. On the evidence surveyed in this chapter,
however, it is an error of timing and balance to say that Stalin
created an atomised mass. It already existed before the 1930s,
although it is true that Stalin played on the political possibilities
inherent in the situation which confronted him. Arendt states that
group formations among the Soviet non-élites had to be abolished,
or else they would have developed interests opposed to the ruling
élite. This generalisation appears to be correct in broad outline,
if one looks at the dangers of kulak influence during NEP in the
network of local Soviets, and in the cooperative and *kustarnyi*
systems. It scarcely holds water with regard to workers' control,
unless the minor threat of syndicalism can be construed as a real
political menace. Kornhauser likewise holds that intermediate
groups are weak, and goes on to label them as 'inclusive', in the
sense that they are manipulated by the ruling élite through 'front'
organisations. Here again the static analysis must be modified.
Initially Lenin did make genuine attempts to nurture non-inclu-
sive groups, but he was defeated by a combination of socio-
economic and political factors.

These reservations on the findings of the three writers are all
connected with the defects of the totalitarian model as they seek
to apply it. It is too static and so glosses over crescive social change,
particularly that which occurs before the emergence of the full-
blown totalitarian state. It exaggerates the dichotomy between a
political élite and a mass society, and although it may be relevant
to a period of rapid industrialisation like the 1930s in Russia, it is
less appropriate to a more advanced industrial system.

1 Preface to Lewin, op. cit., p. 7.
2 From 10,251 million roubles in 1913 to 1410 million roubles in
1920. See R. Hutchings, *Soviet Economic Development* (London,
1971) p. 35, n. 8. For corroboration by Soviet scholarship, see A.
Buzlaeva, *Leninskii plan kooperirovaniia melkoi promyshlennosti
SSSR* (Moscow, 1969) p. 49.

3 See A. V. Chaianov, *The Theory of Peasant Economy*, edited by D. Thormer, B. Kerblay and R. Smith (Homewood, Illinois, 1966). Chaianov favoured the notion of individual peasant production in NEP, together with cooperative sales and purchases; but in 1929 he turned turtle and even outdid Stalin in the race into large-scale enterprises. Chaianov called for single agricultural conglomerates the size of a *volost'*. See N. Jasny, *Soviet Economists of the Twenties: Names to be Remembered* (Cambridge, 1972) pp. 200–3.

4 Until 1925 most of the members of the Politburo had been born in towns, although the majority of those who were in the Politburo between 1917 and 1951 were born in the countryside; however, all of them moved to towns at an early stage in their career. See G. Schueller in H. Lasswell and P. Lerner (editors), op. cit., pp. 109–11.

5 For a lucid discussion of the Bolshevik treatment of class, see Carr, *Socialism in One Country, 1924–1926*, pp. 89–136.

6 The quality of research during NEP into social conditions is assessed in Yu. Arutiunian, 'Rural sociology', in G. Osipov (editor), *Town, Country and People* (London, 1969).

7 This approach has been used with success to cast light on social relations in writings like J. Meijer, 'Town and Country in the Civil War', in Pipes (editor), *Revolutionary Russia*; T. von Laue, 'Russian peasants in the factory 1892–1904', in the *Journal of Economic History* (March 1961) pp. 61–80; R. Zelnik, 'The Peasant and Factory', in W. Vucinich (editor), *The Peasant in Nineteenth-Century Russia* (Stanford, 1968); G. Osipov (editor), *Town, Country and People*. For a comparison with the French Revolution, see A. Cobban, *The Social Interpretation of the French Revolution* (Cambridge, 1964) chap. 9. For lack of data none of these authors has been able to apply precise criteria to his research. Some of the quantitative methods used for examining social movement between country and town are assessed in J. Gibbs (editor), *Urban Research Methods* (New York, 1961).

8. For details of peasant pressure on town labour in the later stages of NEP, see O. Narkiewicz, *The Making of the Soviet State Apparatus*, pp. 99–111, 142–3.

9 For verdicts on this difficulty, see T. Emmons, *The Russian Landed Gentry and the Peasant Emancipation of 1861* (Cambridge, Mass., 1968) and D. Male, *Russian Peasant Organization before Collectivization*.

10 See Y. Taniuchi, *The Village Gathering in Russia in the Mid-1920s* (Birmingham, 1968) pp. 24–6.

11 *The German Ideology* (Moscow, 1968) p. 41.

12 Ibid., p. 44.

13 F. Engels, in F. Mehring (editor), *Aus dem literarischen Nachlass von Karl Marx, Friedrich Engels und Ferdinand Lasalle: Gesammelte Schriften von Karl Marx und Friedrich Engels von Juli 1844 bis November 1847* (Stuttgart, 1902) p. 405.

14 *The German Ideology*, p. 47. A lucid secondary analysis of Marx's and Engels' views on universal society, which includes a survey of all their writings on this subject, is to be found in E. R. Goodman, *The Soviet Design for a World State* (New York, 1960) pp. 2–24.

15 Ibid., p. 90.

16 Ibid., p. 71.

17 See Lenin, *Collected Works*, 4th edn., vol. 3, pp. 183–4, 315n.

18 Ibid., vol. 1, pp. 106–7, 503–4; vol. 3, pp. 233, 314–21, 545. The author is indebted to G. N. Harding for help with the analysis of Lenin's views on small-scale and large-scale units in the prerevolutionary period.

19 Lenin, *Sochineniia*, 4th edn., vol. 18, p. 232.

20 Stalin, *Sochineniia*, vol. 5, p. 158.

21 See Chapter 2, p. 37.

22 See for instance A. Bodganov and I. Stepanov, *Kurs politicheskoi ekonomiki*, vol. 2, *Torgovoi kapitalizm* (Moscow, 1920) ch. 5.

23 Letter to L. Kugelmann, 11 July 1868, in *Selected Works*, vol. 2, p. 461. See also *Das Kapital*, vol. 1 (Vienna, 1932) pp. 368–77, where Marx differentiates the division of labour in society as a whole from the division of labour in the factory.

24 L. Namier, *England in the Age of the American Revolution*, quoted in Carr, 'The Russian Revolution and the Peasant', in *The Proceedings of the British Academy*, vol. 49 (London, 1963).

25 F. Nansen, *Through Siberia* (London, 1914) p. 282.

26 *VKP (b) v tsifrakh (vypusk 8)* (Moscow–Leningrad, 1928) p. 6.

27 E. Volkov, *Dinamika naseleniia SSSR za vosem'desiat' let* (Moscow, 1930) p. 209.

28 The reasoning comes from M. Khataevich, 'Partiia v derevne', in *Na agrarnom fronte*, no. 2 (1925).

29 The Smolensk Archives, file **WKP 248**, referring to an order from A. Andreev, *O podgotovke i perepodgotovke volostnykh i sel'skikh rabotnikov*, 17 February 1925.

30 Petrograd in 1917 was markedly out of line and out of touch with events in the provinces. See an essay by Pethybridge, 'Petrograd and the Provinces', op. cit.

31 The telecommunications system practically always followed the railway lines so that they could be built, serviced and tapped more easily.

32 The author is indebted to an article by R. Hutchings, 'Geographic Influences on Centralization in the Soviet Economy', in *Soviet Studies* (January 1966) pp. 291, 301, for the inference regarding railway construction.

33 For a full treatment of the social, economic and political effects of the breakdown of the railway system in 1917, see R. Pethybridge, 'The Railways', op. cit.,

34 Kritsman, op. cit., p. 172.

35 The proportion of disabled locomotives stood at about 30 per cent at the time of the October coup and rose to 69 per cent by 1920. See L. Pasvolsky, *Economics of Socialism*, p. 362, quoted in M. Dobb, *Soviet Economic Development Since 1917* (London, 1948) p. 99.

36 'Window of Rosta' poster series of 1919.

37 Iu. Rudzutak in the *Manchester Guardian Commercial*, Russian Supplement, 26 June 1924.

38 *Manchester Guardian Commercial Reconstruction Supplement*, 6 July 1922.

39 Iu. Klimov, *V surovye gody dvadsatye: Bol'sheviki severo-zapada v bor'be za provedenie NEPa v 1921–25* (Murmansk, 1968) pp. 67–8.

40 For example, in the northwestern region river transport productivity was 3.4 times better in 1923 than it had been in 1921. The tonnage passing through the port of Petrograd rose by 240 per cent over the same period; Ibid., p. 108.

41 Bol'shakov, op. cit., p. 37 and p. 469, table 33.

42 Ibid., p. 299.

43 *Bol'shaia sovetskaia entsiklopediia*, vol. 35, p. 328.

44 Bol'shakov, op. cit., p. 301.

45 Ibid., pp. 299, 303.

46 See *Voprosy ekonomicheskogo raionirovaniia* (Moscow, 1957) p. 267.

47 *Soveshchanie po voprosam sovetskogo stroitel'stva* (January, 1925) pp. 113–14.

48 *Vlast' sovetov*, no. 12 (1926) p. 24; no. 17 (1926) p. 1. See also *Sovetskoe stroitel'stvo, sbornik*, no. 1 (1925) p. 55.

49 *Soveshchanie po voprosam sovetskogo stroitel'stva* (April 1925) pp. 175–80. This source, and notes 46 and 48, are quoted in Y. Taniuchi, op. cit., p. 34.

50 From the German ambassador's memoirs; H. Schweinitz, *Denkwürdigkeiten*, vol. 2 (Berlin, 1927) p. 223.

51 See pp. 55–6.

52 A. Slepkov, 'Semia i stroitel'stvo sotsializma', in *Byt i molodezh'* (Moscow, 1926) pp. 52, 57.

53 The danger of making generalisations about small-scale social units should be stressed again at this point. For instance, to take but one example, much of Soviet Central Asia was inhabited in the 1920s by polygamous family units.

54 A. Smirnov in *Na agrarnom fronte*, nos. 11–12 (1926).

55 *Piatnadsatyi s" ezd*, VKP(b), *stenograficheskii otchet*, p. 97.

56 See D. Male, op. cit., for a rigorous examination of the *mir* and the *skhod* in the period 1925–30.

57 In L. Leonov's novel, *The Badgers*, which appeared in 1923–4, two villages have been wrangling for 100 years over a disputed plot of land. When the Bolsheviks award the plot to one of them, both sides are equally annoyed. For them the Revolution is viewed as a mere distraction from the local quarrels that make up the real history of Russia.

58 M. Gorky, *O russkom krestian'stve* (Berlin, 1922) pp. 39–40.

59 For the political importance of rumour in the Revolution, see Pethybridge, op. cit., 'Propaganda and Political Rumours'.

60 Bol'shakov, op. cit., p. 301. The two local papers were *Tverskaia derevnia* and *Kimrskaia zhizn'*.

61 Ibid.

62 See D. Kurskii, *Izbrannye stat'i i rechi* (Moscow, 1948) p. 78. *Volost'* courts were said to punish theft seven times more severely than city courts.

63 *Bol'shaia sovetskaia entsiklopediia*, vol. 28 (Moscow, 1930) p. 74.

64 Bol'shakov, op. cit., p. 313.

65 Bogdanov, writing in *Novyi mir* (Moscow, 1918) p. 117.

66 Laslett, *The World We Have Lost*. The danger of neglecting the coexistence in one epoch of overlapping forms of social life emanating from many previous ages must be remembered here. The same applies to psychological attitudes as to socio-economic processes. In his studies of mental reflections and folklore in East Anglia, G. Evans shows the strong though apparently incongruous survival of pre-industrial attitudes in the twentieth-century countryside. See his *The Pattern under the Plough: Aspects of the Folk-life of East Anglia* (London, 1966). The same phenomenon applied to Soviet Russia in even stronger terms.

67 See p. 202 supra.

68 Bukharin, *Historical Materialism*, p. 102.

69 Ibid., pp. 134–5.

70 Ibid., p. 90. See also p. 93 for a longer explanation, based on analogy.

71 See A. P. Zablotsky-Desiatovsky, *Graf P. D. Kiselev*, vol. 2 (St. Petersburg, 1882) p. 149.

72 For a unique description of present day life and methods on collective farms, see A. Amalrik, *Involuntary Journey to Siberia* (London, 1970).

73 See p. 197, supra.

74 *USSR Handbook* (London, 1936) p. 53.

75 B. Semenov Tian-Shansky, 'Russia : Territory and Population : a Perspective on the 1926 Census', in *Geographical Review* (1926) p. 635.

76 *USSR Handbook*, p. 53.

77 Between the end of 1918 and the end of 1920, epidemics, hunger and cold killed approximately 7.5 million Russians, many of them town-dwellers. See P. Sorlin, *The Soviet People and Their Society* (London, 1969).

78 Wells, op. cit., pp. 132–4.

79 See Sir J. Simpson, *The Refugee Problem: Report of a Survey* (London, 1939) pp. 80–2, 559–61, for the lowest figure, which only includes persons formally registered as refugees, with Nansen passports; H. von Rimscha, *Der russische Bürgerkrieg und die russische Emigration 1917–1921* (Jena, 1924) pp. 50–1, gives a total of 2,935,000.

80 On the eve of the Revolution the gentry was only supplying 12 per cent of Russia's bread grain and 21.6 per cent of her trade corn. The kulaks were producing 38 and 50 per cent, respectively. See W. Hoffman-Wilhelmshaven, 'Die russische Gesellschaft nach der bolschewistischen Revolution', in *Schmollers Jahrbuch fur Gesetzgebung, Verwaltung und Volkswirtschaft*, vol. V, 76er Jahrgang, p. 70.

81 See L. Schapiro, *The Origin of the Communist Autocracy* (London, 1955), and *The Communist Party of the Soviet Union*; Carr, *A History of Soviet Russia*; R. Daniels, *The Conscience of the Revolution: Communist Opposition in Soviet Russia* (Cambridge, Mass., 1960); Fainsod, *How Russia is Ruled*.

82 Trotsky, *The New Course* (New York, 1943) p. 154.

83 *Desiatyi s"ezd RKP(b), stenograficheskii otchet* (Moscow, 1933) p. 72.

84 The party census of 1927 revealed that only 0.7 per cent of peasant households included a party member and that the party coverage of 546,747 'rural inhabited points' in the Soviet Union was extremely thin. See Carr, *Foundations of a Planned Economy*, vol. 2, p. 179.

85 See Chapter 2, pp. 57–61.

86 Bukharin, *Programma kommunistov (bol'shevikov)* (Petrograd, 1919) pp. 8–9.

87 See also Chapter 3, p. 76.

88 Smilga, op. cit., p. 10. Smilga thought that if a militia system were attacked from the west of Russia, it would only be able to assemble in time to defend a line on the Volga.

89 Ibid., pp. 9, 16.

90 See, amongst others, O. Anweiler, *Die Rätebewegung in Russland 1905–1921* (Leiden, 1958); Carr, *The Bolshevik Revolution*; Narkiewicz, *The Making of the Soviet State Apparatus*; *Sovety v pervyi period proletarskoi diktatury: oktiabr' 1917 g. – noiabr' 1918 g.* (Moscow, 1967); M. Rezunov, *Selskie sovety i zemelnye obshchestva* (Moscow, 1928).

91 Bukharin, *ABC of Communism*, p. 302.

92 *State and Revolution*, p. 481.

93 See Pethybridge, 'Petrograd and The Provinces', op. cit., for a discussion of Lenin's changing views on revolutionary strategy in geographical terms during 1917.

94 Schapiro has observed (*The Communist Party of The Soviet Union*, p. 242) that the Bolshevik leadership overcame local fragmentation in 1917–18 more through direct collaboration between Bolshevik officials in the Soviet organs than through the looser hierarchy of party committees.

95 *VKP(b) v rezoliutsiakh*, vol. 1 (Moscow, 1941) p. 306.

96 Lenin, *Sochineniia*, vol. 26, p. 208.

97 Ibid., vol. 25, p. 315.

98 Krupskaia, *Pedagogicheskie sochineniia*, vol. 2, p. 76.

99 See *Partiinaia zhizn'*, no. 20 (1957) pp. 80–96.

100 See M. Bockhenhauer, *Die Genossennschaften im Wirtschaftssystem des Soviet Staates* (Leipzig, 1930); E. Fuckner, *Die russische Genossenschaftsbewegung* (Leipzig, 1922); V. P. Miliutin, *Kooperatsiia v SSSR za 10 let* (Moscow, 1928); Ia. Kristanov, *Potrebitel'skaia kooperatsiia SSSR: istoricheskii ocherk* (Moscow, 1951).

101 Lenin, 'O kooperatsii', in *Sochineniia*, vol. 33, pp. 430–1.

102 Lenin, *Sochineniia*, vol. 28, p. 365.

103 M. Bronsky, in *Sotsialisticheskoe khoziaistvo*, no. 5 (1926) pp. 18–19.

104 *Soviet Union Yearbook*, 1930, p. 217.

105 Kristanov, op. cit., pp. 231, 237.

106 Meshcheriakov, *Sovremennaia kooperatsiia* (Moscow, 1923) p. 111.

107 Ibid., pp. 97, 107, 120.

108 See A. Antsiferov, *Ocherki po kooperatsii i lektsii i stat'i* (Moscow, 1915) p. 81.

109 *Kooperatsiia v Rossii do, vo vremia i posle bol'shevikov*

(Frankfurt, 1955) p. 64. The number was reduced to 9000 following an investigation.

110 Ibid., p. 79.

111 *Pravda*, 30 July 1930, quoted in Lewin, op. cit., p. 97.

112 Antsiferov, op. cit., p. 80.

113 *The Communist Manifesto*, p. 66.

114 Lewin, op. cit., p. 100. See also M. Bogdenko, in *Istoricheskie zapiski*, no. 76, p. 36.

115 This is also the case for the prerevolutionary period. See for instance *Kustarnaia promyshlennost' Rossii*, 4 vols. (St. Petersburg, 1913), and the discussion of source materials by N. Filinnov in the introduction to vol. 3.

116 This remains the area of definition in present-day Soviet scholarship. See A. Malinova, 'O sotsialisticheskom preobrazovanii melkotovarnogo uklada v promyshlennosti SSSR', in *Istoriia SSSR*, no. 4 (1963) pp. 23–44.

117 *Vsesoiuznaia perepis' naseleniia 1926 g.* (Moscow, 1928).

118 D. Shapiro, *Problemy ekonomiki*, no. 7–8 (Moscow, 1929) p. 126. The primary sources of data on the *kustari* are few in number, and they sometimes conflict. Only with the census covering the years 1926–7 was a systematic analysis made. Even there the data are confined to gross value of turnover and number of persons employed, both full-time and part-time.

119 See the article on *kustari* in the *Bol'shaia sovetskaia entsiklopediia*, 2nd edn., vol. 24, pp. 136–7.

120 A. Buzlaeva, *Leninskii plan kooperirovaniia* (Moscow, 1969) pp. 50–1. There were also other reasons for the growing importance of small-scale industry during the Civil War and NEP. The famine of 1919–21 forced industrial workers back to the countryside, where they proceeded to apply their skills, encouraged by the local peasantry, thwarted by the lack of industrial consumer goods from the towns. The loss of the Polish and Baltic provinces, which had supplied the Russian market with a large quantity of consumer goods, also served to increase the dependence of the Soviet population on the *kustari*.

121 *Bol'shaia sovetskaia entsiklopediia*. For more details, see *Melkaia promyshlennost' SSSR po dannym vsesoiuznoi perepisi 1929 g.* (Moscow, 1932–3) *vypusk* 1–3.

122 A. Malikova, op. cit., p. 23.

123 I. Gladkov, *Sovetskoe narodnoe khoziaistvo (1921–5)* (Moscow, 1960) p. 204.

124 *Bol'shaia sovetskaia entskilopediia*.

125 N. and M. Sheremeteva, *Samoprialochnyi promysel v Piatovskom kustarnom raione* (Kaluga, 1929) pp. 58–9.

126 See Dobb, *Soviet Economic Development Since 1917*, p. 45.

127 Bogdanov, *Elementy* . . ., p. 27.

128 Trotsky, *Kak vooruzhalas' revoliutsiia*, vol. 1, p. 188.

129 Bukharin, *ABC of Communism*, pp. 274–6.

130 Baron von Haxthausen, *The Russian Empire, Its People, Institutions, and Resources*, vol. 1 (London, 1856) p. 160.

131 *Kustarnaia promyshlennost' Rossii*, vol. 3, p. iii.

132 *KPSS v rezoliutsiiakh i resheniiakh s"ezdov, konferentsii i plenumov Tsk*, vol. 1 (Moscow, 1953) p. 422.

133 Lenin, *Sochineniia*, vol. 24, pp. 332–3.

134 See Buzlaeva, op. cit., p. 70.

135 Bukharin, *Historical Materialism*, p. 136.

136 Malikova, op. cit., p. 23. Roughly half of the 1927 employment in small-scale industry was shifted into large-scale industry between 1927 and 1931. The move was further precipitated by the severe shortage of industrial raw materials, which compelled the government to reduce their supply to the *kustari*. Although this displacement of small-scale industry was undoubtedly massive, part of it may have been illusory because there were changes in the definition of large-scale production which led to incorporation in that sphere of what was formerly treated as small-scale production. See A. Kaufman, *Small-scale Industry in the Soviet Union* (New York, 1962) especially pp. xvi, 42–6.

137 See *Izvestiia Tsk RKP(b)*, no. 10 (1924) pp. 1–2; no. 15–16 (1925) p. 3.

138 Smolensk Archives, file WKP 277, July 1924.

139 *XIII s"ezd RKP(b), mai 1924 g., stenograficheskii otchet*, p. 487.

140 M. Zoshchenko, *Scenes From The Bathhouse and Other Stories of Communist Russia*.

141 See Chapter 4, pp. 163–4.

142 See R. Redfield, *Peasant Society and Culture: An Anthropological Approach to Civilization* (London, 1956) p. 61.

143 M. Tomsky, in *Trud*, 14 November 1924.

144 *Voprosy truda*, no. 7–8 (1924).

145 *Soveshchanie po voprosam sovetskogo stroitel'stva, ianvar' 1925 g.*, p. 137. See also *XIII s"ezd RKP(b), mai 1924 g., stenograficheskii otchet*, pp. 480–1.

146 There are some Soviet studies which refer in passing to this problem. See L. F. Morozov, 'K voprosa o periodizatsii istorii bor'by s nepmanskoi burzhuaziei', in *Voprosy istorii*, no. 12 (1964) pp. 3–17;

and by the same author, *Reshaiushchii etap bor'by s nepmanskoi burzhuaziei* (Moscow, 1960).

147 More information on other aspects of the human links between town and country in NEP may be found in Shanin, op. cit., pp. 180–99.

148 S. Strumilin, *Problemy ekonomiki truda* (Moscow, 1964) pp. 168–71.

149 See R. Robinson, *The First Turkish Republic* (Cambridge, Mass., 1963) p. 59 ff.

150 M. Asquith, *Famine: Quaker Work in Russia 1921–3* (London, 1943).

151 See Chapter 2, p. 65.

152 See Chapter 3, pp. 98–9, for the argument in favour of a decentralised system at the start of War Communism. In a late gloss on Marx, Engels put an almost contrary case : see his 1891 introduction to K. Marx, *The Civil War in France.*

153 H. Arendt, *On Revolution* (London, 1963); R. Aron, 'Social Structure and Ruling Class', in the *British Journal of Sociology*, vol. 1 (1950); W. Kornhauser, *The Politics of Mass Society* (London, 1960).

154 See Conclusion, p. 316.

155 Arendt, *The Origins of Totalitarianism* (London, 1967) p. 318.

156 Kornhauser, op. cit., p. 58; see also p. 62.

6 The Administration of Society

The topic under consideration here brings us to one of the central features of Stalinism as a political phenomenon – the bureaucratic system. As the title of this chapter implies, emphasis is shifted away from the traditional political and economic reasons that have been given for the resurgence of bureaucracy in the teeth of Bolshevik objections to it. Stress is laid here on the social foundations of the new bureaucracy. Another good reason for not opting for the over-used label of bureaucracy in the title is that it causes many ambiguities of definition. This problem cannot be avoided, however. Since an attempt is being made to add a dimension to what is generally known as Stalinist bureaucracy, it must be clear what is meant by this phrase.

The administration of society by the party and state was deeply affected by the developments outlined earlier in this book. The failure to cultivate auxiliary, semi-autonomous organisations between the central authorities and the masses, described in the previous chapter, entailed an over-growing accumulation of central administrative power, as did the demise of workers' control and trade union independence. Entrenched military influences affected both the organisation and the ethos of the bureaucracy, while the continuing illiteracy of a large sector of the Soviet population shored up the need for official scribes acting as political interpreters between the masses and a regime intent on entering the modern industrial world at breakneck speed.

These social pressures will be examined at greater length below. At this stage we must clarify the use of the term bureaucracy as applied to the Soviet political and social system. This is easier said than done. The word 'bureaucracy' merely helps us to identify a whole series of problems concerning the relations of individuals to abstract organisational features. The trouble is that virtually every writer on the Soviet system, from Lenin through Bukharin, Trotsky and Djilas on the one hand, to a plethora of non-communist scholars on the other, has assumed that his own interpretation of the term, which is rarely spelt out, is the definitive version of bureaucracy. A quick glance at the history of the word is enough to dispel any confidence of this kind. Probably the most widespread usage in this century derives from the vapid definition given by R. von Mohl in the nineteenth century. This led critics to regard any system of administration, whether good or bad, as bureaucracy.[1] Although it is often assumed that Max Weber defined the term, in fact he never did. His general concept has to be reconstructed by inference from the passages where he alluded to it.[2] In view of the vague origins of the word, it is hardly surprising that in the mouths of the Bolsheviks, and of many of their opponents, it became an all-embracing term of abuse in the sphere of administration, just as 'kulak' was turned into a multi-purpose label in the agricultural realm. It was noted in the discussion on illiteracy how easy it was for the ruling literate minority to manipulate abstract concepts like bureaucracy.[3] Another reason for emptiness of meaning in the Soviet context was that in the 1920s, and even more so during the 1930s, it was impossible to stabilise the usage of the term. The Soviet Union possessed what has been called a 'development administration'.[4] Whatever this heavy phrase means, rapidly changing conditions certainly ensured that a new concept of bureaucracy had to be thrown up with each major structural change in the running of the country. An example taken from the end of NEP may serve to illustrate the way in which it was used as a convenient umbrella term. When a campaign was being waged against 'bureaucratism', the Fifteenth Party Congress of December 1927 promoted the 'wide use of the *rabsel'kor* [worker and peasant correspondents'] movement in the struggle with bureaucratic distortions'.[5] All this really meant was that the regime encouraged attacks on abuses of any sort that thwarted its aims. Thus in 1928 we find the *rabkors* conducting campaigns in factories against drunkenness and absenteeism, while *sel'kors* were involved in checking grain collections, sowings, self-taxation and contributions to state loans.[6]

A recent writer on the definition of bureaucracy, Martin Albrow, advises his readers to avoid the use of the term altogether, while continuing to pursue research in the areas in which it has been employed.[7] This advice cannot be taken here, since we must first discover what the various critics of 'Stalinist bureaucracy' have meant by the phrase, before going on to look at its social roots. Albrow cites no less than seven modern concepts of bureaucracy, and it does not appear that he is exaggerating. We shall take them briefly in turn, in an attempt to find out which apply to our present analysis, and to what extent. Weber's usual view of bureaucracy as rational organisation may be set aside, since it deals with an ideal type and maintains a non-pejorative approach.[8] Marx, Lenin, other Bolshevik leaders and foreign critics all took a pejorative view of bureaucracy and were concerned with the actual workings of Russian administration. The second definition of bureaucracy, as organisational inefficiency, therefore does fall within the meanings ascribed to bureaucracy by these critics, though we shall see that they concentrated too heavily on political and economic causes while ignoring or underestimating the social reasons for inefficiency.

Two other definitions of bureaucracy are rule by officials and administration by officials. In Marx's pejorative usage of the term it could refer equally to an inefficient system and also to the men who implemented the system, but usually to the latter. The same goes for the Bolsheviks and most scholars who have written on Soviet bureaucracy. Whereas these two definitions can ideally be kept apart, in the Soviet context they became fused, since the party *apparatchiki* who ruled the country were also its chief administrators in the state Commissariats (the origins and function of the party-state bureaucracy are outlined below). The fifth definition of bureaucracy is organisation as a whole, conceived mainly in terms of large-scale structure. This approach concerned the Bolsheviks and their critics and so must concern us here. Indeed, this view has been implicit in the references already made to bureaucracy in the earlier chapters on military influences and on large-scale theories. In its sixth metamorphosis or rather apotheosis, bureaucracy appears as a complete system which characterises a whole society, and so is used as a blanket term like democracy or capitalism. This method was not adopted by Marx, who did not ascribe a dominating role to bureaucracy, nor was it followed by Lenin and other Bolshevik thinkers in the 1920s. Nevertheless it enters into our considerations, because Djilas and many non-communist observers of what they called 'Stalinist bureaucracy' used this definition either explicitly or implicitly. What interests us particularly from the social angle is to what extent these analysts mean a whole society which has itself become a bureaucracy, and in what degree a society permeated by a ruling bureaucracy. Can one possibly mean the former when talking of a society like that of Russia during NEP, in which 70–80 per cent of the population consisted of ignorant peasants? Even in the 1930s, when the balance of employment began to swing faster towards factory workers, the type of Soviet society was firmly stamped on it by the character of its 'bureaucratic' ruling élite.

The final definition of bureaucracy, as public administration, brings us into close proximity with the title given to this chapter. This concept appears to be essentially neutral in nature. Public administration is treated as bureaucracy without reference to the possession of power, with the emphasis taken off the notion of rule by officials. This approach has some purely methodological advantages in the context of this book, since it permits us to lay stress on the historical and social reasons in Russia for the growth of Soviet administration. Some observers have been hypnotised by the phenomenon of power in the administrative structure. This is not surprising, given the amount of power which accrued so rapidly to the Soviet party bureaucracy. They have also been swayed by the usual approach to the concept of bureaucracy, in which too great an accent is laid on the executive group and its current activity, and not enough on the forces which brought both the group and its functions into play in the first place.

In this notion of bureaucracy as administration, the citizen is seen to be closely and actively associated in its management. Bureaucracy is no longer thought to be a barrier between the people and the state. Sidney Webb, who first gave precise meaning in English to the term 'social administration', believed that 'Every increase in the political power of the proletariat will most surely be used by them for their economic and social protection.'[9] This was the theoretical basis for the comments that Sidney and Beatrice Webb were later to make in the 1930s on Soviet society. In their book, *Soviet Communism: A New Civilization*, they told British readers that 'the USSR does not consist of a government and a people confronting each other as all other great societies have hitherto been. It is a highly integrated organization, in which

each individual man, woman or youth is expected to participate ...' [10] They only stayed in Russia from May to August 1932,
but the enormous number of Soviet documents they received were
translated and formed the backbone of their book. They concluded that the Communist Party and its administration were
democratic in their internal structure : their joint function was to
inspire with the passion of community service a diversely moulded
democracy, in which Soviets, trade unions, cooperatives and
other voluntary associations allowed for the individual political
and administrative participation of millions of people.[11] This
opinion is virtually the opposite of the conclusion reached in the
previous chapter of this book concerning the lack of evolution in
auxiliary entities during the 1920s.

The Webbs had some strange bedfellows in the 1930s. Mussolini agreed with their view that bureaucracy viewed as neutral
administration presented no particular political problems. Speaking on the corporate state in 1933, he said that bureaucracy did
not create a gulf between the people and the state, since the population was closely involved in administration.[12] Before the Webbs,
another Englishman had studied social administration without forgetting that it almost always implies rule by officials as well. J. S.
Mill found that the dangers of bureaucracy were the most important reason for protesting against government interference in
society. As a government enveloped more functions, so it could
offer more careers and attract hangers-on. The administration
would become the mecca of all talent, which would eventually en-
throne the ruling élite in a position of permanent dominance.

It is imperative in the Soviet context never to divorce the
problem of power from that of the administration of society. The
central aim of this chapter is to show how the gradual and almost
inevitable accumulation of authority in the hands of a minority
through the onerous task of managing a backward society merely
served to tighten the political strings which manipulated the
bureaucracy, and helped to turn an authoritarian system into a
totalitarian one. It is a commonplace that when a bureaucracy in
the sense of rule by officials amasses enough power to pursue its
own interests, it often tries to mould the social environment to its
convenience. This is what happened in Russia in the 1930s. The
illusion of greater administrative efficiency was thereby created (an
illusion to which the Webbs fell prey in their hurried digestion of

Soviet written propaganda), but harsh realities entailed the use of ever more repressive methods.

Scholars have dwelt on the coercive impact of Soviet bureaucracy on society once it had reached its peak of power under Stalin's control. Instead of proving this over again, we wish to point out the reverse influence (that of society on bureaucracy) at work during NEP. It was a slower, subtler influence, much less coercive but no less determining. In his analysis of bureaucracy, defined primarily as large-scale organisation, E. Strauss tries to distinguish between technical and social defects.[13] This is surely unrealistic, at least in the study of Soviet bureaucracy, because in so many ways technical difficulties and allied political problems arose within it precisely on account of the poverty of the social *milieu*, which after all supplied the personnel and influenced the scope of administration in the vital formative stages of the new bureaucracy.

Before turning to examine the social reasons for the resurgence of large-scale coercive administration in the Soviet period, there is one other point of definition which should be considered. It has already been stated that the Soviet bureaucracy was a fusion of rule and administration by the same officials in a combined party-state system. How did this come about? Both Soviet and foreign historians nearly always assume that the Communist party at once dominated all other possible rivals in the bid for administrative control straight after October 1917. This judgment is perhaps over-simplified, as one or two percipient scholars have shown.[14] What is certain is that from 1919 on, if not before that, a full-time party apparatus greatly increased its administrative scope, infiltrated the Soviets and other institutional structures, and subordinated both local party and government agencies to strong central control. It would be unwise to suppose, however, that a monolithic fusion of party and state administrative personnel and of their ideas and methods took place during NEP. For one thing, political nonconformists like Mensheviks, neo-Narodniks and even Kadets continued to occupy important posts in the administration.[15] For another, it has been argued convincingly for the post-Stalin phase of Soviet administration that agents at different levels of the hierarchy have very different functions and attitudes to the central apparatus.[16] There is no reason to imagine that the situation would be any more homogeneous for the 1920s, even when the discrepancies between the conditions prevailing in the two periods are allowed for.

By the 1930s, however, it can be said that even in those areas where state administration survived as a distinctive structure, it was penetrated and supervised by the party apparatus, which in turn was controlled by one man. In a one-party system permanent party officials can hold permanent jobs in the state administration. In Nazi Germany there was a similar fusion of government and party offices. In fact party-state bureaucracies have been identified as typical byproducts of totalitarian regimes.[17]

Having dealt with questions of definition which are pertinent to our theme, we can now examine the reasons given in turn by early Soviet leaders, internal Bolshevik critics, Communist heretics and non-Marxist writers for the recurrence of a heavily centralised administration in the 1920s and afterwards. It may seem strange that so many groups of opposed thinkers have taken great pains to explain why such a likely development took place. After all, Tsarist Russia had possessed one of the largest state administrative systems in the world. The country retained its enormous size, nearly all its nationalities, and its weak communications network after the Bolshevik revolution. Social and economic problems that had been endemic in Tsarist Russia still cried out for administrative solutions, and the national temperament described by N. Gogol in *The Greatcoat* did not disappear overnight.

The basic reason for such painstaking analysis stems from Marx's, and consequently Lenin's, attitude towards bureaucracy. They maintained that after a proletarian revolution there would be no need to preserve a permanent corpus of administrative officials geared to the requirements of the centralised state and set apart from the masses. Marx took a pejorative view of bureaucracy. His initial stance led to interminable soul-searching when bureaucratic symptoms reappeared in Soviet Russia. Lenin sought for remedies, internal critics looked for explanations, while heretics and outsiders indulged in detailed diagnoses and pointed accusing fingers.

Marx characteristically defined bureaucracy by division of functions and hierarchy,[18] for he saw it as the political expression of the division of labour. He also linked his theory of alienation to this definition, by condemning bureaucracy as the organisational result of the illusion that the state can realise human universality. On a more pragmatic level, Marx feared that the hierarchical traditions of the working class in Germany might prevent the development of a revolutionary proletariat in that country.[19] This supposition alone, however, could not be ascribed major importance in the realm of theory, as it would imply that bureaucracy could act as an independent force and control society in its own interests. The influence of the economic substructure would thus be nullified. Partly for this reason Marx played down the future role of bureaucracy as he defined it. He saw it as an appendage which would die away after a proletarian revolution. Certainly it would lose all political power. Administrative posts would be filled by election and their occupants would be directly responsible to self-governing communities.[20]

Lenin elaborated on this latter theme in *State and Revolution*, written in the late summer of 1917. He took the view that bureaucracy seen as coercive rule by officials could be replaced by neutral non-central public administration. His famous dictum concerning the ability of any literate person to carry out functions previously assigned to trained civil servants ignored the weak social foundations on which the new system would have to be based. In this Lenin was merely repeating the common tendency to underestimate the social factor : but he also forgot momentarily various political influences which he had personally set in motion. In *What is to be Done?* he had already advocated 'bureaucratism' so long as his party was at the helm : 'Bureaucratism *versus* democratism, this is precisely centralism *versus* autonomism, and this is the organizational principle of revolutionary social-democracy as against that of opportunist social-democracy.'[21] Much nearer the time of writing *State and Revolution*, in fact in the late spring of 1917, he abandoned a final attempt in practice to stimulate revolutionary progress by relying on the localities in the manner of the 1905 revolution. He quickly reverted to an emphasis on political and administrative centralism.[22]

However, Lenin continued to assert that old-style bureaucracy in the pejorative sense could be replaced by efficient administration. The vital point for Lenin was not the structure of the mechanism *per se*, but which class operated it, and in whose interests. Since the Bolshevik party represented the proletariat, the new administration could not fail to be beneficial (echoes of the views of the Webbs before him and of Mussolini afterwards). We shall examine later in this chapter the degree to which the factory labour force, through workers' control and other means, breathed life into this notion. For his part, Lenin genuinely struggled until his death for the active participation in the national administration of organs extraneous to the party, so long as they did not threaten the latter's pre-eminence. His efforts with regard to the Soviet network, the cooperatives and the *kustari* were described in Chapter 5. He honestly recognised that bureaucratic features in the pejorative sense were creeping back into Soviet institutions, and he spent much of his declining energy in his last years trying to combat the menace through the establishment of *Rabkrin* and other measures.[23]

Lenin hardly ever understood the mainsprings of inefficient rule by party-state officials. He rarely saw the connection between social underdevelopment and bureaucracy, and perhaps preferred to ignore some of the political reasons, especially those for which he himself was responsible, such as the emphasis on party hierarchy, rigid central control, and the will to permeate all subsidiary institutions with Bolshevik officials. When the new party-state bureaucracy could no longer be ignored, rather vague political reasons were given which pinned the blame firmly either on class or national enemies. At first, stress was laid on the idea that bureaucratic symptoms from the prerevolutionary regime were still infectious. There was some truth in this, as it was natural that the habits of the Petrine system would linger on, particularly as many Tsarist civil servants had had to be retained as *spetsy* by the new government. But as an all-inclusive argument it did not suffice. Nor did another, much vaguer, line, to the effect that the corruptive conditions of capitalism had a bad influence on party administration. A third reason given was the continuing threat of capitalist intervention. The menace was real enough during the Civil War, and definitely did contribute to Lenin's emphasis on central control, but the trouble with this argument was that it was upheld in even stronger terms in the peace which followed, and became Stalin's favourite.

When realities could no longer be denied, euphemistic titles became another way of exorcising the evil, as was the case with the secret police, which likewise underwent a variety of name changes. At the top party level, the term 'apparatus' came into much more frequent use to describe party officials with political powers who ran both party and state organs, sometimes efficiently, sometimes not. The idea caught on at lower levels too. A trade union organiser put it this way : 'We have been accustomed to conceive bureaucracy in terms of lack of progress and sluggishness, whereas this new industrial bureaucracy is characterised by its speed and automatization of labour.' He was not clever enough to change the term completely, but coined a new, hopeful phrase, 'mechanized bureaucracy'.[24]

Lenin was far from being alone among the leading Bolsheviks in his failure to understand and deal with the growth of cumbersome yet powerful administrative forces. For all his sophisticated analysis of early Soviet society in the *ABC of Communism* and *Historical Materialism*, Bukharin too was blinkered in his assessment of bureaucracy. He believed that the emergence of a segregated administrative élite was impossible on account of the 'colossal over-production of organizers, which will nullify the stability of the ruling groups ... The increasing reproduction of technologists and organizers in general, out of the working class itself, will undermine this possible new class alignment.' [25] Unlike Lenin and Stalin, Bukharin was never strictly a party bureaucrat himself, but this lack of experience hardly excuses the bland tone of his optimism. The notion that technical personnel could overwhelm the party 'apparatus' from outside only became a remote chance after 1953, when Stalin's death left behind an atrophied party core that might conceivably have ceded control to an oligarchy relying mainly on government rather than on party agencies for support.[26] One of the perennial features of Soviet society until the very recent period has been the acute shortage of technologists and organisers.

Stalin stood out from nearly all his colleagues in the Bolshevik élite during NEP as a positive supporter of increased party-state administration for its own sake, and for his personal aggrandisement, since he knew how to manipulate it. For most of the time in the 1920s he muted this unpopular opinion, but after his rise to sole power there was less need for caution. At the end of his life, in his *Economic Problems of Socialism in the USSR*, he went so far as to advocate the idea of a permanent body of officials enjoying different working conditions from the proletariat. He hastened to add that a difference of this kind would be inessential, and would be an advantage for society as a whole rather than a retrogressive feature.[27]

The open expression of an opinion of this kind would have been anathema to most Bolshevik leaders in the years 1917–28, and would undoubtedly have led to an increasingly dangerous confrontation with those elements at lower party levels or outside the party altogether that cried out against 'bureaucratism' in the early period. In 1920 the Ninth Party Congress was the scene of a fierce assault on 'bureaucratic centralism'. The critical Kronstadt revolt was sparked off partly on account of resentment at party bureaucratisation. Finally at the Tenth Party Congress the Workers' Opposition called for the Marxist aim of elections to administrative positions. It also condemned party bureaucracy and demanded the expulsion of non-proletarian figures from the administration. None of these three campaigns recognised the social causes of the evils they deplored. They only dimly realised how the authoritarian political structure of the Bolshevik party as established by Lenin was another major reason for 'bureaucratism'. Even if they had delved to this particular root, it was unlikely that they would have dared or wished to launch such a fundamentalist attack on the regime. The same went for the barrage of criticism which came from Soviet literary figures. They satirised the external paraphernalia of administrative mismanagement without penetrating to origins.[28]

Trotsky's interpretation of Soviet bureaucracy cannot be accused of this type of superficiality. He had the advantage of publishing his main broadside, *The Revolution Betrayed*, in 1937, by which time the full outlines of the Stalinist system were clearly apparant. Stalin had successfully accelerated the integration of party-state functions, and encouraged the permanent establishment of officials who supported his personal power. Fast industrialisation and urbanisation had shored up the size and central location of administrative organs. Trotsky in exile could stand back from details and apply his lucid brain to working out a generalised theoretical definition of Stalinist bureaucracy. Yet like most interpreters of bureaucracy, he never defined the term at the outset, and so built a house on shifting sand. He normally followed Marx by taking a pejorative view. He also asserted indirectly that the Soviet phenomenon was a combination of rule *and* administration by officials, and he took bureaucracy to mean a strongly unified organisation, without, however, ever making it clear if he was talking about a vertically integrated series of posts in a hierarchy or about a horizontal group of office holders at the apex of the party-state system.

Trotsky spent very little time in discussing the reasons for the emergence of his version of bureaucracy, but he did alight briefly on two fundamental socio-economic causes, although they were rather constricted within the Marxist framework he used. The first point he made was to remind us that, according to Marxist thought, the level of technology helps to determine the basis of society as much as do the relations of production. Given that 'material forces' in the Soviet Union of the 1930s were not as well developed as in other more advanced capitalist regimes, it was also doubtful whether social relations in Russia could have reached a higher stage. In other words, it would be no surprise to find in Russia a permanent body of officials still set in opposition to the working masses. The second point lays more stress on early social conditions in the Soviet Union. Trotsky realised that the Russian proletariat was 'hardly emerging from destitution and darkness'. Suffering an intrinsic tradition of domination, it fell prey to a bureaucratic group which came to monopolise the control of Soviet society.[29] Whilst this statement is broadly correct, it suffers from a polarisation of the sort so often favoured by Trotsky in his urge for clarity. He forgot that the 'bureaucratic group' at first swallowed up thousands of poorly trained workers into its own ranks.

By far the greater part of Trotsky's energies was devoted to an analysis of full-blown Stalinist bureaucracy rather than to a search for origins. For polemical motives he was mainly concerned with the corruption of Soviet political and social life since the rise of Stalin to sole power. The defeat of his opposition to Stalin in 1923 and his deportation in 1929 were seen by himself and by his later supporters as steps on the decline into bureaucratic government.[30] Trotsky's views are nevertheless of some interest to us in that they concentrate on socio-economic factors. He was obsessed by the crucial Marxist question as to whether Stalinist bureaucracy constituted a new ruling class. He stopped short of admitting this, confining himself to the opinion that it represented a new ruling stratum. There is no need in the context of this chapter to go into the details of his well-known argument, except to point out two exaggerations he made in his eagerness to condemn the new Soviet bureaucracy and its leader in particular.

Trotsky held that the bureaucracy had entered into a position of exploitation vis-à-vis the proletariat. He was careful to admit that members of the bureaucracy had no special property relations of their own, nor could they hand over their right of exploitation to their heirs, who might not become bureaucrats themselves. The supposed economic power of this stratum is weakened further by a fact which Trotsky ignored, namely that in the Soviet system it could not dispose of assets it merely controlled, but did not own, for its own private benefit. Trotsky's successors in this line of thought (Rizzi, Djilas and Schachtman)[31] took a step further, evolving the 'state capitalist' theory, which conceives of the Soviet bureaucracy as a definite class rather than just a stratum. The economic objections listed above apply with greater force to this extended claim, since the classic Marxist definition of social class cannot be fitted into this watered down version bereft of strict economic determinants.

Moreover, both Trotsky and his successors failed to prove in any detail that the socio-economic interests of all the members of the Soviet bureaucracy were unified. It has already been observed that before the 1930s and from 1953 onwards it was not true that party-state management was monolithic in its structure or in the attitudes of its personnel. Even during the period of Stalin's hegemony it would be unsafe to assume that because a monolithic political stance was adopted, *ipso facto* the social and economic ambitions of the ruling hierarchy were also stereotyped. This is not the place to prove this point, but we may assume its likelihood, and in passing note that another erstwhile supporter of Trotsky, Boris Souvarine, devised a social theory which appears to show just the opposite of what the 'state-capitalist' group took to be the reality. Souvarine thought that a social division of interests had taken place within the party-state bureaucracy itself. The best products of 1917 had been absorbed into the less important, but more intellectually demanding, posts by reason of their capabilities. Mediocre men, who could not be so usefully employed, became the top stratum of Soviet society. Those Bolsheviks who proved themselves unfit for responsibility in the vital spheres of national administration ended up by gaining a post in the hierarchy of the party secretaries.[32] Souvarine's theory must remain in the realm of hypothesis, because he never offered any detailed proof. The same goes for the constructs of Trotsky, Djilas and others. Nevertheless their ideas do serve a useful purpose in two ways. They handle the socio-economic aspects of bureaucracy, which is a rare virtue in the Soviet context, and they show, albeit in very general and sometimes exaggerated terms, how socio-economic power sustains an entrenched political system.

The great majority of non-Soviet, non-Marxist analyses of Stalinism follow the more normal Soviet tendency to accentuate political considerations at the expense of other influences in the growth of central administration. As might be expected, they provide a rather different list of political causes. Many scholars mention the appointment of Stalin as General Secretary of the Communist Party in the summer of 1922 and his growing manipulation of party-state structure from then on. Lenin could dare to criticise Stalin's role in this respect, but both before and especially after Lenin's death, the monster (*derzhimorda*) of bureaucracy was more often ascribed to the careerism of lesser individuals in the party hierarchy. Foreign observers also frequently allude to the increasing political arbitrariness of the party in the war climate between October 1917 and the end of the Civil War. Little or no stress is put on those disturbed social conditions which were examined in Chapter 3. Much more attention is paid to acts of high politics which could be carried out because the Bolsheviks were fighting for survival. Examples usually cited include the harsh repression of all the opposing left-wing parties and the speedy centralisation of the Bolshevik party apparatus. However, the heaviest emphasis of all is put on another political factor, which is seen as the real disease, whereas the other influences mentioned above are assessed as secondary symptoms. This is the Leninist conception of the party, stated in *What is To Be Done?*,[33] to which reference has already been made.

This list of reasons is not only too narrowly political. It does not stop to wonder whether in some ways even Lenin's view of the party was in turn just another symptom of a general *malaise* in Russian politics and in the social and economic order which cut right across the apparent dividing line of 1917. In his analysis of the French Revolution, de Tocqueville goes straight to the heart of the matter : 'If the principle of centralization did not perish in the Revolution, it was because that principle was itself the precursor and the commencement of the Revolution.'[34] From the armoury of Tsarist and anti-Tsarist politics, the Bolsheviks could choose between anarchy and over-centralisation. These were the prevailing modes of effective operation in the late Empire. The liberals achieved very little by comparison. In order to oppose a maximalist regime, similarly extreme methods had to be used. In *What Is To Be Done?* Lenin opted for a negative image of the power structure he wished to destroy. He even unconsciously took over the Tsarist state theory of local self-government which was prevalent during the last two decades of the nineteenth century. This theory assumed that there were no specifically local affairs, that they were really state affairs which were delegated by the 'will of the state' to the organs of local government. The state authority (later to be recast as the Bolshevik party-state administration) was one and indivisible and had two arms – the units of the bureaucratic pyramid and the institutions of local self-government.[35]

Of course Lenin diverged completely from prevailing modes of Tsarist political thought with regard to his party's long term *aims*, but his notion of party *structure* owed a certain debt to the prevailing authoritarian model, though he viewed the tight party élite as a temporary cudgel only, by means of which he could destroy the Tsarist regime. He underestimated, as we shall see below, the dragging effect of a backward society after a political revolution which was to have little effect at first on that society. He also minimised certain pervasive political influences. A centralised authoritarian structure of the kind outlined in *What Is To Be Done?*, with no separation of the powers, called for a long-tentacled administrative machine of the type that becomes notorious for its permanence once it is established. Lenin's over-optimistic view about the demise of bureaucracy had unfortunate repercussions after 1917 which all tended to swell the size and significance of central administration. Thus when it was realised that the new Russia could not be managed entirely by Bolshevik personnel, a large body of Tsarist specialists had to be taken on, creating the need for a watchdog system of dual control for security reasons. When at a later stage the tight political dominance of the Bolshevik party leaders did not evaporate, further structural duplications, though of a different kind, were required in order to maintain the myth of proletarian democracy. The successive façades of the Soviet network, the extensive party-state hierarchy, the Party Congress and other organs continued to proliferate, masking the realities of naked power concentrated in ever narrowing circles. Finally, when it became apparent that conflicts of interest between the main social groups and the ruling officials had not in fact been eliminated, administrative organs and problems took on an even greater prominence. The strains resulting from continuing but officially unrecognised social unrest were diagnosed as 'bureaucratic' defects. This is a typical manoeuvre of a monolithic party-state system which does not allow of independent social organisations beyond its compass.

That the type of party structure selected by Lenin and the cumbersome central administration which eventually fused with it, were more symptoms of the Russian disease than the disease itself becomes even clearer when we move on to study the social base which necessitated the survival of highly centralised state management. Nor must the economic foundations be forgotten. They have already been subjected to substantial analysis by non-Soviet scholars and can be summarised very briefly here.

Russia in the nineteenth century faced the immense task of economic modernisation if she was to carry her weight in European affairs. The process would have to be fast and undertaken without the aid of a long-standing and extensive bourgeois class. Witte could not leap over all these hurdles during the reign of Nicholas II, so the Bolsheviks were faced with similar problems. Robert Michels' prediction in 1911 referred equally to existing capitalist and future socialist systems : 'Social wealth cannot be satisfactorily administered in any other manner than by the creation of an extensive bureaucracy.'[36] Industrialisation in any country and under any regime entails a radical reallocation of manpower and leads to a swift increase in the number of administrators, planners, managers, bookkeepers, etc. It also tends to drive a wedge between the administration and those directly employed in large-scale industrial projects. This trend was reinforced in Russia in several ways. The lack of a strong bourgeoisie, the need for speed, and for protective barriers against West European industry, led to the creation of government monopolies run by central administrators. The need for similar instruments did not cease in the early Soviet period, for the same causes were still at work, and new reasons were added. The nationalisation of the 'commanding heights' of the economy meant that, as in all nationalised industries, the number of administrators multiplied. The flight of many individuals belonging to the Tsarist managerial stratum and the grave deficiency in technical expertise due to the disruption of normal training methods during the years 1914–21 led to much inefficiency and further duplication in the economy. On the eve of the first Five-Year Plan S. Ordzhonikidze found that only a third of seventy-six decisions of the Economic Council and the Council of People's Commissars had been fulfilled in 1927: one in ten had been partly implemented. Some of the unfulfilled decisions had been adopted as far back as eighteen months previously. In some cases ten to fifteen people dealt with an insignificant matter that could have been settled quickly by one or two individuals.[37] Because of the dearth of reliable statistics on personnel, it is not possible to make a precise estimate as to how far Soviet industrialisation swelled the ranks of the already large NEP administration. E. H. Carr has provided some useful figures and definitions for the period 1926–9.[38]

Given Lenin's view that the Bolshevik party would have to be the leading element in all aspects of social and economic life, and given also the uninterrupted and growing need for central economic administration before and after 1917, it was natural that the Soviet party-state apparatus should take over the entrepreneurial role of the nineteenth century West European bourgeoisie. From this development flowed the charges of Trotsky and Djilas, coined in social as well as economic terms. Marx, in the third book of *Das Kapital*, provides a concept of managerial capitalism which could possibly be applied to the Soviet system. Marx envisaged a society in which the functions of capitalists in the traditional sense might be taken over by the agents or 'managers' of capital. This new relationship still brings together capital, the exploiting capacity of the means of production and the labour exploited by this means, although individual capitalist owners are no longer involved.

Have we then arrived at the conclusion that Russia's political, economic, and, as we shall see in more detail, social problems rendered centralised, unwieldy administration almost inevitable? This seems to be the position, but it does not predetermine the political uses to which such an administration could be put by an unscrupulous dictator like Stalin. His individual manipulation will be examined at the end of this chapter and in the concluding chapter.

The great authorities on bureaucracy and its relationship to revolution agree on the former's tenacious hold amid swift political change. Weber wrote that 'Once it is fully established, bureaucracy is among those social structures which are the hardest to destroy . . . Where the bureaucratization of administration has been completely carried through, a form of power relation is established that is practically unshatterable.'[39] This power relation had clearly established itself in Russia long before the Revolution. Weber typically failed to appreciate the changing outlines (and occasional diminution) of bureaucracy, since he clung to an ideal and static concept. He wrote two essays on the aftermath of the 1905 revolution in Russia, *Zur Lage der bürgerlichen Demokratie in Russland*, and *Russlands Übergang zum Schein-Konstitutionalismus*, both published in 1906. He concluded that if Nicholas II had ceded genuine power to the Duma, the bureaucracy (i.e. in the Weberian sense of non-pejorative administration by officials) would not have acquired the entrenched position Weber ascribed to it after 1905. He saw it as a fixed and influential entity between Emperor and people. This prophesy turned out to be erroneous in fact, since the administrative functions of the bureaucracy were later eroded by the machinations of individuals like the Empress and Rasputin. But it is important in the light of the Bolshevik experience to remember that these functions were merely short-circuited and not eliminated for good.

De Tocqueville, more of an expert on revolution than on bureaucracy, wrote of the first English Revolution that it 'overthrew the whole political constitution of this country and abolished the monarchy itself, but touched superficially the secondary laws of the land and changed scarcely any of the customs and usages of the nation. The administration of justice and the conduct of public business retained their old forms and followed even their past aberrations'. Of the French Revolution he wrote 'since 1789 the administrative constitution of France has ever remained standing amidst the ruins of her political constitutions'.[40] Now there is no denying the unique features of Russian administration and the Russian Revolution, but the historical examples cited above were repeated in some respects after 1917.

Marx dared to generalise when he stated that 'All revolutions perfected this machine [centralised governmental administrative power] instead of smashing it. The parties that contended in turn for domination regarded the possession of this huge state edifice as the principal spoils of the victor.'[41] Of course Marx was referring to all revolutions except the coming proletarian revolution. He gave his reasons for the exception, but he still underestimated the force of historical experience. If he had survived to witness 1917 and its aftermath, he might have seen that centralised administration would recur, as his preconditions for a successful proletarian revolution did not exist in Russia. Lenin remained blind and optimistic on this subject to the end, although increasingly depressed in his last years. By 1923 the fact of the swelling administration was deliberately kept from him, either to keep alive his illusion or to prevent his wrath. When he wanted to know the findings of the census of civil servants in the larger cities that had been conducted at his own wish, his secretary was forced to tell him that he would not be allowed to see the documents without Stalin's permission.[42] This incident epitomises the shift in the basis of personal power and changing attitudes to administration at the time.

Following on the failure of Soviet Russia to eliminate central administration *and* rule by officials, socialists no longer try to ignore the historical precedents set by all the great revolutions of modern times. Most of them accept with fatalism the apparently universal aspects of contemporary administration – size, an impersonal approach, and strict regulation. Thus J. A. Schumpeter admits: 'I for one cannot visualize, in the conditions of modern society, a socialist organization in any form other than that of a huge and all-embracing bureaucratic apparatus. Every other possibility I can conceive would spell failure and breakdown.'[43]

It is now time to consider the neglected social reasons for the resurgence of highly centralised administration. Many of them can be culled from developments treated in earlier chapters. As always, they cannot be mistaken for the dynamic political motor which willed the return of a centralised system, but they may be said to constitute the heavy, antiquated frame which this motor had to pull into the twentieth century : and the way the motor was built by Lenin and Stalin was determined to a great extent by the shape of the frame. Virtually all those aspects of social backwardness that shored up Soviet centralism were survivals of Tsarist society, and thus preceded the transformed political situation. Indeed, long before Soviet attempts in NEP to create bridges between large-scale administration and local social organs, Tsarist reformers, confronted by a not so dissimilar society, had advocated parallel measures couched in the administrative terms of their own age.[44] Incidentally, they also made the error, repeated by Bolshevik and foreign critics later, of envisaging the Russian 'bureaucracy' as a homogeneous group acting in unison at all levels.[45]

In spite of the fact that the ruling élite of Russia changed beyond recognition in 1917, in some instances the outlines of the pre-existing administrative pattern remained as latent reference signals in the minds of the new élite. When these signals were activated by new information, a strong urge arose to fabricate new structures and methods in the guise of the old. A striking example, noted in Chapter 3, was the way in which the Bolsheviks took over two indigenous organisational controls inherited from the period before October 1917, namely the secret police and the system of political commissars in the army. Trotsky for the army and Latsis for the *Cheka* felt the need to convince critics that the new structures were only like the old ones in form but not in content, but their arguments were not very convincing.[46] Administrative customs rehabilitated in the Soviet period even incorporated old methods in detail. The personal passes that were brought in from 1932 onwards to prevent too great a peasant exodus from the countryside to the towns were a clear reminder of Tsarist practice.

The revolutionaries sometimes found it hard to struggle free from the inertia of existing machinery. Furthermore, their attitude towards social administration was similar to that of many West European Socialists at the turn of the century on at least one important point : Lenin shared the Fabians' distaste for the amateurism and confused welfare management that was typical of their respective governments. Both the Webbs and Lenin longed for the planned reorganisation of society in order that such things as the elimination of poverty and the overhaul of the educational system might be achieved. The crucial thing to notice is that their plans necessarily involved an increase in numbers rather than a diminution of administrative personnel in order to undertake social welfare on a huge scale. The departure from *laissez-faire* in Britain and from authoritarian paternalism or neglect in Russia meant that the machinery of the state would have to be augmented to a great degree in this respect. Both Lenin and the Webbs underestimated the bureaucratic problems that would arise in due course. That is partly why the Webbs, who, unlike Lenin, survived to see Soviet social administration in the 1930s, turned a blind eye to the worst aspects of Stalinist bureaucracy, and believed that they had at last discovered in a far-off land the ideal which they had fore-seen between 1901 and 1911.

The fact that the Webbs thought they had found the embodi-ment of their plans in a remote, little known society, smacks of the irresponsible escapism that sometimes mars the practical applica-tion of noble ideals. We saw in Chapter 2 how the revolutionary and utopian urges of the Bolsheviks led them to ignore Russian society as it actually was and to discount the strength of its histori-cal origins. This in turn led them to underplay the continuing vitality of the weighty administration that had long been required to cope with this society. They also shared with the utopians and Engels the dubious belief that politics could be reduced to adminis-trative problems which could be handled by administrative machinery. This notion lies behind Lenin's devotion to party structure in *What is to Be Done?* and helps in part to explain Stalin's reliance on bureaucratic institutions. The same idea in-spired Lenin's interest in Taylorism and electrification. It dates back in history at least as far as Saint-Simon, who also saw efficient management as a universal panacea. To requote N. Berdiaev's opinion cited in Chapter 2, Lenin 'had a boundless faith in the social regimentation of men. He believed that a compulsory social organization could create any sort of new man.' [47]

Thus the ideas of the early Bolsheviks on society, as well as the backwardness of existing Russian society, tended to ensure the stability of bureaucracy in the sense of large-scale administration. Together with H. G. Wells, the Bolsheviks were the final heirs of a waning tradition intrigued by utopian social models. Lenin, rather more than colleagues like Bukharin, saw the dangers of predicting details. Wells shared his caution, yet some of his factual recom-mendations in *A Modern Utopia* are only slight exaggerations of what actually happened under Stalin's rule. Wells wanted the state to keep a check on its inhabitants by making them all register and notify any change of address, however temporary (shades of the draconic Stalinist labour laws). An elaborate central system would classify the records of each member of the population, with his index number, fingerprint, notes on his movements, parentage, criminal convictions, etc. At death 'would come the last entry of all, his age and the cause of his death and the date and place of his cremation, and his card would be taken out and passed on to the universal pedigree, to a place of greater quiet, to the ever-growing galleries of the records of the dead'.[48] Wells thought that as a tribute to the lucidity of the French mind this vast central index, to be applied to the whole planet, should be housed near Paris. Rather, it distinctly reminds a student of Soviet history of N. Ezhov's central *nomenklatura* files for processing the Great Purge.

The Bolsheviks followed the authoritarian branch of the utopian tradition, hoping to immerse man's selfish individuality in the collective. In the years of the early Five-Year Plans Stalin eliminated all elements of the libertarian branch of utopian thought which survived until then in Bolshevik social policies. The pejorative features of 'bureaucracy' now loomed so large that they could not be wished away as they had been in the first years after the Revolution.

Just as the Bolsheviks' ideas on social administration oiled the wheels of the new bureaucracy, so did the cultural and class background of their leaders. The fact that most of the élite were intellectuals from the middle strata of society with common interests in spite of their renunciation of their social past, placed them in a category apart from the proletariat in whose name they acted, and even further apart from the peasant masses, since the great majority of important Bolsheviks were townsmen. This social isolation was described in Chapter 1. The point to be stressed here is that the influence of this social segregation was ultimately reflected in the hierarchical administrative structures that were created to manage society.

Lenin did his best to ignore this influence. As we have seen, in *State and Revolution* he looked forward to a system in which peasants as well as factory workers would take up commanding roles in the new administration. He never forsook this ideal after coming to power in 1917. Having taken decisive political action in conditions of an inadequate socio-economic base in the Marxist sense, he was not inclined to draw his horns in over the question of proletarian participation in state management. There were four vital differences between workers' control, as analysed in Chapter 2, and administration by workers, which inclined Lenin to continue to promote the latter whilst stamping firmly on the former.

In the first place, workers' control had sprung up prior to the Bolshevik assumption of power and had acquired an independent status of its own in 1917. Secondly, and for this very reason, Lenin had wooed the movement with vague promises of shared authority in the event of a successful revolution : there was never really any question of coequal status for the state administration by the side of the party. A third difference lay in the anarchist elements which permeated workers' control : those workers who sought and were granted administrative posts were not tarred with this brush, and so the Bolshevik *apparat* had nothing to fear from them. Finally the real threat of syndicalism which existed in individual factories never affected the workings of the unified state administration, nor the minds of those who entered into it.

Given these differences between workers' control and the idea of early mass participation in state administration, how did it come about that both failed, despite the fact that Lenin wished to promote the latter? Since the problems connected with workers' control cropped up first, the methods used to deal with them tended to set a precedent for managing the subsequent entry of workers into the central administration. The size of the proletariat was reduced so drastically by decimation in the Civil War, unemployment, disease and famine, that it was difficult for the regime to create a large pool of workers suitable for training as administrators. Either they had damaged their career prospects through their part in workers' control, or they lacked sufficient intelligence and know-how. Lenin's original idea of also drawing on the peasants turned out, in the short term at least, to be impracticable. Most of them lived far away from the administrative centres and were often physically cut off from them in the Civil War. Their political reliability remained in the balance, and their aptitude for paperwork was almost nil.

The methods which the Bolshevik party used to subjugate the trade unions to central political and administrative direction have been described in detail elsewhere.[49] In any case this process is only of interest here insofar as the trade unions veered from their theoretical goal of becoming non-party mass organisations representing the interests of the workers in both nationalised and private enterprises, to grow instead into yet another branch of the party-state administration. As time went on, it became impossible to distinguish union officials from other servants of the state. They defended uncritically every economic and administrative measure, and they did not try to explain them to the rank and file of the workers. The atrophied factory committees spent most of their time and energy at their desks and lost touch with the ordinary worker.[50] While he lived, Lenin did what he could to get more workers from the factory floor into state administration and to prevent those who did enter it from cutting themselves off from their economic and social origins. Stalin did not make such overt efforts subsequently, and during Lenin's lifetime Trotsky's attacks on the trade unions and advocacy of efficient management led to the irony of Stalin himself accusing Trotsky of being the 'patriarch of the bureaucrats'.[51]

The harnessing of the trade unions, and rigorous party control over those workers who entered into the service of the party and the state after 1917, are usually characterised in western scholarship (as has already been seen in the case study of workers' control in Chapter 2) as mainly one-way processes of dictatorial political enforcement from above.[52] This is probably an exaggerated view for three reasons. First, Lenin did make genuine efforts to open the door of state administration to workers. Second, the undeniable fact that the party did exercise close control over the appointment of top union (and management) officials does not necessarily mean that once appointed these men would follow a set line.[53] Neither were directives from the top personnel in the trade unions bound to receive a uniform response at middle, let alone lower, union levels, given that the number of workers who were party members between 1921 and 1928 amounted to less than 10 per cent of the total trade union membership.[54] In the third place, and more central to the present discussion, the social backwardness of the proletariat helped to mould the character and composition of state management almost as much as political machination by the party.

The debacle of workers' control soon proved that the proletariat, even had it not been obstructed politically, was incapable of running the economy. It therefore came as no surprise that the workers were not equal to the greater task of managing the national administration as a whole, covering not only economic affairs but much else besides. The representatives of the proletariat who were elevated to the ranks of the national administration fell between two stools. They were not strong enough in calibre or in numbers to make a major impact on the party-controlled machinery: neither were they able to keep in close touch with the working masses, nor exert any influence in order to support their vital class interests. The administrative organs enrolled some of the best cadres of the railwaymen, the metal workers and the miners. A contemporary Soviet critic observed how, as industry contracted in the Civil War and workers were drafted into administrative tasks, the foreman range of jobs did not contract nearly so fast, as proportionally more were needed in order to oversee the reduced working force.[55]

Hierarchical trends were thus growing in both industry and the state administration, and between the two. Workers transformed into white-collar officials tended, as is so often the case, to ascribe more value to their new privileges than to the function that justified them. There were frequent cases of lower and middle rank personnel exercising petty tyranny over the class from which they had so recently escaped. Moreover, their presence in the administration often served to accelerate its growth, inefficiency and subjugation to higher party authority. These tendencies stemmed from the understandable lack of expertise which ex-workers brought with them. Many of those defects usually ascribed to bureaucratic structures were magnified in the Soviet case due to social backwardness. Lack of initiative was one. It was not possible in psychological terms to turn a worker conditioned by Tsarist factory life into a self-reliant administrator overnight. Procrastination resulted, another typical bureaucratic defect. Both vertical and horizontal buck-passing became a common feature of Soviet administration. It arose from the refusal of the competent official to make a decision, but was often exacerbated by lack of functional competence as well. Unnecessary duplication, a further symptom of inefficient management, was also rife in the Soviet system. This was due in part to the low literacy standards of the proletarian element, as it struggled with unfamiliar paper work. The Smolensk party archive file for 1925 uses up an inordinate amount of space to list the number of party workers who received galoshes from Briansk in that year. Five separate documents were required for transferring the galoshes, and one document alone needed four different signatures[56] – a nice example of Gogol's 'laughter through tears'. If so much red tape was lavished on footwear, it is easy to imagine what happened to more important problems : there is ample evidence during the 1920s in the party-state administration's tirades of self-criticism.[57]

As early as October 1919 the Bolshevik party was able to claim that 52 per cent of its members were 'workers'.[58] The majority of them were employed, not at the factory bench, but in the offices of the party-state administration. Only 11 per cent actually worked in industry. The rift in terms of status and interests between ex-workers in administrative posts and the working masses widened as time went on. Like any government, the Bolsheviks depended upon labour to keep the country going, but after 1917 they were never in a position where this dependence developed into a bargaining point for economic or political concessions to the working class. Due to its ideological stand, the party could claim that in theory at least there was never any danger of such a confrontation, as the party was the champion of the proletariat. Thanks also to its Marxist view of labour, the compulsion to work was written into the Bolshevik ethic and could be used as an argument against free labour, which could threaten party dominance. In the first years after the Revolution a threat of this kind was never available to the proletariat in any case (though it was to the peasantry, which acted on it and helped to push the government into inaugurating NEP). Industry stood in ruins, factory workers were shaken by much hardship, so that they were in no position to haggle over their economic, let alone their political rights, as they certainly had been in 1917.[59]

Another reason for the depression of the proletariat, and its increasing segregation from ex-workers in administrative jobs, was indicated by M. Tomsky at the Fourteenth Party Congress in December 1925. The composition of labour in industry, he noted, had changed; either they were 'children of the Revolution', who had no experience of factory life in prerevolutionary conditions, or they were young peasants fresh from the countryside who were equally inexperienced and often illiterate into the bargain.[60] Their alienation from the proletarian vanguard of 1917, some of whom now worked for the party-state administration, was becoming acute. By 1928 the rank-and-file was not only out of touch with its representatives in the central state offices, but even with its own trade union leaders. At the Eighth Trade Union Congress, held in that year, Tomsky stated that constructive criticism from below was sparse and weak, and that the principle of open elections was fading. Worse than this, industrial workers were resorting to acts of physical violence against their foremen and unemployment officials.[61] If the internal hierarchy of the trade union movement was producing splits of this kind amongst its own membership, there was little chance of maintaining a strong, concerted influence on ex-workers in the central administration, let alone on the higher reaches of the party decision-making process.

In practically every sphere of administration a similar divorce occurred. The Soviets were originally intended to be the archetype for direct management by the proletariat, but as early as March 1919 Lenin admitted that on account of the social backwardness of the masses, particularly with regard to education, 'the Soviets, which according to their programme were organs of government *by the workers*, are in fact only organs of government *for the workers* by the most advanced section of the proletariat, but not by the working masses themselves'.[62] In all areas of administration, and notably in those requiring specialised skills, opportunities for contacts between workers and bureaucrats were more remote, since 'bourgeois' specialists usually held the posts. Time was needed to train workers who could take over, and officials in The People's Commissariat of Education tended to give broad educational causes priority over narrow professional training schemes. Before 1927 no special attention seems to have been paid to the training of engineers and technicians.[63]

Long before Lenin tried to come to grips with the problems outlined above, three perceptive political thinkers of very different persuasions had agreed in general terms on the course administrative processes would probably take after a revolutionary upheaval. De Tocqueville observed with regard to the French Revolution, 'The person of the sovereign or the form of the government was changed, but the daily course of affairs was neither interrupted nor disturbed : every man still remained submissive, in the small concerns which interested himself, to the rulers and usages with which he was already familiar; he was dependent on secondary powers to which it had always been his custom to defer; and in most cases he had still to do with the very same agents; for, if at each Revolution the administration was decapitated, its trunk remained unmutilated and alive; the same public duties were discharged by the same public officers . . .'[64] Max Weber, writing in a more modern context in his essay on socialism, published in 1918, asked the crucial question – who would run the nationalised industries under socialism? He forecast that those best qualified would do so, and men of this sort would feel no solidarity with the proletariat.[65] Finally, Bakunin saw further than Marx and his followers when he criticised them for not realising that their theories were bound to lead to a minority of ex-workers ruling the masses in a powerfully centralised state. Bakunin's pessimism was not deep enough to fit Russia's subsequent experience. In the Soviet party-state structure ex-workers during the 1920s were often secondary in influence to non-proletarian Bolshevik elements and to the bourgeois *spetsy*.

The low educational standards prevalent in the early Soviet period compounded the tendencies that have been described above. In Chapter 4 the general impact of illiteracy on Russian society and politics was considered. At this point its particular influence on the size, character and structure of administrative bodies may be studied.

A society endowed with literacy is able both to transmit speech in written form through space and to conserve it over time. If only one section of a society is literate, then its socio-political powers are at once enhanced in relation to the masses. The same truth applies to education as a whole, but where basic literacy represents the dividing line, the social hiatus is far more clear cut. Intricate administrative structures are heavily dependent upon writing for the organisation of their own activities, and in a backward, largely illiterate country they must also carry the burden of recording the lives of the masses who are handicapped by the transitory nature of oral communication. This responsibility tends to swell the size as well as the importance of central administration, which acts as the scribe for the whole range of human affairs, political, economic, religious and legal.

In the specific case of Russia, certain intrinsic features lent special significance to the central recording agencies. Russia's enormous size made it essential to have a dependable and durable means of passing information between the administrative hub and the peripheries. An early Soviet observer thought that one of the two main reasons for the resuscitation of a large bureaucratic system after the Revolution was the persistence of small-scale economic and social units. They had to be supervised, but it was impossible to scrutinise them at first hand, so a great deal of paper work had to be transmitted from the localities to the centre.[66] Frequent and detailed written reports on the affairs of Russia's many national minorities, most of whom lived round the edges of the country, were also a vital method of averting centrifugal tendencies in a great empire, most of whose component parts remained in the Soviet Union. Reliance on documentation was all the more necessary in a country which in some ways and in a few geographical areas had achieved the complex economic level of Western Europe, but which was still encumbered by a largely illiterate labour force.

Russia's authoritarian political tradition, both after and before 1917, was partly a result of having to deal in a paternal manner with the 'dark people'. An example from the legal sphere may be taken as an illustration of this. In the mid-1920s the Soviet Procuracy, the supreme coordinating legal organ, ordered that all local ordinances without exception be sent to it, together with the protests of the local procurators, so that the central authorities could find out whether the ordinances contained any illegalities, and, if so, whether they had been spotted by the local procurator concerned. The Procuracy's motive was not just one of pursuing tight legal and political control from above, but was based on bitter experience of the low educational standards of all those involved in the law at the local level, from the judges down to the accused.[67]

The power of the written word in the hands of a minority which controls it should not be exaggerated, even where Russia is concerned. Before Trotsky suggested that the Bolsheviks should destroy all Tsarist documents on foreign policy and thereby help to alter the course of the Soviet role in international affairs, Bakunin had believed that by destroying public records the basis of acquired rights and political domination could be totally undermined. In his essay on bureaucracy, Weber disagrees. He shows how in time an official comes to obtain 'precise obedience within his *habitual* activity . . . This discipline increasingly becomes the basis of all order, however great the practical importance on the basis of the filed documents may be.'[68] Weber finds Bakunin's notion naive, since it 'overlooks the settled orientation of *man* for keeping to the habitual rules and regulations that continue to exist independently of the documents'.[69] In Russia many of these 'settled' administrative structures, methods and even personnel, in the shape of the *spetsy*, survived the Revolution, in addition to the bulk of the central archives.

The survival of widespread illiteracy and semi-literacy during NEP undoubtedly shored up the administration's exclusive structure, despite all attempts to prevent it for ideological reasons. For instance it has been shown that white-collar workers used more initiative than the less skilled in their efforts to join the party and enter its administrative offices; they were also far less likely to resign subsequently.[70] An analysis which appeared in 1923 revealed that almost two-thirds of full party members and half the candidate members were employed in non-manual jobs. These proportions pointed to another trend – those entering into the party often shifted from manual to white-collar work after being admitted.[71] These pieces of evidence, together with many others, make it plain that the party and its appendage, the party-state administration, were becoming the bastion of the more articulate and privileged groups of early Soviet society. This process was arrested temporarily in the latter part of the Civil War, but accelerated again in the first years of NEP.[72]

Given the high incidence of illiteracy among the rural population, the number of peasants in the party is a good indication of the correlation between illiteracy and exclusion from influential political and administrative bodies. The proportion of rural party members reached a peak at the end of the Civil War which it never approached again.[73] Large numbers of young peasants who had entered the party while serving in the Red Army went back to their villages after the war. Many quitted the party, and many more were expelled in the 1921 purge.[74] By the start of 1925 under 10 per cent of the Bolshevik party membership were classified as working peasants. As the majority of this small percentage were really officials who only farmed in their spare time, the actual proportion of those who worked in agriculture on a permanent basis was probably as low as 2 or 3 per cent, or one person in three or four thousand of the adult peasant population.[75] Whereas it had been essential in the Civil War to ensure the loyalty of peasant troops at a time when the peasant masses vacillated between the claims of the military protagonists, after the Bolshevik victory and the economic sops granted to the peasants in NEP, the tension subsided. The illiterate peasantry felt more at home and of use in the ranks of the infantry, where it had traditionally fought for centuries, than in the urban offices of the peacetime administration. The customary rift between town and country, literate and illiterate, widened once again. Up until the end of NEP the minority of peasants active in party administration consisted mainly of a small literate or semi-literate élite of local officials and the richer peasants in each community.[76]

Numbers and percentages throw some light on the problem of bureaucratisation in a semi-literate society, but the psychological impact is not clear. Some idea of its influence can be gleaned from contemporary satire in the acute observations of Zoshchenko. Two of his short stories highlight the problems confronting a regime trying to promote equality of opportunity in a backward society. Both stories are concerned with the lower levels of the administrative system, which were hampered most by the lack of education. In *Rachis* an old 'postal specialist' is dismissed from the service after thirty years' service, stretching back over the prerevolutionary period, for interpreting the word 'Paris', written on the back of a foreign telegram, in the Russian script as 'Rachis'. Not only was he ignorant of all foreign languages, but even, apparently, of the difference between the Roman and Cyrillic scripts. In another story called *The Poker*, the manager of a new state institution is troubled by a request from the central heating stoker for five more pokers. In Russian the word for poker (*kochergà*) follows an archaic declension pattern and has grammatical peculiarities. The number five takes the genitive plural of the noun in Russian, and the manager does not know the proper ending for the genitive plural of *kochergà*. Being a bureaucrat and white-collar worker with status, he cannot possibly consult another institution, like, for example, the Academy of Science. None of his colleagues knows the answer either, so in desperation he consults the stoker himself, who is a peasant. The stoker suggests the diminutive form so common in peasant speech, but the manager cannot afford to lose his dignity by using this form and being taken for a peasant in turn. In the end he gets a member of his legal staff to draft a circuitous works order which will secure the five pokers without having to refer to them directly. The answer comes back from the stores department – there are no pokers available anyway. The stores department uses the diminutive form in its reply.

The Bolshevik party strove to close the social gaps caused by low levels of literacy. An enormous effort was made in all fields, as has been noted earlier in this book. The peak of achievement in terms of numbers of those converted to basic literacy took place after Stalin's acquisition of sole power, but the rise of large quantities of previously illiterate persons into administrative posts of any authority naturally occurred even later, due to the extra skills that were required. In a functionally specialised society, like the one which existed for the most part in Russia before and after the Revolution, the occupational structure, together with literacy rates, has a pyramidal shape. Despite the fact that several millions left the occupational summit (and the country as a whole in many cases) after 1917, it was obviously impossible within one or even two generations to turn the truncated pyramid upside down. Neither the slow increase in economic production, nor the lengthy process of education, would allow for it. The goal has still not been achieved in any country in the world today. Specialisation of economic function means that in twentieth century societies there must be more people performing direct and relatively simple manual tasks than engaged in administrative or other work demanding a high level of articulate mental skill.

All this was recognised at an early stage in the Soviet Union, and many efforts were made to accelerate the preparation of workers with very limited schooling or none at all for jobs in administration and other skilled areas. In 1919 Workers' Faculties (the *Rabfaks*) were set up and attached to universities. Their overall successes and failures have been studied by several scholars. What is of interest here is the reason for their failure to provide at a reasonably early stage a corps of confident and efficient ex-workers and peasants who might have some impact on the higher levels of the administrative structure. Organisations sponsoring candidates for the *Rabfak* system tended to hold back their most able members while handing over the others. Once enrolled, proletarian students often found that they could not survive on their paltry stipends and had to take up some kind of paid work. Some students with party ties were drawn into too many extra-mural activities and were frequently of the opinion that party influence would make up for their lack of academic progress.[77] Finally, even the most assiduous students suffered from lack of facilities, poor libraries, and the vagaries of the educational experiments that were so popular in the early postrevolutionary years.

Another method used by the party to encourage mobility was *vydvizhenchestvo*, or promotion from the ranks. The system was aimed in particular at persons with no specialised education. By the end of NEP, however, the relevant authorities had to admit that many of those who had been promoted had later returned to their former jobs. The numbers of those who were successful remained very low, and some of them were not of genuine proletarian or peasant origin.[78]

The disease of bureaucracy, in its pejorative sense of unnecessary hierarchy and duplication of structure, crept into those very bodies which were set up precisely in order to smash the social causes of this disease. At a congress of political educators held in October 1921, Lenin objected to the establishment of a special new organisation with the haughty title of the Central Committee for Political Education (*Glavpolitprosvet*). He expressed unease about the educators' work methods. They adopted an officious stance and sent out directives from the centre without checking in the localities on the impact of their decisions. If only they would actually help illiterates to read, they would be providing a far better service, and at the same time might eventually avoid duplication by rendering redundant another administrative organ, the Extraordinary Commission for the Liquidation of Illiteracy.[79]

The broader implications of the educational gulf for the future of social and political administration in Russia were sometimes seen with considerable clarity by Soviet leaders during the 1920s, and had even been prophesied as early as 1898. Trotsky wrote with regard to what he took to be the evils of bureaucracy in NEP, that they proliferated 'in inverse proportion to the enlightenment, the cultural standards and the political consciousness of the masses'.[80] He did not go so far as Djilas and others, who maintained that the 'bureaucracy' represented a new social class.[81] Trotsky probably realised that such a conclusion would make his arguments about the emancipation of the proletariat look like a hypocritical screen for his desire as an intellectual to rule over the workers and peasants. Djilas may well have taken his idea from J. Machajski, whose theories concerning the intelligentsia's dominating social role have already been referred to in passing.[82] Between 1898 and 1911 Machajski elaborated the theory that the Russian revolutionary intelligentsia, including the Bolsheviks, were not genuine allies of the workers, but represented a new class of potential rulers. They owned a peculiar form of property, namely, education, which they could and did exploit with as much success as bourgeois capitalists wielding the material means of production.[83] Machajski's argument touched a sensitive spot among the prerevolutionary Russian intelligentsia, and it led to controversy and much criticism. After the Revolution he took up a non-political, administrative post as technical editor for the journal of the Supreme Economic Council, so he knew something at first hand about administrative structure and functions. In 1918 he returned to the attack, declaring that a new 'people's bureaucracy' was emerging. The Bolshevik success of October 1917, he declared, was nothing less than 'a counter-revolution of the intellectuals'.[84]

This line of argument appeared to cut very near the bone, especially in the years after Machajski's death in 1926. Certainly a new administrative élite manipulated by the Bolsheviks did spring up, and it did for the most part serve to separate further the educated from the semi-literate and illiterate masses. Whether it formed a new social *class* as such is much more disputable, as is also Machajski's firm conviction that all the Bolshevik intellectuals consciously plotted to exploit the masses by virtue of their mental superiority. In the light of the examination in this book of the literacy campaign, of Lenin's personal attitude, and of the attempts to train uneducated workers for administrative responsibilities, it cannot be maintained that in the early Soviet period, apart from the use of political censorship, there was a deliberate intent to suppress the dissemination of knowledge. Machajski's call for the 'socialisation of knowledge', as well as of the means of production, was in fact heeded by the Bolsheviks, but they were up against enormous social problems, which all but defeated their aims in some respects. The actual result was therefore rather similar to what Machajski prophesied.

There was, however, another important and ironical difference. On the one hand, the organisational details of Machajski's gloomy vision coincided most of all with the characteristics of Stalinist administrative arrangements. Machajski forecast a hierarchical system in which all sectors of the economy would be nationalised and run by office holders and managers whose salaries would be much higher than the wages paid to manual workers. On the other hand, Stalin personally represented the anti-intellectual stream in the Bolshevik leadership and was himself suspicious of the first generation of Old Bolsheviks on account of their higher educational achievements.[85] Souvarine's thesis, mentioned earlier in this chapter, that intellectually mediocre men rose to the top of the Stalinist system, undoubtedly contained a good deal of truth. It also became true after the end of NEP that the massive propaganda machine, combined with a much stricter censor, was used to indoctrinate fertile minds *en route* towards full literacy.[86] In the more cynical climate of the 1930s a deliberate intent to wield knowledge for the benefit of a small élite was far more apparent; but the men who did this were often not intellectuals themselves and had scant respect for true intellectuals. Finally, and also in contrast to Machajski's predictions, these means were only applied after at least ten years' genuine struggle to 'socialise' knowledge. It was clear through the 1930s, however, that at least some of the mud from Machajski's attacks still stuck, despite the discrepancies between his forecasts and what actually happened. Frequent denunciations of 'Machaevism', as it came to be called, were made in the 1930s.[87]

On closer scrutiny, therefore, Machajski's argument is far from being watertight, although it contains a good deal of truth.

A similar elusive quality pertains to the exact nature of the role played by military influences in Soviet political and social life, as was noted in Chapter 3. Although scarcely a whiff of genuine Bonapartism ever affected the political climate, there was no doubt that military ideas were influential in several spheres, including the administration of society.

In terms of the general history of administration, the army appears to be the oldest form of organisation of large-scale activity. It is doubtful whether military arrangements normally have any close application to social and governmental organisational methods, but the Russian experience is unusual. The military model was deeply rooted, as Professor M. Fainsod has pointed out : 'Under Alexander I and Nicholas I there was an increasing disposition to turn to the military to perform functions of civil administration.'[88] Under Alexander III civil affairs were run more often than not by governors-general who were also usually the military district commanders. This tradition was reinforced rather than reversed, despite the Bolsheviks' distaste for both military and hierarchical institutions, under the impact of total war in the revolutionary period. As in other countries involved in the First World War, an extension of the scope of central administration took place. Combined civil-military exercises on a large scale were called for. In Russia the military machine in conjunction with the Bolshevik Party became a stop-gap administrative system in the wake of the collapse of the Tsarist structure. It was observed in

Chapter 3 how the army in the Civil War dealt with problems of national supply and civilian labour recruitment, and also how these stringent controls reappeared in a revised form in the 1930s.

The state of Russia during the Civil War provided a suitable climate for the growth of dictatorial administrative methods. The cruel necessities of internal war allowed the party bureaucracy to adopt a single line of authority based on a highly disciplined hierarchy. The similarity with military procedures was further enhanced by Lenin's deliberate fusion of the military and political commands. This step was made easier by the Bolshevik party's conscious imitation of military organisational methods even prior to 1917.[89]

Military influences permeated into many spheres of administration besides those directly affected by wartime demands. After the introduction of a decree in April 1918, calling for compulsory education for all ranks in the army, the military was converted into one of the leading instruments of the literacy campaign. However, the most permanent influence, which was to survive through NEP and affect the long-term evolution of administrative attitudes, was the nature of the personnel involved. The ideas and values of the Tsarist specialists who were retained in the new administration were bound to have an impact on the new civil servants from proletarian and peasant backgrounds. The prototype of all the *spetsy*, both in time and in importance, were those Tsarist military officers who agreed to fight for the Bolsheviks in the Civil War. The differentiation of rank to which they were accustomed, their hierarchical inclinations and naturally ruthless methods, became part and parcel of the administrative climate and did not die out with the coming of peace. During the Civil War both military and civilian administrators were transferred from one sector or job to another in order to deal with the constant state of emergency. The methods used to control the changing situation were not sanctioned in theory or in practice by any formal decree. The habits formed over three years did not disappear after 1921 : appointments were still made in an authoritarian manner from above, and the special bureau (*Uchraspred*) of the Party Central Committee continued to distribute cadres according to the central requirements of the state.

From 1920 onwards a heated debate arose within the party on

increasing 'bureaucratisation'. One of the most frequently recurring charges was that Civil War conditions and the so-called 'militarisation' of the party had a lot to do with this development.[90] This showed that Bolshevik leaders were far from being unaware of what was happening. They could scarcely avoid noticing. Thirteen members of the Politburo who kept their posts into the 1950s had held combined military-political jobs in the Civil War. Below the political peaks, 4000 military officers were taken into the party at one blow during the Leninist enrolment of 1924.[91] Of course entry into the party did not necessarily lead to a permanent post in party or state administration. A scholar who has compared the personnel of the late Tsarist and Soviet administrations has found that there were fewer men with active military careers serving in the Soviet than in the Tsarist system.[92] Yet although full-time soldiers did not feature widely at all levels, there certainly was a large influx of ex-military men at the close of the Civil War. As Trotsky said, 'the demobilization of the Red Army of five million played no small role in the formation of the bureaucracy. The victorious commanders assumed leading posts in the local Soviets, in the economy, in education, and they persistently introduced everywhere that regime which had ensured success in the Civil War.'[93] Trotsky had a specific axe to grind about the rigid bureaucratic methods he ascribed partly to the influence of such men, and so his opinion cannot be trusted entirely, but it is known from other, less prejudiced, sources that many ex-military men sought and found posts in the peacetime administration.[94] Of particular value to the central authorities were those demobilised soldiers who took back to their localities some knowledge of national affairs and applied it in provincial administration, often in the local Soviets.[95]

Thus whereas it is incorrect to imagine that the dual political-military structure survived after the close of the Civil War, many ex-military personnel imbued with experience rooted in wartime methods continued to serve in administrative posts, and the authoritarian temper of the party leadership did not soften to such an extent in peacetime that any degree of tension or incompatability became apparent between top NEP managers and the administrative veterans of the Civil War.

In the course of the high-level struggle between Lenin's lieutenants shortly before his death, Trotsky argued that the party machine had become encrusted with bureaucratic traditions taken from the Civil War years. He advocated that younger men should be allowed to play a greater role by promoting them to leading positions in the party and its administrative cadres.[96] This was sound advice, if there was to be any genuine long-term democratisation of administrative processes, but Trotsky was also striking out in his personal vendetta with Stalin, who stood most to gain from the tightly-knit structure which he was coming to control. There is a considerable amount of irony in Stalin's and Trotsky's changing views on the dangers of lingering wartime attitudes in the administration. During the Civil War, when Trotsky occupied the leading post on the military side of the national dual command, it was Stalin who vigorously attacked authoritarian ways; but as soon as Trotsky let go of the reins of power, Stalin took over control, retaining many rigid administrative features in the peace that followed. At first they were not very apparent in the laxer atmosphere of NEP, but they became prominent again in the period of collectivisation and the First Five-Year Plan, when draconic social mobilisation took place once more, on a much vaster scale than during the Civil War.

It is not surprising that lingering traces of military attitudes pervaded Soviet social administration. They have been somewhat neglected, partly because of the usual accent in research on purely political and economic matters, partly because direct military coordination of civil affairs disappeared after the Civil War. Another reason is that the army was replaced as an instrument of social coercion by the secret police, but, as was observed in Chapter 3, the police itself emerged in wartime conditions partly under the aegis of the military. If one examines the course of the Chinese Communist Revolution, with its more recent origins and lack of heavy reliance on a secret police force, the social role of the military can be seen in much clearer outline. As in Russia during her Civil War, so in China, but over a much longer period, transport and supply problems have been in the hands of the military. In 1963, fourteen years after the Chinese Revolution, military organisation was consciously adopted as the model for political and social administration. Over twenty local administrative areas were under direct military supervision. Nearly half the membership of the Chinese Communist party consisted of men in military careers. Long-lived military influences in China were due also to the original strength of Mao-Tse-Tung's guerilla forces which became the backbone of the Communist government in a way that would have been impossible in Russia, given the lack of Bolshevik military organisation before 1917.

The breakdown of all attempts to link up small-scale with large-scale activities, which was examined in the preceding chapter, perpetuated an administrative vacuum that was gradually filled by a highly centralised system acting in the name of the localities, as it had done in the Tsarist past. The collapse of central authority in 1917, together with the newly released social and economic aspirations of the peasants and the proletariat, led in the short term to fissiparous trends that threatened both the maintenance of basic law and order and the long-term socio-economic aims of the Bolsheviks. The peasants seized the land on their own initiative, thereby increasing the number of small-scale holdings. At the height of the campaign for workers' control in January 1918, the Bolshevik leadership warned the trade unions that it would be suicidal for them to deal with the socialisation of industry in the crude manner then being adopted by the peasants for the socialisation of the land.[97] Bukharin reiterated the warning in the following year. He insisted that the large number of petty owners who would be thrown up by the system of ownership-sharing envisaged by workers' control, would lead to anarchic competition between them and result in neo-capitalist features.[98]

Thus workers' control, on the face of it one of the most likely viable links between the Bolshevik political centre and the socio-economic grass roots, was discarded as an administrative bridge. But it was the Soviets which were intended to serve as the primary antidote to the large-scale bureaucratic structures of the past.[99] Similar dangers surrounded their role, however. Indeed, they were the chief formal agents in 1917–18 for the organisation of workers' control and the rapid confiscation of the land. Infiltrated with elements hostile to the Bolsheviks and plagued by corruption and inefficiency, the Soviets likewise fell prey to close Communist Party supervision, as the result of decisions taken at the Eighth Party Congress in March 1919.[100]

Subsequently the regime launched an energetic campaign to revitalise the Soviets, but even loyal and efficient Soviets were unable to narrow the administrative margin between the political hub and the localities. Huge distances, poor communications, illiteracy, and lack of local cooperation continued to thwart their efforts. Moreover the fixed Bolshevik doctrine of dual subordination meant that lower Soviet organs were responsible to the Soviet immediately superior to them as well as to their own electors, so that the central authorities exercised great power. During the 1920s the rural Soviets enlarged the areas under their jurisdiction. In the process they weakened their contacts with the day-to-day life of the peasant communes. Most of the energies of the administrators in the Soviets were taken up by directives from the central authorities, and success in this sphere counted more in career terms than attention to local demands. These general trends were enhanced by the administrative reorganisation of the territory of the USSR through the system of regionalisation (*raionirovanie*), which was introduced by the Twelfth Party Congress in 1923. It made reasonable progress in the next three years, and gathered extra impetus, particularly in the RSFSR, in 1928. The process compounded administrative difficulties by increasing still further the size of the lower units and reducing their number.[101]

Into the gap between small-scale and large-scale administration stepped the monolithic Bolshevik party. At first, in the Civil War, it leaned heavily on the only other reliable large-scale administrative structure, the military. Subsequently it moulded in its own centralised image a party and state system which from the start was clearly subordinate to its authority, having been thrown up hurriedly in the postrevolutionary period and composed of elements from widely differing social groups. Without exception all spheres of social affairs and the economy came under Bolshevik scrutiny, given the inclusive nature of Marxist-Leninist thought. The dominant pattern of the rapidly increasing central administration was not influenced by the existence of a great variety of social and economic activity, although this was certainly the case in Russia. This was ignored, and the pattern was based on repetitive extension of similar functions at all levels, a system far better suited to unitary political command than one influenced in its workings by varietal multiplicity. The system of dual subordination ensured the perpetuity of repetitive extension.

The true dimensions of the chasm that lay between small-scale realities and large-scale projects were revealed in the operation of the First Five-Year Plan. At the outset the State Research Institute for Agriculture and Colonisation (*Goszemkolit*) estimated that there were from 24.5 to 32.5 million surplus agricultural labourers.[102] Yet by October 1930 the Peoples' Commissar of Labour was able to issue a statement to the effect that unemployment was liquidated.[103] Even when some allowance for optimism is made, the transition from country to town, from small-scale to large-scale economic and social endeavour, was breathtakingly fast in human terms. After a decade of stagnation and inability to harness one sphere to the other, the change was carried out at an unprecedented speed. In view of the peasants' reluctance or incapacity to engage in activities outside their immediate environment, it is not surprising that administrative compulsion was necessary in the First Five-Year Plan to accomplish overnight what had been hoped for in vain since 1917. Agricultural labourers as often as not were reluctant to move into industry. The difference between the standards of living in the towns and the villages was not large enough to encourage many peasants to leave their localities. Rumours about the impending collectivisation of agriculture also deterred them from moving, since they were afraid of missing their share in the new system of village life.

Naked force was the instrument wielded by the central bureaucracy to bring about *smychka* on a grand scale. The violent background of the Civil War and wartime influences on civilian affairs rendered this move less unexpected than it might otherwise have been. The fast growth of forced labour in the early years of the Five-Year Plans, another reminder of the Civil War years, was closely connected with the absorption of surplus agricultural labour into industry. Villagers predominated among the inmates of the camps.[104]

The question of force in the hands of the administrators introduces us finally to the relationship between Russia's social backwardness, the need for a bureaucracy, and the specific ways in which that bureaucracy was made to work on Soviet society under Stalin's tight grip.

Whenever in this century the leading elements in any society have decided to introduce innovation on a large scale, they have had to resort to bureaucratic methods of administration in order to cope with their complex task. The Bolsheviks represent the clearest and most impressive example of this. They were the greatest innovators, working in the largest country in the world. Given the all-embracing nature of Marx's ideas on economic and social affairs, the Soviet bureaucracy had to be equipped to deal with the comprehensive planning and management of the whole of Russian society. Its size and power were a far cry from the limited functions of, say, a colonial-type bureaucracy merely devoted to upholding basic law and order and collecting revenue. It differed also in that it was intended to be a dynamic instrument for socio-economic change rather than a conserver of the *status quo*. This aim was undoubtedly achieved by the Soviet system in the economic sphere during the 1930s, and had even been carried out with some degree of success in the late Tsarist period in the hands of Count Witte.

It is when one looks at the social and political implications of bureaucratic modernisation (and not in the Soviet case alone) that the resulting benefits become less apparent. Robert Michels argues that any new social ideas must be bureaucratically implemented if they are to find expression in institutional change.[105] Unfortunately, in the process of creating an efficient bureaucratic apparatus, radical ideas are abandoned in favour of more conservative ones. Original objectives are successively discarded in the interest of increased organisational strength. Less attention is paid to external social need, and more to internal self-preservation. Bureaucratic methods become an end rather than a means, so that administrators try to adapt the social environment to their convenience, instead of switching their activities in order to suit changing circumstances. There may be a way out of this *impasse* if a bureaucracy can remain dynamic by continually devising more and more new reforms. That this was broadly the case in the economic sphere can hardly be denied in the Soviet context. But it seems as though the enormous energies required in this direction induced exhaustion in the social and political fields. In any case political progress had been left behind as early as 1921, when the notion of the dictatorship of the proletariat had become a meaningless slogan. Continuing political backwardness was bound to distort subsequent social progress, and to some extent economic modernisation as well.

Rosa Luxemburg foresaw Russia's fate :

Without general elections, without unrestricted freedom of press and assembly, without a free struggle of opinion, life dies out in every public institution, becomes a mere semblance of life, in which only the bureaucracy remains as the active element . . . Yes, we can go ever further : such conditions must cause a brutalization of public life . . .[106]

Rosa Luxemburg did not spell out what she meant by the 'brutalization of public life', but she was correct in this prophesy as well. At this point we return to the question of force and Stalin's part in it. When, at the end of NEP, the central administration hurriedly forsook all previous attempts to inculcate some form of organisational harmony between small-scale realities and large-scale management methods, it proceeded to mould social and economic affairs entirely from the centre. This involved an immediate reduction in *technical* friction over matters of administrative organisation, but soon led to a sharp rise in *social* tension between the ruthless bureaucracy and those sectors of the population that suffered acutely from its arbitrary actions. Here lies the main social reason behind the Great Purge. The bureaucracy under Stalin turned to the pre-existing organs of repression and applied them, with superfluous zeal, to the strained situation. The purges were also useful in the more abstract realm of social ideas. The aim of the Bolsheviks remained what it always had been, to transform constantly the modalities of social and economic organisation. A potential clash appeared between this ideal and the stabilising ethos of the entrenched bureaucracy. The purges were a drastic method of trying to maintain revolutionary dynamism in the face of bureaucratic consolidation.

These two social reasons for the application of widespread coercion coincided nicely with the political and personal motives of the man who in the name of the party controlled both the party and state administration. Stalin had climbed to power through the party administration. By the 1930s he was prepared to cripple the party apparatus through purges in order to ensure his lasting personal hegemony over the party and the state. His temperament was well suited to the use of force, and also to the centralised and seemingly impersonal manner in which it was applied for all ends, political, social and economic, by the administration. Stalin capitalised on the social background in other ways as he set about consolidating a totalitarian system. These methods are outlined in the concluding chapter.

1 Robert von Mohl, *Staatsrecht, Völkerrecht und Politik* (Tübingen, 1862).

2 See M. Albrow, *Bureaucracy* (London, 1970) pp. 40–5.

3. See Chapter 4, p. 182 and note 157.

4 See, for instance, Jerry F. Hough, *The Soviet Prefects: The Local Party Organs in Industrial Decision-Making* (Cambridge, Mass., 1969) pp. 4–6, 292–305.

5 *KPSS v rezoliutsiakh* (1954), vol. 2, p. 445.

6 *Sovetskoe stroitel'stvo*, no. 12 (29) (December 1928) p. 13.

7 Albrow, op. cit., p. 124.

8 The distance between the Soviet party bureaucracy and the classical concept of bureaucracy is clearly measured by L. Schapiro in *The Communist Party of the Soviet Union*, 2nd edn. (London, 1970) pp. 622–4.

9 *Fabian Essays in Socialism* (London, 1890) p. 61.

10 *Soviet Communism: A New Civilization* (London, 1935) p. 450.

11 Beatrice Webb tells us in a later work that the Soviet draft constitution of 1936 was discussed at no less than 527,000 meetings attended by 36,500,000 persons. See *The Truth About Soviet Russia* (London, 1942) p. 24.

12 Benvenuto Mussolini, *The Corporate State* (Florence, 1938) p. 28.

13 E. Strauss, *The Ruling Servants* (London, 1961) pp. 41–2.

14 See for example W. Pietsch, *Revolution und Staat: Institutionen als Träger der Macht in Sowjetrussland 1917–1922* (Cologne, 1969). Pietsch argues that the party jockeyed for control initially with such organisations as the Military Revolutionary Committee, the Council of People's Commissars and the Soviet network.

15 These persons are named, and their influence discussed, in N. Jasny, *Soviet Economists of the Twenties: Names to be Remembered* (Cambridge, 1972). See in particular pp. 28–36.

16 Jerry H. Hough, op. cit.

17 See Fainsod, 'Bureaucracy and Modernization : The Russian and Soviet Case', in J. La Palombara (editor), *Bureaucracy and Political Development* (Princeton, 1963) p. 235.

18 *Selected Works*, vol. 1, pp. 332–3. See also the first draft of *The Civil War in France*, in *Werke*, vol. 18, p. 539.

19 See K. Marx and F. Engels, *Selected Correspondence* (London, 1943) p. 249. Marx wrote to Engels in 1868, 'For the German working class the most necessary thing of all is that it should cease conducting its agitation by kind permission of the higher authorities. A race so schooled in bureaucracy must go through a complete course of "self-help".'

20 *The Civil War in France.*

21 Lenin, *Sochineniia*, vol. 4, p. 313.

22 For the details of this change, see Pethybridge, 'Petrograd and the Provinces', op. cit., pp. 193–7.

23 For an illuminating discussion of Lenin's activities in this field, see M. Lewin, *Lenin's Last Struggle* (London, 1969).

24 A. Gastev, 'Novaia industriia', in *Vestnik Metallista* (January, 1918) p. 24.

25 N. Bukharin, *Historical Materialism*, p. 310.

26 See Pethybridge, *A Key to Soviet Politics: The Crisis of the 'Anti-Party' Group* (London, 1962), for an analysis of this possibility.

27 *Economic Problems of Socialism in the USSR*, 2nd edn. (Moscow, 1953) p. 27.

28 Maiakovsky's play *The Bathhouse* was a typical example. The trappings of Soviet 'bureaucratism' were mocked in the roles of the pompous Pobedonosikov and his secretary Optimistenko, surrounded by heavy armchairs, telephone wires and inefficiency. Other writers who attacked the surface of bureaucracy included Fedin, Zamiatin and Zoshchenko.

29 Trotsky, *The Revolution Betrayed: The Soviet Union, What it is and Where it is going* (London, 1945) p. 248–9.

30 At the time of his personal battle against Stalin within the party, Trotsky, in his *New Course*, published in 1924, encouraged the party youth to put active pressure on the Old Bolsheviks in order to prevent the growth of an ossified bureaucracy. This was naturally seen by Stalin as a pretext for undermining his position.

31 B. Rizzi, *La bureaucratisation du monde* (Paris, 1939); M. Djilas, *The New Class: An Analysis of the Communist System* (London, 1966); M. Schachtman, *The Bureaucratic Revolution* (London, 1962).

32 B. Souvarine, *Stalin: A Critical Survey of Bolshevism* (London, 1940) pp. 473–4.

33 For example, Leonard Schapiro lists the 'careerist' and military symptoms and then continues : 'No one appeared to appreciate that "bureaucratization" flowed inevitably from the administrative role allotted to the party and to the structure which it adopted in order to perform this role. Remedies, therefore, insofar as they were genuine attempts at reform, necessarily attacked the symptoms rather than the disease itself.' (*The Communist Party of the Soviet Union*, p. 254).

34 Alexis de Tocqueville, *On the State of Society in France before the Revolution of 1789* (London, 1856) p. 111.

35 See P. P. Gronsky, 'Teorii samoupravleniia v russkoi nauke', in B. B. Veselovsky and Z. G. Frenkel (editors), *1864–1914, Iubileinyi zemskii sbornik* (St. Petersburg, 1914) pp. 76–85.

36 Robert Michels, *Political Parties* (London, 1962) p. 348.

37 *Vosmoi s"ezd professional'nykh soiuzov SSSR, 10–24 dekabria 1928 g., plenumy i sektsii, polnyi stenograficheskii otchet* (Moscow, 1929) pp. 323–35.

38 See Carr, *A History of Soviet Russia: Foundations of a Planned Economy*, vol. 2 (London, 1971) ch. 51.

39 H. H. Gerth and C. Wright Mills (editors), *From Max Weber: Essays in Sociology* (London, 1948) pp. 228–9.

40 See *On the State of Society in France before the Revolution of 1789*, pp. 367–71.

41 Karl Marx, 'The Eighteenth Brumaire of Louis Napoleon', in K. Marx and F. Engels, *Selected Works in Two Volumes* (Moscow, 1962) vol. 1, p. 333.

42 See Lewin, op. cit., p. 92.

43 J. A. Schumpeter, *Capitalism, Socialism and Democracy* (London, 1950) p. 206. Quoted in M. Albrow, op. cit., p. 82.

44 See, for instance, P. V. Dologorukov, *La vérité sur la Russie* (Paris, 1860) and A. I. Koshelëv, *Kakoi iskhod dlia Rossii iz nyneshnogo ego polozheniia?* (Leipzig, 1862).

45 This view is corrected by M. Raeff in 'The Russian Autocracy and its Officials', in *Harvard Slavic Studies*, vol. 4 (1957) pp. 77–91, and 'L'état, le gouvernement et la tradition politique en Russie impériale avant 1861', in *Revue d'histoire moderne et contemporaine* (October–December 1962) pp. 296–305.

46 See Chapter 3, p. 104.

47 See p. 39.

48 H. G. Wells, *A Modern Utopia*, Nelson edn. (London, 1905?) p. 164.

49 See note 104 on p. 71 for a list of works to consult on this subject.

50 For more details on the 'bureaucratisation' of the trades unions and factory committees see Margaret Dewar, *Labour Policy in the USSR 1917–1928*, op. cit., ch. 3 and 4.

51 See Stalin, *Sochineniia*, vol. 6, p. 29. The taunt was directed against Trotsky's schemes for the militarisation of labour.

52 For example, one writer sums up in this manner the fate of the trade unions: 'Government by dictatorship had an adverse effect on internal union politics. It gave rise to a bureaucracy which was characterized by the usual problems . . .' See J. B. Sorenson, op. cit., p. 187.

53 This point is well put in M. McAuley, *Labour Disputes in Soviet Russia 1957–1965* (Oxford, 1969) pp. 34–5.

54 Sorenson, op. cit., p. 197.

55 L. Kritsman, op. cit., pp. 192–3.

56 File WKP 23, Smolensk archive for 1925.

57 For good secondary accounts of this see Lewin, *Lenin's Last Struggle*, for the earlier period and Carr, *Foundations of a Planned Economy, 1926–1929*, vol. 2, ch. 51, for the later years of NEP.

58 The definition of what a 'worker' meant is very complicated, and cannot be examined at this point. See Carr, *Socialism in One Country 1924–1926*, vol. 1, pp. 89–136.

59 A good example of the combined economic and political pressures in 1917 is provided by the million-strong railway workers. See Pethybridge, *The Spread of the Russian Revolution*, 'The Railways'.

60 *XIV s"ezd vsesoiuznoi kommunisticheskoi partii (B), dekiabria 1925 g., stenograficheskii otchet* (Moscow, 1926) pp. 722 ff.

61 *VIII s"ezd professional'nykh soiuzov SSSR, dekiabria 1928 g., plenumy i sektsii, polnyi stenograficheskii otchet* (Moscow, 1929) pp. 157 ff., 180.

62 *Sochineniia*, vol. 38, p. 170.

63 See Carr and R. W. Davies, *Foundations of a Planned Economy*, vol. 1, pt. 2, pp. 590–1.

64 Alexis de Tocqueville, *On the State of Society in France Before the Revolution of 1789*, p. 371.

65 Max Weber, *Der Sozialismus* (Vienna, 1918) p. 24.

66 Kritsman, op. cit., p. 143.

67 See G. G. Morgan, *Soviet Administrative Legality: The Role of the Attorney General's Office* (Stanford, 1962) p. 61 ff.

68 Max Weber, 'Bureaucracy', in *From Max Weber: Essays in Sociology*, translated and edited by H. H. Gerth and C. Wright Mills (London, 1948) p. 229.

69 Ibid.

70 T. H. Rigby, *Communist Party Membership in the USSR 1917–1967*, p. 108.

71 Ibid., pp. 108–9.

72 Ibid., p. 109.

73 See the table in Rigby, op. cit., p. 491.

74 Ibid., p. 106.

75 Ibid., p. 135.

76 Ibid., p. 171 : 'An ambitious study of rural communists undertaken in 1929 showed that, whereas less than one peasant household in six in the RSFSR had property worth over 800 roubles, the proportion among *communist* peasants was one in four.'

77 See N. Hans and S. Hessen, *Educational Policy in the Soviet Union* (London, 1930) p. 156.

78 G. Nikitsky, 'Voprosy vydvizhenchestva', in M. Steklov (editor), *Sovetskaia demokratiia* (Moscow, 1929) pp. 238–44.

79 See Lenin, *O vospitanii i obrazovanii* (Moscow, 1963) p. 531.

80 See Trotsky, *Sochineniia*, vol. 25, p. 218 ff.

81 See supra, p. 264.

82 Supra, pp. 172–3.

83 See J. W. Machajski, *Burzhuaznaia revoliutsiia i rabochee delo* (St. Petersburg, 1906) p. 86; and also by the same author, *Bankrotstvo sotzializma XIX stoletiia* (Geneva, 1905) p. 28.

84 *Rabochaia revoliutsiia*, no. 1 (June–July 1918) p. 4 ff.

85 See Chapter 1, p. 4.

86 See Chapter 4, p. 179 ff.

87 See *Partiinoe stroitel'stvo*, no. 17, 1931; 'O postanovke partiinoi propagandy v sviazi s vypuskom *Kratkogo Kursa istorii VKP(b)*', *Pravda*, 15 November 1938; and also 'Chto takoe "makhaevsh-china"?', ibid., 18 November 1938.

88 'Bureaucracy and Modernization: The Russian and Soviet Case', in J. LaPalombara, op. cit., p. 245.

89 See Chapter 3, p. 86.

90 Schapiro, op. cit., p. 254.

91 Berkin, op. cit., p. 385.

92 See J. Armstrong, 'Tsarist and Soviet Elite Administrators', in the *Slavic Review* (March 1972) pp. 15–16.

93 Trotsky, *The Revolution Betrayed*, pp. 89–90.

94 For example Frunze's reforms of the central military adminis-tration led to 947 persons losing their jobs out of a total of 3732. Cuts also took place at the lower levels. A considerable proportion of these men entered the civil administration subsequently. See Berkhin, op. cit., p. 154.

95 See A. Divil'kovsky, *Pomogai stroit' sovetskaia vlast'-naputstvie otpusknomu krasnoarmeitsu* (Moscow, 1921) pp. 8–13.

96 *Pravda*, 29 December 1923.

97 *Pervyi vserossiiskii s"ezd professional'nykh soiuzov 7–14 ianvaria 1918: stenograficheskii otchet* (Moscow, 1918) p. 236.

98 Bukharin, *Programma Kommunistov (bol'shevikov)* (Petrograd, 1919) pp. 8–9.

99 See Chapter 5, pp. 222–3.

100 Ibid., pp. 223–4.

101 For more details, see Carr, *Foundations of a Planned Economy 1926–1929*, vol. 2, pp. 213–73. Carr quotes on p. 221 the typical re-action of a local administrator to regionalisation: 'In practice the

result is not to bring the government closer to the population, but to increase the distance, since for every trifle the inhabitant . . . must travel tens of versts to the district or the department.'

102 'The Five-Year Plan and the Regulation of the Labour Market in the USSR', in the *International Labour Review*, no. 27 (1933) p. 353.

103 A. Baykov, *The Development of the Soviet Economic System* (Cambridge, 1947) p. 213.

104 For a detailed account of this period, see S. Swianiewicz, *Forced Labour and Economic Development: An Enquiry into the Experience of Soviet Industrialization* (London, 1965).

105 Michels, op. cit.

106 Luxemburg, op. cit., p. 71.

Conclusion: The Social Ingredients of Stalinism

We have now attempted to trace significant social developments in the early Soviet period that exerted a cumulative influence on the political life of the country. At this stage it is necessary to stand back from details and to ask several general questions. First of all, does it not seem necessary to define another ingredient in what has come to be known as Stalinism? Stalinism is a shorthand term that stands for a certain kind of totalitarian rule whose political, economic and unique personal qualities have been fully analysed. The aim of this book has been to adumbrate some social antecedents which together may add up to a new dimension of Stalinism.

Secondly, we should inquire into the relative weight of the various ingredients of Stalinism, particularly since the traditional balance may now be somewhat upset by the new emphasis implied in this book. The notion of ingredients is used advisedly here, for ingredients are mixed into a compound and so become virtually inextricable. It was stressed at the outset that although for the purposes of analysis it may be useful to separate social from political and other determinants, in the end the exercise must be seen to be partly artificial and the natural compound must be allowed to resolve itself once again into a general, but perhaps slightly new, shape.

Thirdly, we must ask a question that has been posed with regard to all but the social ingredient of Stalinism. To what extent were Lenin and other Old Bolsheviks responsible for what has been ascribed to Stalin? Finally, it would be useful to take a sideways glance at the impact of social development, or lack of it, on another contemporaneous political system which also slid into totalitarianism. Germany presents an interesting problem in this respect. Students of Soviet history and politics have been accused, and perhaps rightly so, of being so mesmerised by the unique characteristics of the Soviet phenomenon that they have remained prisoners of an academic claustrophobia. A brief comparative survey of the social roots of totalitarianism in this century may not provide an instant key to the relationship between all backward societies and dominating political regimes, but should help at least to throw the Soviet example into clearer relief.

The chronological framework of the preceding chapters would be disrupted if an attempt were now made to depict the main outlines of Stalinism as it evolved in the years 1929–53. We remain concerned, above all, with the prelude to Stalinism. However, some assessment of Stalin's personal qualities during, as well as before, the 1930s will be needed in order to weigh the role of the individual in the balance. After all, the very term Stalinism renders this imperative.

The political and economic foundations of Stalinism have been clearly revealed by many writers. The political approach has been the most thoroughly covered,[1] but often in artificial isolation from economic and especially from social influences. Let us take just one example of this tendency. Scholars have shown how Stalin drew on the resources of the party machine, the police and the bureaucracy in moulding the instruments of totalitarian rule, but they have neglected certain social pressures at work within these institutional pillars which affected their development and made them more malleable in the hands of the Leader. We have seen how the secret police could flourish in the social and legal chaos of the Civil War, how the cumbersome bureaucracy was resurrected phoenix-like partly because a still backward society depended on it; and in the introductory chapter it was pointed out how Stalin stood to gain from the changing social composition of the party apparatus in the 1920s.

The economic explanation of Stalinism has for several reasons been more subtly linked to both political and social phenomena. Marxist thought has coloured non-Marxist as well as Soviet historiography. Economic historians, even more than political interpreters, cannot afford to work in isolation, particularly in the case of Soviet Russia, where a political party staged a revolution primarily in order to carry out a fairly specific socio-economic programme, and where the main historical epochs have been given economic labels (War Communism, NEP, the period of the Five-Year Plans). Before the Bolsheviks, Witte realised that political freedom would remain an idle dream in Russia so long as the country lacked a solid industrial base; the whole of Russia's agrarian history through the nineteenth century pointed to this. The men involved in the great economic debate of the 1920s as to how to overcome the oppressive socio-economic dominance of the peasantry looked to political and social freedoms that would result from such a victory. The drastic shift in Marxist-Leninist economic thought that led to Stalin's 'Socialism in One Country' and subsequent fast and ruthless industrialisation brought about a curtailment of the few liberties that survived until the late 1920s. The ways in which collectivisation and industrialisation reinforced political totalitarianism have often been described, both by experts on Soviet Russia and by perceptive outsiders like Simone Weil.[2]

Most writers on totalitarianism agree that several differences in kind can be seen compared with earlier examples of dictatorships. Three of these differences in kind, and one of degree, are due to a considerable extent to social influences. The most important difference in kind is that Stalinism 'belongs to the age of legitimation of power by a democratic formula, to the age of the emergence of mass society'.[3] Lenin's first government claimed to derive its legitimacy from mass approbation, and Stalin's regime continued to use democratic symbols to describe its aims. This posture has received full analysis in political and economic terms, but its social basis has remained less well delineated, like the submerged part of an iceberg. This is strange in a sense, since mass society comprises half of the equation.

In history no political revolution has remained for long in the hands of potential, though not actual, mass organisations, whether they were the Jacobin clubs or the Russian Soviets. Elites have soon taken over the running of the government, but since the age of mass democracy they have normally insisted that they are nothing more than temporary guardians for the rights of the whole people. Lenin's political reasoning on this point was both full and subtle. In reality social pressures, as well as political and economic influences, served to widen the gap between the party apparatus and the rest of the country and to perpetuate the breach. In the first chapter attention was drawn to the social gulf that separated the Old Bolsheviks from the masses and affected their view of state and society. Another social force, or rather vacuum, accentuated this rift. Although there was some degree of social homogeneity among the Old Bolsheviks, this was much diluted after the Revolution in two important respects. Whereas a number of them had already been *raznochintsy* or *déclassés* by origin, they all struggled to become classless later by political inclination. After 1917 the middle to upper class, whose social *mores* and intellectual values the Old Bolsheviks had, in part unwittingly, imbibed, suddenly collapsed. This upheaval and loss of orientation in society was accelerated amongst the second generation of Bolshevik *apparatchiki*. Men of Stalin's caste and choosing came from a lower and more mixed social background. As the party grew in size in the 1920s, more and more proletarians and peasants joined it, rose to white-collar jobs and cut off their ties with their class roots both physically and mentally. The sense of insecurity generated by all these factors, which deprived party men and their families of any settled place in society, may help to account for the rigid cohesion of the party apparatus. It was a response to the need to belong to some kind of integrated group. As time went on this lack of flexibility had serious consequences for the easy relationship of the Bolshevik élite to the masses.[4] Stemming from psychological as well as social causes, this feeling of insecurity proved Pareto's idea that political élites are often irrational, acting against their own original interests and the interests of the classes they claim to represent. It also underlined Pareto's suspicion concerning the wish of élites to become permanent.

On the other side of the democratic equation stand the masses. Totalitarian mass movements have often been successful because they have attracted the loyalty of groups of people who previously had been excluded from the political arena.[5] This fact helps to resolve the apparent paradox outlined in Chapter 4 – that of a government intent on providing universal literacy in Russia as fast as possible, but which subsequently imposed a harsh censor on the uses of literacy once it was acquired. Catherine the Great's dictum that it is easier to govern an ignorant and illiterate people may be correct as far as the enlightened despotism of the eighteenth century is concerned, but it does not hold for modern regimes claiming to respect the tenets of democracy.

It would be too cynical, and an example of blatant Whig history into the bargain, to maintain that the Bolsheviks deliberately fostered basic literacy amongst the population in the 1920s so as to provide mental fodder for the rigid political system of the 1930s. Yet it remains true that the greatest wave of the literacy campaign happened to coincide in time with the imposition of Stalin's muzzle on the free expression of political ideas. Armed with literacy and an elementary education, the majority of the population could now become a profitable recipient of propaganda and act as an efficient servant of the state. This was essential, not only in order to give life to the myth of mass participation, but also to inflate the rediscovered nationalism of the 1930s. Stalin was acting shrewdly, as always, when he added Soviet nationalism to his psychological instruments for moulding the country to his will. At last nearly all the people could consciously grasp in an intellectual sense the significance of their national heritage, and the first realisation of this was, and still is, a heady experience. The peasant no longer needed a Tolstoy to articulate his Russianness.

In the past liberal thinkers have usually believed that education is necessary for the protection of the individual against the state, a political party or a Leader. As intellectuals they naturally had a high level of culture in mind. The swiftly acquired, and necessarily flimsy education of the newly literate in Soviet Russia equipped men to know how to be obedient to the law, and little else. The best brains in the 1930s were harnessed to the urgent need for specialists in industry. The idea of the leisured gentleman with an all-round education was not only frowned on for Marxist reasons – it was a luxury the country could not afford. Narrow experts, just as much as the newly educated and sometimes more so, are likely to swallow political creeds without inquiring more deeply into realities. This was another danger that Russia faced under Stalin. Widespread literacy by the eve of the Second World War was by no means a guarantee for democracy.

If the Bolshevik party was eventually to forsake its role as temporary guardian for the masses, it had to build bridges between itself and the population as a whole. There is little doubt that before and during 1917 Lenin combined an élitist view of the party with a belief in mass political consciousness. A recent scholarly work on the February Revolution makes it clear once and for all that in the early stages of 1917 Russia was being manipulated not by a Dual Government, but by a Triarchy, consisting of the Provisional Government, the Soviet structure and vocal elements among the masses.[6] Shortly afterwards, however, an intricate combination of circumstances put the masses out of the ring again, after the briefest feel of direct power for the only time in Russian history. Some sectors of the active proletariat in 1917 proved to be politically irresponsible, and small wonder in view of their lack of opportunity in the Tsarist period. Other vocal elements were decimated in the course of the Civil War.[7] The crucial test of workers' control shortly after the October *coup d'état* showed two things quite plainly. Lenin was not willing to build this particular bridge between party and people at that point of time, and the proletariat was not independently capable of claiming its own inheritance which was put in trust for an indefinite period.

It was observed in Chapters 5 and 6 how the party failed during NEP to create any other effective links between the political centre and the social community which could lead to the eventual devolution of power from the party élite to the masses. The party swelled in size, and thousands of workers and peasants were brought into it, but the result was to establish a formidable party bureaucracy rather than human ties with the people through ancillary social and political organisations. By the end of NEP, the new Soviet bureaucracy was isolating the party from an atomised society of the type described in general terms by Kornhauser, a society in which individuals were opposed to their rulers without the shield of intermediary institutions. Under Stalin both the party and its bureaucracy were to be bypassed, with the concentration of power in his hands alone. In her brilliant essay on the Russian Revolution, Rosa Luxemburg put her finger on the central sociopolitical danger latent in the events of 1917. She feared that unless Lenin's élitist party soon handed its sovereignty over to the masses, the Bolshevik regime would degenerate into a dictatorship.[8] Perhaps she was naive in imagining that any élite in history voluntarily transferred its powers to the whole people; but she pinpointed the blatant contrast that might (and did in fact) arise in Russia between the vision of the dictatorship of the proletariat and the reality of totalitarian government.

The second difference in kind between earlier dictatorships and twentieth-century totalitarian rule concerns the close relationship between international and internal war, and between military and civil violence. It is no coincidence that both Stalinism and Hitlerism emerged from the ashes of the first total war in history, in which Russia and Germany were defeated and suffered extreme economic and social deprivation. Hannah Arendt makes the point that the First World War became total in nature, i.e., involving both soldiers and civilians indiscriminately, because of the new weapons that were used.[9] This is true, but we have tried to show in the specific details of the Russian experience how many other factors helped to make her involvement in international and internal war total in character. Hannah Arendt stresses that although the interconnection between war and revolution as such is not a novel phenomenon, the fury of total war in this century has meant that no government would be strong enough to survive defeat in war. This in turn has led to a stronger tie between war and revolution. Finally, total war has whipped up so much civilian as well as military violence that the horrors of international war have often been, as in the case of Russia, only the preparatory stage to the violence unleashed by revolution and internal war.

In Chapter 3 emphasis was placed on the impact of violence on Russian society as a whole. The aim was to observe not just how physical suffering lasted from 1914 to 1921, but to see how tolerance of violence and militancy, and new methods and instruments of violence, outlived the Civil War and became part and parcel of the Soviet system. Thus total civilian involvement in violence cleared the ground for subsequent totalitarian political methods. There is far more than a semantic relationship between 'total' and 'totalitarian'. Of course it cannot be denied that wars and revolutions are initiated and managed by political decisions, but the social conditions they have jointly engendered in this century have undoubtedly had a boomerang effect on the conduct of politics in the successor regimes.

A cautionary note should be inserted here. The tie between war and the development of totalitarianism may be close, but a confusion should not be made between military and totalitarian regimes. Neither Stalin nor Hitler were primarily military commanders, nor even Bonapartes turned civilians. Franco had been, and remained, a General, but Spain has not become totalitarian, despite a superficial reliance on Fascist doctrine. No illusion of mass democracy arose in Spain after her Civil War. In the chapter on military influences it was shown how the Soviet system became impregnated with the effects of violence without falling a prey to Bonapartism.

Very rapid developments in technology during this century have given increased power to totalitarian regimes which have controlled them, particularly in the fields of communications and armaments. The uses of technology are a nice illustration of the amalgam with which we are dealing, since political, social and economic spin-offs are inextricably mixed. It is difficult to support the assertion that the introduction of modern technology represents a novel element in totalitarian government in the twentieth century, but its fast growth has made a difference in degree, if not in kind. At first sight it might appear that the prelude to Stalinism was little affected by any link-up between technology and its political manipulation, simply because fast industrial progress was only made with the inauguration of the Five-Year Plans. However, in Chapter 2 it was noted how Russians like Witte were intrigued by the *idea* of technology before the Revolution, as were the intellectuals who inspired the artistic movements of Futurism and Constructivism. The Bolsheviks kindled this enthusiasm. Via Marx they inherited Saint-Simon's interest in a technocratic ruling class whose main objectives would be efficiency in order to eliminate poverty. Lenin's fascination with electric power and Taylorism presaged technological experiments on a far vaster scale in the 1930s when economic and social resources permitted them.

Lenin, consciously, or unconsciously, was following in the intellectual tradition of Saint-Simon. He gave the definite impression when discussing the electrification of the country that politics would eventually be eliminated or left to the competence of technicians. One wonders whether Engels stands midway in this intellectual line, which is clearly influenced by Marx's relegation of politics to the superstructure. Does Engels' famous but mysterious dictum about government being replaced by the administration of things owe more to Saint-Simon than has been noticed? Marx and Engels remained vague on the precise nature of the millennium, indeed far vaguer in many ways than Saint-Simon. The technocratic visions of Lenin also stayed at the same level, partly out of sympathy with the reasons given for restraint by Marx and Engels, partly because Russia's low resources negated any hope of immediate concrete results.

By the 1930s the position had altered. Large-scale industrialisation, managed centrally by a strong bureaucracy without the mediation of any auxiliary organs, transformed technocratic dreams into realities. The industrialisation campaign engulfed the masses for the first time in Russian history, and they were made to participate in the illusion of socialist democracy. The Five-Year Plans involved a vicious circle. They were conducted by totalitarian acts of will, and they also helped to reinforce that will by harnessing hundreds of thousands of workers to the technocratic treadmill, by enlarging the ranks of a subservient bureaucracy with industrial managers, and by producing armaments on an unprecedented scale in the Russian experience.

The political implications of industrialisation remained in embryonic form before the age of Stalinism, though in the realm of the history of ideas the writing was already on the wall. Occasional practical experiments in microcosm, like Trotsky's labour armies at the close of the Civil War, had been tried out and rejected in the more liberal political climate of Lenin's rule. In the 1930s social and political conditions and urgent economic needs ran together to produce a detailed nightmare version of Saint-Simon's generalised optimistic plans. The untutored labour force, as in the early stages of the British industrial revolution, poured into the factories without the defence of skills to bargain with or any intermediary bodies like genuine trade unions to shield them from central bureaucrats. Professor K. Wittfogel has drawn an illuminating comparison between the hydraulic societies of the oriental world and modern totalitarian systems. Mobilisation of the population for enormous work projects was an integral part of the dictatorial method of rule in both these types of societies.[10] The parallel may seem to be far-fetched, given the differences in time and background, but in fact it matters little whether a society is at a primitive or a fairly advanced stage : the accent lies on the military-style mobilisation of men which keeps them busy in some technical venture, either building the Pyramids or the Siberian hydro-electric stations. Indeed, a Menshevik, R. Abramovich, who opposed Trotsky's militarisation of labour at the Third All-Russian Congress of Trade Unions, drew a similar parallel long before Wittfogel, and also spelt out the political consequences in no uncertain terms. He said,

we . . . believe that Socialists should remain in their old position, according to which the construction of socialism should be left to the free initiative of the working masses. This is not a liberalistic superstition but is the essence of human experience, which teaches us that it is impossible to build a planned socialist economy by methods which the Egyptian Pharaohs used in building the pyramids ...[11]

The inhuman aspects of technology harnessed to political lack of scruple under Stalin were a tragic contradiction of the ideals of the young Marx. Marx had realised the dehumanising nature of industrial society. His concept of alienation formed the cornerstone of his later theories. This was a far cry from working and political conditions in Russia by the 1930s. The contours of this side of Stalinism had already been prophesied in NEP by Zamiatin. In his anti-utopian novel, *My*, people become mere numbers. They have to carry metal plates for identification purposes and a watch so that they can synchronise their rigid schedule of work. In their technocratic society, the most distinguished literary masterpiece that is acknowledged from the national heritage is a railway timetable.

The ruthless application of technology depends among other things on the temper of the national manager, and there was a marked discrepancy between the attitudes of Lenin and Stalin. At this point a general comparison may be drawn between the relative involvement of the two men in the social foundations of Stalinism.

The role of the Leader has marked a third difference in kind between traditional despotisms and modern totalitarian systems. Stalin, like Hitler and Mussolini, personally controlled the ideology by which the state was governed. He was also determined to suppress any social group or institution which might conceivably have enough independence to threaten his own power. He thus replaced the party élite by his single authority and usurped the party's position vis-à-vis the masses. The democratic myth survived, but one man virtually embodied it. Lenin never had any intention of doing any of these things on a permanent basis, although on occasion he dealt ruthlessly with opposing factions and nearly single-handedly changed the content of official ideology. The personal rule of Stalin after 1928 therefore caused a radical shift of emphasis which transformed the Leninist regime into a totalitarian structure. This was due to a considerable degree to the psychology of Stalin, which became the driving force of the political mechanism. 'The regime is shaped into a highly complicated instrumentality for acting out the needs of the paranoid leader-personality, whose psychodynamics are politicalized, i.e., expressed in political action,' as Robert Tucker has put it.[12]

One must not fall prey, however, to the sort of optical illusion that often afflicts discussions on the role important men play in history. One could easily substitute Stalin for Napoleon in Plekhanov's observation that

> Napoleon's personal power presents itself to us in an extremely magnified form, for we place to his account the social power which had brought him to the front and supported him . . . And when we are asked, 'What would have happened if there had been no Napoleon?' our *imagination* becomes confused and it seems to us that without him the social movements upon which his power and influence were based could not have taken place.[14]

Plekhanov is right in observing how the personal qualities of famous people are far more noticeable than deeply rooted general causes. The teaching of history, and especially the history of dynastic epochs, which had their 'good' and 'bad' kings, used to be run on this myopic basis. In his essay, 'Was Stalin Really Necessary?', Alec Nove argues convincingly that Stalin could only operate within the logical effects of Leninism, so that Stalinism was situation-determined to a great extent. Stalinism was not inevitable, because some of Stalin's actions once he attained sole power were due above all to his personal ruthlessness, but 'the possibility of a Stalin was a necessary consequence of the effort of a minority group to keep power and to carry out a vast social-economic revolution in a very short time'.[15]

Trotsky overstresses this point of view in his vituperative biography : 'Stalin took possession of power . . . with an impersonal machine. It was not he that created the machine, but the machine that created him.' Here again an unbalanced assessment is being made with the weight on the other side of the scales. Stalin's personality long before 1927–28 had its effect on major developments. Lenin promoted him just because he was known to be tough, and others backed him up for the same reason. The same machine (the party apparatus) which is said to have created Stalin, also 'created' Ia. Sverdlov, N. Krestinsky, E. Preobrazhensky and L. Serebriakov, who were first secretaries before him. Sverdlov, more than all of his four successors, centralised the administration of the

Secretariat, but his motive was efficiency rather than personal power. Stalin sought personal power, but it is also true that he profited greatly from these earlier organisational changes.

In his brilliant essay on the role of the individual in history, Plekhanov writes 'every man of talent who becomes a *social force*, is the product of *social relations*. Since this is the case, it is clear why talented people can . . . change only individual features of events, but not their general trend'. At the time when social relations were 'producing' Stalin, his character was also moulding them to a slight extent. Plekhanov's generalisation holds less water when Stalin's later career as sole dictator is examined. After 1928 his margin of manoeuvrability widened, so that he could and did change the general trend of events. Plekhanov was a Marxist and thus committed to underplaying the influence of the individual. He also wrote prior to the epoch of modern totalitarianism, and it probably appeared inconceivable to a thinker of his era that one man could make such a bold imprint on mass society in the way Stalin and Hitler did.

The economic and political background to the 1930s narrowed Stalin's choices immensely, but the Stalinist purges are in a different category. They amount to a change in the general trend of events. On this subject the fused political, economic and social interpretation of Stalinism must allow elbow-room for psychological analysis as well. In the introductory chapter to his account of the Great Terror, Robert Conquest subscribes to the view that the political and economic antecedents to the purges must be assessed, together with Stalin's personality, in order to understand what happened in the 1930s. Like the majority of scholars, he does not pay sufficient attention to the social component. Indeed he goes so far as to classify a sociological approach with the Marxist view; for him both have their validity restricted to systems which allow of the application of the statistical conception.[16] This is surely an example of misplaced specificity. Conquest's book, like nearly all the primary evidence of those who suffered from the purges, offers virtually no social reasons for how it was possible to enslave a nation of more than 200,000,000 people, whose past record against tyranny had been distinguished and who had offered many martyrs in the cause of political freedom.

The insertion of Stalin's character into our treatment of Stalinism has begun with an emphasis on the fairly well-trodden ground of political and economic affairs. This method has been chosen on purpose in order to provide a solid base before moving on to an exploration of Stalin's conditioning by social influences. The difference between Leninism and Stalinism may also be given a somewhat clearer outline by this exercise.

Both Lenin's and Stalin's freedom of movement was narrowed by the Russian social system as well as by political and economic problems. In fact the weight of inherited tradition remained more burdensome in the social sphere. Whereas the Revolution altered the political leadership immensely, reduced the economic structure to chaos and transformed its commanding heights, the social infrastructure was less disturbed through the 1920s, particularly the peasantry, which comprised the bulk of the population. At the outset of this book it was predicted that it would be necessary time and again to refer back to the prerevolutionary period in order to interpret NEP socially, and so it has proved. Political regimes require certain social structures in so far as they cannot become effective unless the society for which they are designed is organised in certain ways. This does not imply that the social infrastructure 'produces' a definite type of constitution, but only that the social background narrows the range of efficiency of political management. Lenin and Stalin in turn aimed at intervening in social affairs so as to stir up that dynamic progress which according to Marx should follow in the wake of economic change. Both men were well aware that the kind of economic change envisaged by Marx had not taken place in Russia by 1917, but because Lenin took the voluntarist step of a political *coup d'état* in October 1917, he, and Stalin after him, were pushed into adopting a voluntarist stance on social problems. This sequence has been studied with respect to Lenin in Chapter 2. Voluntarism entailed the imposition of personal ideas on the social life of the masses. We have returned to the role of the individual, and also to the battlefield of ideafact confrontation that lies at the centre of this book.

Russia's social backwardness impinged on the personal characteristics of Lenin and Stalin just as it did on the development of political institutions. Stalin's social origins set him apart from the majority of Old Bolsheviks. His lower cultural level affected his views on the uses of literacy, which were very different from those of Lenin.[17] Stalin leaned heavily on the party bureaucracy in NEP as an organisational weapon with which to combat the superior but increasingly isolated intellect of Trotsky. In the Civil War he had fought shy of the utopian and academic social experiments temporarily indulged in by both Trotsky and Lenin. Stalin gathered round him younger men of his own type, so that with the demise of the Old Bolsheviks as an influential group in the purges, new attitudes prevailed on cultural affairs, as well as in many other spheres.

Although Stalin was not interested in the more theoretical aspects of social experimentation in the years immediately after 1917, he was at first compelled by Lenin's previous voluntarism to assume that the Soviet population was capable of carrying out an industrial revolution without sacrificing its political ambitions. During the 1930s, this time in the interests of *Machtpolitik*, he too resorted to an assumption which is basic to utopian schemes. He maintained that conditions had been created which rendered conflicts superfluous, because the party was the ideal guardian of the masses : 'The Party must stand at the head of the working class; it must see farther than the working class.' [18]

The state of harmony induced by such a system is the theoretical goal of the social structure of utopia. Stalinist *practice* was of course very different. When S. Kirov's murder apparently disturbed the millennium in process of realisation, utopian theory conceded the use of terror in order to eliminate what could scarcely be talked about. Stalin attributed the so-called opposition to the relic of a superseded past. He thought up the notorious pseudo-Marxist gloss concerning the sharpening of class conflict as hostile social forces made a final desperate attempt to avoid defeat. The double irony was that Stalin himself inaugurated the purges with no apparent provocation and, secondly, that the purges were not used to smash hostile class elements (none existed that could challenge his power), but rather to wipe out any potential threat from the Old Bolshevik rump of the ruling party. The authoritarian streak that has run through utopian thought in history turned into a stark totalitarian reality.

Lenin's harsh policies in the infant Soviet government were partly conditioned by unavoidable social pressures in time of war, but he personally took advantage of them in order to tighten his grip over political life even further. He ran the party on military lines in the Civil War, temporarily backed up some aspects of Trotsky's labour armies, and allowed the *Cheka* to subvert civilian legal procedures and acquire wide coercive powers at every level of society. Stalin adopted all these willed transformations and magnified their effect. Trotsky's small, short-term labour armies were followed in the First Five-Year Plan by militant mobilisation on a compulsory basis for millions. The difference in scope was caused by economic need, but the style reflected Stalin's personal methods. The enlargement of the secret police was out of all proportion to any objective requirements. Its growth and large-scale punitive work was unnecessary, except as the expression of Stalin's paranoia. Conquest tells us that for every party member who suffered in the purges, eight to ten ordinary citizens went to the cells. Even many of the martyred party men were hardly political creatures in any real sense.[19] The major distinction between Lenin's and Stalin's use of social coercion was its wanton and mass application by the latter.

Stalin inherited a flourishing party bureaucracy, whose detailed administration Lenin had left to lieutenants like Sverdlov and his successors in the Secretariat of the Central Committee. Lenin regretted his earlier negligence near his death and tried too late to stem bureaucratic growth. Stalin merely converted *Rabkrin* – an organ intended to reduce proliferation – into another bureaucratic tool. Both political leaders had to rely on a bureaucracy for the social, economic and political reasons given in Chapter 6, but Stalin worked through it out of personal ambition, thus bolstering it in a way that Lenin, with his enormous prestige, never needed to do. As the years of NEP passed by and no intermediate organisations emerged between party and society, the centralised bureaucracy took on ever greater authority in the name of the party. Lenin's attitude towards better links between the political centre and society as a whole was markedly unlike Stalin's. It is true that Lenin first set the party apparatus on its isolated pinnacle, and remained extremely wary of all groups which contested this position, but the dangerous political climate in the years 1917–24 seemed to call for this. He never failed to look forward to an imminent devolution of authority, and it was seen in Chapter 5 how he tried to promote intermediary organs.

Stalin professed to uphold Lenin's aims in this respect, but there is no evidence of this in actuality. Stalin's fear that any institution or social group might arise which would assail his personal authority became so inflamed that he finally destroyed the party apparatus itself, the chief large-scale coordinator of the nation. The combined party and state bureaucracy was subdued at the same time, and the only remaining large-scale structure, the military, was laid low in the purge devoted to the Red Army. Thus Soviet society became literally atomised into its individual human parts, so that, as the writer Isaak Babel said : 'Today a man only talks freely with his wife – at night, with the blankets pulled over his head.'[20] All the small-scale social and institutional units, including those singled out in the 1920s for eventual collaboration with the party, were infiltrated and infected with lack of trust. Thus not only were the bridges between society and political authority demolished; there was a strong retrogressive tide which swept away even the semi-autonomous but politically harmless small-scale units that survived through NEP. The bravest individuals took refuge in private virtues during the purges. This political indifference, or fear of politics, unfortunately served to call mutely for a dictator to fill the vacuum. If it is a fruitless exercise to analyse the influence of social stratification on high politics in the 1920s, as was argued in Chapter 5, then the effort is even more vain in the 1930s. A man's social status had no impact under the crushing weight of Stalinism. Peasant, worker and intellectual alike were stripped of any means of communicating politically among themselves or with the leadership. They were all cowed into equal submission.

To conclude, both Lenin and Stalin were confined by Russia's social backwardness in the same way as they were forced to adapt to political and economic circumstances. But whereas Lenin often struggled against the malignant effects of social traditions on political development (though sometimes adding to them), Stalin cynically manipulated them for his own purposes.

Having extracted the role of the individual momentarily from the flux of Soviet history, we must now reinsert it. As Plekhanov warns, 'the "factors" theory is unsound in itself, for it arbitrarily picks out different sides of social life, hypostasises them, converts them into forces of a special kind'.[21] He reminds us also that in the 1870s an author called Kablitz, in an article entitled 'The Mind and the Senses as Factors of Progress', even went so far as to try to convert into special sociological hypostases the different parts of the activity of the individual mind. Shrinking from such absurdities, all that can be affirmed is that Stalin's personality worked like cement on the intermingling political, economic and social trends of his time, turning the amalgam into a totalitarian system. One might also conjecture that the years 1922–28 (from the onset of Lenin's physical incapacity to the final defeat of Stalin's chief rivals) were stagnant in many ways, partly for lack of a single dominant personality to pull the strings together. Yet even this may be going too far.

There are clear differences between Leninism and Stalinism, but by no means are all of them due to the proper names in these titles. Political and economic needs changed and required new solutions between Lenin's death and Stalin's hegemony; and even if social development went at a snail's pace, its very slowness created fresh problems as time sped by. Nevertheless one of the essential characteristics of totalitarianism in separate countries which cannot be reduced to accidental coincidences is the need for a Leader. The fact that, as far as is known, no human personality is ever repeated precisely must mean that Hitlerism was different from Stalinism, and by quite a wide margin, given the truism that in a polity governed virtually by one man a large role must be played by the personality of the Leader.

Similar suggestions apply to any general comparison of Soviet and German totalitarianism. Within a broad framework containing common ground many features unique to each country can coexist. By comparing the social influences at work in Nazi Germany and the USSR, we may come upon some developments in both countries which are similar without being fortuitously so, though we shall have to rest content with illumination through contrast on many topics.

The three differences of kind and one of degree that mark out totalitarian rule are equally applicable to Nazism and Stalinism, with some local modifications. Hitler's regime was based on mass appeal, though the component social sectors of the German population were more independent from Hitler and from each other than their Soviet counterparts. They were also far better educated. Germany like Russia had been prostrated by war, though the connections between the common denominator of violence in war and subsequent political rule were of a different sort in Germany. Both systems succumbed to a Leader, who wielded technological means in order to control the nation. Hitler benefited from a far more vigorous industrial base, which soon provided him with heavy armaments (some of which Germany had already been able to afford to pass on to Russia in the 1920s), and a streamlined propaganda machine.

It is when one turns to examine the historical foundations of Stalinism and Nazism that what look like major discrepancies appear. Although Germany suffered defeat in the First World War and subsequent economic disruption, she experienced no more than a short series of abortive revolutionary tremors. She had developed a financially strong middle class and a broad-based socialist party. Above all, she had reached a level of industrial development far in advance of that of Russia. Given these considerations, Russian social history seems to be more at home in the stable of other less developed peasant societies like Turkey. Yet a closer scrutiny of Germany's socio-economic structure reveals flaws that also involve political shortcomings. The assumption is often made that industrialisation opens the door to a liberal society and political leadership. Industrialisation arrived later in Germany than in Britain. It was fast, thorough, and relatively painless in terms of arousing class animosities. Thus it had little impact on the centralised dynastic system under the thumb of Prussia, the most politically archaic of the states which made up Bismarck's united Germany. The Prussian nobility stayed on to control the main levers of state.[22] The bourgeoisie did not succeed in forming a homogeneous social class with high political influence, as was the case in Britain. The aristocracy let into its ranks some of the rising industrialists but otherwise did little to adjust itself to the new socio-economic structure. As was later the case in Tsarist Russia, which embarked on a similar economic phase of fast though uneven industrialisation, the German state took a leading part, as manager and financier. Industrial development in both countries was based on large-scale economic units which were beyond the control of individual bourgeois entrepreneurs. The German state, unlike its Tsarist counterpart, combined political authoritarianism with considerable social benevolence. In practical terms this entailed a proliferation of welfare measures, which helped in some degree to temper the aggressiveness of the Social Democrats' supporters and stemmed the tide of revolution. The mood was one of paternalism, not in the interest of promoting liberal democracy, but in order to oil the wheels for the state's industrial purpose.

Because of the failure to develop politically and socially in step with industrialisation, Germany's record with regard to civil liberties was almost as dark as that of Tsarist Russia. Censorship remained strong. The courts could be induced to rule against the liberties enshrined in the constitution, and there was widespread discrimination against members of certain faiths and other groups. This situation existed for fifty-nine of the seventy-four years from 1871 to 1945. In the freer climate of the Weimar Republic, the scales remained weighted against stable political development. The prewar élite still survived, and economic disaster coupled with abortive political aspirations eventually stifled social rights once again. The masses remained politically apathetic, as they had been prior to the First World War. It is a truism of German history that the great majority of citizens treated political activity as a kind of ritual in which they dutifully participated for brief moments at elections, but which they shunned most of the time. Although far better educated than the Russian public, and with much greater opportunities in history to emerge from their restricted small-scale web of private and family morality, they did not succeed in doing so before the rise of Hitler.

Thus, despite appearances, the social roots of Nazism had various elements in common with the prelude to Stalinism. More than this, German experience in some ways reflected that of Russia with regard to the role of certain theoretical ideas at work on the social organism. It is often said that the mind of the German people is of a different sort from the mind of the West European countries, and that it has more affinity with Russian culture. Karl Buchheim believes that Germany and Russia for similar reasons had to beware of imitating the social and political patterns of the West; 'In this respect, the ideology of many Germans showed traits related to the ideology of the Russians.' [23] There is much truth in this statement. In Russia as in Germany from the period of the Enlightenment onwards, political ideology occupied the same isolated claustrophobic position, cut off from any hope of practical implementation. During the nineteenth century Marx was only one among many German thinkers whose ideas were taken up in Russia. It was noted in Chapter 2 how Russian intellectuals in the first two decades of this century found inspiration in German social theories beyond those of Marx. German pedagogical ideas also had a long tradition of influence over Russian educationalists which extended well past 1917.

Hegelian thought in a vulgarised guise affected the formative stages of German totalitarianism. The notion that the state transcends the structure of civil society and embodies a new political principle of its own passed into the intellectual armoury of German socialism by way of F. Lassalle. The idea survived through the Weimar Republic in terms of the search for a lost synthesis which could solve all political problems; Hitler manipulated it once again by stressing the need for a Leader who was so closely allied with providence that he had the right to direct the affairs of state.[24] Hegel was widely read by the Russian intelligentsia in the nineteenth century, but of course it was Marx who provided the mental fuse for the Russian Social Democrats. Hegel's influence on Marx is undisputed, though its full subtleties have still to be unravelled.[25] Just as Hegel's reputation suffered from the vulgarised and applied versions of his thought that were adopted in Germany, so the Marxist tradition was to undergo a sea change in Russia. In actual political *practice*, Stalin's interpretation of Marx contained some resemblance to Hitler's adoption of pseudo-Hegelian notions. Both of course were distorted, and both laid great stress on the right to diagnose the national interest and to apply it in a socio-political climate devoid of any conflict. While Stalin continued to stake a claim to his role as seer by invoking Marxist materialist philosophy, which in so many ways contradicted Hegel, he unwittingly drew closer to the Hegelian political tradition in Germany by re-emphasising the parts played by the nation-state and the inspired individual interpreter.

A similar yearning for an end to social and political conflict can be detected in Russia and Germany in the 1930s, derived partly from the *dirigiste* philosophies of Marx and Hegel. The Nazi slogan of the 'people's community' had its counterpart in Stalin's belief that it was impossible for him in the name of the party to misinterpret the will of the masses, as he had come to embody this will. In Germany as in Russia, well before the 1930s, there was a similar aversion to democratic conflict in the all-important field of industrial relations. Ralf Dahrendorf goes so far as to maintain that 'Industrial democracy in Germany has always been the search for an industrial utopia'.[26] Even during the Weimar period, the only time the labour movement was directly responsible for controlling political development, the Social Democrats thought they were saving the state when they joined forces with the military and paramilitary groups of the right against the extremism of the left. This move eventually led to the repression of social forces in the name of the state. The trade unions and the labour movement were martyred, as in the infant Soviet state, in the interest of ending (liberal) conflict. In the words of one of the German trade unionists' erstwhile supporters in the 1920s, 'In pursuit of this goal [of economic democracy], trade unions indeed became part and parcel of the administrative machine of the state.'[27]

The administrative involvement of German labour in the state bureaucracy and its subsequent loss of independence of manoeuvre reminds us of the demise of workers' control and the envelopment of the Soviet trade unions. The naked ties between the German Social Democrats and the military in politics did not, indeed could not, come about in Russia because of the careful subjugation of the military to the Bolshevik party, but indirect connections between the socio-economic organisation of labour and the military did exist, as has been seen. The derivation of the German catastrophe under Hitler is often ascribed to the dictatorial tradition inherited from the military-bureaucratic Prussian state.[28] In spite of vigorous efforts, unwelcome military influences from the Tsarist past also returned in the Soviet Union, and these were eventually used, however indirectly, to enhance Stalin's power. Nazism was more clearly penetrated by military influences than Stalinism. The core of Hitler's early supporters were dissatisfied ex-servicemen from the First World War. Unlike Stalin, Hitler also never finally got rid of pressure from high military personnel in the form of the Prussian Junker class. Yet the more subtle aftermath of total violence experienced over the long period 1914–21 inside the social organism influenced Soviet social responses and political structure more deeply than exposure to the First World War affected Germany. Just because the pure military influence was less direct and obvious in the Soviet experience, it does not follow that broader wartime effects were less pervasive in social and political life.

To conclude, pre-existing social traditions and political ideologies favoured a return to earlier historical patterns in both Germany and Russia after the First World War, and further than that, led on to totalitarian systems which had some elements in common. This said, any comparison of Hitlerism and Stalinism is bound to raise a hornet's nest, partly on account of genuine academic doubts regarding the value of such an exercise, partly because of polemical objections from those who are determined never to notice areas of coincidence between the two regimes. It is agreed that any comparison of details is meaningful mainly in order to throw up unique differences through confrontation, but some general similarities in the social and ideological contours of totalitarianism also appear. The fact that Soviet totalitarianism was avowedly on the political left and Nazism on the right does not negate these similarities. Left and right lost their sense under Hitler and Stalin. Nazi ideology strongly advocated a return to tradition, but Hitler was compelled all the same to carry through a social revolution in order to keep his power. He needed to undermine traditional German attachment to units like the family and the local region so that he could gain total control.

It has been fashionable since the advent of Hitler to lay much of the blame for the German tragedy on the natural reaction to the crushing terms of the Treaty of Versailles, and on the consequences of other foreign actions like the withdrawal of international funds from Germany in the 1920s. A similar, though far less elaborate, case has been made out for Stalinism. This tries to show how foreign intervention by the great powers during the Civil War, and later the threat of Nazi expansionist policies, prepared the ground for what happened in the 1930s. It is true that Weimar Germany and the Soviet Union were the pariahs of the international system, and that their isolation affected their internal policies. Herbert Butterfield and others have made out a case for international moral responsibility. The accent in this brief comparison of two totalitarian regimes, and in the book as a whole, has been on domestic social influences, but it must not be forgotten that foreign policy also had a role to play. It has received more than enough emphasis in the case of Germany, but perhaps not sufficient where Russia is concerned. It remains a neglected area, like the study of social causation in the realm of Soviet politics, and deserves closer examination.

The analysis of social conditions underpinning political affairs has normally been associated with the theory of democracy in the past. The sociological theory of totalitarianism is a much more recent approach, particularly with reference to Russia. That is why it was thought worth while to write this book. A great deal more work is needed in order to fathom the social origins of Stalinism.

A group of interconnected topics have been studied here in a modest attempt to diagnose a few significant relationships between ideas, social realities and political action. The role of ideas as catalysts is crucial in the Soviet social and political experience. R. G. Collingwood's view of all human history as the history of thought is exaggerated, but so are those empiricist methodologies which try to produce scientific generalisations on the basis of purely statistical data. The importance of human ideas becomes underestimated in the process.

1 'Most of the serious analyses of totalitarianism have been carried out by political scientists rather than sociologists, and in general they have been concerned to define the structure of the ruling elite.' D. Lane, *The End of Inequality? Stratification under State Socialism* (London, 1971) p. 52.

2 cf. Chapter 2, pp. 29–30, note 10.

3 L. Schapiro, 'The Concept of Totalitarianism', in *Survey* (Autumn 1969) p. 114.

4 For a general description of this phenomenon, see Z. Barbu, *Democracy and Dictatorship: Their Psychology and Patterns of Life* (New York, 1956). A. Koestler specifically interprets the psychology of the dependents in the Moscow Trials in this vein. See his *Darkness At Noon* (New York, 1941).

5 This theme has been elaborated by J. Ortega y Gasset in *La rebelión de las masas* (Madrid, 1926).

6 See M. Ferro, *The Russian Revolution of February 1917* (London, 1972). For an illuminating treatment of Lenin's view of the masses in 1917 see Carr and discussants, 'A Historical Turning Point: Marx, Lenin, Stalin', in R. Pipes (editor), *Revolutionary Russia*, pp. 282–300.

7 See Chapter 1, p. 3.

8 *The Russian Revolution* (Ann Arbor, Michigan, 1961) p. 69 ff.

9 *On Revolution*, p. 5.

10 Karl Wittfogel, *Oriental Despotism. A Comparative Study of Total Power* (New Haven, 1957).

11 *Tretii vserossiiskii s"ezd professional'nykh soiuzov* (Moscow, 1921) pt. 1, pp. 96–7. Other perceptive observers realised before the end of NEP how the accent on technology could have dehumanising effects. See for instance, Maiakovsky, *Moë otkrytie Ameriki*, in his *Collected Works*, vol. 7 (Moscow, 1958) pp. 255–6.

12 *The Soviet Political Mind. Studies in Stalinism and Post-Stalin Change* (London, 1963) p. 16.

13 Felix Kersten, Himmler's masseur, believed that if only he could massage the stomach of Stalin he could bring about universal peace.

14 G. V. Plekhanov, *The Role of the Individual in History* (London, 1940) p. 50.

15 Nove, *Was Stalin Really Necessary? Some Problems of Soviet Political Economy*, p. 32.

16 R. Conquest, *The Great Terror. Stalin's Purge of the Thirties* (London, 1971) p. 98.

17 See Chapter 4, p. 146. Stalin expressed his anti-intellectual feelings in a letter written to the German Communist Party leader Maslow in 1925 : 'We in Russia have also had a dying away of a number of old leaders from among the *littérateurs* and the old "chiefs" . . . This is a necessary process for a renewal of the leading cadres of a living and developing party.' (*Sochineniia*, vol. 7, p. 43).

18 Stalin, 'The Foundations of Leninism' in *Problems of Leninism* (Moscow, 1940) p. 73.

19 Conquest, op. cit., p. 375.

20 Quoted in Ibid., p. 383. Giovanni Gentile, the philosopher of Fascism, tried to make out that this process of atomisation was a liberating one, since the state did not swallow the individual but represented the individual will in its universal and absolute aspect. See his *Genesis and Structure of Society* (Urbana, Illinois, 1960) p. 179.

21 Plekhanov, op. cit., p. 9.

22 The great historian Theodor Mommsen observed that the German nation had contented itself with what he called 'pseudo-constitutional absolutism'. Speaking for the political Left, the Social Democrat Wilhelm Liebknecht labelled Bismarck's methods as 'fig leaves for absolutism'.

23 K. Buchheim, *Leidensgeschichte des zivilen Geistes-oder die Demokratie in Deutschland* (Munich, 1951) p. 5.

24 This theme has been developed by many writers, but the connection between society and the weakness of democracy in Germany is most clearly revealed in R. Dahrendorf, *Society and Democracy in Germany* (London, 1968) ch. 13. Already in the Weimar period the historian Friedrich Meinecke had noted how 'The deep yearning for the inner unity and harmony of all laws of life and events in life remains a powerful force in the German spirit'. See his *Die Idee der Staatsräson in der neueren Geschichte* (Berlin, 1924) p. 490.

25 G. Lukacs' classic, *Geschichte und Klassenbewusstsein*, first

published in 1923, still remains the most illuminating exposition of the relationship of Marx to Hegel in the sphere of social philosophy.

26 Dahrendorf, op. cit., p. 170.

27 Franz Neumann, quoted in Dahrendorf, op. cit., pp. 181–2.

28 See, for example, G. Ritter, *Das deutsche Problem* (Munich, 1962).

Bibliography

The bibliography is arranged according to the successive chapters in the book, so that the reader may more easily follow up the particular theme that is of interest to him.

CHAPTER 1

Aron, R., *Eighteen Lectures on Industrial Society* (London, 1967).

Carr, E. H., *A History of Soviet Russia, Socialism in One Country, 1924–1926*, vol. 1 (London, 1958) pp. 89–136.

Cobban, A., *The Social Interpretation of the French Revolution* (Cambridge, 1965).

Daniels, R. V., 'Intellectuals and the Russian Revolution', in the *American Slavic and East European Review* (1961) pp. 270–8.

Danilov, V. P. and Yakuboskaia, S. I., 'Istochnikovedenie i izuchenie istorii sovetskogo obshchestva', in *Voprosy Istorii*, no. 5 (1961) pp. 3–24.

Feldmesser, R. A., 'The Persistence of Status Advantages in Soviet Russia', in the *American Journal of Sociology* (1953) pp. 21–6.

Gubenko, M. P., and Litvak, B. G., 'Konkretnoe istochnikovedenie istorii sovetskogo obshchestva', in *Voprosy Istorii*, no. 1 (1965) pp. 5–6.

Lane, D., *Politics and Society in the USSR* (London, 1970).

Laqueur, W. Z., *The Fate of the Revolution: Interpretations of Soviet History* (London, 1967).

Mosse, W. E., 'Makers of the Soviet Union', in the *Slavonic and East European Review* (1968) pp. 141–54.

Ossowski, S., *Class Structure in the Social Consciousness* (London, 1963).

Schueller, G. K., in H. D. Lasswell and D. Lerner (editors), *World Revolutionary Elites: Studies in Coercive Ideological Movements* (Cambridge, Mass., 1965).

Sorlin, P., *The Soviet People and Their Society: From 1917 to the Present* (London, 1969).

CHAPTER 2

Aleksinskaia, T., *Zhenshchina v voine i revoliutsii* (Petrograd, 1917).

Balabanova, A., *Ot rabstva k svobode* (Moscow, 1920).

Berdiaev, N., *The Russian Idea* (London, 1947).

——, *The Origin of Russian Communism* (Ann Arbor, 1960).

Berlin, I., 'Political Ideas in the Twentieth Century', in *Foreign Affairs* (April 1950) pp. 365–6.

Biulleteni pervogo vserossiisskogo zhenskogo s"ezda, no. 1 (St. Petersburg, 1908) p. 78.

Bogachev, N., *Sem'ia i gosudarstvo* (Moscow, 1903).

Bogdanov, A. A., 'Voprosy sotsializma', in *Novy Mir* (Moscow, 1918).

——, *Filosofiia zhivogo opyta* (St. Petersburg, 1912).

——, *Vseobshchaia organizatsionnaia nauka* (St. Petersburg, 1913).

——, *Nauka ob obshchestvennom soznanii* (Moscow, 1914).

——, *Sotsializm nauki* (Moscow, 1918).

——, *Iskusstvo i rabochii klass* (Moscow, 1918).

——, *Inzhener Menni* (Petrograd, 1919).

Bonner, V., *Bor'ba protiv prostitutsii v SSSR* (Moscow, 1936).

Bukharin, N., *The ABC of Communism* (Ann Arbor, 1966).

Campanella, T., *Civitas Solis Poetica: Idea Reipublicae Philosophiae* (Frankfurt, 1623).

Carr, E. H., 'The Bolshevik Utopia', in *1917: Before and After* (London, 1969) pp. 60–1.

Cheremin, D., *Zadachi maksimalizma*, no. 2 (Moscow, 1918).

Deutscher, I., *Soviet Trade Unions: Their Place in Soviet Labour Policy* (London, 1950).

Dewar, M., *Labour Policy in the USSR 1917–1928* (London, 1956).

Dodge, N. T., *Women in the Soviet Economy* (Baltimore, 1966).

Engels, F., *The Origin of the Family. Private Property and the State* in K. Marx and F. Engels, *Selected Works* (Moscow, 1951).

Feuer, L. S., 'Lenin's Phantasy – The Interpretation of a Russian Revolutionary Dream', in *Encounter* (December 1970) pp. 23–35.

Friedländer, P., *Polovoi vopros – gosudarstvo i kul'tura* (Petrograd, 1920) pp. 65–7.

Geiger, K., *The Family in Soviet Russia* (Cambridge, Mass., 1968).

Goichbarg, A. G., *Brachnoe, semeinnoe i opekunskoe pravo sovetskoi respubliki* (Moscow, 1920).

Gorev, B. I., *Ot Tomasa Mora do Lenina, 1516–1917* (Moscow, 1922).

Grave, O. K., *Zhenskii vopros* (St. Petersburg, 1907).

Grigorovsky, G., *Grazhdanskii brak: ocherki politiki semeinogo prava* (Petrograd, 1917).

Hammond, T., *Lenin on Trade Unions and Revolution 1893–1917* (New York, 1957).

Kaplan, F., *Bolshevik Ideology and the Ethics of Soviet Labour 1917–1920: The Formative Years* (London, 1969).

Ketlinskaia, V. and Slepkov, V., *Zhizn' bez kontrolia* (Moscow, 1929).

Kollontai, A., *Novaia moral' i rabochii klass* (Moscow, 1918).

Larin, Iu., *Trudovaia povinnost' i rabochii kontrol'* (Petrograd, 1918).

Lenin, V. I., *Philosophical Notebooks*, in *Collected Works*, vol. 38 (Moscow, 1961) pp. 372–3.

——, *Ob elektrifikatsii* (Moscow, 1934).

Muranevich, A. I., *Sem'ia i zhenshchina* (Moscow, 1909).

Nikol'sky, V. K., *Sem'ia i brak v proshlom i nastoiashchem* (Moscow, 1936).

Oktiabr'skaia revoliutsiia i fabzavkomy vol. 1 (Moscow, 1927) p. 171.

Osinsky, N., 'Stroitel'stvo sotsializma, obshchie zadachi organizatsii proizvodstva', in *Kommunist* (Moscow, 1918).

Pervyi vserossiiskii s"ezd professional'nykh soiuzov 7–14 ianvaria 1918 (Moscow, 1918) pp. 221–2.

Posse, V. A., *Brak, sem'ia i shkola* (St. Petersburg, 1913).

Romanov, P., 'Bez cheremukhi', in *Sbornik rasskazov* (Moscow, 1927.)

——, *Chernye lepeshki* (Moscow, 1927).

Rosenfeld, R., *Promyshlennaia politika SSSR* (Moscow, 1926).

Serebrennikov, G. N., *Zhenskii trud v SSSR* (Moscow, 1934).

Smirnov, A., 'Rabochii kontrol', in *Vestnik metallista* (June–August 1918).

Sorenson, J., *The Life and Death of Soviet Trade Unionism, 1917–1928* (New York, 1969).

Sventokhovsky, A., *Istoriia utopii* (Moscow, 1910).

Sverdlov, G., *Brak i sem'ia v SSSR* (Moscow, 1956).

Svobodnaia liubov' (St. Petersburg, 1908).

Toch, H., *The Social Psychology of Social Movements* (London, 1966).

Trotsky, L., *Voprosy byta* (Moscow, 1923).

Trudy pervogo s"ezda po obrazovaniiu zhenshchin, vol. 2 (Petrograd, 1915).

Tyrkova, A., *Osvobozhdenie zhenshchin* (Petrograd, 1917).

Verkhovsky, P. V., *Novye formy braka i sem'i po sovetskomy zakonodatel'stvu* (Leningrad, 1925).

CHAPTER 3

Arendt, H., *On Revolution* (London, 1963).

Berkhin, I., *Voennaia reforma v SSSR (1924–1925 gg.)* (Moscow, 1958).

Bukharin, N., *Ökonomik der Transformationsperiode* (Hamburg, 1922).

——, *Historical Materialism* (London, 1926).

Chorley, K., *Armies and the Art of Revolution* (London, 1943).

Divil'kovsky, A., *Pomogai stroit' sovetskuiu vlast' – naputstvie otpusknomu krasnoarmeitsu* (Moscow, 1921).

Erickson, J., *The Soviet High Command: A Military-Political History 1918–1941* (London, 1962).

——, 'The Origins of the Red Army', in R. Pipes (editor), *Revolutionary Russia* (Cambridge, Mass., 1968) pp. 224–56.

Fraiman, A., *Revoliutsionnaia zashchita Petrograda, fevral'-mart 1918* (Moscow, 1964).

Gavrilov, L., and Kutuzov, V., 'Perepis' russkoi armii 25 oktiabria 1917 goda', in *Istoriia SSSR*, no. 2 (1964) pp. 87–91.

Golovine, N., *The Russian Army in the World War* (New Haven, 1931).

Gorodetsky, E., *Rozhdenie sovetskogo gosudarstva, 1917–1918 gg.* (Moscow, 1965).

Illustrierte Geschichte des Bürgerkrieges in Russland 1917–1921 (Berlin, 1929).

Katkov, G., *Russia 1917: The February Revolution* (London, 1967).

Kolkowicz, R., *The Soviet Military and the Communist Party* (Princeton, 1967).

Kritsman, L., *Geroicheskii period velikoi russkoi revoliutsii*, 2nd edn. (Moscow, 1926).

Latsis, M., *Chrezvychainye Kommissii po bor'be s kontr-revoliutsiei* (Moscow, 1921).

——, 'Tov. Dzerzhinskii i VChK', in *Proletarskaia revoliutsiia*, no. 9 (1926) p. 85.

Muratov, Kh., *Revoliutsionnoe dvizhenie v russkoi armii v 1917 g.* (Moscow, 1958).

Obshchestvennaia rabota v glubokom tylu (Moscow, 1915).

Peters, Ya., 'Vospominaniia o rabote v VChK v pervyi god revoliutsii', in *Proletarskaia revoliutsiia*, no. 10 (1924).

Pietsch, W., *Revolution und Staat: Institutionen als Träger der Macht in Sowjetrussland 1917–1922* (Cologne, 1969).

Pipes, R., review of 'Petrogradskii voenno-revoliutsionnyi komitet. Dokumenty i materialy', in *Kritika* (Spring 1968).

Prodovol'stvennaia politika (Moscow, 1920).

Roberts, P. C., '"War Communism" : A Re-examination', in the *Slavic Review* (June 1970) pp. 238–61.

Seton-Watson, G. H. N., 'Russia. Army and Autocracy', in M. Howard (editor), *Soldiers and Governments* (London, 1957) p. 101 ff.

Shatagin, N., *Organizatsiia i stroitel'stvo Sovetskoi Armii v period inostrannoi interventsii i grazhdanskoi voiny (1918–1920 gg.)* (Moscow, 1954).

Singleton, S., 'The Tambov Revolt (1920–1921)', in the *Slavic Review* (September 1966) pp. 497–512.

Smilga, I., *Ocherednye voprosy stroitel'stva krasnoi armii* (Moscow, 1920).

Sokolov, S. A., *Revoliutsiia i khleb* (Saratov, 1967).

Startsev, V., *Ocherki po istorii petrogradskoi krasnoi gvardii i rabochei militsii* (Moscow–Leningrad, 1965).

Strumilin, S., 'Trudovye poteri Rossii v voine', in *Narodnoe khoziaistvo* (December 1920) p. 105.

Thornton, T., 'Terror as a Weapon of Political Agitation', in H. Eckstein (editor), *Internal War* (New York, 1964) p. 73.

Tishkov, A., *Pervyi Chekist* (Moscow, 1968).

Trotsky, L., *Kak vooruzhalas' revoliutsiia*, 3 vols. (Moscow, 1923).

——, *Organizatsiia krasnoi armii* (Moscow, 1918).

Tukhachevsky, M., *Krasnaia armii i militsiia* (Moscow, 1921).

Vserossiiskii, zemskii soiuz. Sobranie upolnomochennykh gubernskikh zemstv v Moskve 7–9 sentiabria 1915 goda: doklad glavnogo komiteta (Moscow, 1916).

White, D. F., *The Growth of the Red Army* (Princeton, 1944).

Wolfe, B., 'The Influence of Early Military Decisions Upon the National Structure of the Soviet Union', in the *American Slavic and East European Review* (1950).

Wolin, S., and Slusser, R. (editors), *The Soviet Secret Police* (London, 1957).

Zemgor. Poltora goda raboty glavnogo po snabzheniiu armii komiteta vserossiiskikh zemnogo i gorodskogo soiuzov, iun' 1915 g. – fevral' 1917 (Moscow, 1917).

CHAPTER 4

Anan'in, V., and Dmitriev, S. (editors), *Po fabrikam i zavodam: ocherki proizvodstva i byta* (Moscow, 1926).

Bessonova, I., 'Lenin i bor'ba za narodnuiu gramotnost' (1919–1924 gg.)', in *Iz istorii revoliutsionnoi i gosudarstvennoi deiatel'nosti V. I. Lenina* (Moscow, 1960).

Boldyrev, N. I. (editor), *Direktivy VKP (b) i postanovleniia sovet-skogo pravitel'stva o narodnom obrazovanii. Sbornik dokumentov za 1917–1947 gg.*, vol 2 (Moscow, 1947).

Budnikov, V. P., *Bolshevistkaia partiinaia pechat' v 1917 godu* (Kharkov, 1959).

Chto chitaiut vzroslye rabochie i sluzhashchie po belletristike (Moscow, 1928).

Cipolla, C. M., *Literacy and Development in the West* (London, 1969).

Ekonomicheskaia otsenka narodnogo obrazovanii (St. Petersburg, 1896).

Fanger, D., 'The Peasant in Literature', in W. S. Vucinich (editor), *The Peasant in Nineteenth-Century Russia* (Stanford, 1968) pp. 231–62.

Film und Filmkunst in der UDSSR 1917–1928 (Moscow, 1928).

Fitzpatrick, S., *The Commissariat of Enlightenment* (Cambridge, 1971).

Gerschenkron, A., 'A Neglected Source of Economic Information on Soviet Russia', in the *American Slavic and East European Review*, vol. 9 (1950) pp. 1–19.

Graaff, F. de, *Serge Ésénine (1895–1925), Sa vie et son oeuvre* (Leiden, 1933).

Johnson, W. H. E., *Russia's Educational Heritage* (New Brunswick, 1950).

Kahan, A., 'Determinants of the Incidence of Literacy in Rural Nineteenth-Century Russia', in C. A. Anderson (editor), *Education and Economic Development* (London, 1965) p. 302.

Kak naladit' rabotu stennoi gazety, published by *Gudok* (Moscow, 1926).

Kazamias, A. M., *Education and the Quest for Modernity in Turkey* (London, 1966).

'Khoziaistvennoe znachenie narodnogo obrazovaniia' in *Planovoe khoziaistvo*, nos. 9–10 (1924).

Kirsanev, L., and Shishkin, A., *Klassovaia bor'ba v derevne i politiko-prosvetitel'naia rabota* (Moscow, no date).

Krupskaia, N., *Pedagogicheskie sochineniia v desiati tomakh* (Moscow, 1957–62).

Kumanev, V. A., *Sotsializm i vsenarodnaia gramotnost'* (Moscow, 1967).

Lebedev, N. A., *Ocherk istorii kino SSSR* (Moscow, 1947).

Lenin, V. I., *O narodnom obrazovanii. Stat'i i rechi* (Moscow, 1957).

Likvidatsiia bezgramotnosti (Moscow, 1920).

Lorimer, F., *The Population of the Soviet Union* (Geneva, 1946).

Lozinsky, E., *Chto zhe takoe, nakonets, intelligentsiia* (St. Petersburg, 1907).

Lunacharsky, A. V., *O narodnom obrazovanii* (Moscow, 1958).

Machajski, J. W., *Umstvennyi rabochii*, pt. 2 (Geneva, 1904–5).

Maguire, R. A., *Red Virgin Soil: Soviet Literature in the 1920's* (Princeton, 1968).

Narodnoe prosveshchenie, nos. 59–61 (1920); nos. 9–10 (1924).

Narodnoe prosveshchenie v piatiletnem plane sotsialisticheskogo stroitel'stva (Moscow, 1930).

Nearing, S., *Education in Soviet Russia* (London, 1926).

O kul'turnom pod"eme SSSR za gody pervoi piatiletki (Moscow, 1933).

Ozerov, I., *Na bor'bu s narodnoi t'moi* (Moscow, 1967).

Pethybridge, R. W., essays on the press and propaganda in 1917, in *The Spread of the Russian Revolution – Essays on 1917* (London, 1972).

Petrov, A. A., *Pamiatka rabochego samoobrazovaniia* (Moscow, 1924).

Piaget, J., *Comments on Vygotsky's Critical Remarks Concerning the Language and Thought of the Child, and Judgment and Reasoning in the Child* (Boston, 1962).

Plakate der russischen Revolution, 1917–1929 (Berlin, 1966).

Postanovlenie Tsk VKP (b) i Sovnarkom. O rabote po obucheniiu negramotnykh i malogramotnykh (Moscow, 1936).

Prosveshchenie Sibiri, no. 1 (1930).

Rashin, A. G., 'Gramotnost' i narodnoe obrazovanie v Rossii v XIX i nachale XX v.', in *Istoricheskie zapiski* (1951) pp. 39–49.

Rimskii, S. L., 'Udarnaia politicheskaia zadacha', in *Narodnoe prosveshchenie*, no. 12 (1929).

Romanov, G., Likvidatsiia negramotnosti nakanune XVI partsëzda', in *Narodnoe prosveshchenie*, no. 7/8, (1930) pp. 17–21.

Serman, I. Z., 'Problema krest'ianskogo romana v russkoi kritike serediny XIX veka', in B. I. Bursov and I. Z. Serman (editors), *Problemy realizma russkoi literatury XIX veka* (Moscow, 1961) pp. 162–82.

Simmons, E. J. (editor), *Through the Glass of Soviet Literature: Views of Russian Society* (New York, 1961).

Smiriagin, A., *Intelligentsiia i narod* (St. Petersburg, 1903).

Smolensk Archives, especially files WKP 2, 3, 10, 23, 25, 26, 126, 248, 249, 275 and 286.

Sovetskii bukvar' dlia vzroslykh (Ekaterinburg, 1919).

Sputnik professionalista. Zapisnaia knizhka na 1922 g. (Moscow, 1922).

Strumilin, S. G., *Izbrannye proizvedeniia v piati tomakh*, vol. 3, *problemy ekonomiki truda* (Moscow, 1964).

Troinitsky, A. A. (editor), *Pervaia vseobshchaia perepis' naseleniia rossiiskoi imperii*, vol. 1 (St. Petersburg, 1905).

Veselov, A. N., 'Nizshee professional'no-teknicheskoe obrazovanie v Rossii v kontse XIX i nachale XX veka', in *Sovetskaia pedagogika*, no. 1 (1953).

Vsesoiuznaia perepis' naseleniia 1926 g. (Moscow, 1928–33).

Vygotsky, L., *Thought and Language* (Boston, 1962).

Zeman, Z. A. B., *Nazi Propaganda* (London, 1964).

CHAPTER 5

Antsiferov, A., *Ocherki po kooperatsii i leksii i stat'i* (Moscow, 1915).

Anweiler, O., *Die Rätebewegung in Russland 1905–1921* (Leiden, 1958).

Arutiunian, Yu., 'Rural Sociology', in G. Osipov (editor), *Town, Country and People* (London, 1969).

Bockenhauer, M., *Die Genossenschaften im Wirtschaftssystem des Soviet Staates* (Leipzig, 1930).

Bol'shaia sovetskaia entsiklopediia, 2nd edn., vol. 24 (Moscow, 1953) article on *Kustari*, pp. 136–7.

Bol'shakov, M., *Derevnia 1917–27* (Moscow, 1927).

Buzlaeva, A., *Leninskii plan kooperirovaniia melkoi promyshlennosti SSSR* (Moscow, 1969).

Carr, E. H., 'The Russian Revolution and the Peasant', in *The Proceedings of the British Academy*, vol. 49 (London, 1963).

Chaianov, A. V., *The Theory of Peasant Economy*, ed. by D. Thormer, B. Kerblay and R. Smith (Homewood, Illinois) 1966.

Debiuk, A., 'del'nyi ves melkoi promyshlennosti Soiuza SSR v obshchem promyshlennom proizvodstve', in *Statisticheskoe obozrenie*, no. 2 (1939) pp. 28–32.

Fuckner, E., *Die russische Genossenschaftsbewegung* (Leipzig, 1922).

Gladkov, I., *Sovetskoe narodnoe khoziaistvo (1921–5)* (Moscow, 1960).

Gorky, M., *O russkom krestian'stve* (Berlin, 1922).

Gukhman, B., 'K ischisleniiu produktsii melkoi promyshlennosti', in *Planovoe khoziaistvo*, no. 6 (1924) pp. 52–94.

Hutchings, 'Geographic Influences on Centralization in the Soviet Economy', in *Soviet Studies*, January, 1966, pp. 291, 391.

Iakhiel, N., *Gorod i derevnia* (Moscow, 1968).

Kaufman, A., *Small-scale Industry in the Soviet Union* (New York, 1962).

Khalturin, N., 'Osnovnye momenty v istorii promkooperatsii', *Vestnik promyslovoi kooperatsii*, no. 5 (1932) pp. 3–8.

Khataevich, M., 'Partiia v derevne', in *Na agrarnom fronte*, 1925.

Klimov, Iu., V. *surovye gody dvadsatye: Bol'sheviki severo-zapada v bor'be za provedenie NEPa v 1921–25* (Murmansk, 1968).

Kooperatsiia v Rossii do, vo vremia i posle bol'shevikov (Frankfurt, 1955).

Kornhauser, W., *The Politics of Mass Society* (London, 1960).

Kristanov, Ia., *Potrebitel'skaia kooperatsiia SSSR: istoricheskii ocherk* (Moscow, 1951).

Kustarnaia promyshlennost' Rossii, 4 vols. (St. Petersburg, 1913).

Kuz'min, V. I., 'Osushchestvlenie Leninskikh idei NEPa v SSSR', in *Voprosy Istorii* (April, 1970).

Laue, T. von, 'Russian peasants in the factory 1892–1904', in the *Journal of Economic History* (March 1961) pp. 61–80.

Lenin, V. I., 'O kooperatsii', *Sochineniia*, vol. 33, pp. 430–1.

Lewin, M., *Russian Peasants and Soviet Power* (London, 1967).

Male, D. J., *Russian Peasant Organization Before Collectivization* (Cambridge, 1971).

Malinova, A., 'O sotsialisticheskom preobrazovanii melkotovarnogo uklada v promyshlennosti SSSR', in *Istoriia SSSR*, no. 4 (1963) pp. 23–44.

Meijer, J., 'Town and Country in the Civil War', in R. Pipes (editor), *Revolutionary Russia* (Cambridge, Mass.) 1968.

Melkaia promyshlennost' SSSR po dannym vsesoiuznoi perepisi 1929 g., vypusk 1–3 (Moscow, 1932–3).

Melkaia i kustarno-remeslennaia promyshlennost' Soiuza SSR v 1925 godu: Trudy TsSU vol. 33 (Moscow, 1926).

Miliutin, V. P., *Kooperatsiia v SSSR za 10 let* (Moscow, 1928).

Morgenshtern, A., 'Melkaia promyshlennost' v 1921 godu', in *Narodnoe khoziaistvo SSSR*, no. 4 (1922) pp. 42–53.

Morozov, L. F., 'K voprosa o periodizatsii istorii bor'by s nepmanskoi burzhuaziei', in *Voprosy istorii*, no. 12 (1964) pp. 3–17.

——, *Reshaiushchii etap bor'by s nepmanskoi burzhuaziei* (Moscow, 1960).

Narkiewicz, O., *The Making of the Soviet State Apparatus* (Manchester, 1970).

Pethybridge, R. W., 'Petrograd and the Provinces' and 'The Railways', in *The Spread of the Russian Revolution: Essays on 1917* (London, 1972).

——, Review article on V. I. Kuz'min, 'Lenin's Ideas of NEP and their Practical Realization in the USSR', in the *European Studies Review*, no. 1 (1971) pp. 84–8.

Petrov, G. P., *Promyshlennaia kooperatsiia i kustar'* (Petrograd, 1916).

Redfield, R., *Peasant Society and Culture: An Anthropological Approach to Civilization* (London, 1956).

Rezunov, M., *Selskie sovety i zemelnye obshchestva* (Moscow, 1928).

Rimscha, H. von, *Der russische Bürgerkrieg und die russische Emigration 1917–1921* (Jena, 1924).

Rybnikov, A. A., *Melkaia promyshlennost' i eë rol' v vosstanovlenii russkogo narodnogo khoziaistva* (Moscow, 1922).

Semenov Tian-Shansky, B., 'Russia : Territory and Population : a Perspective on the 1926 Census', in the *Geographical Review* (1926) p. 635.

Sen'ko, A., 'Melkaia i kustarnaia promyshlennost' na putiakh sotsialisticheskoi rekonstruktsii', in *Puti industrializatsii*, nos. 5–6 (1931) pp. 70–85.

Shanin, T., *The Awkward Class: Political Sociology of Peasantry in a Developing Society: Russia 1910–1925* (Oxford, 1972).

Sheremeteva, N. and M., *Samoprialochnyi promysel v Piatovskom kustarnom raione* (Kaluga, 1929).

Slepkov, A., 'Semia i stroitel'stvo sotsializma', in *Byt i molodezh'* (Moscow, 1926) pp. 52, 57.

Sorlin, P., *The Soviet People and Their Society* (London, 1969).

Soveshchanie po voprosam sovetskogo stroitel'stva (January, 1925).

Sovetskoe stroitel'stvo, sbornik, no. 1 (1925).

Sovety v pervyi period proletarskoi diktatury: oktiabr' 1917 g. – noiabr' 1918 g. (Moscow, 1967).

Strel'nikov, I., 'S"ezd kustarno-promyslovoi kooperatsii', *Vestnik sel'skokhoziaistvennoi kooperatsii*, no. 11 (1923) pp. 42–4.

Taniuchi, Y., *The Village Gathering in Russia in the Mid-1920s* (Birmingham, 1968).

Volkov, E., *Dinamika naseleniia SSSR za vosem'desiat' let* (Moscow, 1930).

Vsesoiuznaia perepis' naseleniia 1926 g. (Moscow, 1928).

Zelnik, R., 'The Peasant and Factory', in W. Vucinich (editor), *The Peasant in Nineteenth-Century Russia* (Stanford, 1968).

CHAPTER 6

Albrow, M., *Bureaucracy* (London, 1970).

Avineri, S., *The Social and Political Thought of Karl Marx* (London, 1968).

Bendix, R., 'Socialism and the Theory of Bureaucracy', in the *Canadian Journal of Economics and Political Science* (1950) pp. 501–14.

Carr, E. H., *A History of Soviet Russia: Foundations of a Planned Economy*, vol. 2 (London, 1971) ch. 51.

Djilas, M., *The New Class: An Analysis of the Communist System* (London, 1966).

Fainsod, M., 'Bureaucracy and Modernization : The Russian and Soviet Case', in J. La Palombara (editor), *Bureaucracy and Political Development* (Princeton, 1963) p. 235.

Friedrich, C., 'Some Observations on Weber's Analysis of Bureaucracy', in R. K. Merton *et al* (editors), *Reader in Bureaucracy* (London, 1952) pp. 27–33.

Gerth, H. H. and Wright Mills, C. (editors), *From Max Weber: Essays in Sociology* (London, 1948).

Gronsky, P. P., 'Teorii samoupravleniia v russkoi nauke', in B. B. Veselovsky and Z. G. Frenkel (editors), *1864–1914, Iubileinyi zemskii sbornik* (St. Petersburg, 1914) pp. 76–85.

Handman, M., 'The Bureaucratic Culture Pattern and Political Revolutions', in the *American Journal of Sociology* (1933) pp. 301–13.

Hough, J. F., *The Soviet Prefects: The Local Party Organs in Industrial Decision-Making* (Cambridge, Mass. 1969).

Ikonnikov, S., *Organizatsiia i deiatel'nost' RKI v 1920–1925 gg.* (Moscow, 1960).

Lenin, V. I., *State and Revolution* (Moscow, 1965).

Lewin, M., *Lenin's Last Struggle* (London, 1969).

Litvak, E., and Meyer, H., 'A Balance Theory of Coordination Between Bureaucratic Organizations and Community Primary Groups', in the *Administrative Science Quarterly* (1966–7) pp. 31–58.

Luxemburg, R., *The Russian Revolution* (Ann Arbor, Mich., 1961).

Machajski, J. W., *Bankrotstvo sotzializma XIX stoletiia* (Geneva, 1905).

——, *Burzhuaznaia revoliutsiia i rabochee delo* (St. Petersburg, 1906).

Marx, K., *The Civil War in France* (New York, 1968).

Mohl, R. von, *Staatsrecht, Völkerrecht und Politik* (Tübingen, 1862).

Morgan, G. G., *Soviet Administrative Legality: The Role of the Attorney General's Office* (Stanford, 1962).

Mussolini, B., *The Corporate State* (Florence, 1938).

Nikitsky, G., 'Voprosy vydvizhenchestva', in M. Steklov (editor), *Sovetskaia demokratiia* (Moscow, 1929) pp. 238–44.

Pietsch, W., *Revolution und Staat: Institutionen als Träger der Macht in Sowjetrussland 1917–1922* (Cologne, 1969).

Presthus, R. V., 'Weberian v. Welfare Bureaucracy in Traditional

Society', in the *Administrative Science Quarterly* (1961–2) pp. 1–24.

Raeff. M., 'The Russian Autocracy and its Officials', in *Harvard Slavic Studies*, vol. 4 (1957) pp. 77–91.

——, 'L'état, le gouvernement et la tradition politique en Russie impériale avant 1861', in *Revue d'histoire moderne et contemporaine* (October–December 1962) pp. 296–305.

Rigby, T. H., *Communist Party Membership in the USSR 1917–1967* (Princeton, 1968).

Rizzi, B., *La bureaucratisation du monde* (Paris, 1939).

Schachtman, M., *The Bureaucratic Revolution* (London, 1962).

Schumpeter, J. A., *Capitalism, Socialism and Democracy* (London, 1950).

Souvarine, B., *Stalin: A Critical Survey of Bolshevism* (London, 1940).

Strauss, E., *The Ruling Servants* (London, 1961).

Trotsky, L., *New Course* (Moscow, 1924).

——, *The Revolution Betrayed: The Soviet Union, What it is and Where it is Going* (London, 1945).

Webb, B., *The Truth About Soviet Russia* (London, 1942).

Webb, S., *Fabian Essays in Socialism* (London, 1890).

Webb, S. and B. Webb, *Soviet Communism: A New Civilization* (London, 1935).

Yaney, G. L., *The Systematization of Russian Government: Social Evolution in the Domestic Administration of Imperial Russia, 1711–1905* (Chicago, Ill., 1973).

CONCLUSION

Barbu, Z., *Democracy and Dictatorship: Their Psychology and Patterns of Life* (New York, 1956).

Buchheim, K., *Leidensgeschichte des zivilen Geistes oder die Demokratie in Deutschland* (Munich, 1951).

Carr, E. H., 'A Historical Turning Point : Marx, Lenin, Stalin', in R. Pipes (editor), *Revolutionary Russia* (London, 1968) pp. 282–300.

Conquest, R., *The Great Terror. Stalin's Purge of the Thirties* (London, 1971).

Dahrendorf, R., *Society and Democracy in Germany* (London, 1968).

Lane, D., *The End of Inequality? Stratification under State Socialism* (London, 1971).

Meinecke, F., *Die Idee der Staatsräson in der neueren Geschichte* (Berlin, 1924).

Nove, A., *Was Stalin Really Necessary? Some Problems of Soviet Political Economy* (London, 1964).

Plekhanov, G. V., *The Role of the Individual in History* (London, 1940).

Ritter, G., *Das deutsche Problem* (Munich, 1962).

Schapiro, L., 'The Concept of Totalitarianism', in *Survey* (Autumn, 1969).

——, *Totalitarianism* (London, 1972).

Tucker, R., *The Soviet Political Mind. Studies in Stalinism and Post-Stalin Change* (London, 1963).

Wittfogel, K., *Oriental Despotism. A Comparative Study of Total Power* (New Haven, 1957).

Index

DATE			
APR 19 1983			